Meaning and Relevance

When people speak, their words never fully encode what they mean, and the context is always compatible with a variety of interpretations. How can comprehension ever be achieved? Wilson and Sperber argue that comprehension is a process of inference guided by precise expectations of relevance. What are the relations between the linguistically encoded meanings studied in semantics and the thoughts that humans are capable of entertaining and conveying? How should we analyse literal meaning, approximations, metaphors and ironies? Is the ability to understand speakers' meanings rooted in a more general human ability to understand other minds? How do these abilities interact in evolution and in cognitive development? *Meaning and Relevance* sets out to answer these and other questions, enriching and updating relevance theory and exploring its implications for linguistics, philosophy, cognitive science and literary studies.

DEIRDRE WILSON is Emeritus Professor of Linguistics at University College London, and Research Professor at the Centre for the Study of Mind in Nature at the University of Oslo.

DAN SPERBER is Emeritus 'Directeur de Recherche' at the Institut Jean Nicod, CNRS, Paris, and part-time university professor in the Departments of Philosophy and Cognitive Science at the Central European University, Budapest.

we got lost in interpretations
are we really capable of
convey A THOUGHT?
can our minds communicate?

Meaning and Relevance

Deirdre Wilson and Dan Sperber

CAMBRIDGE
UNIVERSITY PRESS

CAMBRIDGE
UNIVERSITY PRESS

University Printing House, Cambridge CB2 8BS, United Kingdom

Published in the United States of America by Cambridge University Press, New York

Cambridge University Press is part of the University of Cambridge.

It furthers the University's mission by disseminating knowledge in the pursuit of education, learning and research at the highest international levels of excellence.

www.cambridge.org
Information on this title: www.cambridge.org/9780521747486

First published 2012
Reprinted 2013

Printed in the United Kingdom by Clays, St Ives plc

A catalogue record for this publication is available from the British Library

Library of Congress Cataloging in Publication data
Wilson, Deirdre.
Meaning and relevance / Deirdre Wilson and Dan Sperber.
    p.   cm.
ISBN 978-0-521-74748-6 (pbk.)
1. Semantics.   2. Relevance.   3. Inference.   4. Cognition.   I. Sperber,
Dan.   II. Title.
P325.W479   2012
401'.43–dc23

2011032500

ISBN 978-0-521-76677-7 Hardback
ISBN 978-0-521-74748-6 Paperback

Contents

Figures

Tables

Preface

When Mary speaks to Peter, she has in mind a certain meaning that she intends to convey: say, that the plumber she just called is on his way. To convey this meaning, she utters certain words: say, 'He will arrive in a minute'. What is the relation between Mary's *intended meaning* and the *linguistic meaning* of her utterance? A simple (indeed simplistic) view is that for every intended meaning there is a sentence with an identical linguistic meaning, so that conveying a meaning is just a matter of encoding it into a matching verbal form, which the hearer decodes back into the corresponding linguistic meaning. But this is not what happens, at least in practice. There are always components of a speaker's meaning which her words do not encode: for instance, the English word 'he' does not specifically refer to the plumber Mary is talking about. Indeed, we would argue that the idea that for most, if not all, possible meanings that a speaker might intend to convey, there is a sentence in a natural language which has that exact meaning as its linguistic meaning is quite implausible.

An apparently more realistic view is that the speaker typically produces an utterance which encodes some, but not all, of her meaning. Certain components of her meaning – in Mary's utterance the referent of 'he' or the place where 'he' will arrive, for instance – are not encoded, and have to be inferred by the hearer; so while it might seem that a speaker's meaning should in principle be fully encodable, attempts to achieve such a full encoding in practice leave an unencoded, and perhaps unencodable, residue.*

We have argued for a long time that this widely accepted view is still too simple, and that utterances do not encode the speaker's meaning – not even some of it. The function of the linguistic meaning of an utterance is not to encode the speaker's meaning, but to provide *evidence* of her meaning. For instance, when Mary says that the plumber will arrive in 'a minute', the linguistic meaning of the phrase 'a minute' is not part of her intended meaning: she uses this expression not to encode her meaning, but merely to indicate to Peter that she means an amount of time as trivial in the circumstances as a minute would be. In more standard approaches, this use of language would be treated as a case of hyperbole and analysed, along with metaphor and irony, as a departure from the normal practice of using the linguistic meanings of words to encode the speaker's intended

our mental reality can't be translate into a language reality outside the mind

meaning. We have argued that hyperbole, metaphor and irony are normal uses of language, which involve no special device or procedure.

If we are right, then the goal of pragmatics – the study of utterance comprehension in context – is to investigate an inferential *process* which takes as input the production of an utterance by a speaker, together with contextual information, and yields as output an interpretation of the speaker's intended meaning. Since we believe that inferential processes are best approached from the perspective of cognitive psychology, using tools provided by that framework, we have put forward hypotheses about the basic cognitive dispositions and mechanisms recruited in utterance interpretation, and have helped to promote the development of experimental pragmatics (see Noveck and Sperber 2004). However, pragmatics can not only benefit from cognitive psychology, but can contribute to it in worthwhile ways. Pragmatic processes are of special interest among higher cognitive processes because their inputs and outputs are highly structured and complex, yet, thanks to the development of linguistics, and semantics in particular, we are in a position to give rich and precise descriptions of at least the linguistic components of these inputs.

Indeed, the formalisation of semantics is so far advanced that it is tempting to try and treat pragmatics as an extension of formal semantics, giving rise to similar problems, to be tackled using similar methods. However, the price for this is quite high. In our view, it can only be achieved by abandoning (or at least backgrounding) the cognitive psychology framework, and idealising away the most fundamental aspect of pragmatics – the joint inferential processing of an utterance and an open-ended context (reminding us rather of the way methodological rigour was achieved in behaviourist psychology by idealising away the mental). To repeat: pragmatics is first and foremost about a process, and not about a set of abstract formal relationships between linguistic meaning, context and intended meaning. Moreover, the context used in utterance comprehension is vast and open-ended. Understanding how a context of this type can be exploited and co-ordinated across interlocutors is a crucial problem for pragmatics, which is bypassed when the context is idealised into a small closed set of items. While we are open to the possibility that some apparently pragmatic problems have semantic solutions, we believe that Paul Grice, the founder of modern pragmatics, was right to argue that many semantic problems have more parsimonious pragmatic solutions. In any case, if (as we claim) linguistic meanings are used not to encode the speaker's meaning but merely to provide evidence of it, then the relation between semantics and pragmatics will have to be rethought, and in a more systematic and constructive way than the current series of border skirmishes and sorties.

In our 1986 book *Relevance: Communication and Cognition*, we described in some detail a cognitive approach to pragmatics, relevance theory, which this book revisits, updates and expands. Since then, work on relevance theory has become a collective endeavour, with more than thirty books – here we will just mention the most deservedly influential of them, Robyn Carston's *Thoughts and Utterances* (2002) – and hundreds of articles in linguistics, psychology, philosophy and literary studies. The theory has been widely debated, with occasional misunderstandings and caricatures, but also highly relevant comments, for which we are grateful.

Apart from a Postface to the 1995 second edition of *Relevance* which revised and clarified some of our basic assumptions, we ourselves have contributed to the development of the theory through a series of articles written together, singly or with other collaborators. We have selected for this volume what we see as our most useful contributions to the updating, revision and exploration of the consequences of the theory for various areas of research.

After an introductory chapter outlining the main tenets of theory and setting it within a broader philosophical and linguistic context, the book falls into three main parts. Part I, 'Relevance and Meaning', is concerned with the relation between coding and inference in communication and the nature of the inference processes involved. Its central themes are the capacity of humans to entertain and communicate concepts which are not the encoded meaning of any public word, and the inadequacy of the traditional distinction between literal and figurative meaning. We defend the view that there is a continuum of cases between literal, loose and metaphorical uses of language, and that the interpretation of metaphorical uses involves no special principles or mechanisms beyond those required for the interpretation of ordinary 'literal' utterances. We end this part with a new chapter on the relevance-theoretic account of irony and its relation to some alternative accounts.

Relevance theorists were among the earliest defenders of the so-called 'linguistic underdeterminacy' thesis (the claim that pragmatic processes contribute much more to the explicit side of communication than was traditionally assumed), and Part II, 'Explicit and Implicit Communication', explores some of the arguments for this approach. We start by surveying the various ways in which information can be conveyed by an utterance, and then look in more detail at the temporal and causal connotations sometimes carried by conjoined utterances, at approaches to the analysis of 'bridging' reference, the semantics and pragmatics of non-declarative utterances, and the contribution of metarepresentational processes to the interpretation of utterances in general, and to explicit content in particular.

Part III, 'Cross-Disciplinary Themes', considers some of the broader implications of the theory. We present arguments for a modular approach to comprehension, report some experiments designed to test the main tenets of the theory, and reassess current treatments of so-called 'scalar implicatures' in both theoretical and experimental terms. The book ends with a discussion of the implications of relevance theory for the evolution of language.

Several chapters in this volume briefly re-introduce the basic ideas of relevance theory, leading to some overlap in content. Since the original versions of these chapters are often discussed elsewhere, we felt that removing these short summaries would detract from coherence; we therefore decided to retain the summaries, but in a smaller font, giving access to the full article while at the same time indicating to readers familiar with the theory that they can be passed over more quickly. For the same reason, we have kept the content as close as possible to the original versions, merely correcting obvious mistakes, updating references to forthcoming work and making minor stylistic revisions to improve readability.

Acknowledgements

We have benefited enormously from the encouragement and comments of others over the years. We would like to thank Diane Blakemore, Robyn Carston, Pierre Jacob, Ruth Kempson, François Recanati and Neil Smith for constant help and inspiration from the very beginnings of the theory. We are also grateful to our co-authors Tomoko Matsui, Ira Noveck, Gloria Origgi and Jean-Baptiste Van der Henst for their valuable contributions and insights, and for kindly allowing us to reprint four papers jointly written with them. Others who have helped in more ways than we can fully acknowledge include Aoife Ahern, Nicholas Allott, Helen Santos Alves, Nicholas Asher, Jay Atlas, Anne Bezuidenhout, Regina Blass, Richard Breheny, Noel Burton-Roberts, Herman Cappelen, Susan Carey, Peter Carruthers, Coralie Chevallier, Billy Clark, Herb Clark, Annabel Cormack, Gergo Csibra, Greg Currie, Jonathan Dancy, Martin Davies, Steven Davis, Dan Dennett, Jean-Louis Dessalles, Bill Downes, Alan Durant, Vicky Escandell-Vidal, Nigel Fabb, Ingrid Lossius Falkum, Thorstein Fretheim, Uta Frith, Chris Frith, Anne Furlong, Gyuri Gergely, Ray Gibbs, Sam Glucksberg, Marjolein Groefsema, Steven Gross, José Luis Guijarro, Jeanette Gundel, Ernst-August Gutt, Sam Guttenplan, Alison Hall, Francesca Happé, He Ziran, Isao Higashimori, Larry Horn, Richard Horsey, Elly Ifantidou, Kunihiko Imai, Corinne Iten, Mark Jary, Maria Jodlowiec, Istvan Kecskes, Marta Kisielewska-Krysiuk, Eliza Kitis, Georg Kjoll, Patricia Kolaiti, Ernie Lepore, Stephen Levinson, Eric Lormand, Ewa Mioduszewska, Mo Aiping, Jacques Moeschler, Stephen Neale, Yuji Nishiyama, Eun-ju Noh, Milena Nuti, Nicky Owtram, Manuel Padilla Cruz, Anna Papafragou, Adrian Pilkington, Agnieszka Piskorska, Guy Politzer, Anna Pollard, George Powell, Geoff Pullum, Ran Yongping, Anne Reboul, Villy Rouchota, Paul Rubio Fernandez, Louis de Saussure, Kate Scott, Thom Scott-Phillips, Barry Smith, Rob Stainton, Jason Stanley, Marie Taillard, Michiko Takeuchi, C.C.W. Taylor, Seiji Uchida, Christoph Unger, Rosa Vega Moreno, Begoña Vicente, Ewa Wałaszewska, Daniel Wedgwood, Tim Wharton, Yan Jiang, Francisco Yus Ramos, Vlad Zegarac and Theodore Zeldin.

Deirdre Wilson would like to thank students and colleagues at University College London and the Centre for the Study of Mind in Nature at the University of Oslo for friendship and support over the years. Dan Sperber would like to thank the members of the Institut Jean Nicod and in particular his students in the Groupe Nash and the members of the departments of philosophy and cognitive science at the Central European University, Budapest. We are also grateful to members of the relevance e-mail list, the UCL Pragmatics reading group and relevance groups in China, Japan, Norway, Poland, Spain and Switzerland.

Finally, we would like to thank the publishers for permission to re-use the following papers: 'Pragmatics', in F. Jackson and M. Smith (eds.), *Oxford Handbook of Contemporary Analytic Philosophy* (Oxford University Press, 2005, 468–501); 'The mapping between the mental and the public lexicon', in P. Carruthers and J. Boucher (eds.), *Language and Thought: Interdisciplinary Themes* (Cambridge University Press, 1998, 184–200); 'Truthfulness and relevance', *Mind* 111 (2002, 583–632); 'Rhetoric and relevance', in J. Bender and D. Wellbery (eds.), *The Ends of Rhetoric: History, Theory, Practice* (Stanford University Press, 1990, 140–56); 'A deflationary account of metaphors', in R. Gibbs (ed.), *The Cambridge Handbook of Metaphor and Thought* (Cambridge University Press, 2008, 84–105); 'Linguistic form and relevance', *Lingua* 90 (1993, 1–25); 'Pragmatics and time', in R. Carston and S. Uchida (eds.), *Relevance Theory: Applications and Implications* (John Benjamins, 1998, 1–22); 'Recent approaches to bridging: Truth, coherence, relevance', in J. de Bustos Tovar, P. Charaudeau, J. Alconchel, S. Iglesias Recuero and C. Lopez Alonso (eds.), *Lengua, Discurso, Texto* (Visor Libros, 2000, 103–32); 'Mood and the analysis of non-declarative sentences', in J. Dancy, J. Moravcsik and C. C. W. Taylor (eds.), *Human Agency: Language, Duty and Value* (Stanford University Press, 1988, 77–101); 'Metarepresention in linguistic communication', in D. Sperber (ed.), *Metarepresentations: A Multidisciplinary Perspective* (Oxford University Press, 2000, 411–48); 'Pragmatics, modularity and mindreading', *Mind & Language* 17 (2002, 3–23); 'Testing the cognitive and communicative principles of relevance', in I. Noveck and D. Sperber (eds.), *Experimental Pragmatics* (Palgrave, 2004, 141–71); 'The why and how of experimental pragmatics', in N. Burton-Roberts (ed.), *Pragmatics* (Palgrave, 2007, 184–212); 'A pragmatic perspective on the evolution of language', in R. Larson, V. Déprez and H. Yamakido (eds.), *The Evolution of Human Language: Biolinguistic Perspectives* (Cambridge University Press, 2010, 124–32).

1   Introduction: pragmatics

Dan Sperber and Deirdre Wilson

Pragmatics is often described as the study of language use, as opposed to language structure. In this broad sense, it covers a variety of loosely related research programmes ranging from formal studies of deictic expressions to sociological studies of ethnic verbal stereotypes. In a more focused sense – the one we will use here – pragmatics contrasts with semantics, the study of linguistic meaning, and is the study of how contextual factors interact with linguistic meaning in the interpretation of utterances. Here we will briefly highlight a range of closely related, fairly central pragmatic issues and approaches that have been of interest to linguists and philosophers of language in the past thirty years or so. Pragmatics, as we will describe it, is an empirical science, but one with philosophical origins and philosophical import.

References to pragmatics are found in philosophy since the work of Charles Morris (1938), who defined it as the study of the relations between signs and their interpreters. However, it was the philosopher Paul Grice's William James Lectures at Harvard in 1967 that led to the real development of the field. Grice introduced new conceptual tools – in particular the notion of implicature – in an attempt to reconcile the concerns of the two then dominant approaches to the philosophy of language, Ideal Language Philosophy and Ordinary Language Philosophy (on the philosophical origins of pragmatics, see Recanati 1987, 1998, 2004a, 2004b). Ideal language philosophers in the tradition of Frege, Russell, Carnap and Tarski were studying language as a formal system. Ordinary language philosophers in the tradition of the later Wittgenstein, Austin and Strawson were studying actual linguistic usage, highlighting in descriptive terms the complexity and subtlety of meanings and the variety of forms of verbal communication. For ordinary language philosophers, there was an unbridgeable gap between the semantics of formal and natural languages. Grice showed that the gap could at least be reduced by drawing a sharp distinction between sentence meaning and speaker's meaning, and explaining how relatively simple and schematic linguistic meanings could be used in context to convey richer and fuzzier speaker's meanings, consisting not only of what was said, but also of what was implicated. This became the foundation for most of modern pragmatics.

1

Grice (1967/1989: 47) proposed a rather vague general principle (Modified Occam's Razor) for deciding whether some aspect of interpretation is semantic or pragmatic: *Senses are not to be multiplied beyond necessity*. However, judgements about what is necessary have too often been affected by disciplinary parochialism and opportunistic considerations. When the work of Montague and Davidson suggested that natural language semantics could be directly studied as a formal system, Gricean pragmatics offered a rationale for dismissing a variety of hard-to-handle intuitions as irrelevant to semantics. A good example is Nathan Salmon's claim that failure of substitutivity in belief contexts is only apparent, and can be explained away in terms of Gricean implicatures (Salmon 1986). However, when formal semanticists feel they have the tools to handle some specific regularity in interpretation, they tend to treat it as *ipso facto* semantic, and to see a pragmatic account as inferior and unnecessary. Thus, the treatment of natural language conditionals has proved a rich field for formal elaboration (e.g. Jackson 1991), while the Gricean pragmatic approach to conditionals has been neglected. By the same token, pragmaticists tend to assume that whatever they feel able to account for is automatically pragmatic, on the ground that pragmatic explanations are more general, albeit vaguer. A more principled and generally accepted division of labour between semantics and pragmatics will involve more collaborative work. The recent development of formal pragmatics (Stalnaker 1999; Kadmon 2001; Blutner and Zeevat 2003; Asher and Lascarides 2003) is to be welcomed in this context.

1.1   Three approaches to pragmatics

The approaches to pragmatics we will consider here all accept as foundational two ideas defended by Grice (1989: chapters 1–7; 14; 18) (for representative collections, see Davis 1991; Kasher 1998; Horn and Ward 2004). The first is that sentence meaning is a vehicle for conveying a speaker's meaning, and that a speaker's meaning is an overtly expressed intention which is fulfilled by being recognised.[1] In developing this idea, Grice opened the way to an inferential alternative to the classical code model of communication. According to the classical view, utterances are signals encoding the messages that speakers intend to convey, and comprehension is achieved by decoding the signals to obtain the associated messages. On the inferential view, utterances are not signals but pieces of evidence about the speaker's meaning, and comprehension is achieved by inferring this meaning from evidence provided not only by the utterance but also by the context. An utterance is, of course, a linguistically coded piece of evidence, so that comprehension involves an element of decoding. How far does linguistic decoding take the hearer towards an interpretation of the speaker's meaning? Implicitly for Grice and explicitly for John Searle (1969: 43), the output of decoding is normally a sense that is close to being fully propositional, so that only reference assignment is needed to determine what is said, and the main role of inference in comprehension is to recover what is implicated. Following Recanati (2004a), we will call this a *literalist* approach to semantics. However, a major development in pragmatics over the past thirty years (which has gone much further than Grice envisaged) has been to show that the explicit content of an utterance, like the implicit content, is largely underdetermined by the linguistically encoded meaning, and its recovery involves a substantial element of pragmatic inference. Following Recanati (2004a), we will call this a *contextualist* approach.[2]

The second foundational idea defended by Grice is that, in inferring the speaker's meaning, the hearer is guided by the expectation that utterances should meet some specific standards. The standards Grice proposed were based on the assumption that conversation is a rational, cooperative activity. In formulating their utterances, speakers are expected to follow a Cooperative Principle, backed by maxims of Quantity (informativeness), Quality (truthfulness), Relation (relevance) and Manner (clarity) which are such that 'in paradigmatic cases, their observance promotes and their violation dispromotes conversational rationality' (Grice 1989: 370):

Cooperative Principle (Grice 1967/1989: 26–27)
Make your contribution such as is required, at the stage at which it occurs, by the accepted purpose or direction of the talk exchange in which you are engaged.

Quantity maxims
1. Make your contribution as informative as is required (for the current purposes of the exchange).
2. Do not make your contribution more informative than is required.

Quality maxims
Supermaxim: Try to make your contribution one that is true.
1. Do not say what you believe to be false.
2. Do not say that for which you lack adequate evidence.

Maxim of Relation
  Be relevant.

Manner maxims
Supermaxim: Be perspicuous.
1. Avoid obscurity of expression.
2. Avoid ambiguity.
3. Be brief (avoid unnecessary prolixity).[3]
4. Be orderly.

When an utterance has several linguistically possible interpretations, the best hypothesis for the hearer to choose is the one that best satisfies the Cooperative Principle and maxims. Sometimes, in order to explain why a maxim has been (genuinely or apparently) violated, the hearer has to assume that the speaker believes, and was trying to communicate, more than was explicitly said. Such implicitly communicated propositions, or implicatures, are widely seen – along with presuppositions and illocutionary force – as the main subject matter of pragmatics.[4]

Most current pragmatic theories share Grice's view that inferential comprehension is governed by expectations about the behaviour of speakers, but differ as to what these expectations are. Neo-Griceans such as Gazdar (1979), Levinson (1983, 1987, 2000), Horn (1984, 1989, 1992, 2000, 2004, 2006) and Atlas (2005) stay relatively close to Grice's maxims. For instance, Levinson (2000) proposes the following principles, based on Grice's Quantity and Manner maxims (and given here in abridged form):

Q-Principle (Levinson 2000: 76)
Do not provide a statement that is informationally weaker than your knowledge of the world allows.

I-Principle (Levinson 2000: 114)
Produce the minimal linguistic information sufficient to achieve your communicational ends.

M-Principle (Levinson 2000: 136)
Indicate an abnormal, nonstereotypical situation by using marked expressions that contrast with those you would use to describe the corresponding normal, stereotypical situations.

Each principle has a corollary for the audience (e.g. 'Take it that the speaker made the strongest statement consistent with what he knows') which provides a heuristic for hearers to use in identifying the speaker's meaning.

For many philosophers and linguists, an attraction of the neo-Gricean programme is its attempt to combine an inferential account of communication with a view of language strongly influenced by formal semantics and generative grammar. The aim is to solve specifically linguistic problems by modelling pragmatics as closely as possible on formal semantics, assigning interpretations to sentence–context pairs without worrying too much about the psychological mechanisms involved. The following comment by Gerald Gazdar gives a flavour of this approach:

The tactic adopted here is to examine some of the data that would, or should, be covered by Grice's quantity maxim and then propose a relatively simple formal solution to the problem of describing the behaviour of that data. This solution may be seen as a special case of Grice's quantity maxim, or as an alternative to it, or as merely a conventional rule for assigning one class of conversational meanings to one class of utterances. (Gazdar 1979: 49)

Accordingly, neo-Griceans have tended to focus on *generalised* conversational implicatures, which are 'normally (in the absence of special circumstances)' carried by use of a certain form of words (Grice 1967/89: 37), and are therefore codifiable to some degree. For example, the utterance in (1a) would normally convey a generalised implicature of the form in (1b):[5]

(1)   a. Some of my friends are philosophers.
        b. Not all of my friends are philosophers.

Levinson (2000) treats generalised implicatures as assigned by default to all utterances of this type, and contextually cancelled only in special circumstances. *Particularised* implicatures, by contrast, depend on 'special features of the context' (Grice 1967/1989: 37), and cannot be assigned by default. For example, the speaker of (2a) would not normally implicate (2b), but this implicature might be conveyed if (2a) were uttered (in England) in response to the question 'Are the pubs open?':

(2)   a. It's midnight.
        b. The pubs are closed.

Neo-Griceans, and formal pragmaticists in general, have little to say about particularised implicatures.[6] The result is a significant narrowing in the domain of pragmatic research, which has yielded valuable descriptions of data from this domain, but is driven largely by methodological considerations.

Relevance theory (Sperber and Wilson 1995; Carston 2002a; Wilson and Sperber 2002, 2004), while still based on Grice's two foundational ideas, departs from his framework in two important respects. First, while Grice was mainly concerned with the role of pragmatic inference in implicit communication, relevance theorists have consistently argued that the explicit side of communication is just as inferential and worthy of pragmatic attention as the implicit side (Wilson and Sperber 1981). This has implications not only for the nature of explicit communication but also for semantics. As noted above, Grice and others such as Searle and Lewis who have contributed to the development of an inferential approach to communication have tended to minimise the gap between sentence meaning and speaker's meaning. They treat sentences as encoding something as close as possible to full propositions, and explicit communication as governed by a maxim or convention of truthfulness, so that the inference from sentence meaning to speaker's meaning is simply a matter of assigning referents to referring expressions, and perhaps of deriving implicatures. Relevance theorists have argued that relevance-oriented inferential processes are efficient enough to allow for a much greater slack between sentence meaning and speaker's meaning, with sentence meaning typically being quite fragmentary and incomplete, and speaker's explicit meaning going well beyond the minimal proposition arrived at by disambiguation and reference assignment.

Relevance theory also departs substantially from Grice's account of the expectations that guide the comprehension process. For Griceans and neo-Griceans, these expectations derive from principles and maxims: that is, rules of behaviour that speakers are expected to obey but may, on occasion, violate (for instance, because of a clash of maxims, or in order to trigger an implicature, as in Grice's account of tropes). For relevance theorists, the very act of communicating raises precise and predictable expectations of relevance, which are enough on their own to guide the hearer towards the speaker's meaning. Speakers may fail to be relevant, but they can not, if they are genuinely communicating (as opposed, say, to rehearsing a speech), produce utterances that do not convey a presumption of their own relevance.

Relevance theory starts from a detailed account of relevance and its role in cognition. Relevance is defined as a property of inputs to cognitive processes (whether external stimuli, which can be perceived and attended to, or internal representations, which can be stored, recalled, or used as premises in inference). An input is *relevant* to an individual when it connects with available contextual assumptions to yield *positive cognitive effects*: for example, true contextual implications, or warranted strengthenings or revisions of existing assumptions. Everything else being equal, the greater the positive cognitive effects achieved, and the smaller the mental effort required (to represent the input, access a context and derive these cognitive effects), the greater the relevance of the input to the individual at that time.

Relevance theory is based on two general claims about the role of relevance in cognition and communication:

Cognitive Principle of Relevance (Sperber and Wilson 1995: 260–66)
Human cognition tends to be geared to the maximisation of relevance.

Communicative Principle of Relevance (pp. 266–72)
Every act of overt communication conveys a presumption of its own optimal relevance.

As noted above, these principles are descriptive rather than normative. The first, or Cognitive, Principle of Relevance yields a variety of predictions about human cognitive processes. It predicts that human perceptual mechanisms tend spontaneously to pick out potentially relevant stimuli, human retrieval mechanisms tend spontaneously to activate potentially relevant assumptions, and human inferential mechanisms tend spontaneously to process them in the most productive way. This principle has essential implications for human communication. In order to communicate, the communicator needs her audience's attention. If attention tends automatically to go to what is most relevant at the time, then the success of communication depends on the audience taking the utterance to be relevant enough to be worthy of attention. Wanting her communication to succeed, the communicator, by the very act of communicating, indicates that she wants the audience to see her utterance as relevant, and this is what the Communicative Principle of Relevance states.

According to relevance theory, the presumption of optimal relevance conveyed by every utterance is precise enough to ground a specific comprehension heuristic which hearers may use in interpreting the speaker's meaning:

Presumption of optimal relevance (Sperber and Wilson 1995: 266–78)
(a) The utterance is relevant enough to be worth processing.
(b) It is the most relevant one compatible with the communicator's abilities and preferences.

Relevance-guided comprehension heuristic (Sperber, Cara and Girotto 1995: 51)
(a) Follow a path of least effort in constructing an interpretation of the utterance (and in particular in resolving ambiguities and referential indeterminacies, in going beyond linguistic meaning, in supplying contextual assumptions, computing implicatures, etc.).
(b) Stop when your expectations of relevance are satisfied.

A hearer using the relevance-theoretic comprehension heuristic during online comprehension should proceed in the following way. The aim is to find an interpretation of the speaker's meaning that satisfies the presumption of optimal relevance. To achieve this aim, the hearer must enrich the decoded sentence meaning at the explicit level, and complement it at the implicit level by supplying contextual assumptions which will combine with it to yield enough conclusions (or other positive cognitive effects) to make the utterance relevant in the expected way. What route should he follow in disambiguating, assigning reference, constructing a context, deriving conclusions, and so on? According to the relevance-theoretic comprehension heuristic, he should follow a path of least effort, and stop at the first overall interpretation that satisfies his expectations of relevance. This is the key to relevance-theoretic pragmatics.

The Gricean, neo-Gricean and relevance-theoretic approaches are not the only theoretical approaches to pragmatics (even in the restricted sense of the term that we are using here). Important contributors to pragmatic theorising with original points of view include Searle (1969, 1975b, 1979); Stalnaker (1974, 1999); Fauconnier (1975, 1985, 1997); Travis (1975, 2001); Harnish (1976, 1994); Kasher (1976, 1982, 1984, 1998); Clark (1977, 1993, 1996); Katz (1977); Bach and Harnish (1979); Hobbs (1979, 1985, 2004); Lewis (1979, 1983); Dascal (1981); van der Auwera (1981, 1985, 1997); Anscombre and Ducrot (1983); Ducrot (1984); Bach (1987, 1994a, 1999, 2001, 2004); Recanati (1987, 1995, 2002a, 2004a); Neale (1990, 1992, 2004, in press); Sweetser (1990); Vanderveken (1990–91); Hobbs, Stickel, Appelt and Martin (1993); Asher and Lascarides (1995, 1998, 2003); van Rooy (2003); Blutner and Zeevat (2003). However, the approaches outlined above are arguably the dominant ones.

In the rest of this chapter, we will briefly consider four main issues of current interest to linguists and philosophers of language: literalism versus contextualism in semantics (1.2), the nature of explicit truth-conditional content and the borderline between explicit and implicit communication (1.3), lexical pragmatics and the analysis of metaphor, approximation and narrowing (1.4), and the communication of illocutionary force and other non-truth-conditional aspects of meaning (1.5). We will end with some comments on the prospects for future collaboration between philosophy and pragmatics.

1.2   Literalism and contextualism in semantics

Grice's distinction between saying and implicating is a natural starting point for examining the semantics–pragmatics distinction.[7] One of Grice's aims was to show that his notion of speaker's meaning could be used to ground traditional semantic notions such as sentence meaning and word meaning (Grice 1967/89: chapter 6). In his framework, a speaker's meaning is composed of *what is said* and (optionally) *what is implicated*, and Grice sees sentence meaning as contributing to both. What a speaker *says* is determined by truth-conditional aspects of linguistic meaning, plus disambiguation, plus reference assignment. Thus, identifying what the speaker of (3) has said would involve decoding the truth-conditional meaning of the sentence uttered, disambiguating the ambiguous word 'pupil' and assigning reference to the indexicals 'I' and 'now':

(3)   *I* have two *pupils now.*

The resulting proposition is sometimes called the literal meaning of the utterance, or the proposition expressed. Grice saw the truth value of a declarative utterance like (3) as depending on whether this proposition is true or false. By contrast, the meanings of non-truth-conditional expressions such as 'but', 'moreover' or 'so' are seen as contributing to what is *conventionally implicated* rather than what is said; in Grice's terms, conventional implicatures involve the performance of 'higher-order' speech acts such as contrasting, adding and explaining, which are parasitic on the 'central, basic' speech act of saying (Grice 1989: 359–68).[8] For Grice, the semantics–pragmatics distinction therefore cross-cuts the saying–implicating distinction, with semantics contributing both to what is said and to what is implicated.

However, although he allows for semantic contributions to implicit content, and although his Quality maxims ('Do not say what you believe to be false', 'Have adequate evidence for what you say') are presented as applying at the level of what is said, Grice seems not to have noticed, or at least not to have pursued the idea, that pragmatic inference might contribute to explicit content apart (perhaps) from helping with disambiguation or reference assignment. It therefore seemed quite feasible to many (apparently including Grice himself) to combine a literalist approach to semantics with a Gricean approach to pragmatics.[9] The result was a division of labour in which pragmaticists concentrated on implicatures, semanticists concentrated on literal meaning, and neither paid sufficient attention to potential pragmatic contributions to the proposition expressed.

As noted above, literalist approaches to semantics treat sentences as encoding something close to full propositions. Extreme forms of literalism, found in early versions of formal semantics, were adopted by neo-Griceans such as Gazdar (1979), whose slogan *Pragmatics = meaning minus truth conditions* was very influential. On an extreme literalist approach, the sense and reference of (3) are seen as determined by purely linguistic rules or conventions, whose output would generally coincide with the intended sense and reference, but might override them in the case of a clash. More moderate literalists see the output of semantics as a logical form with variables for indexicals and other referential expressions, needing only reference assignment to yield a fully propositional form.

On a contextualist approach to semantics, by contrast, sentence meaning is seen as typically quite fragmentary and incomplete, and as falling far short of determining a complete proposition even after disambiguation and reference assignment have taken place. A considerable body of work in semantics and pragmatics over the last thirty years suggests strongly that the gap between sentence meaning and proposition expressed is considerably wider than Grice thought, and is unlikely to be bridged simply by assigning values to referential expressions. Thus, consider (4a)–(4b):

(4)   a. The sea is *too cold*.
        b. That book is *difficult*.

Even after disambiguation and reference assignment, sentences (4a) and (4b) are semantically incomplete: in order to derive a complete, truth-evaluable proposition, the hearer of (4a) must decide what the speaker is claiming the sea is too cold for, and the hearer of (4b) must decide whether the speaker is describing the book as difficult to read, understand, write, review, sell, find, etc., and by comparison with what. It is quite implausible that these aspects of truth-conditional content are determined by purely linguistic rules or conventions, and fairly implausible that they are determined merely by assigning values to linguistically specified variables. Given an inferential system rich enough to disambiguate, assign reference and derive implicatures, it is more natural (and parsimonious) to treat the output of semantics as a highly schematic logical form, which is fleshed out into fully propositional form by pragmatic inferences that go well beyond what is envisaged on a literalist approach. The result is a division of labour in which semanticists deal with decoded meaning, pragmaticists deal with inferred meaning, and pragmatic inference makes a substantial contribution to truth-conditional content.

In fact, the contribution of pragmatic inference to the truth-conditional content of utterances goes much further than examples (3)–(4) would suggest. Consider (5a)–(5c):

(5)   a. I'll bring a *bottle* to the party.
        b. I'm *going to* sneeze.
        c. If you leave your window open and a burglar *gets in*, you have no right to *compensation*.

Whereas in (4a)–(4b) inferential enrichment is needed to complete a fragmentary sentence meaning into a fully propositional form, in (5a)–(5c), inferential enrichment of a fully propositional form is needed to yield a truth-conditional content that satisfies pragmatic expectations (e.g. the presumption of optimal relevance from section 1.1). Thus, the speaker of (5a) would normally be understood as asserting not merely that she will bring some bottle or other, but that she will bring a *full* bottle of *alcohol*; the speaker of (5b) would normally be understood as asserting not merely that she is going to sneeze at some time in the future, but that she is going to sneeze *very soon*; and the speaker of (5c) would normally be understood as asserting that if a burglar gets in *through the window as a result of its being left open by the hearer*, the hearer has no right to compensation *for any consequent loss*. Enrichments of this type are surely driven by pragmatic rather than semantic considerations. They argue for a contextualist approach to semantics, combined with an inferential pragmatics which makes a substantial contribution to the proposition expressed.

From a radical literalist perspective, on which the semantics–pragmatics borderline should coincide with the borderline between saying and implicating, examples such as (4)–(5) show unexpected 'intrusions' of pragmatic inference into the domain of semantics. As Levinson (2000: 195) puts it, 'there is no consistent way of cutting up the semiotic pie such that "what is said" excludes "what is implicated"'. Literalists see this as a problem. Levinson's solution is to abandon Grice's view that saying and implicating are mutually exclusive. From a contextualist perspective, on which the semantics–pragmatics distinction coincides with the borderline between decoding and inference, examples such as (4)–(5) come as no surprise. An obvious way of handling these cases is to abandon the assumption that sentences are the primary bearers of truth conditions, and to break down the assignment of truth conditions to utterances into two theoretically distinct phases. In one phase of analysis, utterances of natural-language sentences would be seen as decoded into schematic logical forms, which are inferentially elaborated into fully propositional forms by pragmatic processes geared to the identification of speakers' meanings.[10] These propositional forms would be the primary bearers of truth conditions, and might themselves provide input, in another phase of analysis, to a semantics of conceptual representations (what Fodor calls 'real semantics') which maps them onto the states of affairs they represent. On this approach, there is no pragmatic 'intrusion' into a homogeneous truth-conditional semantics. Rather, there are two distinct varieties of semantics – linguistic semantics and the semantics of conceptual representations – of which the first, at least, is contextualist rather than literalist.[11]

1.3   Explicit and implicit communication

In much of contemporary philosophy of language and linguistics, the notions of saying and literal meaning are seen as doing double duty, characterising, on the one hand, the (minimally enriched) output of semantics and, on the other, what is explicitly communicated by an utterance. We have already argued that the traditional notions of saying and literal meaning are inadequate for semantic purposes: sentence meaning is much more schematic than literalist approaches to semantics suggest. We now want to argue that they are also inadequate for pragmatic purposes: what is explicitly communicated by an utterance typically goes well beyond what is said or literally meant, and may be vaguer and less determinate than is generally assumed.

In analysing the notion of speaker's meaning, Grice introduced the terms 'implicate' and 'implicature' to refer to what is implicitly communicated, but rather than use the symmetrical 'explicate' and 'explicature', or just talk of what is explicitly communicated, he chose to contrast what is implicated with the ordinary-language notion 'what is said'. This terminological choice reflected both a presupposition and a goal. The presupposition was that 'what is said' is an intuitively clear, common-sense notion. The goal was to argue against a view of meaning that ordinary-language philosophers were defending at the time. As noted above, to achieve this goal, Grice wanted to show that what is said is best described by a relatively parsimonious semantics, while much of the complexity and subtlety of utterance interpretation should be seen as falling on the implicit side. We share Grice's desire to relieve the semantics of natural language of whatever can be best explained at the pragmatic level, but we take a rather different view of how this pragmatic explanation should go.

We suggested in section 1.2 that the intuitive truth-conditional content of an utterance – what the speaker would normally be taken to assert – may go well beyond the minimal proposition obtained by decoding, disambiguation and reference assignment. We will develop this claim in more detail by considering an example in which Lisa drops by her neighbours, the Joneses, one evening as they are sitting down to supper, and the following exchange takes place:

(6)   a. ALAN JONES: Do you want to join us for supper?
        b. LISA: No, thanks. I've eaten.

On a standard Gricean account, what Lisa has said in uttering (6b) is that she has eaten something or other at some time or other. However, what she would normally be understood as asserting is something stronger: namely, that she has eaten *supper* on the *evening of utterance*. Inferential elaborations of this type, which seem to be performed automatically and unconsciously during compre-hension, are ruled out by Grice's account of what is said.

The term 'explicature' was introduced into relevance theory, on the model of Grice's 'implicature', to characterise the speaker's explicit meaning in a way that allows for richer elaboration than Grice's notion of 'what is said':

Explicature (Sperber and Wilson 1995: 182)
A proposition communicated by an utterance is an *explicature* if and only if it is a development of a logical form encoded by the utterance.

The process of *developing* a logical form into a fully propositional form may involve not only reference assignment but other types of pragmatic enrichment illustrated in (4)–(6). The implicatures of an utterance are all the other propositions that make up the speaker's meaning:

Implicature (Sperber and Wilson 1995: 182)
A proposition communicated by an utterance, but not explicitly, is an *implicature*.

Thus, Lisa's meaning in (6b) might include the explicature that she has eaten supper on the evening of utterance[12] and the implicature that she doesn't want to eat with the Joneses because she's already had supper that evening.

Explicatures are recovered by a combination of decoding and inference. Different utterances may convey the same explicature in different ways, with different proportions of decoding and inference involved. Compare Lisa's answer in (6b) (repeated below) with the three alternative versions in (6c)–(6e):

(6)   a. ALAN JONES: Do you want to join us for supper?
         b. LISA: No, thanks. I've eaten.
         c. LISA: No, thanks. I've already eaten supper.
         d. LISA: No, thanks. I've already eaten tonight.
         e. LISA: No, thanks. I've already eaten supper tonight.

All four answers communicate not only the same overall meaning but also the same explicature and implicatures. If this is not immediately obvious, there is a standard test for deciding whether some part of the speaker's meaning is part of the explicit truth-conditional content of the utterance or merely an implicature. The test involves checking whether the item falls within the scope of logical operators when embedded into a negative or conditional sentence: explicit truth-conditional content falls within the scope of negation and other logical operators, while implicatures do not (Carston 2002a: chapter 2.6.3). Thus, consider the hypothesis that the explicature of (6b) is simply the trivial truth that Lisa has eaten something at some point before the time of utterance, and that she is merely *implicating* that she has eaten that evening. The standard embedding test suggests that this hypothesis is false. If Lisa had replied 'I haven't eaten', she would clearly not have been asserting that she has never eaten in her life, but merely denying that she has eaten supper that very evening. So in replying 'I've eaten', Lisa is explicitly communicating that she has eaten supper that very evening.

Although all four answers in (6b)–(6e) convey the same explicature, there is a clear sense in which Lisa's meaning is least explicit in (6b) and most explicit in (6e), with (6c) and (6d) falling in between. These differences in *degree of explicitness* are analysable in terms of the relative proportions of decoding and inference involved:

Degrees of explicitness (Sperber and Wilson 1995: 182)
The greater the relative contribution of decoding, and the smaller the relative contribution of pragmatic inference, the more explicit an explicature will be (and inversely).

When the speaker's meaning is quite explicit, as in (6e), and in particular when each word in an utterance is used to convey one of its encoded meanings, what we are calling the explicature is close to what might be common-sensically described as the explicit content, or what is said, or the literal meaning of the utterance. The less explicit the meaning, the more responsibility the hearer must take for the interpretation he constructs: in relevance-theoretic terms, explicatures may be *stronger* or *weaker*, depending on the degree of indeterminacy introduced by the inferential aspect of comprehension. Whether the explicature is strong or weak, the notion of explicature applies straightforwardly. However, the same is not true of the notions of literal meaning and what is said. When asked what Lisa has *said* by uttering (6b) ('I've eaten') with a relatively weak explicature, people's intuitions typically waver. The weaker the explicature, the harder it is to paraphrase what the speaker was saying except by transposing it into an indirect quotation ('She said she had eaten'), which is always possible but does not really help to specify the content of what was communicated. In such cases, the notions of explicature and degrees of explicitness have clear advantages over the traditional notions of literal meaning and what is said.[13]

According to our account, the recovery of both explicit and implicit content may involve a substantial element of pragmatic inference. This raises questions about how explicatures and implicatures are identified, and where the borderline between them is drawn. We have argued that the linguistically encoded meaning of an utterance gives no more than a schematic indication of the speaker's meaning. The hearer's task is to use this indication, together with background knowledge, to construct an interpretation of the speaker's meaning, guided by expectations of relevance raised by the utterance itself. This overall task can be broken down into a number of sub-tasks:

Sub-tasks in the overall comprehension process
(a) Constructing an appropriate hypothesis about explicatures by developing the linguistically encoded logical form.
(b) Constructing an appropriate hypothesis about the intended contextual assumptions (*implicated premises*).
(c) Constructing an appropriate hypothesis about the intended contextual implications (*implicated conclusions*).

These sub-tasks should not be thought of as sequentially ordered. The hearer does not *first* decode the sentence meaning, *then* construct an explicature and identify an appropriate context, and *then* derive a range of implicated conclusions. Comprehension is an online process, and hypotheses about explicatures, implicated premises and implicated conclusions are developed in parallel, against a background of expectations which may be revised or elaborated as the utterance unfolds. In particular, the hearer may bring to the comprehension process not only a general presumption of relevance, but more specific expectations about how the utterance will be relevant to him (what implicated conclusions he is expected to derive), and these may contribute, via backwards inference, to the identification of explicatures and implicated premises. The overall process is guided by the relevance-theoretic comprehension heuristic presented in section 1.1 ('Follow a path of least effort in constructing an interpretation that satisfies your expectations of relevance').

A crucial point about the relation between explicatures and implicatures is that implicated conclusions must be deducible from explicatures together with an appropriate set of contextual assumptions. A hearer using the relevance-theoretic comprehension heuristic is therefore entitled to follow a path of least effort in developing the encoded schematic sentence meaning to a point where it combines with available contextual assumptions to warrant the derivation of enough conclusions to make the utterance relevant in the expected way. This is what happens in Lisa's utterance (6b) (repeated below):

(6)   a. ALAN JONES: Do you want to join us for supper?
        b. LISA: No thanks. I've eaten.

Lisa's utterance 'No thanks' should raise a doubt in Alan's mind about why she is refusing his invitation, and he can reasonably expect the next part of her utterance to settle this doubt by offering an explanation of her refusal. From encyclopaedic information associated with the concept EATING, he should find it relatively easy to supply the contextual assumptions in (7):

(7)   a. People don't normally want to eat supper twice in one evening.
        b. The fact that one has already eaten supper on a given evening is a good reason for refusing an invitation to supper that evening.

These would suggest an explanation of Lisa's refusal, provided that the encoded meaning of her utterance is enriched to yield an explicature along the lines in (8):

(8)   Lisa has already eaten supper on the evening of utterance.

By combining (7) and (8), Alan can derive the implicated conclusion that Lisa is refusing his invitation because she has already had supper that evening (which may in turn lead on to further implications), thus satisfying his expectations of relevance. On this approach, explicatures and implicatures are constructed by mutually adjusting tentative hypotheses about explicatures, implicated premises and implicated conclusions in order to satisfy the expectations of relevance raised by the utterance itself.[14]

The mutual adjustment process suggests an account of how implicated premises may be 'accommodated' in the course of comprehension (Lewis 1979). Consider the exchange in (9):

(9)   a. BILL: I hear you've moved from Manhattan to Brooklyn.
        b. SUE: The rent is lower.

In interpreting Sue's utterance in (9b), Bill will expect it to be relevant to his preceding remark, for instance by disputing it, elaborating on it or answering a question it raises (e.g. 'Why did you move?'). In ordinary circumstances, the easiest way to arrive at a sufficiently relevant interpretation (and hence at the interpretation favoured by the relevance-theoretic comprehension heuristic) would involve interpreting 'the rent' to mean *the rent in Brooklyn*, and 'cheaper' to mean *cheaper than in Manhattan*.[15] (9b), understood in this way and combined with an assumption such as (10), provides the answer to an implicit question raised by Bill:

(10)   A lower rent is a reason to move.

Of course, not everyone would be prepared to move in order to get a lower rent, and Bill may not have known Sue's preferences in advance; in Lewis's terms, in interpreting her utterance he may have to *accommodate* an assumption such as (10). In the relevance-theoretic framework, what Lewis calls accommodation involves adding a new (i.e. previously unevidenced or under-evidenced) premise to the context in the course of the mutual adjustment process geared to satisfying the hearer's expectations of relevance. Which premises are added will depend on the order in which they can be constructed, via a combination of backward inference from expected conclusions and forward inference from information available in memory. By encouraging the hearer to supply some such premises in the search for relevance, the speaker takes some responsibility for their truth.[16]

Implicatures, like explicatures, may be stronger or weaker, depending on the degree of indeterminacy introduced by the inferential element of comprehension. When the hearer's expectations of relevance can be satisfied by deriving any one of a range of roughly similar conclusions, at roughly comparable cost, from a range of roughly similar premises, the hearer also has to take some responsibility for the particular premises he supplies and the conclusions he derives from them. In interpreting Sue's utterance in (9b), for example, Bill might have supplied any of the premises in (11), or many others of a similar tenor:

(11)   a. A substantially lower rent for an otherwise comparable residence is a good
           reason to move.
        b. Sue could not afford her Manhattan rent.

    c. Sue would rather spend as little as possible on rent.
    d. The relative benefit of living in Manhattan rather than Brooklyn was not worth the high rent Sue was paying.

The implicated conclusion that Bill will derive from Sue's utterance depends on the particular implicated premise he supplies. Still, it is clearly part of Sue's intention that Bill should provide some such premise and derive some such conclusion. In other words, Sue's overall meaning has a clear gist, but not an exact paraphrase. The greater the range of alternatives, the *weaker* the implicatures, and the more responsibility the hearer has to take for the particular choices he makes. Much of human communication is weak in this sense, a fact that a pragmatic theory should explain rather than idealise away.

Grice comments in passing on the indeterminacy of implicatures:

Since to calculate a conversational implicature is to calculate what has to be supposed in order to preserve the supposition that the Cooperative Principle is being observed, and since there may be various possible specific explanations, a list of which may be open, the conversational implicatum [implicature] in such cases will be a disjunction of such specific explanations; and if the list of these is open, the implicatum will have just the kind of indeterminacy that many actual implicata [implicatures] do in fact seem to possess. (1967/1989: 39–40)

However, he did not pursue the idea, or suggest how the indeterminacy of implicatures might be compatible with their calculability, which he also regarded as an essential feature. In the Gricean and neo-Gricean literature, this problem is generally idealised away:

Because indeterminacy is hard to handle formally, I shall mostly ignore it in the discussion that follows. A fuller treatment of implicatures would not be guilty of this omission, which is really only defensible on formal grounds. (Gazdar 1979: 40)

Relevance theory argues that indeterminacy is quite pervasive at both explicit and implicit levels, and provides an analysis that fits well with Grice's intuitive description.

1.4   Lexical pragmatics: metaphor, approximation and narrowing

The claim that an utterance does not encode the speaker's meaning but is merely a piece of evidence for it has implications at the lexical level. Metaphors and other tropes are the most obvious cases where the meaning conveyed by use of a word goes beyond the linguistically encoded sense. Relevance theory gives a quite different account of these lexical-pragmatic phenomena from the standard Gricean one. Gricean pragmatics is often seen as shedding new light on the distinction between literal and figurative meaning, which goes back to classical rhetoric. Among the central assumptions of classical rhetoric (rephrased in modern terms) were that:

(a) Linguistic expressions have a literal meaning.
(b) They are normally used to convey this literal meaning.
(c) Literal meanings are primary; figurative meanings are produced by systematic departures from literal meaning along dimensions such as similarity (in the case of metaphor), part–whole relationships (in the case of synecdoche), contradiction (in the case of irony), and so on.
(d) Figurative meanings are paraphrasable in literal terms, and can therefore be literally conveyed.
(e) When a meaning is conveyed figuratively rather than literally, it is in order to please or impress the audience.

Much of the contemporary philosophy of language shares these assumptions, from which it follows that only literal meaning matters to the study of meaning. Metaphor, irony, and other tropes are seen as more relevant to aesthetics and the study of literature than to philosophy of language.

The classical view of figurative meaning was challenged by the Romantics. Against the view of figures as mere ornaments, they claimed that tropes have no literal paraphrases and language is figurative through and through. The Romantic rejection of the literal–figurative distinction has had more influence on literary studies and continental philosophy than on analytic philosophy. However, recent work in cognitive psychology and pragmatics (e.g. Lakoff 1987; Gibbs 1994a; Glucksberg 2001) also challenges the classical view in a variety of ways, some of which should have philosophical relevance.

Grice's account of tropes is closer to the classical than the Romantic approach. Suppose that the speaker of (12) or (13) manifestly could not have intended to commit herself to the truth of the propositions literally expressed: it is common knowledge that she knows that John is not a computer, or that she thinks the weather is awful:

(12)   John is a computer.

(13)   It's lovely weather.

She is therefore overtly violating Grice's first maxim of Quality ('Do not say what you believe to be false'). According to Grice, such overt violation or *flouting* of a maxim indicates a speaker's intention: the speaker intends the hearer to retrieve an implicature which brings the full interpretation of the utterance (i.e. what is said, plus what is implicated) as close as possible to satisfying the Cooperative Principle and maxims. In the case of tropes, the required implicature is related to what is said in one of several possible ways, each characteristic of a different trope. With metaphor, the implicature is a simile based on what is said; with irony, it is the opposite of what is said; with hyperbole, it is a weaker proposition, and with understatement, a stronger one.[17] Thus, Grice might analyse (12) as implicating (14) below, and (13) as implicating (15):

(14)   John processes information like a computer.

(15)   The weather is bad.

As in the classical rhetorical approach, literal meanings are primary, and figurative meanings are associated with literal meanings in simple and systematic ways. What Grice adds is the idea that figurative meanings are derived in the pragmatic process of utterance comprehension and that this derivation is triggered by the fact the literal interpretation is an overt departure from conversational maxims.

However, there is a problem with explaining the interpretation of tropes in terms of standard Gricean implicatures. In general, the recovery of an implicature is meant to restore the assumption that the maxims have been observed, or that their violation was justified in the circumstances (as when a speaker is justified by her ignorance in providing less information than required) (Grice 1989: 370). In the case of tropes, the first maxim of Quality seems to be irretrievably violated, and the implicature provides no circumstantial justification whatsoever: what justification could there be for implicitly conveying something true by saying something blatantly false, when one could have spoken truthfully in the first place? In fact, there is some textual evidence to suggest that Grice had in mind a slightly different treatment, on which the speaker in metaphor or irony does not actually *say*, but merely 'makes as if to say' what the sentence she utters literally means (Grice 1967/89: 34). But in that case, since nothing is genuinely said, the first Quality maxim is not violated at all, and an account in terms of overt violation does not go through.

A Gricean way to go (although Grice himself did not take this route) would be to argue that what is violated is not the first maxim of Quality but the first maxim of Quantity ('Make your contribution as informative as is required'), since if nothing is said, no information is provided. The implicature could then be seen as part of an overall interpretation that satisfies this maxim. However, this creates a further problem, since the resulting interpretations of figurative utterances would irretrievably violate the Manner maxims. In classical rhetoric, where a metaphor such as (12) or an irony such as (13) is merely an indirect and decorative way of communicating the propositions in (14) or (15), this ornamental value might help to explain the use of tropes (in so far as classical rhetoricians were interested in explanation at all). Quite sensibly, Grice does not appeal to ornamental value. His supermaxim of Manner is not 'Be fancy' but 'Be perspicuous'. However, he does assume, in accordance with classical rhetoric, that figurative meanings, like literal meanings, are fully propositional, and paraphrasable in literal terms. Which raises the following question: Isn't a direct and literal expression of what you mean *always* more perspicuous (and in particular less obscure and less ambiguous, cf. the first and second Manner maxims) than an indirect figurative expression?

There are deeper problems with any attempt (whether classical or Gricean) to treat language use as governed by a norm of literalness, and figurative utterances as overt departures from the norm. Apart from creative literary metaphors and aggressive forms of irony, which are indeed meant to be noticed, ordinary language use is full of tropes which are understood without attracting any more attention than strictly literal utterances. This familiar observation has now been experimentally confirmed: reaction-time studies show that most metaphors take no longer to understand than their literal counterparts (Gibbs 1994a; Glucksberg 2001; see also Noveck, Bianco and Castry 2001). This does not square with the view that the hearer of a metaphor first considers its literal interpretation, then rejects it as blatantly false or incongruous, and then constructs a figurative interpretation.

Moreover, while there is room for argument about which metaphors are noticed as such and which are not, ordinary discourse is full of utterances which would violate the first maxim of Quality if literally understood, but are not perceived as violations by ordinary language users. We are thinking here of approximations and loose uses of language such as those in (16)–(19) (discussed in greater detail in Wilson and Sperber 2002):

(16)   The lecture starts *at five o'clock*.

(17)   Holland is *flat*.

(18)   SUE: I must *run* to the bank before it closes.

(19)   JANE: I have a terrible cold. I need a *Kleenex*.

If the italicised expressions in (16)–(19) are literally understood, these utterances are not strictly true: lectures rarely start at exactly the appointed time, Holland is not a plane surface, Sue must hurry to the bank but not necessarily run there, and other brands of disposable tissue would do just as well for Jane. Despite the fact that hearers do not normally perceive them as literally false, such loose uses of language are not misleading. This raises a serious issue for any philosophy of language based on a maxim or convention of truthfulness. In some cases, it could be argued that the words are in fact ambiguous, with a strict sense and a more general sense, both known to competent language users. For instance, the word 'Kleenex', originally a brand name, may also have come to mean, more generally, a disposable tissue. However, such ambiguities ultimately derive from repeated instances in which the original brand name is loosely used. If 'Kleenex' now has TISSUE as one of its lexical senses, it is because the word was often loosely used to convey this broader meaning before it became lexicalised.

Approximations such as (16) and (17) are generally treated in philosophy of language under the heading of *vagueness*. Vagueness can itself be analysed in semantic or pragmatic terms. There are certainly words with vague linguistic senses – 'old' or 'ovoid', for instance – and vagueness is therefore at least partly a semantic phenomenon. With other expressions, such as 'five o'clock', 'hexagonal' or 'flat', it seems more appropriate to assign a precise semantics and propose a pragmatic explanation of why they are frequently understood as approximations. David Lewis argues that in such cases, 'the standards of precision in force are different from one conversation to another, and may change in the course of a single conversation. Austin's "France is hexagonal" is a good example of a sentence that is true enough for many contexts but not true enough for many others' (1979/1983: 245).

Both standard semantic and pragmatic treatments of vagueness presuppose that there is a continuum or a fine-grained series of cases between narrower and broader interpretations. This may indeed be true of semantically vague terms such as 'old' or 'ovoid', and terms such as 'flat', 'hexagonal' or 'five o'clock', which are often understood as approximations (Gross 2001). However, with 'run' in (18) and 'Kleenex' in (19), no such continuum exists. There is a sharp discontinuity, for instance, between running (where both feet leave the ground at each step) and walking (where there is always at least one foot on the ground). Typically (though not necessarily), running is faster than walking, so that 'run' may be loosely used, as in (18), to indicate the activity of going on foot (whether walking or running) at a speed more typical of running. But walking at different speeds is not equivalent to running relative to different standards of precision. 'Run', 'Kleenex' and many other words have sharp conceptual boundaries, frequent loose interpretations, and no ordered series of successively broader extensions which might be picked out by raising or lowering some standard of precision. Such cases of loose use seem to call for a special kind of pragmatic treatment, since they are non-literal, but neither the Gricean account of figurative interpretation nor the standard pragmatic treatment of vagueness applies to them.

Do we need four different kinds of analysis for literal, vague, loose and figurative meanings? Relevance theory is unique in proposing a unified account of all these cases. From the general claim that an utterance is a piece of evidence about the speaker's meaning, it follows, at the lexical level, that the function of words in an utterance is not to encode but merely to indicate the concepts which are constituents of the speaker's meaning. We are not denying that words do encode concepts (or at least semantic features), and that they are (at least partly) decoded during the comprehension process; however, we are claiming that the output of decoding is merely a point of departure for identifying the concepts intended by the speaker. The presence in an utterance of an expression with a given sense licenses a variety of (typically non-demonstrative) inferences. Some of these inferences contribute to satisfying the hearer's expectations of relevance, and are therefore drawn. Others don't, and aren't. In the process, there is a mutual adjustment between explicatures and implicatures. The decoded content helps to identify the inferences that make the utterance relevant as expected, and is readjusted so as to warrant just those inferences that contribute to the relevance of the utterance as a whole. In particular, the constituent concepts of the explicature are constructed ad hoc, starting from the linguistically encoded concepts, but quite often departing from them so as to optimise the relevance of the overall interpretation (Carston 1997, 2002a: chapter 5; Sperber and Wilson 1998a, 2008; Wilson and Sperber 2002; Wilson 2003; Wilson and Carston 2007).

Suppose, for instance, you have a lecture one afternoon, but don't know exactly when it is due to start. You are told, 'The lecture starts at five o'clock'. From this utterance, and in particular from the phrase 'at five o'clock', together with contextual premises, you can derive a number of implications that make the utterance relevant to you: that you will not be free to do other things between five and seven o'clock, that you should leave the library no later than 4.45, that it will be too late to go shopping after the lecture, and so on. None of these inferences depends on 'five o'clock' being strictly understood. There are inferences that depend on a strict interpretation (for instance, that the lecture will have begun by 5.01), but they don't contribute to the relevance of the utterance, and you don't draw them. According to the relevance-theoretic approach, you then take the speaker to be committed to the truth of a proposition that warrants just the implications you did derive, a proposition which might be paraphrased, say, as 'The lecture starts between five o'clock and ten past', but which you, the hearer, would have no need to try and formulate exactly in your mind. Note that if the speaker had uttered the more accurate 'between five o'clock and ten past' instead of the approximation 'at five o'clock', the overall effort required for comprehension would have been increased rather than reduced, since you would have had to process a longer sentence and a more complex meaning without any saving on the inferential level. Note, too, that one cannot explain how this approximation is understood by assuming that the standard of precision in force allows for, say, a variation of ten minutes around the stated time. If the lecture might start ten minutes *earlier* than five o'clock, then the inferences worth drawing would not be the same.

This process of ad hoc concept construction via mutual adjustment of explicatures and implicatures is quite general. It works in the same way with metaphors. Consider the metaphor 'John is a computer' used in two different exchanges:

(20)   a. PETER: Is John a good accountant?
          b. MARY: John is a computer.

(21)   a. PETER: How good a friend is John?
          b. MARY: John is a computer.

In each case, the encoded sense of 'computer' draws the hearer's attention to some features of computers that they may share with some human beings. Like the best accountants, computers can process large amounts of numerical information and never make mistakes, and so on. Unlike good friends, computers lack emotions, and so on. In each case, Peter builds an ad hoc concept indicated, though not encoded, by the word 'computer', such that John's falling under this concept has implications that answer the question in (20a) or (21a). Note that Mary need not have in mind the precise implications that Peter will derive, as long as her utterance encourages him to derive the kind of implications that answer his question along the intended lines. So the Romantics were right to argue that the figurative meaning of a live metaphor cannot be properly paraphrased. However, this is not because the meaning is some non-truth-conditional set of associations or 'connotations'. It is because it consists of an ad hoc concept that is characterised by its inferential role and not by a definition, and moreover this inferential role, to a much greater extent than in the case of mere approximations, is left to the hearer to elaborate. Metaphorical communication is relatively weak communication.

In the case of approximations or metaphors, concept construction results in a broadening of the encoded concept; in other cases, as in (5a) ('I'll bring a bottle') and (6b) above, it results in a narrowing. Recall that in (6), Lisa has dropped by her neighbours, the Joneses, who have just sat down to supper:

(6)   a. ALAN JONES: Do you want to join us for supper?
          b. LISA: No, thanks. I've eaten.

As noted above, in order to produce a relevant interpretation of Lisa's answer 'I've eaten', some enrichment of the encoded sentence meaning must take place. In particular, the time span indicated by the perfect 'have eaten' must be narrowed down to the evening of utterance, and 'eaten' must be understood as conveying the ad hoc concept EAT SUPPER. If Lisa has eaten supper on the previous day, or eaten an olive that evening, she would literally *have eaten*, but not in a relevant sense. In still other cases, the result of the same process of meaning construction is that the concept indicated as a constituent of the intended meaning by use of the word 'eaten' is the very one it encodes. If Lisa is supposed to follow a religious fast and says 'I've eaten', then the concept EAT that is part of her meaning is just the linguistically encoded one: a single olive is enough to break a fast.

The comprehension process itself does not involve classifying interpretations as *literal, approximate, loose, metaphorical* and so on. These classifications belong to linguistic theories, including folk and philosophical theories, and play a role in metalinguistic arguments. However, a pragmatic approach suggests that these notions may denote regions on a continuum rather than sharply distinct categories, and may play no role in a proper theory of language use.

1.5   Procedural meaning: speech acts, presuppositions and indexicals

We have tried to show that a contextualist approach to semantics, combined with a relevance-oriented approach to pragmatics, can yield appropriate accounts of speaker's meaning. Starting with the strongest candidates for literalist treatment – constructions which are plausibly analysed as encoding concepts that contribute to explicit truth-conditional content – we have argued that even with these strongest candidates, the case for literalism does not go through. Many aspects of explicit truth-conditional content are not encoded at all, and utterances do not always communicate the concepts they encode. Moreover, a wide range of linguistic constructions contribute to other aspects of speaker's meaning than explicit truth-conditional content, or encode aspects of meaning that are not plausibly analysed in conceptual terms. Examples include illocutionary-force indicators, presupposition triggers, indexicals and demonstratives, focusing devices, parentheticals, discourse connectives, argumentative operators, prosody, interjections, and so on. Because these constructions fall outside the scope of standard literalist approaches, their linguistic meaning is sometimes characterised as 'pragmatic' rather than semantic (although the proposed analyses have rarely shown much concern for how they might contribute to a properly inferential pragmatics). We see these items as providing strong evidence for a contextualist approach to semantics combined with a relevance-oriented pragmatics, and will end by briefly considering how they might be approached within the framework we have outlined.

Speech-act theorists such as Austin, Searle, Katz and Bach and Harnish underlined the fact that a speaker's meaning should be seen not merely as a set of (asserted) propositions, but as a set of propositions each with a recommended propositional attitude or illocutionary force. The treatment of illocutionary and attitudinal meaning has developed in parallel to the treatment of explicit truth-conditional content, with early literalist accounts replaced by more contextualist accounts in which the role of speakers' intentions and pragmatic inference is increasingly recognised.[18] In relevance theory, these non-truth-conditional aspects of speaker's meaning are analysed as *higher-level* explicatures constructed (like the basic explicatures considered in section 1.4) by development of encoded schematic sentence meanings. In uttering (22), for example, Mary might convey not only the basic explicature in (23a), which determines the explicit truth-conditional content of her utterance, but a range of higher-level explicatures such as (23b)–(23d) (any of which might contribute to overall relevance):

(22)   Confidentially, I didn't enjoy the meal.

(23)   a. Mary didn't enjoy the meal.
        b. Mary is telling Peter confidentially that she didn't enjoy the meal.
        c. Mary is admitting confidentially to Peter that she didn't enjoy the meal.
        d. Mary believes she didn't enjoy the meal.

As this example shows, higher-level explicatures, like basic explicatures, are recovered through a combination of decoding and inference, and may be more or less explicit. Thus, Mary could have made her meaning more explicit by uttering (24), and left it less explicit by merely indicating through her behaviour or tone of voice that she was speaking to Peter in confidence:

(24)   I tell you confidentially, I didn't enjoy the meal.

Speech-act theorists distinguish *describing* from *indicating*. Descriptive expressions may be seen as encoding concepts in the regular way (although we have argued that the encoded concept gives no more than a schematic indication of the speaker's meaning). Indicators are seen as carrying other types of information, which contribute to speaker's meaning in other ways than by encoding regular concepts. As illustrated by (22)–(24) ('Confidentially, I didn't enjoy the meal', 'I tell you confidentially, I didn't enjoy the meal'), higher-level explicatures may be conveyed by a mixture of describing and indicating. While illocutionary adverbials and parentheticals such as 'confidentially', 'I tell you confidentially', 'I tell you in total and utter confidence' clearly have descriptive content, mood indicators such as declarative or interrogative word order, imperative, indicative or subjunctive verb morphology, and exclamatory or interrogative intonation fall on the indicating side. How is their encoded meaning to be analysed, if not in conceptual terms? We would like to suggest that their semantic function is to guide the hearer in the inferential construction of higher-level explicatures by narrowing the search space, increasing the salience of certain candidates, and diminishing the salience of others. In some cases, the search space may be reduced to a single plausible candidate, while in others, there may be several, so that the resulting explicatures may be stronger or weaker. As expected, conceptual encoding leads to stronger communication than linguistic indication (Wilson and Sperber 1988a, 1993; Sperber and Wilson 1995: chapter 4.10; Ifantidou 2001).

As noted at the beginning of this section, languages have a rich variety of indicators, which contribute to other aspects of speaker's meaning than illocutionary force; in the framework we have outlined, these would be analysed on similar lines to mood indicators, as contributing to relevance by guiding the hearer towards the intended explicit content, context or conclusions. Consider, for instance, the contribution of the indexical or demonstrative 'here' to the explicit truth-conditional content of (25):

(25)   I have been *here* for two hours.

The semantic function of 'here' is simultaneously to indicate that a referent is required and to restrict the search space to a certain class of candidates, some of which may be made more salient by gesture, direction of gaze or discourse context (and will therefore be more accessible to the relevance-theoretic comprehension heuristic). Even when all these clues are taken into account, they may not determine a unique interpretation. For example, (25) may be true (and relevant) if 'here' is understood to mean 'in this library', but false if understood to mean 'in this room' or 'on this spot'. The encoded meaning of 'here' is only a clue to the speaker's meaning, which is recovered, as always, by mutual adjustment of explicatures and implicatures in the search for optimal relevance.

Finally, a range of items such as 'even', 'still', 'but', 'indeed', 'also' and 'after all', which have been seen as encoding information about 'presuppositions', conventional implicatures or argumentative orientation instead of (or as well as) descriptive information,[19] may be analysed as restricting the search space for implicated premises and conclusions, or as indicating what type of inferential process the hearer is intended to go through in establishing relevance. To give just one illustration, compare (26a) and (26b):

(26)   a. John is a philosopher and he enjoys detective stories.
        b. John is a philosopher but he enjoys detective stories.

As these examples show, although 'and' and 'but' are descriptively equivalent, they orient the hearer towards different types of interpretation (Ducrot 1984; Blakemore 1987, 2002; Hall 2004, 2007). The use of 'and' in (26a), for example, is compatible with an interpretation in which the fact that John enjoys detective stories is unsurprising given that he is a philosopher, while the use of 'but' in (26b) suggests an interpretation in which the fact that John is a philosopher makes it surprising that he enjoys detective stories. The effect of 'but' is to narrow the search space for inferential comprehension by facilitating access to certain types of context or conclusion: it may therefore be seen, like mood indicators and indexicals, as indicating a rather abstract property of the speaker's meaning: the direction in which relevance is to be sought.[20]

The few attempts that have been made to provide a unified account of indicators have been based on the speech act distinction between conditions on *use* and conditions on *truth* (Recanati 2004b). However, as noted above, not all indicators are analysable in speech-act terms, and the distinction between conditions on truth and conditions on use runs the risk of becoming trivial or non-explanatory when removed from the speech-act framework. While it is clear why certain acts have felicity conditions (e.g. only someone with the appropriate authority can give an order, perform a baptism and so on), it is not clear why linguistic expressions such as 'it' and 'that', or 'even' and 'also', which have no obvious analysis in speech-act terms, should have conditions on their appropriate use. By contrast, if the function of indicators is to contribute to inferential comprehension by guiding the hearer towards the speaker's meaning, the conditions on their use fall out as a natural consequence. More generally, from a radical literalist perspective, it is surprising to find any items at all that contribute to meaning without encoding concepts. From the perspective outlined in this chapter, there is no presumption that all linguistic meaning should be either conceptual or truth-conditional: the only requirement on linguistic meaning is that it guide the hearer towards the speaker's meaning by indicating the direction in which relevance is to be sought.

1.6   Conclusion

When pragmatics emerged as a distinct discipline at the end of the 1960s, analytic philosophy was dominated by philosophy of language, and the cognitive sciences were still in their infancy. Since then, as the cognitive sciences have matured and expanded, priority in philosophy has shifted from philosophy of language to philosophy of mind. The development of pragmatics reflects this shift. Part of Grice's originality was to approach meaning as a primarily psychological phenomenon and only derivatively a linguistic one. By underlining the gap between sentence meaning and speaker's meaning, he made it possible, of course, for ideal language philosophers to ignore many context-dependent features of speaker's meaning that ordinary language philosophers had used as evidence against formal approaches. However, far from claiming that linguistic meaning was the only type of meaning amenable to scientific treatment and worthy of philosophical attention, he suggested that speaker's meaning was relevant to philosophy and could be properly studied in its own right. As pragmatics has developed, it has become increasingly clear that the gap between sentence meaning and speaker's meaning is wider than Grice himself thought, and that pragmatic inference contributes not only to implicit content but also to truth-conditional aspects of explicit content. While the effect may be to remove from linguistic semantics more phenomena than some semanticists might be willing to give up, it does not make the field any less challenging: in fact, the semantics–pragmatics interface becomes an interesting interdisciplinary area of research in its own right. However, as the gap between sentence meaning and speaker's meaning widens, it increasingly brings into question a basic assumption of much philosophy of language, that the semantics of sentences provides straightforward, direct access to the structure of human thoughts. We have argued that linguistic meanings are mental representations that play a role at an intermediate stage in the comprehension process. Unlike speaker's meanings (which they resemble in the way a skeleton resembles a body), linguistic meanings are not consciously entertained. In other words, whereas speakers' meanings are salient objects in personal psychology, linguistic meanings only play a role in sub-personal cognition.

Within pragmatics itself, there is a tension between more linguistically oriented and more cognitively oriented approaches. By idealising away from properties of the context which are hard to formalise, and focusing on aspects of interpretation (e.g. 'presuppositions' or 'generalised implicatures') which exhibit a kind of code-like regularity, it is possible to extend the methods of formal semantics to a sub-part of the pragmatic domain (assuming that these phenomena are genuinely pragmatic, which is in some cases contentious) (Kadmon 2001; Blutner and Zeevat 2003). Good or bad, the resulting analyses are unlikely to generalise to the whole domain of pragmatics. The cognitive approach, and in particular relevance theory (on which we have focused here), approaches verbal comprehension as a psychological process. The challenge is precisely to explain how the closed formal system of language provides effective pieces of evidence which, combined with further evidence from an open and dynamic context, enable hearers to infer speakers' meanings. The methods to be used are those of cognitive psychology, including modelling of cognitive processes, experimental tests, studies of communication pathologies (e.g. autism), and evolutionary insights. Pragmatics so conceived is relevant to linguistics because of the light it throws on the semantics–pragmatics interface. Its main relevance is to cognitive psychology, and in particular to the study of mindreading and inference mechanisms. Its implications for the philosophy of language are largely cautionary and deflationary, amounting mainly to downplaying the philosophical significance of linguistic meanings. Its main philosophical relevance is to philosophy of mind. In particular, by describing comprehension, a very common, easy, everyday process, as a form of richly context-dependent inference, pragmatics provides an illustration of how to approach central cognitive processes, which, precisely because of their context-dependence, have been treated by Fodor as a major mystery for cognitive psychology and philosophy of mind.

Part I

Relevance and Meaning

2 The mapping between the mental and the public lexicon

Dan Sperber and Deirdre Wilson

2.1 Introduction

There are words in the language we speak and concepts in our minds. For present purposes, we can use a relatively common-sense, unsophisticated notion of a linguistic word. A bit more needs to be said, now and later, about what we mean by a concept. We assume that mental representations have a structure not wholly unlike that of a sentence, and combine elements from a mental repertoire not wholly unlike a lexicon. These elements are mental concepts: so to speak, 'words of mentalese'. Mental concepts are relatively stable and distinct structures in the mind, comparable to entries in an encyclopaedia or permanent files in a data-base. Their occurrence in a mental representation may determine matching causal and formal (semantic or logical) relationships. On the one hand, there are relationships between the mind and the world. The activation of a concept may play a major role in causal interactions between the organism and external objects that fall under that concept. On the other hand, there are relationships among representations within the mind. The occurrence of a concept in a mental representation may play a causal role in the derivation of further representations, and may also contribute to the justification of this derivation.

2.2 Three types of mapping

What kind of mapping is there (if any) between mental concepts and public words? One extreme view is that natural languages such as English or Swahili are the sole medium of thought. In this case, there is obviously a genuine one-to-one correspondence between public words and mental concepts. An opposite extreme view is that there are no such things as individual mental concepts at all, and therefore no conceptual counterparts to public words. We will ignore these extreme views. We assume that there are mental concepts, and that they are not simply internalisations of public words, so that the kind and degree of correspondence between concepts and words is a genuine and interesting empirical issue.

In principle, the mapping between mental concepts and public words might be exhaustive (so that every concept corresponds to a word and conversely), or partial. If it is partial, this may be because some concepts lack a corresponding word, some words lack a corresponding concept, or both. The mapping between words and concepts may be one-to-one, one-to-many, many-to-one, or a mixture of these. However, the idea that there is an exhaustive, one-to-one mapping between concepts and words is quite implausible.

Some words (for instance the third person pronoun 'it') are more like placeholders, and do not encode concepts at all. Many words seem to encode not a full-fledged concept but what might be called a pro-concept (e.g. 'my', 'have', 'near', 'long' – while each of these examples may be contentious, the existence of the general category should not be). Unlike pronouns, these words have some conceptual content. As with pronouns, their semantic contribution *must* be contextually specified for the associated utterance to have a truth value. For instance, 'This is my book' may be true if 'my book' is interpreted as meaning *the book I am thinking of*, and false if it means *the book I wrote* (and since there are indefinitely many possible interpretations, finding the right one involves more than merely disambiguation). Similarly, whether 'The school is near the house' is true or false depends on a contextually specified criterion or scale; and so on. We believe that pro-concepts are quite common, but the argument of this chapter does not depend on that assumption (or even on the existence of pro-concepts). What we will argue is that, quite commonly, all words behave *as if* they encoded pro-concepts: that is, whether or not a word encodes a full concept, the concept it is used to convey in a given utterance has to be contextually worked out.

Some concepts have no corresponding word, and can be encoded only by a phrase. For instance, most of us arguably have a non-lexicalised concept of an *uncle-or-aunt*. We have many beliefs and expectations about uncles-or-aunts (i.e. siblings of parents, and, by extension, their spouses). It makes sense to assume that these beliefs and expectations are mentally stored together in a non-lexicalised mental concept, which has the lexicalised concepts of UNCLE and AUNT as subcategories. Similarly, people who do not have the word 'sibling' in their public lexicon (or speakers of French, where no such word exists) may nonetheless have the concept of SIBLING characterised as *child of the same parents*, and object of many beliefs and expectations – a concept which has BROTHER and SISTER as subcategories. So it seems plausible that not all words map onto concepts, and not all concepts map onto words.

The phenomenon of polysemy is worth considering here. Suppose Mary says to Peter:

(1)   Open the bottle.

In most situations, she would be understood as asking him to uncork or uncap the bottle. One way of accounting for this would be to suggest that the general meaning of the verb 'open' gets specified by the properties of its direct object:

thus, opening a corked bottle means uncorking it, and so on. However, this cannot be the whole story. Uncorking a bottle may be the standard way of opening it, but another way is to saw off the bottom, and on some occasion, this might be what Mary was asking Peter to do. Or suppose Mary says to Peter:

(2)   Open the washing machine.

In most situations, she will probably be asking him to open the lid of the machine. However, if Peter is a plumber, she might be asking him to unscrew the back; in other situations, she might be asking him to blow the machine open, or whatever.

The general point of these examples is that a word like 'open' can be used to convey indefinitely many concepts. It is impossible for all of these to be listed in the lexicon. Nor can they be generated at a purely linguistic level by taking the linguistic context, and in particular the direct object, into account. It seems reasonable to conclude that a word like 'open' is often used to convey a concept that is encoded neither by the word itself nor by the verb phrase 'open X'. (For discussion of similar examples from alternative perspectives, see Caramazza and Grober 1976; Lyons 1977; Searle 1980, 1983; Lehrer 1990; Pinkal 1995; Pustejovsky 1995; Pustejovsky and Boguraev 1996; Fodor and Lepore 1998.)

So far, we have argued that there are words which do not encode concepts and concepts which are not encoded by words. More trivially, the existence of synonyms (e.g. 'snake' and 'serpent') shows that several words may correspond to a single concept, and the existence of homonyms (e.g. 'cat' or 'bank') shows that several concepts may correspond to a single word. So the mapping between concepts and words is neither exhaustive nor one-to-one.

Although the mapping between words and concepts is imperfect, it is not haphazard. Here are three contrasting claims about what this imperfect mapping might be like:

(3)   Nearly all individual concepts are lexicalised, but many words encode com-
        plex conceptual structures rather than individual concepts. So there are fewer
        concepts than words, and the mapping is partial mostly because many words
        do not map onto individual concepts.

(4)   Genuine synonyms, genuine homonyms, non-lexicalised concepts and words
        that do not encode concepts are all relatively rare, so there is roughly a one-to-
        one mapping between words and concepts.

(5)   The mapping is partial, and the main reason for this is that only a fraction of the
        conceptual repertoire is lexicalised. Most mental concepts do not map onto
        words.

In *The Language of Thought* (1975), Jerry Fodor famously argued against (3) and in favour of (4). According to the version of claim (3) he criticised, words correspond in the mind to definitions couched in terms of a relatively compact repertoire of primitive concepts: for example, the word 'bachelor' might have as its conceptual counterpart the complex mental expression UNMARRIED MAN; the word 'kill' might have as its conceptual counterpart the complex mental expression CAUSE TO DIE, and so on. Many words – perhaps most – would be abbreviations for complex conceptual expressions, rather than encoding individual concepts. Against this view, Fodor argued that most words have no plausible definitions and must therefore correspond to mental primitives. There are psycholinguistic reasons for thinking that even a word like 'bachelor', which seems to have a definition, is best treated as encoding a single concept BACHELOR, which would itself be a (mental rather than public) abbreviation for a complex mental expression (1975: 152).

As Fodor points out, verbal comprehension is fast, and unaffected by the alleged semantic complexity of lexical items. 'Kill' is no harder to process than 'die', and 'bachelor' is no harder than 'unmarried', even though it might be argued that the meaning of 'die' is included in the meaning of 'kill', and the meaning of 'unmarried' is included in the meaning of 'bachelor'. All this suggests to Fodor that the structure of mental messages is very close to that of the public sentences standardly used to communicate them. 'It may be that the resources of the inner code are rather directly represented in the resources we use for communication' (Fodor 1975: 156).

Fodor's argument against (3), combined with a rather traditional view of linguistic communication, seems to weigh in favour of (4). Fodor does, as he says himself, view language 'the good old way':

A speaker is, above all, someone with something he intends to communicate. For want of a better term, I shall call what he has in mind a message. If he is to communicate by using a language, his problem is to construct a wave form which is a token of the (or a) type standardly used for expressing that message in that language. (Fodor 1975: 106)

Here, Fodor is adopting an updated version of what we have called the code theory of verbal communication (Sperber and Wilson 1995). The classical code theory was based on the following assumptions:

(6)   For every thought that can be linguistically communicated, there is a sentence identical to it in content.

(7)   The communication of a thought is achieved by uttering a sentence identical to it in content.

Assumption (7) is clearly too strong. Sentences with pronouns are obvious counterexamples: they are used to communicate different thoughts on different occasions, and are not identical in content to any of these thoughts.

The updated code theory accepts (6), but rejects (7) in favour of the weaker assumption (8):

(8)   The communication of any thought *can be* achieved by uttering a sentence identical to it in content.

For the classical code theory, the only way to communicate thoughts is to encode them. For the updated code theory, this is still the basic way, but there are also inferential short cuts. The updated theory admits that the basic coding–decoding process can be speeded up, supplemented, or even bypassed by use of contextually informed inferential routines. Though full encoding is possible, the theory goes, it is often unnecessary. By exploiting shared contextual information and inferential abilities, communication can succeed even when a name or description is replaced by a pronoun, a phrase is ellipsed, or a whole thought is indirectly suggested rather than directly encoded.

Still, on both classical and updated versions of the code theory, the semantic resources of a language must be rich enough to encode all communicable thoughts. Every concept that can be communicated must be linguistically encodable. There may be a few non-lexicalised concepts (e.g. UNCLE-OR-AUNT) which are encodable only by a phrase; but it is reasonable to think that, in general, the repeated use of a concept in communication would favour the introduction and stabilisation of a corresponding word in the public language.

Because Fodor uncritically accepts the code theory of communication, and because he does not even consider claim (5), let alone argue against it, his excellent arguments against claim (3) do not unequivocally point to the conclusion in (4). Claim (5) might still be correct. We want to argue that it is, and hence that most mental concepts do not map onto words.

There are two interpretations of (5) on which it would be trivially true, or at least easily acceptable. First, it is clear that the number of perceptual stimuli that humans can discriminate is vastly greater than the number of words available to name them: for instance, it has been claimed that we can discriminate anything up to millions of colours, while English has a colour vocabulary of a few hundred non-synonymous terms, only a dozen of which are in frequent use (Hardin 1988: 182–83). If we have a concept for every colour that we can discriminate (or even for every colour that we have had the opportunity to discriminate), it is clear that we have many more concepts than words. However, a discrimination is not the same as a conceptualisation of the items discriminated. Someone may discriminate two shades of vermilion, and even think, *here are two shades of vermilion*, without forming a distinct mental structure, let alone a stable one, for each of these two shades.

A concept, as we understand the term, is an enduring elementary mental structure, which is capable of playing different discriminatory or inferential roles on different occasions in an individual's mental life. We are not considering ephemeral representations of particulars (e.g. an individual tree, an individual person, a particular taste), attended to for a brief moment and then forgotten.

Nor are we considering complex conceptual structures, built from more elementary mental concepts, which correspond to phrases rather than words, and are not stored in long-term memory. Even so, it might be argued that people do form many idiosyncratic, non-lexicalised concepts on the basis of private and unshareable experience. For example, you may have a proper concept of a certain kind of pain, or a certain kind of smell, which allows you to recognise new occurrences, and draw inferences on the basis of this recognition, even though you cannot linguistically express this concept, or bring others to grasp and share it. More generally, it is arguable that each of us has ineffable concepts – perhaps a great many of them. This would again make claim (5) trivially true.

We will return to this point later, and argue that effability is a matter of degree. For the time being, we will restrict ourselves to effable concepts: concepts which can be part of the content of a communicable thought. We want to argue that, even on this interpretation, claim (5) is true: there are a great many *stable* and *effable* mental concepts that do not map onto words.

2.3   Inference and relevance

The alternative to a code theory of verbal communication is an inferential theory. The basic idea for this comes from the work of Paul Grice (1967); we have developed such a theory in detail in our book *Relevance: Communication and Cognition* (1995). According to the inferential theory, all a communicator has to do in order to convey a thought is to give her audience appropriate evidence of her intention to convey it. More generally, a mental state may be revealed by a behaviour (or by the trace a behaviour leaves in the environment). Behaviour which is capable of revealing the content of a mental state may also succeed in *communicating* this content to an audience. For this to happen, it must be used ostensively: that is, it must be displayed so as to make manifest an intention to inform the audience of this content.

Peter asks Mary if she wants to go to the cinema. Mary half-closes her eyes and mimes a yawn. This is a piece of ostensive behaviour. Peter recognises it as such and infers, non-demonstratively, that Mary is tired, that she wants to rest, and that she therefore does not want to go to the cinema. Mary has communicated a refusal to go to the cinema, and a reason for this refusal, by giving Peter some evidence of her thoughts. The evidence was her mimed yawn, which she could expect to activate in Peter's mind the idea of her being tired. The ostensive nature of her behaviour could be expected to suggest to Peter that she *intended* to activate this idea in his mind. Mary thought that the idea activated, and the manifestly intentional nature of its activation, would act as the starting point for an inferential process that would lead to the discovery of her meaning. She might have achieved roughly the same effect by saying 'I'm tired'. This would also have automatically activated the idea of her being tired (this time by linguistic decoding). Moreover, it would have done so in a manifestly intentional way, thus providing Peter with strong evidence of Mary's full meaning.

In general, inferential communication involves a communicator ostensively engaging in some behaviour (e.g. a piece of miming or the production of a coded signal) likely to activate in the addressee (via recognition or decoding) some specific conceptual structure or idea. The addressee takes this deliberately induced effect, together with contextual information, as the starting point for an inferential process which should lead to the discovery of the message (in the sense of proposition plus propositional attitude) that the communicator intended to convey.

The idea activated and the message inferred are normally very different. The idea is merely a trigger for discovery of the message. Often, the triggering idea is a fragment, or an incomplete schematic version, of the message to be communicated. The inferential process then consists in complementing or fleshing out the triggering idea.

It is possible, at least in principle, for the idea activated by the communicator's behaviour to consist of a proposition and a propositional attitude (i.e. a full thought) which is exactly the message she intended to convey. In this limiting case, the inferential process will simply amount to recognising that this is all the communicator meant. The classical code theory treats this limiting case as the only one. Every act of communication is seen as involving the production of a coded signal (e.g. a sentence token) which encodes exactly the intended message. No inferential process is needed. The sentence meaning (or, more generally, the signal meaning) is supposed to be identical to the speaker's meaning. The updated code theory treats this limiting case as the basic and paradigmatic one. Hearers should assume by default that the sentence meaning is the speaker's message, but be prepared to revise this assumption on the basis of linguistic evidence (the sentence does not encode a full message) or contextual evidence (the speaker could not plausibly have meant what the sentence means).

Since the classical code theory is patently wrong, the updated code theory might seem more attractive. However, the classical theory had the advantage of offering a simple, powerful and self-contained account of how communication is possible at all. The updated theory loses this advantage by invoking an inferential mechanism to explain how more can be communicated than is actually encoded. The updated theory offers two distinct mechanisms – coding–decoding and inference – which may be singly or jointly invoked to explain how a given message is communicated. Why should the first of these be fundamental and necessary to human linguistic communication, while the second is peripheral and dispensable? The classical theory, which treats coding–decoding as the *only* explanation of communication, entails as a core theoretical claim that every communicable message is fully encodable. In the updated theory, this is a contingent empirical claim, with little empirical support and no explanatory purchase.

What is the role of inference in communication? Is it merely to provide short cuts along the normal paths of coding–decoding (in which case any inferentially communicated message could have been fully encoded)? Or does inference open up new paths, to otherwise inaccessible endpoints, making it possible to communicate meanings that were not linguistically encodable? (By 'not linguistically encodable' we mean *not encodable in the public language actually being used*, rather than *not encodable in any possible language*.) In the absence of any plausible account of the inferential processes involved in comprehension, the reasonable, conservative option might be to assume that inference does not enrich the repertoire of communicable meanings. For example, if all we had to go on was Grice's ground-breaking but very sketchy original account (in his 1967 William James Lectures, published in Grice 1989), we would have very little idea of how inferential comprehension processes actually work, how powerful they are, and whether and in what ways they might extend the range of communicable concepts.

Relevance theory (Sperber and Wilson 1995) offers a more explicit account of comprehension processes, which claims that what can be communicated goes well beyond what can be encoded. Here, we will give a brief, intuitive outline of relevant aspects of the theory.

The basic ideas of the theory are contained in a definition of relevance and two principles. Relevance is defined as a property of inputs to cognitive processes. The processing of an input (e.g. an utterance) may yield some cognitive effects (e.g. revisions of beliefs). Everything else being equal, the greater the effects, the greater the relevance of the input. The processing of the input (and the derivation of these effects) involves some mental effort. Everything else being equal, the greater the effort, the lower the relevance. On the basis of this definition, two principles are proposed:

(9)   *Cognitive principle of relevance:* Human cognition tends to be geared to the maximisation of relevance.

(10)   *Communicative principle of relevance:* Every act of ostensive communication communicates a presumption of its own relevance.

More specifically, we claim that the speaker, by the very act of addressing someone, communicates that her utterance is the most relevant one compatible with her abilities and preferences, and is at least relevant enough to be worth his processing effort.

As noted above, ostensive behaviour automatically activates in the addressee some conceptual structure or idea: for example, the automatic decoding of an utterance leads to the construction of a logical form. This initial step in the comprehension process involves some mental effort. According to the communicative principle of relevance, the effort required gives some indication of the effect to expect. The effect should be enough to justify the effort (or at least enough for it to have seemed to the speaker that it would seem to the hearer to justify the effort – but we will ignore this qualification, which plays a role only when the speaker deliberately or accidentally fails to provide the hearer with sufficiently relevant information; see Sperber 1994a).

2.4   Relevance and meaning

The communicative principle of relevance provides the motivation for the following comprehension procedure, which we claim is automatically applied to the online processing of attended verbal inputs. The hearer takes the conceptual structure constructed by linguistic decoding; following a path of least effort, he enriches this at the explicit level and complements it at the implicit level, until the resulting interpretation meets his expectations of relevance; at which point, he stops.

We will illustrate this procedure by considering the interpretation of Mary's utterance in (11):

(11)   PETER: Do you want to go to the cinema?
         MARY: I'm tired.

Let's assume (though we will soon qualify this) that Peter decodes Mary's utterance as asserting that Mary is tired. By itself, the information that Mary is tired does not answer Peter's question. However, he is justified in trying to use it to draw inferences that would answer his question and thus satisfy his expectations of relevance. If the first assumption to occur to him is that Mary's being tired is a good enough reason for her not to want to go to the cinema, he will assume she meant him to use this assumption as an implicit premise and derive the implicit conclusion that she doesn't want to go to the cinema because she is tired. Peter's interpretation of Mary's utterance contains the following assumptions:

(12)   a. Mary is tired.
         b. Mary's being tired is a sufficient reason for her not to want to go to the cinema.
         c. Mary doesn't want to go to the cinema because she is tired.

Mary could have answered Peter's question directly by telling him she didn't want to go to the cinema. Notice, though, that the extra (inferential) effort required by her indirect reply is offset by extra effect: she conveys not just a refusal to go, but a reason for this refusal. There may, of course, be many other conclusions that Peter could derive from her utterance – for example, those in (13):

(13)   a. Mary had a busy day.
         b. Mary wouldn't want to do a series of press-ups.

But even if these conclusions were highly relevant to Peter, they would not help to satisfy the specific expectations of relevance created by Mary's utterance. The fact that she was replying to his question made it reasonable for him to expect the kind and degree of relevance that he himself had suggested he was looking for by asking this question, and no more.

However, there is a problem. How plausible is it that the fact that Mary is tired is a good enough reason for her not to want to go to the cinema? Why should Peter accept this as an implicit premise of her utterance? Does Mary never want to go to the cinema when she is tired, even if she is just a little tired, tired enough for it not to be false to say that she is strictly speaking tired? Surely, in these or other circumstances, Peter might have been aware that Mary was somewhat tired, without treating it as evidence that she didn't want to go to the cinema.

As noted above, a hearer using the relevance-theoretic comprehension procedure should follow a path of least effort, enriching and complementing the decoded conceptual structure until the resulting interpretation meets his expectations of relevance. We have shown how this procedure would apply to Mary's utterance in (11) to yield the implicatures (12b) and (12c). This is a case where the explicit content is complemented at the implicit level. However, for this complementation to make sense, some enrichment must also take place at the level of what is explicitly communicated.

If comprehension is to be treated as a properly inferential process, the inferences must be sound (in a sense that applies to non-demonstrative inference). From the mere fact that Mary is tired, Peter cannot soundly infer that she doesn't want to go to the cinema. For the implicatures (12b) and (12c) to be soundly derived, Mary must be understood as asserting something stronger than that she is tired *tout court*: her meaning must be enriched to a point where it warrants the intended inferences. The process is one of parallel adjustment: expectations of relevance warrant the derivation of specific implicatures, for which the explicit content must be adequately enriched.

Mary is therefore conveying something more than simply the proposition that she is tired, which would be satisfied by whatever is the minimal degree of tiredness: she is conveying that she is tired enough not to want to go to the cinema. If she were 'technically' tired, but not tired enough for it to matter, her utterance would be misleading, not just by suggesting a wrong reason for her not wanting to go to the cinema, but also by giving a wrong indication of her degree of tiredness. Suppose Peter thought that she was being disingenuous in using her tiredness as an excuse for not going to the cinema. He might answer:

(14)   Come on, you're not *that* tired!

He would not be denying that she is tired: merely that she is tired to the degree conveyed by her utterance.

How tired is that? Well, there is no absolute scale of tiredness (and if there were, no specific value would be indicated here). Mary is communicating that she is tired enough for it to be reasonable for her not to want to go to the cinema on that occasion. This is an *ad hoc*, circumstantial notion of tiredness. It is the degree of tiredness that has this consequence.

In saying (11), Mary thus communicates a notion more specific than the one encoded by the English word 'tired'. This notion is not lexicalised in English. It may be that Mary will never find another use for it, in which case it will not have the kind of stability in her mental life that we took to be a condition for mental concepthood. Alternatively, she may recognise this particular sort of tiredness, and have a permanent mental 'entry' or 'file' for it, in which case it is a proper concept. In the same way, Peter's grasp of the notion of tiredness Mary is invoking may be ephemeral, or he may recognise it as something that applies to Mary, and perhaps others, on different occasions, in which case he has the concept too.

It might be argued that the word 'tired' in Mary's utterance, when properly enriched, just means *too tired to want to go to the cinema*. This is a meaning which is perfectly encodable in English, even though it is not lexicalised. Suppose this were so, and that Mary has a stable concept of this kind of tiredness: her utterance would still illustrate our point that there may be many non-lexicalised mental concepts. The fact that this concept is encodable by a complex phrase would be no reason to think Mary does not have it as an elementary concept, any more than the fact that 'bachelor' can be defined is any reason to think we have no elementary mental concept of BACHELOR.

In any case, it is unlikely that Mary's answer in (11) is really synonymous with her answer in (15):

(15)   PETER: Do you want to go to the cinema?
       MARY: I'm too tired to want to go to the cinema.

Mary's answer in (11) has a degree of indeterminacy that is lost in (15). Quite apart from this, the apparent paraphrasability of her answer in (11) is linked to the fact that she is answering a *yes–no* question, which drastically narrows down the range of potential implicatures and the enrichment needed to warrant them. Yet the enrichment mechanism is itself quite general, and applies in contexts where the range of implicatures is much vaguer, as we will show with two further examples.

Suppose that Peter and Mary, on holiday in Italy, are visiting a museum. Mary says:

(16)   MARY: I'm tired!

As before, if her utterance is to be relevant to Peter, she must mean more than just that she is strictly speaking tired. This time, though, the implications that might make her utterance relevant are only loosely suggested. They might include:

(17)   a. Mary's enjoyment of this visit is diminishing.
        b. Mary would like to cut short their visit to the museum.
        c. Mary is encouraging Peter to admit that he is also tired and wants to cut short the visit.
        d. Mary would like them to go back to their hotel after this visit to the museum, rather than visiting the Duomo, as they had planned.

If these and other such conclusions are implicatures of her utterance, they are only weak implicatures: implications that Peter is encouraged to derive and accept, but for which he has to take some of the responsibility himself (for the notion of *weak implicature*, see Sperber and Wilson 1995: chapter 4). Whatever implicatures he ends up treating as intended (or suggested) by Mary, he will have to adjust his understanding of her explicit meaning so as to warrant their derivation. Mary will be understood as having conveyed that she is tired to such a degree or in such a way as to warrant the derivation of these implicatures. This overall interpretation is itself justified by the expectation of relevance created by Mary's utterance (i.e. by this particular instantiation of the communicative principle of relevance).

    That evening, at a trattoria, Mary says to Peter:

(18)   I love Italian food!

She does not, of course, mean that she loves all Italian food; nor does she merely mean that there is some Italian food she loves. So what does she mean? It is often suggested that in a case like this, the expression 'Italian food' denotes a proto-type, here *prototypical Italian food*. This presupposes that there is a readily available and relatively context-independent prototype. In the situation described above, it so happens that Mary is a vegetarian. Moreover, her understanding of Italian food is largely based on what she finds in an 'Italian' vegetarian restaurant in her own country where she sometimes goes with Peter, which serves several dishes such as 'tofu pizza' that are definitely not Italian. Mary's utterance achieves relevance for Peter by implicating that she is enjoying her food, and sees it as belonging to a distinct category which the expression 'Italian food' suggests but does not describe.

    Even if Mary's use of the term 'Italian food' were less idiosyncratic, it would not follow that all Peter has to do to understand it is recover a prototype. Much recent research has cast doubt on the view that word meanings can be analysed in terms of context-independent prototypes, and suggests instead that *ad hoc* meanings are constructed in context (see e.g. Barsalou 1987; Franks and Braisby 1990; Franks 1995; Butler 1995). We would add that this contextual construction is a by-product of the relevance-guided comprehension process. The explicit content of an utterance, and in particular the meaning of specific expressions, is adjusted so as to warrant the derivation of implicatures which themselves justify the expectations of relevance created by the utterance act. These occasional meanings may stabilise into concepts, for the speaker, the hearer, or both.

These examples are designed to show how a word which encodes a given concept can be used to convey (as a component of a speaker's meaning) another concept that neither it nor any other expression in the language actually encodes. There is nothing exceptional about such uses: almost any word can be used in this way. Quite generally, the occurrence of a word in an utterance provides a piece of evidence, a pointer to a concept involved in the speaker's meaning. It may so happen that the intended concept is the very one encoded by the word, which is therefore used in its strictly literal sense. However, we would argue that this is no more than a possibility, not a preferred or default interpretation. Any interpretation, whether literal or not, results from mutual adjustment of the explicit and implicit content of the utterance. This adjustment process stabilises when the hypothesised implicit content is warranted by the hypothesised explicit content together with the context, and when the overall interpretation is warranted by (the particular instantiation of) the communicative principle of relevance.

This approach sheds some light on the phenomenon of polysemy illustrated by the example of 'open' above. A verb like 'open' acts as a pointer to indefinitely many notions or concepts. In some cases, the intended concept is jointly indicated by the verb and its direct object (as with the ordinary sense of 'open the washing machine'), so that the inferential route is short and obvious. There may be cases where such routinely reachable senses become lexicalised. In general, though, polysemy is the outcome of a pragmatic process whereby intended senses are inferred on the basis of encoded concepts and contextual information. These inferred senses may be ephemeral notions or stable concepts; they may be shared by few or many speakers, or by whole communities; the inference pattern may be a first-time affair or a routine pattern – and it may be a first-time affair for one interlocutor and a routine affair for another, who, despite these differences, manage to communicate successfully. (For relevance-theoretic accounts of polysemy, see Deane 1988; Groefsema 1995a; Carston 1997, 1998b; Papafragou 1998a; Wilson and Sperber 1998a.)

2.5   Implications

Our argument so far has been that, given the inferential nature of comprehension, the words in a language can be used to convey not only the concepts they encode, but also indefinitely many other related concepts to which they might point in a given context. We see this not as a mere theoretical possibility, but as a universal practice, suggesting that there are many times more concepts in our minds than words in our language.

Despite their different theoretical perspectives, many other researchers in philosophy, psychology and linguistics have converged on the idea that new senses are constantly being constructed in context (e.g. Barsalou 1987; Franks and Braisby 1990; Goschke and Koppelberg 1991; Gibbs 1994a; Franks 1995; Recanati 1995; Nunberg 1996; Carston 1997, 1998b). However, it is possible to believe that new senses can be contextually constructed without accepting that there are more mental concepts than public words.

It might be argued, for example, that the only stable concepts are linguistically encodable ones. Unless a new sense constructed in context is linguistically encodable, it cannot be a stable concept of the speaker's, and will never stabilise as a mental concept in the hearer. When Mary says at the museum that she is tired, the understanding that she and Peter have of her kind and degree of tiredness cannot be divorced from their understanding of the whole situation. They do not construct or use an *ad hoc* concept of tiredness. Rather, they have a global representation of the situation, which gives its particular contextual import to the ordinary concept of tiredness.

We would reply as follows. We do not deny – indeed, we insist – that most occasional representations of a property (or an object, event or state) do not stabilise into a concept. Most contextually represented properties are not recognised as having been previously encountered, and are not remembered when the situation in which they were represented is itself forgotten. However, some properties are recognised and/or remembered even when many or all of the contextual elements of their initial identification are lost. For example, you look at your friend and recognise the symptoms of a mood for which you have no word, which you might be unable to describe exactly, and whose previous occurrences you only dimly remember; but you know that mood, and you know how it is likely to affect her and you. Similarly, you look at the landscape and the sky, and you recognise the weather, you know how it will feel, but you have no word for it. Or you feel a pain, you recognise it and know what to expect, but have no word for it; and so on. You are capable not just of recognising these phenomena but also of anticipating them, imagining them, regretting or rejoicing that they are not actual. You can communicate thoughts about them to interlocutors who are capable of recognising them, if not spontaneously, at least with the help of your communication. Your ability to recognise and think about the mood, the weather, the pain, is evidence that you have a corresponding stable mental file or entry, i.e. a mental concept. The evidence is not, of course, conclusive, and there might be a better hypothesis. However the suggestion that what has been contextually grasped can only be remembered with all the relevant particulars of the initial context is not that better hypothesis.

There is a more general reason for believing that we have many more concepts than words. The stabilisation of a word in a language is a social and historical affair. It is a slow and relatively rare process, involving co-ordination among many individuals over time. A plausible guess is that, in most relatively homo-geneous speech communities in human history, less than a dozen new words (including homonyms of older words and excluding proper names) would sta-bilise in a year. On the other hand, the addition of new concepts to an individual's mind is comparatively unconstrained. It is not a matter of co-ordinating with others, but of internal memory management. There is no question that we are capable of acquiring a huge amount of new information every day. Do we store it all in pre-existing files, or do we sometimes – perhaps a few times a day – open a new file, i.e. stabilise a new concept? Notice that this would not involve adding extra information to long-term memory but merely organising information that we are going to add anyhow in a different, and arguably more efficient way.

Information filed together tends to be accessed together, and efficient memory management involves not only filing together what is generally best accessed together, but also filing separately what is generally best accessed separately. Thus, you may be able to recognise a certain type of food (which the public linguistic expression 'Italian food' may hint at in an appropriate context but does not describe), and this ability may play a role in your mental life: say in deciding what to eat or cook on a given occasion. Where is information about this kind of food stored in your memory? Does it have its own address, or does it have to be reassembled from information filed elsewhere every time it is used?

How and how often we open new files, and thus stabilise new mental concepts, is an empirical question, to be investigated with the methods of psychology. However, the hypothesis that we can open a new file only when we have a public word that corresponds to it is a costly one, with no obvious merit. It amounts to imposing an arbitrary and counter-productive constraint on memory management. (This is not, of course, to deny the converse point that on encountering a new word you may stabilise a new concept, and that many of our concepts originate partly or wholly from linguistic communication – a point for which there is much evidence, in particular developmental, e.g. Gelman and Markman 1986.)

While the kind of collective co-ordination needed to stabilise a word in a speech community is an elaborate affair, the typically pairwise co-ordination involved in any given communicative act is a relatively simpler achievement – the kind of achievement that a pragmatic theory such as relevance theory aims to explain. This co-ordination may be somewhat loose. When Mary says at the museum that she is tired, her utterance gets its explicit meaning through adjust-ment to a set of weak implicatures: that is, implicatures whose exact content is not wholly determined by the utterance. The *ad hoc* concept of tiredness that Peter constructs (i.e. the concept of tiredness which warrants the derivation of these weak implicatures) is unlikely to be exactly the same as the one Mary had in mind (since she did not foresee or intend precisely these implicatures). This is not a failure of communication. It is an illusion of the code theory that communication aims at duplication of meanings. Sometimes it does, but quite ordinarily a looser kind of understanding is intended and achieved. The type of co-ordination aimed at in most verbal exchanges is best compared to the co-ordination between people taking a stroll together rather than marching in step.

Returning to the question of effability, we would maintain that this is a matter of degree. Some concepts are properly shared, and can be unequivocally expressed: a mathematical discussion would provide good examples. Other concepts are idiosyncratic, but as a result of common experience or communication, are close enough to the idiosyncratic concepts of others to play a role in the co-ordination of behaviour. Still other concepts may be too idiosyncratic to be even loosely communicated. The fact that a public word exists, and is successfully used in communication, does not make it safe to assume that it encodes the same concept for all successful users; and in any case, the concept communicated will only occasionally be the same as the one encoded. Communication can succeed, despite possible semantic discrepancies, as long as the word used in a given situation points the hearer in the direction intended by the speaker. Thus, Peter and Mary might differ as to the exact extension of 'tired': Peter might regard as genuine though minimal tiredness a state that Mary would not regard as tiredness at all. Mary's successful use of the term in no way depends on their meaning exactly the same thing by it. Similarly, their concepts of Italy might pick out different entities in space or time (for example, is Ancient Roman history part of Italian history? That depends on what you mean by 'Italy'). Mary's successful use of the term 'Italian' should be unaffected by these discrepancies.

More generally, it does not much matter whether or not a word linguistically encodes a full-fledged concept, and, if so, whether it encodes the same concept for both speaker and hearer. Even if it does, comprehension is not guaranteed. Even if it does not, comprehension need not be impaired. Whether they encode concepts or pro-concepts, words are used as pointers to contextually intended senses. Utterances are merely pieces of evidence of the speaker's intention, and this has far-reaching implications, a few of which we have tried to outline here.

3   Truthfulness and relevance

Deirdre Wilson and Dan Sperber

3.1   Introduction

Here are a couple of apparent platitudes. As speakers, we expect what we say to be accepted as true. As hearers, we expect what is said to us to be true. If it were not for these expectations, if they were not often enough satisfied, there would be little point in communicating at all. David Lewis (who has proposed a convention of truthfulness) and Paul Grice (who has argued for maxims of truthfulness), among others, have explored some of the consequences of these apparent platitudes. We want to take a different line and argue that they are strictly speaking false. Of course hearers expect to be informed and not misled by what is communicated; but what is communicated is not the same as what is said. We will argue that language use is not governed by any convention or maxim of truthfulness in what is said. Whatever genuine facts such a convention or maxim was supposed to explain are better explained by assuming that communication is governed by a principle of relevance.

According to David Lewis (1975), there is a regularity (and a moral obligation) of truthfulness in linguistic behaviour. This is not a convention in Lewis's sense, since there is no alternative regularity which would be preferable as long as everyone conformed to it. However, for any language £ of a population *P*, Lewis argues that there is a convention of *truthfulness and trust in £* (an alternative being a convention of truthfulness and trust in some other language £´):

> My proposal is that the convention whereby a population *P* uses a language £ is a convention of *truthfulness* and *trust* in £. To be truthful in £ is to act in a certain way: to try never to utter any sentences of £ that are not true in £. Thus it is to avoid uttering any sentence of £ unless one believes it to be true in £. To be trusting in £ is to form beliefs in a certain way: to impute truthfulness in £ to others, and thus to tend to respond to another's utterance of any sentence of £ by coming to believe that the uttered sentence is true in £. (Lewis 1975/1983: 167)

Lewis considers the objection that truthfulness might not be the only factor which has to be taken into account, and replies as follows:

Objection: Communication cannot be explained by conventions of truthfulness alone. If I utter a sentence σ of our language £, you – expecting me to be truthful in £ – will conclude that I take σ to be true in £. If you think I am well informed, you will also conclude that probably σ is true in £. But you will draw other conclusions as well, based on your legitimate assumption that it is for some good reason that I chose to utter σ rather than remain silent, and rather than utter any of the other sentences of £ that I also take to be true in £. I can communicate all sorts of misinformation by exploiting your beliefs about my conversational purposes, without ever being untruthful in £. Communication depends on principles of helpfulness and relevance as well as truthfulness.

Reply: All this does not conflict with anything I have said. We do conform to conversational regularities of helpfulness and relevance. But these regularities are not independent conventions of language; they result from our convention of truthfulness and trust in £ together with certain general facts – not dependent on any convention – about our conversational purposes and our beliefs about one another. Since they are by-products of a convention of truthfulness and trust, it is unnecessary to mention them separately in specifying the conditions under which a language is used by a population. (Lewis 1975/1983: 185)

However, Lewis does not explain how regularities of relevance might be by-products of a convention of truthfulness. One of our aims will be to show that, on the contrary, expectations of truthfulness – to the extent that they exist – are a by-product of expectations of relevance.

Paul Grice, in his William James Lectures (delivered at Harvard in 1967 and published in Grice 1989) sketched a theory of utterance interpretation based on a Cooperative Principle and maxims of Quality, Quantity, Relation and Manner (truthfulness, informativeness, relevance and clarity). The Quality maxims went as follows:

(1)   Grice's maxims of Quality
        Supermaxim: Try to make your contribution one that is true.
        (i) Do not say what you believe to be false. [maxim of truthfulness]
        (ii) Do not say that for which you lack adequate evidence.

The supermaxim of Quality is concerned with the speaker's overall contribution (what is communicated, either explicitly or implicitly), while the first and second maxims of Quality relate only to what is said (the proposition explicitly expressed or asserted). Grice saw the first maxim of Quality, which we will call the maxim of truthfulness, as the most important of all the maxims. He says in the William James Lectures:

It is obvious that the observance of some of these maxims is a matter of less urgency than is the observance of others; a man who has expressed himself with undue prolixity would, in general, be open to milder comment than would a man who has said something he believes to be false. Indeed, it might be felt that the importance of at least the first maxim of Quality is such that it should not be included in a scheme of the kind I am constructing; other maxims come into operation only on the assumption that this maxim of Quality is satisfied. While this may be correct, so far as the generation of implicatures is concerned, it seems to play a role not totally different from the other maxims, and it will be convenient, for the present at least, to treat it as a member of the list of maxims. (Grice 1967/1989: 27)

In his 'Retrospective Epilogue', written twenty years later, this view is apparently maintained:

The maxim of Quality, enjoining the provision of contributions which are genuine rather than spurious (truthful rather than mendacious), does not seem to be just one among a number of recipes for producing contributions; it seems rather to spell out the difference between something's being and (strictly speaking) failing to be, any kind of contribution at all. False information is not an inferior kind of information; it just is not information. (Grice 1989: 371)

Notice, though, an interesting shift. While he talks of 'the maxim of Quality', Grice's concern here is with the speaker's contribution as a whole; indeed, there is room for doubt about whether he had the first maxim of Quality or the supermaxim in mind. We believe that this is not a minor detail. One of our aims is to show that the function Grice attributes to the Quality maxims – ensuring the quality of the speaker's overall contribution – can be more effectively achieved in a framework with no maxim of truthfulness at all.

There is a range of apparent counterexamples to the claim that speakers try to tell the truth. These include lies, jokes, fictions, metaphors and ironies. Lewis and Grice are well aware of these cases, and discuss them in some detail. Grice (1967/1989: 30), for instance, notes that his maxims may be violated, and lists several categories of violation, each with its characteristic effects. Lies are examples of *covert violation*, where the hearer is meant to assume that the maxim of truthfulness is still in force and that the speaker believes what she has said. Jokes and fictions might be seen as cases in which the maxim of truthfulness is overtly *suspended* (the speaker overtly *opts out* of it); the hearer is meant to notice that it is no longer operative, and is not expected to assume that the speaker believes what she has said. Metaphor, irony and other tropes represent a third category: they are *overt violations* (*floutings*) of the maxim of truthfulness, in which the hearer is meant to assume that the maxim of truthfulness is no longer operative, but that the supermaxim of Quality remains in force, so that some true proposition is still conveyed.

We will grant that a reasonable – if not optimal – treatment of lies, jokes and fictions might be developed along these lines. Tropes, and more generally loose uses of language (e.g. approximations, sense extensions), present a much more pressing challenge. After all, many, if not most, of our serious declarative utterances are not strictly and literally true, either because they are figurative, or simply because we express ourselves loosely.

An utterance may be said to have a literal meaning which is capable of being either true or false when the result of combining its linguistic sense with its reference is a proposition. We ourselves do not claim that all utterances have a literal meaning, and we will be arguing that even when a literal meaning is available, it is not automatically the preferred interpretation of an utterance. In fact, literalness plays no role in our account of language comprehension, and nor does the notion of *what is said*. By contrast, to those who argue that there is an expectation of truthfulness in what is said, literal meanings matter. For Grice, what is said (as distinct from what is implicated) is the literal meaning of an utterance. For Lewis, what is said is specifiable on the basis of the utterance's literal meaning. Without such an appeal to literal meaning in the determination of what is said, the claim that there is a maxim or convention of truthfulness in what is said would be, if not vacuous, at least utterly vague.

3.2   The case of tropes

Lewis (1975) considers the case of tropes:

Objection: Suppose the members of a population are untruthful in their language £ more often than not, not because they lie, but because they go in heavily for irony, metaphor, hyperbole, and such. It is hard to deny that the language £ is used by such a population.
    Reply: I claim that these people are truthful in their language £, though they are not *literally truthful* in £. To be literally truthful in £ is to be truthful in another language related to £, a language we can call literal-£. The relation between £ and literal-£ is as follows: a good way to describe £ is to start by specifying literal-£ and then to describe £ as obtained by certain systematic departures from literal-£. This two-stage specification of £ by way of literal-£ may turn out to be much simpler than any direct specification of £. (Lewis 1975/1983: 183)

Lewis's reply rests on a widely shared view which dates back to classical rhetoric. On this view,

(2)   a. Literal and figurative utterances differ not in the kind of meanings they have
            (thus, if literal meanings are truth-conditional, so are figurative meanings),
            but in the way these meanings are generated.
         b. The meanings of figurative utterances are generated by systematic depar-
            tures from their literal meanings.

For example, consider (3) and (4), where (3) is a metaphor and (4) is intended as a hyperbole:[1]

(3)   The leaves danced in the breeze.

(4)   You're a genius.

Lewis might want to say that in literal-English, sentences (3) and (4) have just their literal meanings. In actual English, the language in which a convention of truthfulness and trust holds among English speakers, (3) and (4) are ambiguous:

they have their literal meanings plus other, figurative meanings. Thus, (3) has the metaphorical meaning in (5), and (4) the hyperbolic meaning in (6):

(5)   The leaves moved in the breeze as if they were dancing.

(6)   You're very clever.

However, it is not as if any language £ (in the sense required by Lewis, where the sentences of £ can be assigned truth-conditional meanings) had ever actually been specified on the basis of a corresponding 'literal-£'. So what is the justification for accepting something like (2a) and (2b)? How are figurative meanings derived from literal meanings, and under what conditions do the derivations take place? Lewis does not explain, and there are no generally accepted answers to these questions. We have argued (Sperber and Wilson 1986b, 1990a, 1995, 1998a) that figurative interpretations are radically context-dependent, and that the context is not fixed independently of the utterance but constructed as an integral part of the comprehension process. If so, then the very idea of generating the sentences of a language £ on the basis of a corresponding 'literal-£' is misguided.

Grice is often seen as having provided an explanation of how figurative interpretations are conveyed. Consider a situation where the speaker of (3) or (4) manifestly could not have intended to commit herself to the truth of the propositions literally expressed: it is common knowledge that she knows that leaves never dance, or that she does not regard the hearer as a genius. She is therefore overtly violating the maxim of truthfulness: in Grice's terms, she is *flouting* it. Flouting a maxim indicates a speaker's intention: the speaker intends the hearer to retrieve an implicature which brings the full interpretation of the utterance (i.e. what is said plus what is implicated) as close as possible to satisfying the Cooperative Principle and maxims. In the case of tropes, the required implicature is related to what is said in one of several possible ways, each characteristic of a different trope. With metaphor, the implicature is a simile based on what is said; with irony, it is the opposite of what is said; with hyperbole, it is a weaker proposition, and with understatement, a stronger one. Thus, Grice might analyse (3) as implicating (5) above, and (4) as implicating (6).

Note that this treatment of tropes does not differ radically from Lewis's, or from the classical rhetorical account. Grice's approach, like Lewis's, is based on assumption (2a) and, more importantly, on assumption (2b) (that the meanings of figurative utterances are generated by systematic departures from their literal meanings). The only difference is that Lewis sees these departures as systematic enough to be analysed in code-like terms: the figurative meaning of a sentence is a genuine linguistic meaning specified in the grammar of £ by a derivation which takes the literal meaning of the sentence as input. The sentences of £ (unlike those of literal-£) are systematically ambiguous between literal and figurative senses. For Grice, by contrast, sentences have only literal meanings.

Figurative meanings are not sentence meanings but utterance meanings, derived in a conversational context. However, the derivations proposed in Grice's pragmatic approach to tropes are the same as those hinted at by Lewis in his linguistic approach, and neither differs seriously from the classical rhetorical account.

Grice's treatment of tropes leaves several questions unanswered, and we will argue that it is inconsistent with the rationale of his own enterprise. In particular, there is room for doubt about what he meant by the maxim of truthfulness, and the role it was intended to play in his framework. This doubt is created by two possible interpretations of his notion of *saying*. On the first interpretation, saying is merely expressing a proposition, without any necessary commitment to its truth. Understood in this way, the maxim of truthfulness means 'Do not express propositions you believe to be false'. The function of this maxim, and more generally of the Quality maxims, would be to account for the fact – to the extent that it is a fact – that a speaker actually commits herself to the truth of what she says. Tropes would then be explained by the claim that flouting the maxim triggers the recovery of an implicature in the standard Gricean way. However, there is a problem. In general, the recovery of implicatures is meant to restore the assumption that the maxims have been observed, or that their violation was justified in the circumstances (as when a speaker is justified by her ignorance in providing less information than required) (Grice 1989: 370). In the case of tropes, the first Quality maxim is irretrievably violated, and the implicature provides no circumstantial justification whatsoever.

On the second, and stronger, interpretation, saying is not merely expressing a proposition but asserting it: that is, committing oneself to its truth. Understood in this way, the maxim of truthfulness means 'Do not *assert* propositions you believe to be false'. On this interpretation, saying already involves speaker commitment, and the function of the maxim of truthfulness, and more generally of the Quality maxims, would be to ensure that speakers do not make spurious commitments. This seems to fit with Grice's above remark that the function of the Quality maxim is to guarantee that contributions are genuine rather than spurious. However, understood in this way, it is hard to see why a maxim of truthfulness is needed at all. It seems to follow from the very notion of an assertion as a commitment to truth (perhaps together with a proper understanding of commitment) that your assertions should be truthful. In fact, the only pragmatic function of the first Quality maxim, on this interpretation, is to be violated in metaphor and irony, thus triggering the search for an implicature. Without it, Grice would have no account of figurative utterances at all.

Which notion of saying did Grice have in mind in proposing the maxim of truthfulness? There is evidence of some hesitation. On the one hand, he treats the tropes as 'Examples in which the first maxim of Quality is flouted' (Grice 1967/1989: 34). On the other, he comments that in irony the speaker 'has said *or has made as if to say*' [our italics] something she does not believe, and that in metaphor what is communicated must be obviously related to what the speaker *'has made as if to say'* (p. 34). If the speaker of metaphor or irony merely 'makes as if to say' something, then the stronger notion of saying must be in force; on the other hand, if the speaker of a trope merely 'makes as if' to say something, then surely the maxim of truthfulness is not violated. But if the maxim of truthfulness is not violated, how does Grice's analysis of metaphor and irony go through at all?

Elsewhere in his philosophy of language, where the notion of saying plays a central role, it was the stronger rather than the weaker notion that interested Grice. He says, for example, 'I want to say that (1) "U (utterer) said that p" entails (2) "U did something x by which U meant that p"' (Grice 1967/1989: 87). For Grice, what is *meant* is roughly co-extensive with what is *intentionally communicated*: that is, with the information put forward as true. On this interpretation, saying involves speaker commitment: that is, it means asserting. Among his commentators, Stephen Neale (1992) treats these broader considerations as decisive: 'If U utters the sentence "Bill is an honest man" ironically, on Grice's account U will *not* have said that Bill is an honest man: U will have *made as if to say* that Bill is an honest man' (Neale 1992: 523).

How can we reconcile these two claims: that metaphor and irony are deliberate violations of the maxim of truthfulness, and hence must *say* something, and that in metaphor and irony the speaker merely *makes as if to say* something? A possible answer would be to distinguish two phases in the utterance interpretation process. In the first, the utterance of a declarative sentence would provide prima facie evidence for the assumption that an assertion is being made. In the second, this assumption would be evaluated and accepted or rejected. In the case of metaphor and irony, this second phase would involve an argument of the following sort: if it is common ground that the utterer U doesn't believe p, then U cannot assert p; it is common ground that U doesn't believe p; hence, U hasn't asserted p. In this way, we get a consistent interpretation of the notion of saying, and we can see why Grice hesitates between 'saying' and 'making as if to say'.

However, if this interpretation is correct, then a trope involves no real violation of the maxim of truthfulness at any stage: since the speaker was not saying p, she was not saying what she believed to be false. A flouting, so understood, is a mere appearance of violation. So why should it be necessary to retrieve an implicature in order to preserve the assumption that the maxims have been respected? The Gricean way to go (although Grice himself did not take this route) would be to argue that it is not the maxim of truthfulness but some other maxim that is being violated. Quite plausibly, the maxim of Relation ('Be relevant') is being violated, for how can you be relevant when you speak and say nothing? Surely the first maxim of Quantity ('Make your contribution as informative as is required') is being violated, for if nothing is said, no information is provided. The implicature should thus be seen as a way of providing a full interpretation of the utterance in which these maxims are respected.

The problem with this analysis of tropes (and also with the alternative analysis on which floutings of the maxim of truthfulness are genuine violations) is that it leads to an interpretation of figurative utterances which irretrievably violates the Manner maxims. In classical rhetoric, a metaphor such as (3) or a hyperbole such as (4) is merely an indirect and decorative way of communicating the propositions in (5) or (6). This ornamental value might be seen as explaining the use of tropes, insofar as classical rhetoricians were interested in explanation at all. Quite sensibly, Grice does not appeal to ornamental value. His supermaxim of Manner is not 'Be fancy' but 'Be perspicuous'. He assumes, this time in accordance with classical rhetoric, that figurative meanings, like literal meanings, are fully propositional, and always paraphrasable by means of a literal utterance. Which raises the following question: Isn't a direct and literal expression of what you mean *always* more perspicuous (and in particular less obscure and less ambiguous, cf. the first and second Manner maxims) than an indirect figurative expression? (Remember: you cannot appeal to the subtle extra effects of tropes, since they are not considered, let alone explained, within the Gricean framework.)

It would be presumptuous to attribute Grice's apparent hesitation between two senses of *saying* to a lack of conceptual rigour on his part. We see it rather as arising from the difficulty of deploying a notion of *saying* which is both close enough to common usage to justify the choice of this word, and yet precise enough to make a contribution to a theory of language use. We will argue in section 3.7 that there is no such notion. We ourselves do not use 'saying' as a theoretical term, except in rendering the views of others.

3.3   The case of loose use

Tropes are the most striking examples of serious utterances where the speaker is manifestly not telling the strict and literal truth. Even more common are loose uses of language (e.g. rough approximations, sense extensions), where an expression is applied to items that fall outside its linguistically determined denotation, strictly understood. Consider the examples in (7)–(10):

(7)   The lecture starts *at five o'clock*.

(8)   Holland is *flat*.

(9)   SUE: I must *run* to the bank before it closes.

(10)   JANE: I have a terrible cold. I need a *Kleenex*.

If the italicised expressions in (7)–(10) are understood in the most restrictive way (and ignoring issues of ambiguity or polysemy for a moment), these utterances are not strictly and literally true: lectures rarely start at exactly the appointed time, Holland is not a plane surface, Sue must hurry to the bank but not necessarily run there, and other brands of disposable tissue would do just as well for Jane. Such loose uses of language are very common. Some are tied to a particular situation, produced once and then forgotten. Others may be regular and frequent enough to give rise to an extra sense, which may stabilise in an individual or a population: lexical broadening (along with lexical narrowing and metaphorical transfer) has been seen as one of the main pragmatic factors driving semantic change (Lyons 1977: sections 13.4, 14.5). What concerns us here is not so much the outcome of these historical macro-processes as the nature of the pragmatic micro-processes that underlie them, and we will largely abstract away from the question of whether, or when, a word such as 'flat', or 'run', or 'Kleenex' may be said to have acquired an extra stable sense (see Sperber and Wilson 1998a for some discussion).

How should loose uses such as those in (7)–(10) be analysed? Are they lapses, the result of sloppy speech or thought, accepted by hearers whose expectations have been reduced to realistic levels by repeated encounters with normal human failings? Is it reasonable to assume that there really is a convention or maxim of truthfulness, although speakers quite commonly fall short of strictly obeying it? As hearers, would we always – and as speakers, should we always – prefer the strictly true statements in (11)–(14) to the loose uses in (7)–(10)?

(11)   The lecture starts at or shortly after five.

(12)   Holland has no mountains and very few hills.

(13)   I must go to the bank as fast as if I were running.

(14)   I need a Kleenex or other disposable tissue.

Clearly not. In most circumstances, the hearer would not be misled by strictly untrue approximations such as (7)–(10), and their strictly true counterparts in (11)–(14) would not provide him with any more valuable information. Indeed, since these strictly true counterparts are typically longer, the shorter approximations may be preferable.

Loose uses of language present few problems for speakers and hearers, who are rarely even aware of them; but they do raise a serious issue for any philosophy of language based on a maxim or convention of truthfulness. We have suggested above that appeals to ambiguity (or polysemy) merely defer the problem, since such ambiguities ultimately derive from repeated instances of loose use (for further discussion, see section 3.6 below). In this section, we will consider other solutions proposed in the literature, paying particular attention to Lewis's treatment of pragmatic vagueness. We will argue that no single solution, nor any combination of proposed solutions, is adequate to handle the full variety of loose uses of language, which go well beyond the types of pragmatic vagueness dealt with on Lewis's account.

In Grice's framework, loose uses such as (7)–(10) apparently violate either the maxim of truthfulness or the second maxim of Quality ('Have adequate evidence for what you say'). However, they do not really fit into any of the categories of violation listed in section 3.1 above. They are not covert violations, designed to deceive the hearer into believing the proposition strictly and literally expressed. They are not like jokes or fictions, which suspend the maxims entirely. One might try to analyse them as floutings: overt violations (real or apparent), designed to trigger the search for a related implicature (here, a hedged version of what was literally said or quasi-said); but the problem is that loose uses are not generally perceived as violating the Quality maxims at all. In classical rhetoric, they were not treated as tropes involving the substitution of a figurative for a literal meaning. They do not have the striking quality that Grice associated with floutings, which he saw as resulting in figurative or quasi-figurative interpretations. Loose talk involves no *overt* violation, real or apparent; or at least it does not involve a degree of overtness in real or apparent violation which might trigger the search for an implicature. While we are all capable of realising on reflection that utterances such as (7)–(10) are not strictly and literally true, these departures from truthfulness pass unattended and undetected in the normal flow of discourse. Grice's framework thus leaves them unexplained.

Perhaps we should reconsider the apparent platitudes we started with. Maybe we should have said that as speakers, we expect what we say to be accepted as *approximately* true, and as hearers, we expect what is said to us to be *approximately* true. But this is far too vague to do the required work of explaining how speakers and hearers manage to communicate successfully. Approximations differ both in kind and in degree, and their acceptability varies with content and context. There is no single scale on which the degrees of approximation in disparate statements such as (7)–(10) can be usefully compared. The same statement may be an acceptable approximation in one situation and not in another. Thus, suppose the speaker of (7) expects the lecture to start sometime between five o'clock and 5.10: then (7) would be an acceptable approximation to a student who has just asked whether the lecture starts at five or six o'clock, but not to a radio engineer preparing to broadcast the lecture live. Moreover, as we will argue below, there are cases where the notion of 'degrees of approximation' does not really apply.

A convention of truthfulness and trust in a language (if there were one) might play a valuable role in explaining how linguistic expressions acquire their conventional meanings, and how speakers and hearers use these meanings to communicate successfully. If all that speakers and hearers are entitled to are vague expectations of approximate truth, it is hard to see how the resulting convention of approximate truthfulness could be robust enough to establish common meanings. As we have shown, the same approximation may be differently intended and understood in different circumstances. Unless it is supplemented with some account of how speakers and hearers can converge on these more specific understandings – an account which might then be doing most of the explanatory work – a convention of approximate truthfulness and trust is inadequate to explain how the co-ordination necessary for successful communication is achieved. Still, this is the direction that David Lewis proposes to explore. He writes:

When is a sentence true enough? . . . this itself is a vague matter. More important for our present purposes, it is something that depends on context. What is true enough on one occasion is not true enough on another. The standards of precision in force are different from one conversation to another, and may change in the course of a single conversation. Austin's 'France is hexagonal' is a good example of a sentence that is true enough for many contexts but not true enough for many others. (1979/1983: 244–45)

We agree with Lewis (and Unger 1975: chapter 2) that 'hexagonal' and 'flat' are semantically absolute terms, and that their vagueness should be seen as pragmatic rather than semantic (so in our terms they are genuine cases of loose use). However, Lewis's analysis of pragmatically vague terms such as 'flat' is very similar to his analysis of semantically vague terms such as 'cool'.[2] For Lewis, a semantically vague term has a range of possible sharp delineations, marking different cut-off points between, say, 'cool' and 'warm'. 'This is cool' may be true at some but not all delineations, and depending on our purposes, we may be willing or unwilling to assert it: hence its vagueness (1970/1983: 228–29). On Lewis's account, semantically absolute but pragmatically vague terms are handled on similar lines, except that semantic delineations are replaced by contextually determined standards of precision (so if 'flat' were semantically rather than pragmatically vague, the analysis would not be very different). On this approach, 'Holland is flat' would be true according to some fairly low standard of precision, but false given higher standards.

Semantic vagueness clearly exists ('bluish' and 'flattish' are good examples); its analysis raises problems of its own, about which we have nothing to say here (see Williamson 1994; Keefe and Smith 1997). What we do want to argue against is the idea that loose use can be successfully treated as a pragmatic analogue of semantic vagueness. As we have suggested above (and will argue in more detail below), there are many varieties of loose use, not all of which can be satisfactorily handled by appeal to contextually determined standards of precision. For the cases that cannot be handled on Lewis's lines, an alternative analysis must be found. We will propose such an analysis, and argue that it generalises straightforwardly to all varieties of loose use (and indeed to all utterances, literal, loose, or figurative), making the appeal to standards of precision as a component of conversational competence unnecessary.

In fact, there are problems even in some cases where the appeal to contextually determined standards of precision looks initially plausible. Consider a situation where (7) ('The lecture starts at five o'clock') would be accepted as true enough if the lecture started somewhere between five o'clock and 5.10. On Lewis's account, it might be claimed that here the contextually determined standard of precision allows for a give or take of, say, fifteen minutes around the stated time. It should then follow that a hearer in the same situation, with the same standard of precision in force, would be equally willing to accept (7) as true enough if the lecture started somewhere between 4.50 and five o'clock. But there is an obvious asymmetry between the two cases. Intuitively, the reason is clear enough: the audience won't mind or feel misled if they get to the lecture a few minutes early, but they will if they get there a few minutes late, so the loosening is acceptable only in one direction. In a different situation – when the speaker is talking about the end of the lecture rather than the beginning, for example – there may be an asymmetry in the other direction. Again, the reason is intuitively clear: the audience won't mind or feel misled if they can get away a bit earlier than expected, but they will if they have to stay longer. It is hard to explain these obvious intuitions by appeal to the regular notion of contextually determined standards of precision as described above. One might, of course, try building the asymmetries into the standards of precision themselves, but then two different standards would have to be invoked to explain how (15) is quite naturally understood to mean something like (16):

(15)   The lecture starts at five o'clock and ends at seven o'clock.

(16)   The lecture starts at five o'clock or shortly after and ends at seven o'clock or shortly before.

This is clearly *ad hoc*. It would be better to find an alternative account of these asymmetries – but such an account might make the appeal to contextually determined standards of precision redundant.

A more serious problem for Lewis is that in some cases of loose use, the appeal to contextually determined standards of precision does not seem to work at all. Lewis's account works best when there is a continuum (or ordered series) of cases between the strict truth and the broadest possible approximation. 'Flat' is a good example, since departures from strict flatness may vary in degree. 'Five o'clock' also works well in this respect, since departures from exactness may vary in degree. But with 'run' in (9) ('I must run to the bank') and 'Kleenex' in (10) ('I need a Kleenex'), no such continuum exists. There is a sharp discontinuity between running (where both feet leave the ground at each step) and walking (where there is always at least one foot on the ground). Typically (though not necessarily), running is faster than walking, so that 'run' may be loosely used, as in (9), to indicate the activity of going on foot (whether walking or running) at a speed more typical of running. But walking at different speeds is not equivalent to running relative to different standards of precision. Similarly, 'Kleenex' is a brand name: other brands of disposable tissue are not Kleenex. The word 'Kleenex' may be loosely used, as in (10), to indicate a range of tissues similar to Kleenex. But there is no continuum on which being similar enough to Kleenex amounts to actually being Kleenex relative to stricter or looser standards of precision. 'Run', 'Kleenex' and many other words have sharp conceptual boundaries and no ordered series of successively broader extensions which might be picked out by raising or lowering some standard of precision. Yet these terms are often loosely used. This supports our claim that looseness is a broader notion than pragmatic vagueness.[3]

Again, for someone with no particular theoretical axe to grind, it is easy enough to see intuitively what is going on. Suppose you have a lecture one afternoon, but don't know exactly when it is due to start. Someone tells you, 'The lecture starts at five o'clock'. From the literal content of the utterance, together with other premises drawn from background knowledge, you can derive a number of conclusions that matter to you: that you will not be free to do other things between five and seven o'clock, that you should leave the library no later than 4.45, that it will be too late to go shopping after the lecture, and so on. To say that these conclusions matter to you is to say that you can use them to derive still further non-trivial contextual implications, of a practical or a theoretical nature. These initial conclusions are the main branches of a derivational tree with many further branches and sub-branches. All these direct and indirect conclusions would have been derivable from the strictly true utterance 'The lecture starts at or shortly after five o'clock', but at the extra cost required to process a longer sentence and a more complex meaning. There are other conclusions – false ones this time – that would have been derivable from the approximation, 'The lecture starts at five o'clock', but not from its strictly true counterpart: that the lecture will have begun by 5.01, for instance. But you are unlikely to derive them. They don't matter, because they are derivational bare branches which yield no further non-trivial implications.

To illustrate: Peter and Mary, who are both rather unfit, are discussing where to go on their next cycling holiday. Mary suggests Holland, adding, 'Holland is flat'. From the strictly false proposition that Holland is flat – just as easily as from the strictly true hedged proposition that Holland is approximately flat – Peter can derive the true conclusion that cycling in Holland would involve no mountain roads and would not be too demanding. Unlike the true hedged proposition, the false approximation also has false implications (for instance, that there are no hills at all in Holland). But it is unlikely that Peter would even contemplate deriving any of these.

Sue, chatting with friends in the street, looks at her watch and says, 'I must run to the bank before it closes'. Her friends will take her to mean that she must break off their chat and hurry to the bank. For them, that much information is worth deriving. Whether she will actually get to the bank by running, walking fast or a mixture of both does not matter to them, and they will simply not attend to this aspect of the literal meaning of her utterance.

Jane and Jack are at the cinema waiting for the film to start. In saying, 'I have a terrible cold. I need a Kleenex', Jane provides a premise from which Jack can infer that she wants to borrow a tissue to use in dealing with her cold. Her utterance also provides a premise from which he could derive the possibly false conclusion that she does not want a tissue of any other brand than Kleenex. However, he is unlikely to draw such a conclusion, since his expectations of relevance in this context are satisfied by the weaker interpretation (and in a context where his expectations of relevance would encourage an interpretation on which Jane was specifically requesting a Kleenex – e.g. if she was angrily throwing away tissues of another brand – the utterance would not be understood as a case of loose talk).

As these examples show, hearers have no objection to strictly false approximations as long as the conclusions they bother to derive from them are true. In fact, they might prefer the shorter approximations to their more long-winded but strictly true counterparts for reasons of economy of effort. There is some evidence that speakers take into account the perceived preferences of their audience in deciding how strictly or loosely to speak. In a series of experiments on truthfulness and relevance in telling the time, Van der Henst, Carles and Sperber (2002) showed that when asked for the time by a stranger in a public place, people tend to give an answer that is either accurate to the minute or rounded to the nearest multiple of five, depending on how useful in the circumstances they think a more accurate answer would be. This applies even to people with digital watches, which make it particularly easy to read off a time that is accurate to the minute. These people have to make an extra effort to produce a rounded answer which, to the best of their knowledge, is not strictly true, but is easier for their audience to process.

Anticipating the arguments of the next section, let us say that an utterance is *relevant* when the hearer, given his cognitive dispositions and the context, is likely to derive some genuine knowledge from it (we will shortly elaborate on this). Someone interested in defending a maxim or convention of truthfulness might then suggest that expectations of relevance do play a role in comprehension, but in a strictly limited way. It might be claimed, for example, that while utterances in general create expectations of truthfulness, approximations alone create expectations of relevance, which play a role in loose talk, but only there. This account – apart from being unparsimonious – raises the following problem. As noted above, while we are all capable of realising on reflection that an utterance was an approximation rather than a strictly literal truth, the fact that an approximation has been used is simply not noticed in the normal flow of discourse, and is surely not recognisable in advance of the comprehension process. But in that case, how could loose talk and literal talk be approached and processed with different expectations?

Here is the answer. It is not just approximations but all utterances – literal, loose or figurative – that are approached with expectations of relevance rather than truthfulness. Sometimes, the only way of satisfying these expectations is to understand the utterance as literally true. But just as an utterance can be understood as an approximation without being recognised and categorised as such, so it can be literally understood without being recognised and categorised as such. We will argue that the same is true of tropes. Literal, loose, and figurative interpretations are arrived at in the same way, by constructing an interpretation which satisfies the hearer's expectations of relevance (for earlier arguments along these lines, see Sperber and Wilson 1986b, 1990a, 1995, 1998a).

No special machinery is needed to explain the interpretation of loose talk. In particular, contextually determined standards of precision play no role in the interpretation process. They do not help with cases such as 'run', or 'Kleenex', which are neither semantically nor pragmatically vague; and to appeal to them in analysing cases such as 'flat' or 'at five o'clock', which might be seen as involving a pragmatic form of vagueness, would be superfluous at best.

3.4   Relevance: theory

Grice's maxim of truthfulness was part of what might be called an inferential model of human communication. This contrasts with a more classical code model, which treats utterances as signals encoding the messages that speakers intend to convey. On the classical view, comprehension is achieved by decoding signals to obtain the associated messages. On the inferential view, utterances are not signals but pieces of evidence about the speaker's meaning, and comprehension is achieved by inferring this meaning from the evidence provided. An utterance is, of course, a linguistically coded piece of evidence, so that the comprehension process will involve an element of decoding. But the linguistically encoded sentence meaning need not be identical to the speaker's meaning – and we would argue that it never is – since it is likely to be ambiguous and incomplete in ways the speaker's meaning is not. On this approach, the linguistic meaning recovered by decoding is just one of the inputs to an inferential process which yields an interpretation of the speaker's meaning.

Grice, Lewis and others who have contributed to the development of an inferential approach to communication have tended to minimise the gap between sentence meaning and speaker's meaning; they treat the inference from sentence meaning to speaker's meaning as merely a matter of assigning referents to referring expressions, and perhaps of calculating implicatures. While the slack between sentence meaning and speaker's explicit meaning cannot be entirely eliminated, a framework with a maxim or convention of truthfulness has the effect of reducing it to a minimum. But why should this be something to be a priori expected or desired? Comprehension is a complex cognitive process. From a cognitive point of view, how much of the work is done by inference and how much by decoding depends on how efficient the inferential processes are. We have argued (Wilson and Sperber 1981, 1993, 2004; Sperber and Wilson 1995, 1998a) that relevance-oriented inferential processes are efficient enough to allow for a much greater slack between sentence meaning and speaker's meaning than is generally assumed. Here, we summarise the theory briefly for purposes of the present discussion.

We characterise *relevance* as a property of inputs to cognitive processes which makes them worth processing. ('Relevance' is used in a technical sense which is not meant to capture any of the ordinary senses of the word.) These inputs may be external stimuli (e.g. a smell, the sound of an utterance), or internal representations which may undergo further processing (e.g. the recognition of a smell, a memory, the linguistic decoding of an utterance). At each point in our cognitive lives, there are many more potential inputs available than we can actually process: for example, we perceive many more distal stimuli than we can attend to, and have many more memories than we can reactivate at a single time. Efficiency in cognition is largely a matter of allocating our processing resources so as to maximise cognitive benefits. This involves processing inputs that offer the best expected cost/benefit ratio at the time.

Here we will consider only one type of cognitive benefit: improvements in knowledge (theoretical or practical). This is plausibly the most important type of cognitive benefit. There may be others: improvements in memory or imagination, for example (although it might be argued that these are benefits only because they contribute indirectly to improvements in knowledge; better memory and imagination lead to better non-demonstrative inference, and therefore to better knowledge). In any case, for our present purposes, there is another important reason for identifying cognitive benefits with improvements in knowledge.

In a situation where it is clear to both participants that the hearer's goal in listening to the speaker's utterances is not the improvement of knowledge – say, he just wants to be amused – there is no reason why the speaker should be expected to tell the truth. Thus, one way of challenging the maxim or convention of truthfulness would be to start by questioning whether humans are much interested in truth (e.g. Stich 1990). Here, we want to present a more pointed challenge to Grice's and Lewis's ideas, based on the nature of human communication rather than the goals of cognition. We will therefore grant that one of the goals of most human communication (though certainly not the only one) is the transmission of genuine information and the improvement of the hearer's knowledge. We will consider only cases where hearers are interested in truth.

Our claim is that even in these cases, hearers do not expect utterances to be literally true.

The processing of an input in the context of existing assumptions may improve the individual's knowledge not only by adding a new piece of information, but by revising his existing assumptions, or yielding conclusions not derivable from the new piece of knowledge alone or from existing assumptions alone. We define an input as *relevant* when and only when it has such positive cognitive effects.[4] Relevance is also a matter of degree, and we want to characterise it not only as a classificatory notion but also as a comparative one. There are inputs with at least some low degree of relevance all around us, but we cannot attend to them all. What makes an input worth attending to is not just that it is relevant, but that it is more relevant than any alternative potential input to the same processing resources at that time. Although relevance cannot be measured in absolute terms, the relevance of various inputs can be compared.

For our purpose, which is to characterise a property crucial to cognitive economy, the relevance of inputs must be comparable not only in terms of benefits (i.e. positive cognitive effects), but also in terms of costs (i.e. processing effort). We therefore propose the following comparative notion of relevance:

(17)   Relevance of an input to an individual at a time
        a. Everything else being equal, the greater the positive cognitive effects achieved in an individual by processing an input at a given time, the greater the relevance of the input to that individual at that time.
        b. Everything else being equal, the smaller the processing effort expended by the individual in achieving those effects, the greater the relevance of the input to that individual at that time.

Here is a brief and artificial illustration. Peter wakes up feeling unwell and goes to the doctor. On the basis of her examination, she might make any of the following true statements:

(18)   You are ill.

(19)   You have flu.

(20)   You have flu or 29 is the square root of 843.

The literal content of all three utterances would be relevant to Peter. However, (19) would be more relevant than either (18) or (20). It would be more relevant than (18) for reasons of cognitive effect, since it yields all the consequences derivable from (18) and more besides. This is an application of clause (a) of the characterisation of relevance in (17). It would be more relevant than (20) for reasons of processing effort: although (19) and (20) yield exactly the same consequences, these consequences are easier to derive from (19) than from (20), which requires an additional effort of parsing and inference (in order to realise that the second disjunct is false and the first is therefore true). This is an application of clause (b) of the characterisation of relevance in (17).

Given this characterisation of relevance, it is, *ceteris paribus*, in the individual's interest to process the most relevant inputs available. We claim that this is what people tend to do (with many failures, of course). They tend to do it not because they realise that it is in their interest (and they certainly do not realise it in those terms), but because they are cognitively endowed evolved organisms. In biological evolution, there has been constant pressure on the human cognitive system to organise itself so as to select inputs on the basis of their expected relevance (Sperber and Wilson 2002). Hence:

(21)   *The First, or Cognitive, Principle of Relevance*
            The human cognitive system tends towards processing the most relevant inputs available.

The tendency described in the cognitive principle of relevance is strong enough, and manifest enough, to make our mental processes at least partially predictable to others. We are in general fairly good at predicting which of the external stimuli currently affecting some other individual's nervous system she is likely to be attending to, and which of the indefinitely many conclusions that she might draw from it she will in fact draw. What we do, essentially, is assume that she will pay attention to the potentially most relevant stimulus, and process it so as to maximise its relevance: that is, in a context of easily accessible background assumptions, where the information it provides will carry relatively rich cognitive effects.

This mutual predictability is exploited in communication. As communicators, we provide stimuli which are likely to strike our intended audience as relevant enough to be worth processing, and to be interpreted in the intended way. A communicator produces a stimulus – say an utterance – which attracts her audience's attention, and she does so in an overtly intentional way. In other words, she makes it manifest that she wants her audience's attention. Since it is also manifest that the audience will tend to pay appropriate attention only to an utterance that seems relevant enough, it is manifest that the communicator wants her audience to assume that the utterance is indeed relevant enough. There is thus a minimal level of relevance that the audience is encouraged to expect: the utterance should be relevant enough to be worth the effort needed for comprehension.

Is the audience entitled to expect more relevance than this? In certain conditions, yes. The communicator wants to be understood. An utterance is most likely to be understood when it simplifies the hearer's task by demanding as little effort from him as possible, and encourages him to pay it due attention by offering him as much effect as possible. The smaller the effort, and the greater the effect, the greater the relevance. It is therefore manifestly in the communicator's interest for the hearer to presume that the utterance is not just relevant enough to be worth his attention, but more relevant than this. How much more? Here, the communicator is manifestly limited by her own abilities (to provide appropriate information, and to present it in the most efficient way). Nor can she be expected to go against her own preferences (e.g. against the goal she wants to achieve in communicating, or the rules of etiquette she wishes to follow). Still, it may be compatible with the communicator's abilities and preferences to go beyond the minimally necessary level of relevance. We define a notion of *optimal relevance* (of an utterance, to an audience) which takes these ideas into account, and propose a second principle of relevance based on it:

(22)   Optimal relevance of an utterance
         An utterance is optimally relevant to the hearer iff:
         a. It is relevant enough to be worth the hearer's processing effort;
         b. It is the most relevant one compatible with the speaker's abilities and
            preferences.

(23)   *The Second, or Communicative, Principle of Relevance*
         Every utterance conveys a presumption of its own optimal relevance.

In interpreting an utterance, the hearer invariably has to go beyond the linguistically encoded sentence meaning. There will be ambiguities and referential indeterminacies to resolve, and other underdeterminate aspects of explicit content that we will look at shortly. There may be implicatures to identify, illocutionary indeterminacies to resolve, metaphors and ironies to interpret. All this requires an appropriate set of contextual assumptions. The communicative principle of relevance and the definition of optimal relevance suggest a practical procedure for constructing a hypothesis about the speaker's meaning. The hearer should consider interpretive hypotheses (disambiguations, reference assignments, implicatures, etc.) in order of accessibility – that is, follow a path of least effort – and stop when he arrives at an interpretation which satisfies the expectations of relevance raised by the utterance itself.[5]

What makes it reasonable for the hearer to follow a path of least effort is that the speaker is expected (within the limits of her abilities and preferences) to make her utterance as easy as possible for the hearer to understand. Since relevance varies inversely with effort, the very fact that an interpretive hypothesis is easily accessible gives it an initial degree of plausibility (an epistemic advantage specific to communicated information).

What makes it reasonable for the hearer to stop at the first interpretation which satisfies his expectations of relevance is that either this interpretation is close enough to what the speaker meant, or she has failed to communicate her meaning. A speaker who produced an utterance with two or more significantly different interpretations, each yielding the expected level of cognitive effect, would put the hearer to the gratuitous and unexpected extra effort of choosing among them, and the resulting interpretation (if any) would not satisfy clause

(b) of the presumption of optimal relevance.[6] Thus, when a hearer following the path of least effort finds an interpretation that satisfies his expectations of relevance, in the absence of contrary evidence, this is the best possible interpretive hypothesis. Since comprehension is a non-demonstrative inference process, this hypothesis may well be false. Typically, this happens when the speaker expresses herself in a way that is inconsistent with the expectations she herself has raised, so that the normal inferential routines of comprehension fail. Failures in communication are common enough: what is remarkable and calls for explanation is that communication works at all.

This relevance-theoretic account not only describes a psychological process but also explains what makes this process genuinely inferential: that is, likely to yield true conclusions (in this case, intended interpretations) from true premises (in this case, from the fact that the speaker has produced a given utterance, together with contextual information). On the descriptive level, it has testable implications, some of which have been tested and confirmed by a growing body of research in experimental pragmatics.[7] On the explanatory level, it claims that what makes this relevance-guided process genuinely inferential is the fact that it typically yields a single interpretation for a given quadruple of speaker, hearer, utterance and situation. Given that such interpretations are predictable by the speaker, the best utterance for a speaker to produce is the one that is likely to be interpreted in the intended way, and the best interpretation for a hearer to choose is the one arrived at by use of the relevance-guided procedure, which is therefore likely to have been predicted and intended by the speaker. Communication is a form of co-ordination, and runs into co-ordination problems which are partly standard, and partly specific to communication. Relevance-guided comprehension takes advantage of the communication-specific aspects of these problems, and provides a solution which is, of course, imperfect, but is nonetheless effective (for further discussion, see Sperber and Wilson 2002).

3.5   Relevance: illustration

An utterance has two immediate effects: it indicates that the speaker has something to communicate, and it determines an order of accessibility in which interpretive hypotheses will occur to the hearer. Here is an illustration.

Lisa drops by her neighbours, the Joneses, who have just sat down to supper:

(24)   ALAN JONES: Do you want to join us for supper?
         LISA: No, thanks. I've eaten.

A standard semantic analysis of the second part of Lisa's utterance would assign it the following truth condition:

(25)   At some point in a time span whose endpoint is the time of utterance, Lisa has eaten something.

Clearly, though, Lisa means something more specific than this. She means that she has eaten that very evening, and not just anything, but a supper or something equivalent: a few peanuts wouldn't do.[8]

Here is our explanation of how Alan understands Lisa's meaning. Her utterance activates in his mind, via automatic linguistic decoding, a conceptual structure which articulates in the grammatically specified way the concepts of Lisa, of eating, and of a time span whose endpoint is the time of utterance.[9] He does not have to reason, because it is all routine, but he might reason along the following lines: she has caused me a certain amount of processing effort (the effort required to attend to her utterance and decode it). Given the communicative principle of relevance, this effort was presumably not caused in vain. So the conceptual structure activated by her utterance must be a good starting point for inferring her meaning, which should be relevant to me.

Lisa's utterance, 'I've eaten', immediately follows her refusal of Alan's invitation to supper. It would be relevant to Alan (or so she may have thought) to know the reasons for her refusal, which have implications for their relationship: Did she object to the offer? Would she accept it another time? It all depends on the reasons for her refusal. The use of the perfect 'have eaten' indicates a time span ending at the time of utterance and starting at some indefinite point in the past. Alan narrows the time span by assuming that it started recently enough for the information that Lisa has eaten during that period to yield adequate consequences: here, the relevant time span is that very evening (see Wilson and Sperber 1998a). He does the same in deciding what she ate. In the circumstances, the idea of eating is most easily fleshed out as eating supper, and this, together with the narrowing of the time span, yields the expected level of cognitive effect. Alan then assumes that Lisa intended to express the proposition that she has eaten supper that evening, and to present this as her reason for refusing his invitation. Although this attribution of meaning is typically a conscious event, Alan is never aware of the process by which he arrived at it, or of a literal meaning equivalent to (25).

The process by which Alan interprets Lisa's meaning may be represented as in Table 3.1, with Alan's interpretive hypotheses on the left, and his basis for arriving at them on the right. We have presented the hypotheses in English, but for Alan they would be in whatever is the medium of conceptual thought, and they need not correspond very closely to our paraphrases.

We do not see this as a sequential process, starting with (26a) and ending with (26g). For one thing, interpretation is carried out 'online', and begins while the utterance is still in progress. Some tentative or incomplete interpretive hypotheses may be made and later revised or completed in the light of their apparent consequences for the overall interpretation. We assume, then, that interpretive hypotheses about explicit content and implicatures are developed in parallel, and stabilise when they are mutually adjusted, and jointly adjusted with the hearer's expectations of relevance.

Table 3.1. *Interpretation of Lisa's utterance, 'I have eaten'*

(26a) Lisa has said to Alan 'I have eaten'.	*Decoding of Lisa's utterance.*
(26b) Lisa's utterance is optimally relevant to Alan.	*Expectation raised by the recognition of Lisa's utterance as a communicative act, and acceptance of the presumption of relevance it automatically conveys.*
(26c) Lisa's utterance will achieve relevance by explaining her immediately preceding refusal of Alan's invitation to supper.	*Expectation raised by (b), together with the fact that such an explanation would be most relevant to Alan at this point.*
(26d) The fact that one has already eaten supper on a given evening is a good reason for refusing an invitation to supper that evening.	*First assumption to occur to Alan which, together with other appropriate premises, might satisfy expectation (c). Accepted as an implicit premise of Lisa's utterance.*
(26e) Lisa has eaten supper this evening.	*First enriched interpretation of Lisa's utterance as decoded in (a) to occur to Alan which might combine with (d) to lead to the satisfaction of (c). Accepted as Lisa's explicit meaning.*
(26f) Lisa is refusing supper with us because she has already had supper this evening.	*Inferred from (d) and (e), satisfying (c) and accepted as an implicit conclusion of Lisa's utterance.*
(26g) Lisa might accept an invitation to supper another time.	*From (f) plus background knowledge. One of several possible weak implicatures of Lisa's utterance which, together with (f), satisfy expectation (b).*

In the present case, Alan assumes in (26b) that Lisa's utterance, decoded as in (26a), is optimally relevant to him. Since what he wants to know at this point is why she refused his invitation, he assumes in (26c) that her utterance will achieve relevance by answering this question. In this context, Lisa's utterance, 'I've eaten', provides easy access to the piece of common background knowledge in (26d) – that people don't normally want to eat supper twice in one evening. This could be used as an implicit premise in deriving the expected explanation of Lisa's refusal, as long as her utterance is interpreted on the explicit side as conveying the information in (26e): that she has eaten supper that evening. By combining the implicit premise in (26d) and the explicit premise in (26e), Alan arrives at the implicit conclusion in (26f), from which further weaker implicatures, including (26g) and others, may be derived (on the notion of a weak implicature, see below). This overall interpretation satisfies Alan's expectations of relevance. On this account, explicit content and implicatures (implicit premises and conclusions) are arrived at by a process of mutual adjustment, with hypotheses about both being considered in order of accessibility.

There is a certain arbitrariness about the way we have presented Alan's interpretive hypotheses. This is partly because, as noted above, we had to put into English thoughts which may not have been articulated in English. Another reason is that Lisa's utterance licenses not a single interpretation but any one of a range of interpretations with very similar import. By constructing any particular interpretation from this range, Alan achieves comprehension enough, and has no reason to look for a better interpretation. Thus, he might take Lisa to mean either that she has had supper that evening or, more cautiously, that, whether or not what she has eaten can properly be described as supper, she has eaten enough not to want supper now. He may take her to be implicating (26g), or some conclusion similar to (26g), or nothing of the sort. In each case his interpretation is reasonable, in the sense that Lisa's utterance has encouraged him to construct it.

If Alan interprets Lisa as meaning that she has had supper, or as implicating something like (26g), he has to take some of the responsibility for the interpretation he has chosen. But this is something that hearers often do, and that speakers intend (or at least encourage) them to do. Often, the hearer will be unable to find an interpretation which is relevant in the expected way without taking some of the responsibility for it: that is, without going beyond what the speaker commits herself to acknowledging as exactly what she meant. This is typical in loose use and creative metaphor, both of which involve the communication of weak implicatures (implicatures which the hearer is given some encouragement but no clear mandate to construct). Nor is this sharing of responsibility a sign of imperfect communication: it may be just the degree of communication that suits both speaker and hearer.

Lisa's explicit meaning, as understood by Alan, logically implies the literal, unenriched meaning of her utterance: if she has eaten supper that evening, she has eaten *tout court*. Her utterance might therefore be classified as literal, for whatever good it might do. However, Alan does not attend to the literal meaning at any stage, and the fact that the utterance is literal plays no role in the communication process. This is even more obvious in the following alternative version of the dialogue:

(27)   ALAN JONES: Do you want to join us for supper?
         LISA: I'd love to. I haven't eaten.

Here, if the literal meaning of Lisa's utterance, 'I haven't eaten', is the negation of (25) (i.e. the proposition that she has never eaten anything), then her utterance is patently false. However, this absurd interpretation never crosses Alan's or Lisa's mind.

One way of avoiding such counterintuitive assignments of literal meaning would be to treat the perfect 'has eaten' as containing a hidden linguistic constituent denoting a contextually determinate time span. In (27), Lisa might then be seen as referring, via this hidden constituent, to the evening of utterance, and the fact that she has eaten plenty in her lifetime would not falsify her statement, even literally understood. We will argue below that this move is *ad hoc* and unnecessary, but let us accept it here for the sake of argument.

Assume, then, that the literal meaning of Lisa's utterance in (27) is that she has not eaten anything that evening. Now suppose that she has in fact eaten a couple of peanuts, so that her utterance is strictly speaking false. Although it may be false, it is not misleading. Rather, it is a case of loose use. Alan takes Lisa to be saying that she has not eaten supper that evening. He arrives at this interpretation by taking the concept of eating, which has been activated in his mind by automatic linguistic decoding, and narrowing it down to the concept of eating supper, which yields an overall interpretation that satisfies his expectations of relevance. The procedure is the same as for dialogue (24), but since the narrowed concept falls within the scope of a negation, the result is a loosening rather than a narrowing of the literal meaning.

It might be argued, of course, that Lisa's utterance contains a second hidden linguistic constituent denoting the food she has eaten. On this interpretation, the linguistically determined truth-conditional meaning of 'I have eaten' is equivalent not to 'I have eaten something', but to 'I have eaten x', where the value of x (like the referent of the pronoun 'I' and the time of utterance) must be specified before the sentence token can be said to express a proposition.

In other situations, what the speaker means by saying that she has or hasn't eaten might also involve a specification of the place of eating, some manner of eating, and so on:

(28)   'I've often been to their parties, but I've never eaten anything' [*there*]

(29)   'I must wash my hands: I've eaten' [*using my hands, rather than, say, being spoon-fed*]

To deal with all such cases, one might postulate more and more hidden constituents, so that every sentence would come with a host of hidden constituents, ready for all kinds of ordinary or extraordinary pragmatic circumstances. In this way, the very idea of loose use could be altogether avoided. We see this as a *reductio* which goes all the way to challenging what we accepted earlier for the sake of argument: that the use of the perfect carries with it a hidden constituent denoting a given time span. There is no need to postulate such a hidden constituent: the same process that explains how 'eating' is narrowed down to 'eating supper' also explains how the time span indicated by the perfect is narrowed down to the evening of utterance. Moreover, the postulation of such hidden constituents is *ad hoc*: its role is to reduce to a minimum the slack between sentence meaning and speaker's meaning, a slack which is uncomfortable from certain theoretical viewpoints. However, we read the evidence as showing that the slack actually *is* considerable, and we adopt a theoretical viewpoint which might help us describe and understand this fact.[10]

3.6   The explicit communication of unencoded meanings

We are exploring the idea that the linguistically encoded sentence meaning gives no more than a schematic indication of the speaker's meaning. The hearer's task is to use this indication, together with background knowledge, to construct an interpretation of the speaker's meaning, guided by expectations of relevance raised by the utterance itself. The conceptual resources brought to this task include all the concepts encoded in the hearer's language, but they go well beyond this (Sperber and Wilson 1998a). In particular, a concept may be recognised in context as a constituent of the speaker's explicit[11] meaning even though there is no expression in the sentence uttered, or indeed in the language, which has this concept as its linguistically encoded meaning. This happens regularly in cases of loose use.

Consider Sue chatting to her friend Jim in the street. She looks at her watch and says:

(30)   I can't stay. I must run to the bank.

The process by which Jim interprets Sue's utterance, 'I must run to the bank', may be represented as in Table 3.2.

What Jim takes to be Sue's explicit meaning may be described as in (31e):

(31)   e. Sue must RUN* to the bank (where RUN* is the meaning indicated by 'run', and is such that Sue's having to RUN* to the bank is relevant-as-expected in the context).

This is not, of course, a proper paraphrase – let alone a proper analysis – of Sue's meaning (as understood by Jim). The notions of *a meaning indicated by a word* and of *relevance-as-expected in a context* are not constituents of Sue's meaning, and Jim does not have to use them in understanding her utterance. As it stands, (31e) is not an interpretation but merely a description of Sue's meaning. It attributes to Sue's utterance the property of indicating rather than encoding her meaning, and to Sue's meaning the property of warranting the derivation of enough cognitive effects to make her utterance worth processing for Jim. However, it goes without saying that if Jim succeeds at all in understanding Sue's utterance, the outcome of the comprehension process will be not a description but an interpretation of Sue's meaning: that is, a mental representation which, if not identical to Sue's meaning, has a content similar enough for this to count as a case of successful comprehension. In particular, Jim's interpretation must contain an unglossed version of the concept RUN*, which on our account was not encoded but merely indicated by her use of the word 'run'.

Assuming that a satisfactory account can be given of the nature of these concepts, and of how hearers may grasp them (we will return to this below), an analysis along the lines in (31) shows how a word like 'run', or 'Kleenex',

Table 3.2. *Interpretation of Sue's utterance, 'I must run to the bank'*

(31a) Sue has said to Jim, 'I must run to the bank'.	*Decoding of Sue's utterance.*
(31b) Sue's utterance is optimally relevant to Jim.	*Expectation raised by the recognition of Sue's utterance as a communicative act, and acceptance of the presumption of relevance it automatically conveys.*
(31c) Sue's utterance will achieve relevance by explaining why she must break off their chat.	*Expectation raised by (b), together with the fact that such an explanation would be most relevant to Jim at this point.*
(31d) Having to hurry to the bank on urgent business is a good reason for breaking off a chat.	*First assumption to occur to Jim which, together with other appropriate premises, might satisfy expectation (c). Accepted as an implicit premise of Sue's utterance.*
(31e) Sue must RUN* to the bank (where RUN* is the meaning indicated by 'run', and is such that Sue's having to RUN* to the bank is relevant-as-expected in the context).	*(Description of) the first enriched interpretation of Sue's utterance as decoded in (a) to occur to Jim which might combine with (d) to lead to the satisfaction of (c). Interpretation accepted as Sue's explicit meaning.*
(31f) Sue must break off their chat because she must hurry to the bank on urgent business.	*Inferred from (d) and (e), satisfying (c) and accepted as an implicit conclusion of Sue's utterance.*
(31g) Sue is afraid that if she stays chatting any longer, the bank may close before she gets there.	*From (f) plus background knowledge. One of several possible weak implicatures of Sue's utterance which, together with (f), satisfy expectation (b).*

which is neither semantically nor pragmatically vague, and which (as we argued in section 3.3 above) cannot be satisfactorily analysed by appeal to contextually determined standards of precision, may be loosely used and understood. As we will show, the analysis is straightforwardly generalisable to the full range of cases, including 'flat' and 'five o'clock', making the appeal to contextually determined standards of precision unnecessary.

Consider Peter and Mary discussing their next cycling trip. Peter has just said that he feels rather unfit. Mary replies:

(32)   We could go to Holland. Holland is flat.

The process by which Peter interprets Mary's utterance, 'Holland is flat', may be schematically represented as in Table 3.3.

What Peter takes to be Mary's explicit meaning may be described as in (33e):

(33)   e. Holland is FLAT* (where FLAT* is the meaning indicated by 'flat', and is such that Holland's being FLAT* is relevant-as-expected in the context).

Table 3.3. *Interpretation of Mary's utterance, 'Holland is flat'*

(33a) Mary has said to Peter, 'Holland is flat'.	*Decoding of Mary's utterance.*
(33b) Mary's utterance is optimally relevant to Peter.	*Expectation raised by the recognition of Mary's utterance as a communicative act, and acceptance of the presumption of relevance it automatically conveys.*
(33c) Mary's utterance will achieve relevance by giving reasons for her proposal to go cycling in Holland, which take account of Peter's immediately preceding complaint that he feels rather unfit.	*Expectation raised by (b), together with the fact that such reasons would be most relevant to Peter at this point.*
(33d) Cycling on relatively flatter terrain which involves little or no climbing is less strenuous, and would be enjoyable in the circumstances.	*First assumption to occur to Peter which, together with other appropriate premises, might satisfy expectation (c). Accepted as an implicit premise of Mary's utterance.*
(33e) Holland is FLAT* (where FLAT* is the meaning indicated by 'flat', and is such that Holland's being FLAT* is relevant-as-expected in the context).	*(Description of) the first enriched interpretation of Mary's utterance as decoded in (a) to occur to Peter which might combine with (d) to lead to the satisfaction of (c). Interpretation accepted as Mary's explicit meaning.*
(33f) Cycling in Holland would involve little or no climbing.	*Inferred from (d) and (e). Accepted as an implicit conclusion of Mary's utterance.*
(33g) Cycling in Holland would be less strenuous, and would be enjoyable in the circumstances.	*Inferred from (d) and (f), satisfying (b) and (c) and accepted as an implicit conclusion of Mary's utterance.*

As noted above, this is not an interpretation but merely a description of Mary's meaning. It attributes to Mary's utterance the property of indicating rather than encoding her meaning, and to Mary's meaning the property of warranting the derivation of enough cognitive effects to make her utterance worth processing for Peter. However, the outcome of the comprehension process must be an interpretation rather than a description of Mary's meaning. In particular, it must contain an unglossed version of the concept FLAT*, which on our account was not encoded but merely indicated by her use of the word 'flat'.

What might this concept FLAT* be? It is not too difficult to give a rough answer. As Mary means it, a terrain is FLAT* if travelling across it involves little or no climbing. Being FLAT* is quite compatible with small-scale unevenness, and indeed with being not plane but convex because of the curvature of the Earth.[12] However, the concept FLAT* indicated by Mary's utterance is more specific than this. It has to do with cycling when rather unfit, which determines what will count as cases of climbing. On another occasion, when travelling by car and hoping to see mountain scenery, Mary might describe the south of England as 'flat': what she would then mean is not FLAT* but some other concept FLAT**, which would be appropriately indicated in this different context by her use of the word 'flat'.

How does Peter grasp the concept FLAT* indicated by Mary's utterance? We claim that, in appropriate circumstances, the relevance-theoretic comprehension procedure should automatically guide the hearer to an acceptably close version of the concept conveyed. As noted above, the hearer's expectations of relevance warrant the assumption that the speaker's explicit meaning will contextually imply a range of specific consequences (made easily accessible, though not yet implied, by the linguistically encoded sentence meaning). Having identified these consequences, he may then, by a process of backwards inference, enrich his interpretation of the speaker's explicit meaning to a point where it does carry these implications.

The claim that Holland is FLAT* carries a range of implications which Mary expects to satisfy Peter's expectations of relevance. The concept FLAT* is individuated (though not, of course, defined) by the fact that, in the situation described, it is the first concept to occur to Peter which determines these implications. If Mary has correctly predicted which implications Peter will actually derive from her utterance, he should arrive by a process of spontaneous backwards inference at an appropriate understanding of her explicit meaning, and in particular of the concept FLAT*.

The implications that Mary expects Peter to derive need not be individually represented and jointly listed in her mind. In normal circumstances, they would not be. She might merely expect him to derive some implications which provide reasons for going cycling in Holland and are similar in tenor to those she herself has in mind (again without necessarily having a distinct awareness of each and every one of them). To the extent that her expectations about the implications Peter will derive are indeterminate, the same will go for the concept she intends him to arrive at by backwards inference from these implications. Notice that a difference in implications need not lead to a difference in concepts: from a somewhat different set of implications than the one envisaged by Mary, Peter may in fact arrive at the same concept FLAT* that she had in mind (i.e. a mental representation which picks out the same property). Suppose, however, that Peter constructs some concept FLAT** which differs slightly from FLAT*, but has roughly the same import in the situation. This would not be a case of imperfect communication or insufficient understanding. As noted above, it is quite normal for communicators to aim at such a relatively loose fit between speaker's meaning and hearer's interpretation.

We have described Mary's remark that Holland is flat as a case of loose use. We could also have described it as a case of hyperbole (that is, as a trope). After all, taken literally, it would be a gross exaggeration. Nothing of substance hinges on whether Mary's utterance is categorised in one way or the other. Literal, loose, hyperbolic or metaphorical interpretations are arrived at by

Table 3.4. *Interpretation of Mary's utterance, 'Holland is a picnic'*

(35a) Mary has said to Peter, 'Holland is a picnic'.	*Decoding of Mary's utterance.*
(35b) Mary's utterance is optimally relevant to Peter.	*Expectation raised by the recognition of Mary's utterance as a communicative act, and acceptance of the presumption of relevance it automatically conveys.*
(35c) Mary's utterance will achieve relevance by giving reasons for her proposal to go cycling in Holland, which take into account Peter's immediately preceding complaint that he feels rather unfit.	*Expectation raised by (b), together with the fact that such reasons would be most relevant to Peter at this point.*
(35d) Going on a picnic takes little effort.	*First assumptions to occur to Peter which, together with other appropriate premises, might satisfy expectation (c). Accepted as implicit premises of Mary's utterance.*
(35e) Going on a picnic is a pleasant and relaxed affair.	
(35f) Holland is a PICNIC* (where PICNIC* is the meaning indicated by 'picnic', and is such that Holland's being a PICNIC* is relevant-as-expected in the context).	*(Description of) the first enriched interpretation of Mary's utterance as decoded in (a) to occur to Peter which, together with (d) and (e), might lead to the satisfaction of (c). Interpretation accepted as Mary's explicit meaning.*
(35g) Going to Holland would take little effort.	*Inferred from (d) and (f), contributing to the satisfaction of (b) and (c), and accepted as an implicit conclusion of Mary's utterance.*
(35h) Going to Holland would be a pleasant and relaxed affair.	*Inferred from (e) and (f), contributing to the satisfaction of (b) and (c), and accepted as an implicit conclusion of Mary's utterance.*

exactly the same process, and there is a continuum of cases which cross-cut these categories.

Consider again the case of Peter and Mary discussing their next cycling trip. Peter has just said that he feels rather unfit. In this version, Mary replies:

(34)   We could go to Holland. Holland is a picnic.

This is clearly a metaphorical use of 'picnic'. The process by which Peter interprets Mary's utterance may be represented as in Table 3.4.

Mary uses the word 'picnic' to indicate the concept PICNIC*, which is part of what she wants to convey. Peter reconstructs this concept by treating the word 'picnic' and its associated mental encyclopaedic entry as a source of potential implicit premises such as (35d) and (35e). From these implicit premises and a still-incomplete interpretation of Mary's explicit meaning, he tentatively derives the implicit conclusions in (35g) and (35h), which make the utterance relevant as expected in the situation. He then arrives by backwards inference at the full interpretation of the explicit content in (35f), and its constituent concept PICNIC*.

There is an unavoidable arbitrariness about the way we have listed the implicit premises and conclusions in (35). The more metaphorical the interpretation, the greater the responsibility the hearer has to take for the construction of implicatures (i.e. implicit premises and conclusions), and the weaker most of these implicatures will be. Typically, poetic metaphors have a wide range of potential implicatures, and the audience is encouraged to be creative in exploring this range (a fact well recognised in literary theory since the Romantics). Communication need not fail if the implicatures constructed by the hearer are not identical to those envisaged by the speaker. Some freedom of interpretation is allowed for, and indeed encouraged, by those who speak metaphorically.

The concepts FLAT* and PICNIC* conveyed by Mary's utterances in (32) and (34) are neither encoded nor encodable in English as spoken by Mary and Peter at the time of their exchange. There is no single word or phrase of English which has FLAT* or PICNIC* as one of its linguistically encoded senses. However, once Mary and Peter have successfully communicated one of these concepts, they may be able to co-ordinate more or less tacitly and adopt a new word or phrase to encode it, or add to the polysemy of an existing word (e.g. by giving the word 'flat' the additional stable sense FLAT*).

Different degrees of difficulty are involved in entertaining a linguistically unencodable concept such as FLAT* or PICNIC*, communicating it, and lexicalising it. Entertaining a currently unencodable concept (i.e. a concept not encodable given the resources of the language at that time) is a relatively easy, everyday affair. As individuals, we engage in such a cognitive practice every time we discriminate and think about a property not describable by a word or phrase in our public language, which may well be several times a day. Communicating such an unencodable concept is a matter of co-ordinating the cognitive activities of two individuals so that they simultaneously attend to the same property or object. This is harder than doing it separately, but is still a relatively frequent affair. Stabilising a word in the public language to encode such a concept involves co-ordinating cognitive dispositions in a community over time. This is much harder, and does not normally happen more than, say, a few times a year in a homogeneous speech community (see Sperber and Wilson 1998a).

3.7   Rethinking 'explicit,' 'literal' and 'what is said'

If the above analysis is correct, the notions *explicit, literal* and *what is said*, which Grice and Lewis saw as relatively unproblematic, will have to be rethought. In this final section, we will suggest some lines on which such a rethinking might be approached.

For Grice, a speaker's meaning consists of *what is said* and (optionally) *what is implicated*. He introduced the terms 'implicate' and 'implicature' to refer to what is implicitly communicated, but rather than use the symmetrical 'explicate' and 'explicature', or just talk of what is explicitly communicated, he chose to contrast what is implicated with the ordinary-language notion *what is said*. This terminological choice reflected both a presupposition and a goal. The presupposition was that *what is said* is an intuitively clear, common-sense notion.[13] The goal was to argue against a view of meaning that ordinary-language philosophers were defending at the time. To achieve this goal, Grice wanted to show that *what is said* is best described by a relatively parsimonious semantics, while much of the complexity and subtlety of utterance interpretation should be seen as falling on the implicit side (Carston 1998b, 2002a). We share Grice's desire to relieve the semantics of natural language of whatever can be best explained at the pragmatic level, but we take a rather different view of how this pragmatic explanation should go.

In our account, we give a theoretical status to the notions of *explicature* and *implicature* (roughly, the explicit and implicit contents of utterances), but not to the notions of *literal meaning* or *what is said*. Indeed, we introduced the term 'explicature', on the model of Grice's 'implicature', because we doubt that there is any common-sense notion of *what is said* capable of playing a useful role in the study of verbal comprehension. In our framework, explicatures are arrived at by a combination of decoding and inference, while implicatures are wholly inferred. Identifying the explicature[14] of an utterance is a matter of disambiguating, enriching and fine-tuning the semantic schema obtained by linguistic decoding. Inferring the implicatures is a matter of identifying implicit premises and conclusions which yield an overall interpretation that is relevant in the expected way. As we have shown above, explicatures and implicatures are typically constructed in parallel, via mutual adjustment of interpretive hypotheses guided by considerations of relevance.

We have already argued that implicatures may vary in strength. The same is true of explicatures. The identification of an explicature involves a certain amount of inference. Since the inference process is non-demonstrative and draws on background knowledge, the hearer must take a certain degree of responsibility for how it comes out. How much responsibility he has to take varies from utterance to utterance: explicatures may be weaker or stronger, depending on the degree of indeterminacy introduced by the inferential aspect of comprehension. To illustrate, let us return to dialogue (24) and consider three new versions of Lisa's answer in (36a)–(36c):

(24)   ALAN JONES: Do you want to join us for supper?
         LISA: No, thanks. I've eaten.

(36)   a. LISA: No, thanks. I've already eaten supper.
         b. LISA: No, thanks. I've already eaten tonight.
         c. LISA: No, thanks. I've already eaten supper tonight.

In identifying the explicit content of all four answers, a certain amount of inference (and hence a certain degree of indeterminacy) is involved. It might be thought that the only inferences involved in (36c) are automatic – just a matter of fixing the referents of 'I' and 'tonight' – but this would be a mistake. When Lisa describes what she has eaten as supper, she may be speaking loosely. She may have had a sandwich, and be unwilling to eat again for that reason. So Alan might reasonably take 'supper' to mean SUPPER*: that is, say, enough food to act as a substitute for supper. If, instead, he takes 'supper' to mean SUPPER (i.e. a regular evening meal), this is no less inferential. Whichever of the two interpretations is the first to come to mind will yield an overall interpretation that is relevant as expected, and will therefore be accepted.

Note that the first meaning to occur to Alan need not be the encoded meaning SUPPER. Suppose he knows that Lisa generally has a salad or a sandwich instead of supper: then by saying that she has eaten 'supper', she may make SUPPER* more easily accessible than SUPPER. More generally, the most accessible sense need not be the linguistically encoded one, so when an encoded lexical sense is in fact chosen, the same process is involved as when a word is taken to convey a non-encoded sense. In each case, the first sense accessed and found to contribute to a relevant-as-expected interpretation is taken to be the intended one.

All four answers in (24) and (36a)–(36c) communicate not just the same overall content but also the same explicature and implicatures. If this is not immediately obvious, there is a standard test for deciding whether some part of the communicated content is explicitly or implicitly conveyed. The test involves checking whether the item falls within the scope of logical operators when embedded into a negative or conditional sentence: explicatures fall within the scope of negation and other logical operators, while implicatures do not (Carston 1988; Recanati 1989; Wilson and Sperber 1998a; Ifantidou 2001). Thus, consider the hypothesis that the explicature of (24b) is simply the trivial truth that Lisa has eaten at some point before the time of utterance, and that she is merely *implicating* that she has eaten that evening. The standard embedding test suggests that this hypothesis is false. If Lisa had produced the utterance, 'I haven't eaten' (as in dialogue (27)), she would clearly not have been saying that she has never eaten in her life, but merely denying that she has eaten 'supper' (i.e. SUPPER or SUPPER*) that very evening. So in saying, 'I've eaten,' Lisa is explicitly communicating that she has eaten 'supper' that very evening.

Although all four answers convey the same explicature – that Lisa has eaten SUPPER (or SUPPER*) that evening – there is a clear sense in which it is weaker in (24) than in (36a) or (36b), and stronger in (36c). The greater the inferential element involved (and hence the greater the indeterminacy), the weaker the explicature will be. In particular, *ceteris paribus*, the greater the gap between the encoded meaning of the word and the concept conveyed by use of that word, the weaker the explicature will be. With metaphors, explicatures are at their weakest.

When the explicature is quite strong, and in particular when each word in an utterance is used to convey (one of) its encoded meaning(s), what we are calling the explicature is close to what might be common-sensically described as the explicit content, or what is said, or the literal meaning of the utterance. Whether the explicature is strong or weak, the notion of explicature applies straightforwardly. However, things go differently with the common-sense notions of *literal meaning* and *what is said*.

The notion of literal meaning, which plays such a central role in most theories of language use, is unclear in many respects. Suppose we define the literal meaning of a sentence as one of its linguistically encoded senses. Then the literal meaning of a sentence never coincides with what the speaker explicitly communicates by uttering this sentence (except in the case of genuine 'eternal sentences', if such things exist or are ever used). A speaker's meaning is typically propositional, and at the very least, reference resolution is needed to get from a sentence meaning to a proposition. It seems more appropriate, then, to define the literal meaning of an utterance (rather than a sentence) as the proposition obtained by combining its linguistic sense with its reference. When the speaker's meaning coincides with this proposition, we do indeed have a prototypical case of literalness. Suppose an anthropologist confesses:

(37)   I have eaten human flesh.

In most situations, (37) would be relevant enough if it were understood as explicitly communicating its literal meaning, without any narrowing of the time span or the way in which the eating of human flesh is understood to have taken place. This is then a prototypical case where literal meaning (understood as sense plus reference) coincides with speaker's explicit meaning, or explicature. However, such cases are the exception rather than the rule.

In the first place, there are cases where the explicature cannot simply correspond to the combination of linguistic sense plus reference, because this is not enough to determine a unique proposition. Consider (38):

(38)   His car is too big.

Even when the linguistic sense is combined with appropriate referents for the pronoun 'his' and the present tense, the result is not a complete proposition.[15] 'His car' might be the car he owns, the car he is renting, the car he is thinking about, and so on, and deciding which it is meant to be is not a matter of disambiguation or reference assignment, but of enriching the linguistically encoded meaning. Similarly, 'too big' is indeterminate unless some contextual criterion is supplied for deciding what counts as big enough in this case. Such cases are sometimes dealt with by redefining the literal meaning of an utterance as determined by a combination of sense, plus reference, plus obligatory enrichment (sometimes known as the 'minimal proposition' expressed by an utterance).[16] Suppose, then, that (38) is enriched as in (39):

(39)   The car Bob is planning to steal is too big to hide in the lorry.

Is this the literal meaning of (38) on that occasion, or is there some other, simpler literal meaning? If so, what is it? In such cases, intuitions about literalness become quite unclear.

Even leaving aside the problem of obligatory enrichment (and other related problems discussed in Searle 1979: chapter 5), and considering only sentences where the combination of sense plus reference determines a complete proposition, the fact is that in most cases, the explicature of an utterance goes well beyond this. The identification of an explicature may involve enrichment of the encoded meaning, loosening of the encoded meaning, or some combination of enrichment and loosening. Such cases are sometimes dealt with by drawing a distinction between *literal meaning* and *literal use*, and treating an utterance as a case of literal use provided that the explicature departs from the literal meaning only by being richer or more specific (e.g. Katz 1990: 144–6). So when Lisa says, 'I've eaten', in response to Alan's invitation to supper, the literal meaning of her utterance (the proposition that Lisa has eaten at some point in a time span ending at the time of utterance) is determined in the regular way by combining sense with reference. Since her actual meaning (that she has eaten supper that evening) is an enrichment of the literal meaning, this would count as a case of literal use.[17]

This proposal also runs into problems. If enrichment of meaning preserves literalness of use, then (40) must be treated as a case of literal use:

(40)   [*Antony praising Brutus in* Julius Caesar] This was a man!

However, in classical rhetoric, (40) would be classified as a case of figurative use (more precisely, as a variety of synecdoche). Here again, intuitions are probably not clear enough to decide, so the decision would have to be made on theoretical grounds. But we have argued that a notion of literalness has no role to play in a theory of language use. The interpretation of every utterance involves a process of meaning construction, which is the same whether the result is an enriched, loosened, enriched-and-loosened, or literal interpretation. Yes, literalness can be defined, or at least characterised, in terms of a prototype, but, no, verbal understanding does not involve paying any attention to literal meaning, let alone to literal use. There is no theoretical basis for sharpening our characterisation of literalness. On the other hand, as we will see, there may be social pressure to do so.

Similar problems arise with the notion of *what is said*. Given that a speaker has produced some utterance U as an act of verbal communication, what is the proper completion of (41)?

(41)   The speaker said that ...

The idea that there is a theoretically adequate and useful notion of *what is said* implies that there is a correct completion of (41) (or a set of semantically equivalent completions) which uniquely captures what is said by uttering *U*. (This is, of course, compatible with recognising that different completions may be pragmatically acceptable in different situations. For instance, the dots might be replaced by an exegesis, a summary or a sarcastic rendering of *U*. However, these would not fit the intended notion of *what is said*.) Prototypical instances of the intended notion are easy to find: they are the same as the prototypical instances of *literal meaning*. Thus, what was said by the speaker of (37) is unproblematically rendered as (42):

(42)   The anthropologist said that she has eaten human flesh.

Here, the speaker's explicit meaning can be straightforwardly rendered by a transposition from direct to indirect quotation. However, this is not always so.

When Lisa produces the utterance in (24b), 'I've eaten' (with an explicature rather weaker than the one conveyed by (36c), 'I've already eaten supper tonight'), what is she saying? Intuitions typically waver. *Saying* is often understood in an indirect-quotational sense, where what is said is properly rendered by an indirect quotation of the original utterance. It might thus be claimed that in uttering (24b), Lisa is merely saying that she has eaten; but this would not adequately capture her meaning as we have described it above. *Saying* can also be understood in a commitment sense, where what is said is what the speaker is committing herself to in producing an utterance. This is typically the sense invoked when, precisely, the competence or sincerity of the speaker's commitment is being challenged. Suppose Alan replies to Lisa's utterance (24b), 'What you just said is false: I happen to know that you haven't eaten a thing since lunch.' By common-sense standards, Alan is not misusing the word 'said'. However, his response makes sense only if he was taking Lisa to have said not just that she has eaten, but that she has eaten that very evening. Of course, Lisa might then reply that she had so much lunch that she didn't feel like eating anything more that day. While this might be seen as disingenuous, the explicature of her utterance is weak enough to leave room for reasonable doubt. On the other hand, if she had not eaten for days, then in uttering (24b) in this situation, she would undoubtedly be saying something false.

The weaker the explicature of an utterance, the harder it is to paraphrase what the speaker was saying except in the indirect-quotational sense. It is always safe to quote the speaker's words (either directly or indirectly), but this is of limited use. It would be more useful to paraphrase the speaker's meaning, except for the element of arbitrariness involved. This vacillation between a quotational and a commitment sense of 'saying' is particularly obvious in the case of metaphor.

On the one hand, we may feel that here the only safe sense is the quotational one. When Mary produces the utterance in (34), 'Holland is a picnic', we would all immediately agree that she is saying that Holland is a picnic. However, this does not provide a truth-evaluable content which can be crisply and confidently paraphrased and which Mary is clearly committing herself to. On the other hand, it is quite possible to disagree with what is being said (in an everyday sense) without being able to paraphrase it. If Peter disagrees with Mary's utterance, 'Holland is a picnic', he may well tell her, 'What you say is false'. Here, he would be expressing disagreement with Mary's explicature, however vague, rather than making the obvious point that Holland is a country and not a social event.

Speakers commit themselves, and they can be criticised for their commitments. Often, however, the exact character of their commitment can be disputed. This happens quite regularly at home, in public life, and in court. Arguing about what was said – both its content and its truthfulness – is a social practice conducted within the framework of 'folk linguistics'. The notions of *literal meaning* and *what is said* come from folk linguistics, and they may well play a useful (or even indispensable) role within this framework. Most people are more interested in the norms governing linguistic communication than in the mechanisms by which it is achieved. The apparent platitudes listed at the beginning of this chapter – as speakers, we expect what we say to be accepted as true, as hearers, we expect what is said to us to be true – are versions of one of these folk-linguistic norms, a norm of truthfulness in what is said.

In the situations where it is typically appealed to, the norm of truthfulness is a reasonable requirement on verbal communication. It is generally invoked when the audience suspects that it is being violated, and it is very rare for a speaker accused of violating it to dispute its applicability. By contrast, disagreements about what was actually said are not rare at all. The notion of literal meaning is typically invoked in the context of such disputes. It is often easier to agree on the literal meaning of an utterance, and on its literal truth or falsity, than on what the speaker meant, or what the hearer could reasonably have understood. A speaker can retreat behind the literal meaning of her utterance, which may have been true even if the utterance was misleading. A hearer can point out that what was literally said was false, and the speaker may reply that she was not intending to be taken so literally. Many such arguments are never settled. This shows the limitations of any description of the speaker's commitment in terms of the folk-linguistic notion of *saying*.

The very idea that what a speaker says should always (with the possible exception of poetry) be either literal or paraphrasable by means of a literal utterance is an illusion of folk linguistics. Western folk linguistics, at least, is committed to a code model of communication from which it follows that what is said should always be transparent or paraphrasable. Efforts to bring communicative practice into line with this ideal have had some effect on language use. In forms of verbal interaction where the speaker's commitments are particularly important from a social point of view (in science or law, for example), there is a demand that speech should in general be literal, and that occasional departures from literalness should be overt and obvious: occasional metaphors are acceptable, but not the loose uses found in ordinary exchanges. How well the demand is actually satisfied is another matter. In general, folk-linguistic theories about communicative practice have rather limited and peripheral effects on the natural processes of speech and comprehension, where so many of the sub-processes involved are automatic and impenetrable (cf. Levelt 1989).

It may have seemed reasonable to philosophers such as Paul Grice or David Lewis to base their philosophy of language on a reformulated norm of truthfulness. However, their reformulations did not go far enough. Both Grice and Lewis took for granted that truthfulness based on the conventional meaning of utterances is expected (for Grice, conventional meaning is just literal meaning; for Lewis, it is literal or figurative meaning, with figurative meaning being derived from literal meaning). This assumption played a central role in Lewis's explanation of how linguistic meaning could be conventional, and in Grice's account of how non-conventional meanings could be conveyed.[18]

We agree that, at least in most cases, a hearer who attends to an utterance expects to be informed of something. We agree with Grice that 'false information is not an inferior kind of information; it just is not information' (Grice 1989: 371). So, yes, hearers expect to be provided with true information. But there is an infinite supply of true information which is not worth attending to. Actual expectations are of relevant information, which (because it is information) is also true.[19] However, we have argued that there just is no expectation that the true information communicated by an utterance should be literally or conventionally expressed, as opposed to being explicated or implicated in the sense we have discussed here.

Linguistically encoded meaning is far too schematic and fragmentary to be capable of being true or false: it is just an input to further processing. Contrary to the standard view, this further processing does not consist simply in combining linguistic sense with contextual reference in order to determine a literal meaning. The fact that the speaker has produced this utterance with this linguistic meaning is expected to provide a relevant piece of evidence and a point of departure for inferring the speaker's meaning. The resulting explicatures and implicatures are in turn expected to provide worthwhile input for further processing: that is, to be relevant (and therefore true).

4   Rhetoric and relevance

Dan Sperber and Deirdre Wilson

4.1   A paradox and a dilemma

The student of rhetoric is faced with a paradox and a dilemma. We will suggest a solution to the dilemma, but this will only make the paradox more blatant.

Let us start with the paradox. Rhetoric took pride of place in formal education for two and a half millennia. Its very rich and complex history is worth detailed study, but it can be summarised in a few sentences. Essentially the same substance was passed on by eighty generations of teachers to eighty generations of pupils. If there was a general tendency, it consisted merely in a narrowing of the subject matter of rhetoric: one of its five branches, *elocutio*, the study of figures of speech, gradually displaced the others, and in some schools, became identified with rhetoric *tout court*. (We will also be guilty of this and several other simplifications.) The narrowing was not even offset by a corresponding increase in theoretical depth. Pierre Fontanier's *Les Figures du Discours* is not a radical improvement on Quintilian's *Institutio Oratoria*, despite the work of sixty generations of scholars in between.

This combination of institutional success and intellectual barrenness is puzzling, particularly since the history of rhetoric cuts across major social changes: the eighty generations of pupils had little in common, yet Greek politicians, Roman lawyers, mediaeval clerks, Renaissance aristocrats and nineteenth-century bourgeois were all taught the same thing. The extraordinary institutional resilience of an otherwise ossified rhetoric turns puzzle into paradox.

Then came the Romantics, and the end of rhetoric – or so it seemed. The Romantics were particularly scathing about the classical treatment of metaphor, irony, and other figures of speech. In classical rhetoric, figures were seen as ornaments added to a text, which made it more pleasant and therefore more convincing, but without altering its content. In particular, tropes were described as achieving their ornamental effect through the replacement of a dull literal expression of the author's thought by a more attractive figurative expression (i.e. an expression whose literal meaning is set aside and replaced by a figurative meaning).

A mother says to her child:

(1)   You're a piglet!

A classical rhetorician would analyse 'piglet' in this context as a metaphor with the figurative meaning *dirty child*. Or the mother might say:

(2)   You're such a clean child!

Here, a rhetorician would analyse 'clean child' as a case of irony with the same figurative meaning, *dirty child*. The figurative meaning of the metaphorical or ironical expression is seen as identical to the literal meaning of the ordinary expression it replaces. In general, on this view, every figure has a non-figurative paraphrase.

Against the notion of a figure as a mere ornament, the Romantics maintained that a felicitous trope cannot be paraphrased. According to Coleridge, the 'infallible test of a blameless style' is

its *untranslatableness* in words of the same language without injury to the meaning. Be it observed, however, that I include in the *meaning* of a word not only its correspondent object but likewise all the associations which it recalls. (Coleridge 1907, vol. II: 115)

In her modest way, the mother who calls her child a piglet achieves some unparaphrasable effects: for instance, she appears more forgiving than if she had called him a dirty child. Similarly, the mother who says 'You're such a clean child!' conveys not only that the child is dirty but also – with a light touch that would be lost in the explicit paraphrase – that he ought to be clean.

The Romantic critics were unquestionably right to point out the richness and importance of those effects of figures of speech which are not maintained under paraphrase. These effects were merely noted by classical rhetoricians, who did not describe, let alone explain them. But for all their well-taken criticisms and subtle observations, the Romantics were content to talk about metaphor in metaphorical terms, and provided no explicit theory; if anything, they cast doubt on the very possibility of a non-metaphorical theory of metaphor by entirely rejecting the notion of a literal meaning – the 'proper meaning superstition' as I. A. Richards (1936: 11) calls it.

The Romantic critics' objections have generally been accepted by the contemporary academic heirs to the classical rhetorical tradition. It is now almost a commonplace that, in Jonathan Culler's words, 'one can never construct a position outside tropology from which to view it; one's own terms are always caught up in the processes they attempt to describe' (1981: 209).

The incorporation of Romanticism into academic theorising led – paradoxically – to a resurgence of classical rhetoric. For if 'words are equal, free, of age', as Victor Hugo said, scorning rhetorical typologies (1985: 265), then the words found in these typologies are inferior to none, and can be freely used. And so we find, in modern literary studies, a Romantic use of classical rhetorical terms: they no longer have 'proper meanings', but they suggest subtle distinctions and evoke scholarly sophistication and historical depth.

Let us make our position clear: we see nothing wrong with a free use of all the resources of language – poetic use or rhetorical terminology included – in interpreting particular experiences or texts. However, we do not believe that interpretations of particulars generalise into proper theories. Proper theories are not interpretive: they are descriptive and explanatory.[1] We realise that post-Romantic, post-structuralist sophisticates have even less faith in proper theories than they do in proper meanings. However, we are not sophisticates. We see it as a worthwhile goal to develop a theory of the kind of phenomena that classical rhetoricians tried to describe, but with an even greater explicitness than they aimed to achieve.

So here is the dilemma: it seems we must either hold onto the relative rigour of a rhetorical approach and miss an essential – maybe *the* essential – dimension of language use, or start from the Romantic intuition that linguistic creativity cannot be reduced to a mere set of combinatorial rules, and give up any ambition to produce an adequate scientific theory. More specifically: on the one side we have the view that an utterance or text has a literal meaning which it is presumed to convey in the absence of contrary indications. This makes it possible to provide a neat definition of semantics as the study of literal meaning, and of tropology as the study of departures from literal meaning. On the other side, we have the view of meaning as mishmash in motion, analytically unappealing, but true to life.

It is worth noting that both classical rhetoricians and their Romantic critics take for granted that if there is such a thing as literal meaning, then utterances come with a presumption of literalness. We disagree. We will argue that it is possible to hold onto a notion of literal meaning, which is analytically useful, while dropping the presumption of literalness, which is implausible, by appealing to a presumption of relevance. In this way, theory and intuition can be reconciled.

4.2   Relevance theory

The rhetorician's dilemma is a special case of an even more fundamental problem in the study of human communication. From ancient rhetoric through to modern semiotics, communication was analysed as a coding–decoding process in which the communicator encodes a message into a signal that the audience then decodes. The existence of a common code has been seen as a necessary and essentially sufficient condition for communication. The code model of communication has an appealing simplicity; but it has become increasingly obvious that human communication cannot be fully explained in terms of this model alone.

Given a rich enough code – and human languages are certainly rich enough in the required sense – anything that can be encoded in one way can be encoded in another (i.e. whatever can be encoded can be paraphrased). The fact that communication achieves some unparaphrasable effects – which particularly interested the Romantics – strongly suggests that more is communicated than is actually encoded. Moreover, as modern pragmatics has repeatedly shown, communicators often succeed in conveying implicitly (i.e. without encoding it) information that they *could* have explicitly encoded.

How are (unencodable) poetic effects and (encodable but unencoded) *implicatures* communicated? In the case of implicatures, modern pragmatics suggests an answer: they are inferred by the audience using a combination of linguistic decoding, contextual information and general expectations about the communicator's behaviour. Inference, then, is seen as a supplement to encoding and decoding, designed to economise on effort. However, the special flavour and uses of implicit communication, and also of poetic effects, are just as mysterious in modern pragmatics as they were in classical rhetoric.

In *Relevance: Communication and Cognition* (1986a), we have proposed a novel approach to human communication, grounded in a general view of cognition. We will try to show how this new approach helps resolve both the classical rhetorician's dilemma and its modern pragmatic counterpart.

Rather than seeing the fully coded communication of a well-defined paraphrasable meaning as the norm, we treat it as a limiting case that is never encountered in reality. Rather than seeing a mixture of explicitness and implicitness, and of paraphrasable and unparaphrasable effects, as a departure from the norm, we treat them as typical of ordinary, normal communication. We see communication not as a process by which a meaning in the communicator's head is duplicated in the addressee's, but as a more or less controlled modification by the communicator of the audience's mental landscape – his *cognitive environment,* as we call it – achieved in an intentional and overt way.

The cognitive environment of an individual can be modified by adding a single piece of new information, but it can equally well be modified by a diffuse increase in the saliency or plausibility of a whole range of assumptions, yielding what will be subjectively experienced as an *impression.* On our approach, between the two extremes – communication of specific information and communication of an impression – lies a continuum of cases. Thus, instead of contrasting 'meaning' with 'rhetorical effects', or 'denotation' with 'connotation', we subsume both under a single unitary notion of *cognitive effects.* The communication of cognitive effects is essentially inferential. Decoded meaning structures are not directly adopted by the audience as thoughts of their own; rather, they provide very rich evidence which can be exploited by largely unconscious inferential processes to arrive at comprehension proper. How exactly are these decoded meanings exploited? What guides the comprehension process? This is where considerations of relevance come in.

Human information processing requires some mental effort and achieves some cognitive effect. The effort required is an effort of attention, memory and reasoning. The effect achieved is to modify the individual's cognitive environment by adding new beliefs, cancelling old ones, or merely altering the saliency or strength of existing beliefs. We may characterise a comparative notion of relevance in terms of effect and effort, as follows:

Relevance
(a) Everything else being equal, the greater the cognitive effect achieved by the processing of a given piece of information, the greater its relevance for the individual who processes it.
(b) Everything else being equal, the greater the mental effort involved in the processing of a given piece of information, the less its relevance for the individual who processes it.

We claim that humans automatically aim at maximal relevance: that is, maximal cognitive effect for minimal processing effort. This is the most general factor that determines the course of human information processing. It determines which information is attended to, which background assumptions are retrieved from memory and used as context, and which inferences are drawn.

An act of communication starts out as a request for attention. People will not pay attention to a phenomenon unless they expect it to be relevant enough to them. Hence, to communicate is to imply that the phenomenon being displayed (the linguistic utterance, for instance) is relevant enough to be worth the audience's attention. Any utterance addressed to someone automatically conveys a presumption of its own relevance. This fact, we call the Communicative Principle of Relevance.

A communicator puts a conceptual structure into her audience's head – say, by a piece of mimicry that calls to mind a description of the act or object it resembles, or by producing an utterance which is automatically decoded into a semantic representation. If the presumption of relevance conveyed by this act of communication is to be satisfied, the effort needed to build this conceptual structure must not be wasted. In other words, the structure must yield enough cognitive effects to justify the effort: a request for effort amounts to a promise of adequate effect (how well the promise is kept is another matter).

The audience's task, then, is to identify the effects that the communicator could have both foreseen and used as the basis for guaranteeing the relevance of her communication. Those effects which are (or may have seemed to the communicator to be) sufficient to make the signal adequately relevant to the audience are the intended ones. Taken together, they make up an interpretation consistent with the fact that a presumption of relevance has been communicated: we describe this as an interpretation consistent with the communicative principle of relevance. Consistency with the communicative principle of relevance is the guiding criterion in the comprehension process. (Note, incidentally, that the interpretation selected by this criterion is not the most relevant one, but the one that is relevant enough to confirm the presumption of relevance.)

In *Relevance*, we work out in detail how the communicative principle of relevance guides inferential comprehension and enables the audience to identify the explicit and implicit content of an utterance. Here, we will merely indicate how it gives rise to metaphorical or ironical interpretations.[2]

4.3   Literalness, looseness and metaphor

If verbal communication were guided by a presumption of literalness, every second utterance would have to be seen as an exception. If it is guided by a presumption of relevance (or, more precisely, by a criterion of consistency with the communicative principle of relevance), there are no exceptions: the interpretation of every successful act of communication, including utterances in particular, satisfies this criterion.

At a party in San Francisco, Marie meets Peter. He asks her where she lives, and she replies,

(3)   I live in Paris.

It so happens that Marie lives in Issy-les-Moulineaux, a block outside the city limits of Paris. Her answer is literally false, but not blatantly so. If Peter presumed it was literal, he would be misled.

In normal circumstances, though, Marie's answer would be quite appropriate and not misleading at all. This is easily explained in terms of relevance theory. A speaker wants the hearer, as a result of her utterance, to take a certain set of propositions to be true, or probably true. Suppose these propositions are all easily derivable as implications of a proposition Q. Q has other implications which the speaker does not accept, and whose truth she does not want to guarantee. Still, as long as the hearer has some way of selecting those logical and contextual implications that the speaker intends to convey, while ignoring the rest, the best way of achieving her aim may be to express the single proposition Q.

We claim that such a selection process is *always* at work, and plays a role in the understanding of *every* utterance. Whenever a proposition is expressed, the hearer assumes that some subset of its implications are also implications of the thought being communicated, and aims to identify this subset. He assumes (or at least assumes that the speaker assumed) that this subset will yield enough cognitive effects to make the utterance worth his attention. He also assumes (or assumes that the speaker assumed) that there was no obvious alternative way of achieving these effects for less effort. His goal is to find an interpretation consistent with these assumptions (i.e. consistent with the communicative principle of relevance). When only a single interpretation (or a few closely similar interpretations with no important differences between them) satisfies this criterion, communication succeeds.

In our example, Peter can infer quite a lot of true or plausible information from Marie's reply: that she spends most of her time in the Paris area, that she knows Paris quite well, that she lives an urban life, that he might try to meet her on his next trip to Paris, and so on. These (or similar) cognitive effects make Marie's utterance relevant enough to be worth his processing effort, in a way that Marie could manifestly have foreseen. Peter is therefore entitled to assume that Marie intended him to interpret her utterance along these lines. He would be misled only if he were to conclude from her utterance that she lives within the city limits of Paris. But it is clear that Marie had no reason to assume that he would have to derive such a conclusion in order to establish the relevance of her utterance. Hence, her utterance does not warrant it.

Typically, utterances such as Marie's are loosely understood. The loose interpretation is not arrived at by first considering a strictly literal interpretation, then rejecting it in favour of a looser one. In interpreting Marie's reply in (3), Peter would have no ground for rejecting the literal interpretation in the first place. In fact, at no point is literalness presumed.

Utterances can, of course, be literally understood, but in that case, the literal interpretation emerges only at the end of the comprehension process rather than at the beginning, and only when required by considerations of relevance. Suppose that Marie is asked where she lives, not at a party in San Francisco, but at an electoral meeting for a Paris local election. In that case, if she replies as in (3) above, the proposition that she lives in Paris will itself be crucially relevant; her utterance will therefore be understood literally, and Marie will have lied.

The same procedure – deriving enough cognitive effects to make up an interpretation consistent with the communicative principle of relevance – yields a literal interpretation in some cases, and a loose one in others. In still other cases, it yields a figurative interpretation. Suppose an author describing a character writes:

(4)   Clarissa's face was a perfect oval.

If there were a presumption of literalness, the reader of this description would have first to consider the literal interpretation of (4), and then reject it, given that it is common knowledge that no human face is a perfect oval. He would then look around for a figurative interpretation, and would somehow recognise that in this case the utterance is a hyperbole: what the author presumably means is that Clarissa's face was remarkably close to being oval. It is obvious that (4) should be interpreted as a case of hyperbole rather than, say, a case of irony; but exactly why this is so is not obvious at all in the classical approach.

According to relevance theory, the reader does not first consider and then reject the hypothesis that the writer meant to assert that Clarissa's face was a perfect oval. He simply uses the idea the writer has expressed as a source of cognitive effects: that is, he builds a mental representation of Clarissa's face which contains enough of the implications of the idea of its being a perfect oval – the general shape, a striking degree of regularity and symmetry – to justify the presumption of relevance. Understood in this way, the utterance produces enough effects for a minimum of effort. If the author had spelled out an interpretation along these lines instead of relying on her readers' abilities, the effect would have been roughly similar, but the processing effort would have been much greater, and so the relevance would have been much reduced.

Let us return to our example of a mundane metaphor (repeated here for convenience):

(1)   MOTHER TO CHILD: You're a piglet!

While calling someone a pig is quite standard – the metaphor is *lexicalised* – calling a child a piglet puts the hearer to some extra processing effort, which justifies a search for added effect. For instance, young animals are endearing, even when the adults of the species are not; so the child may feel encouraged to derive not only the obvious contextual implication that he is dirty, but also the further implication that he is, nevertheless, endearing.

The wider the range of cognitive effects, and the greater the degree of initiative left to the hearer (or reader) in constructing them, the more creative the metaphor: 'piglet' is, if only marginally, more creative than 'pig'. In the richest and most successful cases, the hearer can do more than merely explore the immediate context and directly evoked background knowledge, accessing a wider area of knowledge, entertaining *ad hoc* assumptions which may themselves be metaphorical, and discovering more and more suggested effects. The result is a quite complex picture, for which the hearer has to take a large share of the responsibility, but whose discovery has been triggered by the speaker (or writer).

Take Prospero's words to his daughter Miranda:

> The fringed curtains of thine eye advance
> And say what thou see'st yond. (Shakespeare: *The Tempest* I ii)

Coleridge argues, against Pope and Arbuthnot, that these words should not be taken as equivalent in meaning to 'Look what is coming yonder'. They are uniquely appropriate to the characters and situation:

Prospero sees Ferdinand and wishes to point him out to his daughter not only with great but with scenic solemnity . . . Something was to appear to Miranda on the sudden, and as unexpectedly as if the hearer of a drama were to be on the stage at the instant when the curtain is elevated . . . Turning from the sight of Ferdinand to his thoughtful daughter, his attention was first struck by the downcast appearance of her eyes and eyelids . . . (Coleridge 1987: 527–28)

Coleridge's comments are indeed illuminating, but they invite an objection and a question. The objection is that it is possible to appreciate Shakespeare's metaphor without understanding it exactly as Coleridge does. The question is how such an understanding is arrived at.

Our answer to the question also deals with the objection. To understand Prospero's metaphor, the hearer must bring to bear his knowledge of the appearance of eyelids, on the one hand, and curtains – theatre curtains in particular – on the other. But this is not enough, because merely selecting the most obvious implication – that Prospero is telling Miranda to raise her eyelids – would yield an interpretation that requires too much effort for too little effect. A more attentive hearer will invest a little more effort and get much more effect. This extra effort may involve creating a metaphor of his own – such as Coleridge's metaphor of the hearer of a drama being brought on stage – and adopting some of the implications jointly derivable from Prospero's metaphor and his own. In doing so, the hearer takes on a large share of the responsibility for the conclusions he arrives at. Different hearers, with different background knowledge and different imaginations, will follow somewhat different routes. However, they are all encouraged and guided by the text, and they all proceed by exploring the implications of the text as relevantly as they can.

How does this approach to metaphor compare with the classical and Romantic accounts? In many ways, we are on the Romantic side. If we are right, metaphors are based on fundamental and universal psychological mechanisms. They are in no sense departures from a norm, or, as modern pragmatics would have it, breaches of a rule or maxim of communication. We also reject the classical claim that tropes in general, and metaphor in particular, have a purely decorative function. For us, as for the Romantics, tropes have a genuine cognitive content which – particularly with the more creative metaphors – is not paraphrasable without loss. We have proposed to analyse this content in terms of a wide array of weak cognitive effects whose recovery is triggered by the speaker, but whose content the hearer actively helps to determine.

Despite our general sympathy with the Romantic view of metaphor, we differ sharply from the Romantics over the nature of language and meaning. For us, the existence of loose uses does not mean that language is irremediably vague, and the pervasiveness of metaphor does not make it an aspect of word and sentence meaning. Similarly, the fact that hearers approach utterances without fixed expectations as to their literalness, looseness or metaphorical character does not mean that literalness, looseness and metaphor cannot be distinguished from each other. However, we regard the distinction as one of degree, not of kind. Words and sentences have a literal meaning, but this literal meaning is a tool for communi-cation, and does not itself constitute the content of communicative acts. What hearers expect is that the literal meaning of an utterance will help them infer, with a minimum of effort, the thought that the speaker intends to convey. This expect-ation itself derives from, and is warranted by, a more basic expectation of relevance, which is automatically encouraged by any act of communication.

4.4   Echoing and irony

Just as we reject the view that the literal meaning of an utterance constitutes its preferred interpretation, we challenge the view that the grammatical mood of an utterance (declarative, imperative, interrogative, etc.) determines its speech-act type (assertion, request, question, etc.). What is encoded by grammatical mood is not an illocutionary force but a more abstract piece of evidence about the speaker's intentions, which points the hearer in a certain direction but is not conclusive on its own.[3] Thus, the same imperative sentence might be used to express a request, as in (5),

(5)   MOTHER TO SON: Be a good boy!

as the antecedent of a conditional assertion, as in (6),

(6)   Be a good boy and you will become a good man.

to report someone else's utterance, as in (7),

(7)   GIRL: What did Mummy tell you?
       BOY: Be a good boy!

or to echo a preceding utterance, as in (8):

(8)   MOTHER TO SON: Be a good boy!
       SON TO MOTHER: Be a good boy! Be a good boy! I *am* being a good boy!

In a more extended sense of the term, it may also be used to echo someone else's utterance or thought (or the speaker's own past thoughts or utterances, or public opinion, etc.), however far removed in time, as in (9):

(9)   SHE: What kind of an upbringing did you have?
       HE: Oh, you know, be a good boy! and all that sort of thing.

In each case, the utterance will be taken to have whatever illocutionary force is required to arrive at an interpretation that is relevant in the expected way.

What makes an *echoic* utterance relevant? An echoic utterance indicates to the hearer that the speaker is paying attention to a representation (rather than to a state of affairs); it indicates that one of the speaker's reasons for paying attention to this representation is that it has been entertained (and perhaps expressed) by someone; it also indicates the speaker's attitude to the representation echoed. An echoic utterance achieves relevance by allowing the hearer to recognise, and perhaps to emulate, the speaker's interest in, and attitude to, someone else's thought.

The speaker may express any one of an indefinite variety of attitudes to the representation echoed. The attitude expressed may be one of approval, or even of reverence, as when a speaker echoes popular wisdom or holy scriptures, hoping thereby to command greater acquiescence than if she were merely to speak in her own voice. The attitude may be one of surprise, or even disbelief, as when a speaker echoes some amazing statement. There is also an attitude – or rather a range of attitudes – that may properly be called ironical: the representations echoed with such an ironical attitude are worth paying attention to because of their very inappropriateness, falsity, or even absurdity, and, moreover, because they have been or are being entertained by someone (or some group) as true beliefs or as realistic expectations in spite of their inappropriateness, falsity or absurdity.

Irony, then, rests on the perception of a discrepancy between a representation and the state of affairs it purports to represent. This is true of all varieties of irony, from Socratic irony (where the discrepancy is between the self-confidence and sense of superiority that Socrates allows his interlocutor to indulge in and the true *rapport de force*) to Romantic irony (where all representations – and in particular the poet's own ambitions – are seen as illusory).

When verbal irony is viewed as the use of a linguistic expression to convey the opposite of its literal meaning, not only its value as a rhetorical device but also its relationship to irony as an attitude are obscured. The mystery dissolves when verbal irony is seen as the echoing of an utterance or thought to which an ironical attitude is expressed.

In verbal irony, the ironical attitude is tacitly rather than explicitly conveyed. As a result, the hearer who recognises and shares this ironical attitude will feel that he and the speaker are superior to the victims of the irony: those who accept the echoed representation at face value. In the special case where the echoed representation is a belief or expectation of the hearer's own, or a norm that he has failed to conform to, the hearer is not given the option of sharing a sense of superiority with the speaker: he is himself the victim of the irony.

Thus, the mother who says ironically, as in (2) above (repeated here for convenience),

(2)   You're such a clean child!

is drawing attention to a discrepancy between the norm of cleanliness that the child is supposed to satisfy and his actual appearance. This, incidentally, explains why there are many fewer situations in which it would be appropriate for the mother to say ironically to a *clean* child:

(10)   You're such a dirty child!

Unless the child had been expected to be dirty for some reason, there would be no antecedent representation to echo. What makes irony moralistic is not, as Muecke (1970: 63) suggests, that 'all literature is moral', but that an easy way of achieving relevance through the use of irony is to echo a moral norm at the precise moment when it is being violated.

Echoic utterances are a well-defined type. Ironical utterances, by contrast, are a loosely defined sub-class of echoic utterances: there is a wide variety of ironical attitudes, which shade off imperceptibly into other attitudes, such as anger or aloofness. As a result, the same representation can be echoed several times in the same discourse, with slightly different attitudes: the utterance type and content remain the same, but the speaker's disposition evolves and relevance is renewed.

In a famous speech, Shakespeare's Mark Antony says four times, 'Brutus is an honourable man'. The first time, all are agreed that his audience is not intended to take the utterance ironically. The fourth occurrence, on the other hand, is blatantly sarcastic. What happens in between? Wayne Booth, despite his subtlety as an interpreter, is hampered by the classical model of irony (vastly enriched though it is in his treatment):

For the populace, when Mark Antony says for the first time that 'Brutus is an honorable man,' the invitation is simply to agree or disagree. If any of them takes the further step of judging that Mark Antony does not believe what he says, they will probably decide that he is a liar, not an ironist . . . (Booth 1974: 42)

Booth considers only two alternatives: either Mark Antony is making a literal assertion, or else he is being ironical; and since irony is excluded at that stage, it must be a literal assertion (and therefore a lie). For lack of intermediate forms between literalness and irony, a total reversal of meaning must take place at the second or third utterance of 'Brutus is an honourable man'. In order to provide a richer account of the passage than classical rhetorical tools allow, Booth has to resort to metaphor. Mark Antony's hearers, he writes,

do not just translate into the opposite conclusion: 'Brutus is really *dis*honorable.' They are forced to make the ironical leap in order to stand with Mark Antony on his platform (a good deal higher, one might say, than the literal one on which he stands) and they must feel themselves drawn to his conclusions by the acrobatic skill which they themselves have shown. (p. 42)

Relevance theory offers a more powerful analytical tool, which makes it possible to provide a more explicit and fine-grained account of Mark Antony's rapidly evolving mood. When he first says that Brutus is an honourable man, we do not have to describe him as *asserting* his own opinion, and still less as asking his audience to agree. They are already on Brutus's side (''Twere best he speak no harm of Brutus here', a citizen cautions). What Mark Antony does is *echo* their opinion with what they must see, at this stage, as a conciliatory attitude. Considerations of relevance lead Mark Antony's audience to understand him not as *telling* them that Brutus is honourable, but as *granting* them that Brutus is honourable (and granting what you do not believe is not lying, and may even be the moral thing to do).

Then, as he provides his audience with reasons for abandoning the favourable opinion of Brutus that he repeatedly echoes, Mark Antony conveys a more and more scornful attitude to that opinion (and to Brutus himself, who would like to be thought of as honourable). The utterance type remains the same: it is echoic throughout. Only the attitude changes. Neither the fact that the utterance is echoic nor the speaker's gradually changing attitude is encoded, and neither can therefore be decoded: the audience recognises them by looking for a *relevant* interpretation.

Again, we are on the side of the Romantics: irony is not an occasional device, but a fundamental attitude. Unlike the Romantics, however, we believe that the linguistic expression of this attitude can be analysed and explained without appeal to further tropes, and in terms of an unambiguous and testable model.

4.5   The relevance of rhetoric

If relevance theory is right, it offers a solution to the rhetorician's dilemma: a way of being precise about vagueness, of making literal claims about metaphors and ironies, without abandoning any of the Romantics' intuitions. However, rhetoricians could not adopt this solution without jeopardising the foundations of rhetoric itself. For what our proposal implies is that metaphor and irony are not rhetorical devices involving codified departures from the ordinary use of language, but ordinary exploitations of basic processes of verbal communication. Moreover, metaphor and irony exploit quite different basic processes, and are more closely related to other forms of speech – metaphor to loose talk and irony to a variety of echoic uses – than to each other. The very notion of a trope is better abandoned. If so, then rhetoric has no proprietary subject matter to study, or to teach.

Rhetoric has no proprietary subject matter to study because the phenomena and issues it claims as its own amount to a disparate set of items rather than an autonomous category. The set should be dismantled and the individual items studied within the broader framework of a cognitive approach to human communication. Rhetoric has no proprietary subject matter to teach because its effects and procedures are familiar to every human communicator. Teaching metaphor or irony – or, for that matter, the more esoteric-sounding antapodosis or zeugma – has only one indisputable consequence: it makes people do self-consciously what they were already doing spontaneously. From an aesthetic point of view, no-one nowadays would argue that self-conscious use of rhetorical devices is an unmixed blessing. From a cognitive point of view, the teaching of rhetoric turns out to have been a source not so much of self-understanding as of self-misunderstanding.

Because rhetorical effects are achieved in the normal course of the ever-present pursuit of relevance, the institution of rhetoric as a separate subject for teaching and study defeats its avowed purpose. Of course, this makes the historical resilience of rhetoric all the more paradoxical. What covert role, what addictive power, what indirect relevance, should we attribute to rhetoric in order to resolve the paradox?

5   A deflationary account of metaphors

Dan Sperber and Deirdre Wilson

5.1   Introduction

Are metaphors departures from a norm of literalness? According to classical rhetoric and most later theories, including Gricean pragmatics, they are. No, metaphors are wholly normal, say the Romantic critics of classical rhetoric and a variety of modern scholars ranging from hard-nosed cognitive scientists to postmodern critical theorists. On the metaphor-as-normal side, there is a broad contrast between those, like the cognitive linguists Lakoff, Talmy or Fauconnier, who see metaphor as pervasive in language because it is constitutive of human thought, and those, like the psycholinguists Glucksberg or Kintsch, or relevance theorists, who describe metaphor as emerging in the process of verbal communication.[1] While metaphor cannot be both wholly normal and a departure from normal language use, there might be distinct, though related, metaphorical phenomena at the level of thought, on the one hand, and verbal communication, on the other. This possibility is being explored (for instance) in the work of Raymond Gibbs.[2] In this chapter, we focus on the relevance-theoretic approach to linguistic metaphors.

Relevance theory's approach to metaphor is deflationary. Most rhetorical, literary and philosophical traditions emphasise both the importance and the distinctiveness of metaphor. We acknowledge its importance but dispute its distinctiveness. Metaphors are indeed ubiquitous in language use and contribute to what Barthes called 'le plaisir du texte'. Specific uses of metaphors by individual authors or in given literary genres are certainly worthy of study, and so is the very idea of metaphor as a culturally salient notion with a long and very rich history. Still, we see metaphors as simply a range of cases at one end of a continuum that includes literal, loose and hyperbolic interpretations. In our view, metaphorical interpretations are arrived at in exactly the same way as these other interpretations. There is no mechanism specific to metaphors, no interesting generalisation that applies only to them. In other terms, linguistic metaphors are not a natural kind, and 'metaphor' is not a theoretically important notion in the study of verbal communication. Relevance theory's account of metaphor is on the lean side, and is bound to disappoint those who feel that verbal metaphor deserves a full-fledged theory of its own, or should be at the centre of a wider theory of language, or even of thought.

The widespread view that language use is governed by a norm of literalness (which is violated by metaphor and other figurative uses – hence their distinctiveness) follows straightforwardly from the even more widespread view that the function of language in communication is to allow the speaker to encode her meaning and the hearer to decode it. Loosening the grip of this 'code model' view of human communication is a necessary first step towards putting metaphor in a proper perspective.

5.2   The function of language in communication

A code is a systematic pairing of messages and signals. Encoding a message into a signal that a recipient can then decode is a very simple way to communicate very simple messages. Non-human animals do it all the time. Formally speaking, human languages are also codes: they are systems of sound–sense pairs generated by an underlying grammar. But although they are codes, human languages are vastly different from the codes of animal communication. First, and most obvious, they are incomparably richer. Languages not only contain a vast repertoire of expressive elements – the lexicon – with no counterpart in animal signalling systems, but these elements are combined by a syntax with unbounded generative capacities.

Human languages differ from animal codes in another respect that should be equally obvious but is hardly ever mentioned: they are grossly defective as codes. For communication to be achieved purely by coding and decoding, each signal in the code must unambiguously convey exactly the same content on all occasions. Ambiguity – where the same signal is paired with several messages – will stall the decoding process. True, there are cases even in animal communication where the precise message encoded by a given signal varies with the context. In the 'bee dance', for instance, the orientation of the bees' communicative movements indicates the direction in which pollen is to be found, but this indication is relative to the position of the sun at the time. Limited context-sensitivity of this type can be handled by automatic code-like rules of disambiguation and accommodated in a coding–decoding system. However, the interpretation of the linguistic utterances that humans use to communicate is far too context-sensitive to be automatically achieved in purely code-like terms. The sentences of a natural language are typically multiply ambiguous; they contain referential expressions whose values cannot be assigned by decoding alone; the senses they ambiguously encode are often elliptical or incomplete; and there are still other ways in which the encoded meaning of a sentence falls short of determining what it may be used to communicate.

So although a language is formally a code, and human communication involves linguistic coding and decoding, there is a considerable gap between the semantic structure a sentence encodes and the meaning a speaker manages to convey by uttering that sentence in a given situation. In the case of metaphors and other tropes, this gap is often acknowledged as if it were an exception, and described in terms of a distinction between literal and figurative meaning.[3] We claim that metaphors are not exceptional, and that the linguistic content of all utterances, even those that are literally understood, vastly underdetermines their interpretation.

When we say that human languages are defective as codes, we do not mean to imply that there is something wrong with them, or that we should want to improve on them (as some philosophers in the analytic tradition once proposed). On the contrary, we assume that human languages are exquisitely well suited to performing their function in communication. It is just that this function cannot be to encode speakers' intended meanings.

Humans communicate not only by using language but also by producing a variety of what we call 'ostensive stimuli': that is, actions (e.g. gestures or speech) or traces of actions (e.g. writings) that are manifestly intended to attract an addressee's attention and convey some content. Many of these ostensive stimuli do not belong to a code, and hence do not properly speaking encode anything. By using ostensive stimuli, humans are capable of communicating without language, and indeed without any other code. How can a stimulus convey a meaning that it doesn't encode? By providing evidence that the communicator intends to convey this meaning.

Suppose Mary is angry with Peter and doesn't want to talk to him. When he tries to engage her in conversation, she might

(1)   stare pointedly at the ceiling

(2)   open a newspaper and start reading it.

These actions do not draw on any established code. Still, what staring at the ceiling or opening a paper suggests to Peter is that Mary would rather do these things than talk to him at that time. Given that these actions are ostensive stimuli (i.e. are performed in order to attract his attention and convey some content to him), Peter understands Mary to *mean* that she doesn't want to talk to him. He interprets her in this way not because of some underlying code that systematically pairs stimuli of this type to a meaning of this type, but because her actions bring this interpretation to mind, and the best possible explanation of Mary's behaviour is to assume that this is just what it was intended to do. A stimulus can convey a meaning it does not encode by providing evidence that the communicator intends to convey this meaning. Here, the meaning is recovered not by decoding but by inference.

What is true of uncoded communicative stimuli is also true of coded stimuli used in human communication: they too convey their producer's intended meaning not by directly encoding it but by encoding some evidence of it. In the situation described above, Mary might

(3)   look angrily at Peter and clamp her mouth firmly shut

(4)   look angrily at Peter, put a finger to her lips, and whisper 'Shhh!'

In (3) and (4), Mary makes a gesture conventionally used to convey a request for silence, from which Peter can infer that she does not want to talk to him. Unlike the actions in (1) and (2), clamping one's mouth firmly shut or whispering 'Shhh' may be seen as encoding some meaning, but this encoded meaning is much vaguer than Mary's own meaning. For instance, the same gestures might be used in other situations to convey a request for secrecy. In the present situation, though, they are enough to indicate Mary's meaning.

In the same situation as before, Mary might also

(5)   say 'I am deaf and dumb'

(6)   say 'I won't talk to you'.

Obviously, the decoded linguistic content of Mary's utterance in (5) does not directly yield her meaning, but it provides a starting point for inferring her meaning that is not too different in effect from the gesture of clamping one's mouth shut, as in (3). In both cases, what is activated in Peter's mind is the idea of its being impossible to talk, an idea whose import is easy enough to work out in the situation.

What about Mary's utterance in (6)? Surely this, at least, encodes her exact meaning? In fact, it too falls some way short of doing so: the future tense does not indicate when Mary won't talk to Peter; the declarative sentence form does not indicate whether she is expressing a prediction, a warning, a threat or what. On another occasion, she might use the same sentence to promise Peter that she will talk to the whole group rather than just to him. Still, in the situation described, Peter can reconstruct Mary's full meaning by starting from the linguistic content of her utterance and specifying it further so as to reach a contextually plausible interpretation.

What these examples illustrate is the general point that, whether or not it involves the use of a language or some other code, human communication is inferential communication. The communicator provides some evidence of her meaning and the addressee infers this meaning on the basis of this evidence and the context. The evidence may or may not be coded, and if it is coded, it may or may not be linguistic, but in each case it provides input to an inferential process whose goal is to understand the communicator's meaning. Which raises the following question: What is the point of using a language at all, if the kind of thing it can be used to achieve can also be achieved without it? The point is that a language provides an unbounded repertoire of evidence of the speaker's meaning, evidence that can be as nuanced, as complex, as richly structured as the speaker likes. Non-verbal kinds of evidence are much more limited. With language (and only with language) people can communicate about anything they can think about, whether they can point to it or not, imitate it or not, and they can do this with endless refinement. The fact that the interpretations of utterances are not encoded but merely evidenced by their linguistic meaning does not detract from the richness of linguistic communication, but, on the contrary, enhances it: every single sentence can give rise to an open array of interpretations which go well beyond the encoded senses. Some of the best illustrations of this are, of course, creative metaphors.

5.3   How relevance guides inferential comprehension

What we have sketched so far is a view of verbal communication suggested by the work of the philosopher Paul Grice, but more radical than his. Grice charac-terised a speaker's meaning as an overt intention to cause a certain cognitive effect in an audience via their recognition of one's intention to cause this effect (Grice 1989: chapters 5, 6, 14, 18). A speaker's meaning, so understood, is an intention, a mental state. The mental states of others cannot be simply perceived or decoded, but must be inferred from their behaviour, together with background information. What is special about a speaker's meaning as compared with other mental states (which people usually keep to themselves) is that speakers intend their audience to discover their meaning, and provide evidence to that effect, in the form of communicative behaviour. This raises the possibility that there might be an inferential procedure uniquely adapted to comprehension.

Grice tended to take for granted – and Searle explicitly argued – that when someone uses language to communicate, she is presumed to express her mean-ing literally. It can then be assumed by default that the literal linguistic meaning of the utterance is *her* meaning, or at least the explicit part of her meaning (Grice's *what is said*), with only the implicit part (Grice's *implicatures*) left to be inferred. This amounts, in practice, to saying that part of the speaker's meaning is decoded and part is inferred. Metaphors and other tropes, where the linguistic meaning of the utterance is not even part of the speaker's meaning, are excep-tional in this respect: Grice suggested that in metaphor, the speaker is not really saying what she appears to be saying, but merely 'makes as if to say' it, so that in this case, the speaker's meaning must be wholly inferred. We claim, by contrast, that verbal comprehension involves no presumption of literalness and no default interpretation, and that metaphors are in no way exceptional. All human inten-tional communication works in the way outlined above: the communicator produces a piece of evidence of her meaning – the ostensive stimulus – and the addressee infers her meaning from this piece of evidence and the context. Linguistic utterances are just one type of ostensive stimulus. Verbal communication is always context-sensitive and inferential.

How exactly does inferential comprehension work? Relevance theory draws on a precise characterisation of relevance and its role in human cognition to put forward a testable account of the comprehension mechanism, an account in which expectations of relevance play a crucial role.

We analyse *relevance* not just as a property of utterances or other ostensive stimuli, but as a property that any input to a cognitive process might possess: sights, sounds, utterances, thoughts, memories, suppositions may all be relevant to an individual at a given time. When is an input relevant? When processing it in the context of previously available information yields new cognitive effects. The input may answer a question the individual had in mind, it may raise or settle a doubt, suggest a hypothesis or a course of action, confirm or disconfirm a suspicion, correct a mistake. All these cognitive effects involve a fruitful interaction between the input and the context in which it is processed. However, the interaction may be more or less fruitful; inputs may be more or less relevant.

What makes one input more relevant than another? Suppose you are a caterer making lunch for a group of ten people, and all you need to know is how many will want the vegetarian menu. Then the information that three of them are vegetarian would be more relevant to you than the information that three of them are Buddhists (from which it follows that they are probably, though not definitely, vegetarian). In general, it is more informative to discover that someone is a Buddhist than to discover that he is a vegetarian, but if the context is such that only his food preferences are consequential, then the less informative input is more relevant. The greater the cognitive effects produced by processing an input, the greater its relevance (to the person processing it, at the time).

However, cognitive effects are only one of two factors that affect the relevance of an input. The other is the processing effort involved in achieving these effects. Some effort of perception, memory or inference is required to represent the input, access contextual information, and derive cognitive effects. In the situation described above, suppose that the choice is between a straightforward statement that three of the guests are vegetarian and a brochure with a short biography of all ten guests, mentioning inter alia whether or not they are vegetarian. In this case, the brochure would be less relevant than the straightforward statement: although both would contain all the information required, extracting this information from the brochure would involve more effort for the same effect, hence less relevance. In a nutshell:

Degrees of relevance:
(a) The greater the *cognitive effects* achieved by processing an input, the greater its relevance.
(b) The smaller the *processing effort* required to achieve these effects, the greater the relevance.

At every moment in their waking lives, humans have a huge variety of inputs competing for their attention: things and events they perceive, previous thoughts that have not been fully digested, pending goals, and so on. For contexts to use in processing these inputs, they have a vast mental encyclopaedia of accumulated knowledge on which to draw. At any given moment, most of these inputs are not worth processing, and, for any given input, most of this background information is not worth activating: the resulting process would yield too few cognitive effects to be worth the effort. Cognitive efficiency is very much a matter of selecting the most relevant inputs available at each point, and processing them in the context of background information that will most enhance their relevance. In fact, if there were not a strong tendency to select maximally relevant inputs, cognition would be an extremely wasteful activity. We assume that, among the many selective pressures that have driven the evolution of human cognitive capacities, there has been a constant pressure on the cognitive system as a whole, on its component parts, and on their articulation, towards an efficient use of brain resources. We therefore put forward the following claim:

Cognitive Principle of Relevance:
Human cognition tends to be geared to the maximisation of relevance.

We are not claiming that humans always succeed in maximising relevance, but only that they have a sufficient tendency to do so to make their massive investment in cognition evolutionarily worthwhile. More specifically, we are claiming that human perceptual mechanisms tend to pick out potentially relevant stimuli, human retrieval mechanisms tend to activate potentially relevant background assumptions, and human inferential mechanisms tend to process them in the most productive way, so that, overall, attention tends to go to the inputs with the greatest expected relevance. These claims have a variety of experimentally testable consequences (see Van der Henst and Sperber 2004). Here we are only concerned with the consequences of the cognitive principle of relevance for human communication.

Given the indefinite variety of possible objects of attention and courses of thought, it would be impossible for one person to predict what others will attend to, and what the resulting thoughts will be, if their attention and thought processes were not guided by considerations of relevance. The tendency to maximise relevance is crucial to making human mental processes relatively interpretable and predictable. Given this tendency, it is possible not only to interpret and predict the mental processes of others, but also to manipulate them by producing a stimulus which will predictably attract their attention and be interpreted in foreseeable ways. Jill knows it is relevant to Peter that all his guests should be happy, so she leaves her empty glass in his line of sight, anticipating that he will pay attention and conclude that she would like another drink. This is not yet a case of inferential communication, because, although Jill intends Peter to come to this conclusion, she provides evidence only that she is thirsty, and not that she intends to inform Peter that she is thirsty. If she had instead established eye contact with him and waved her empty glass, or said to him 'My glass is empty', then the stimulus would be ostensive, and her behaviour would be properly communicative.

Use of an ostensive stimulus as opposed to a regular non-ostensive one provides the addressee with information not only about some state of affairs (e.g. the fact that Jill would like another drink) but also about the communicator's intention to convey this information, and to do so overtly. By producing an ostensive stimulus, the communicator openly requests the addressee's attention. Since attention tends to go to the most relevant inputs available, the communicator implicitly conveys that her message is such an input. The central claim of relevance-theoretic pragmatics is that use of an ostensive stimulus raises expectations of relevance not raised by other inputs, and that these expectations guide the comprehension process. More specifically, we claim:

> *Communicative Principle of Relevance*
> Every act of inferential communication conveys a presumption of its own optimal relevance.

The presumption of optimal relevance mentioned in the communicative principle has a precise content. The utterance (or other communicative act) is presumed to be relevant enough to be worth processing, from which it follows that it must be more relevant than other inputs competing for the addressee's attention at the time. In some conditions, it can be presumed to be even more relevant than that. Communicator and addressee have at least one common goal: for communication to succeed, that is, for the addressee to understand what the communicator meant. The more relevant the utterance, and in particular the less processing effort it requires, the more likely the addressee is to understand it successfully. The communicator can therefore be expected, within the limits of her expressive abilities, and without going against her own goals (and in particular the goal she is pursuing in communicating), to have aimed at maximal relevance. So when we say that every act of inferential communication conveys a presumption of its own optimal relevance, we mean something quite precise: as much relevance as is compatible with the communicator's abilities and preferences, and, in any case, enough relevance to be worth processing.

The communicative principle of relevance suggests both a path for the addressee to follow in constructing the interpretation of an utterance, and a stopping point. Since effort is one of the two factors affecting relevance, the appropriate path to follow is one of least effort. The stopping point is the point at which the current interpretation (i.e. what the speaker is taken to have conveyed, either explicitly or implicitly) satisfies the expectations of relevance raised by the utterance itself. From the speaker's point of view, the easiest way to increase the relevance of her communication, and hence the chances of being properly understood, is to express herself (within the limits of her abilities and preferences) so that the interpretation she intends to convey is the first interpretation found by an addressee following the path of least effort that meets the expectations of relevance she herself has raised.

To illustrate, consider the following exchange:

(7)   PETER: For Billy's birthday party, it would be nice to have some kind of show.
        MARY: Archie is a magician. Let's ask him.

Suppose that 'magician' is ambiguous for Peter, with two senses: (a) *someone with supernatural powers who performs magic*, and (b) *someone who does magic tricks to amuse an audience.* In the context of a discussion about a show for a child's birthday party, the second sense is likely to be activated first, and the information (or reminder) that their friend Archie is a magician in this sense is likely to satisfy Peter's expectations of relevance by implying that he might perform at Billy's birthday party. In presuming that her utterance would be relevant to Peter, Mary must have expected him to derive this implication, which can therefore be seen as an implicit part of her meaning, i.e. an implicature. The disambiguation of 'magician' as someone who does magic tricks dovetails with this implicature, and the two confirm one another by jointly yielding an interpretation that is relevant in the expected way.

The linguistic meaning of the sentence 'Let's ask him' is very schematic and gappy, leaving the second part of Mary's utterance wide open to an indefinite range of interpretations. 'Him' may refer to Archie, to Billy, or to someone else. 'Ask' may be understood as asking for advice, help, an opinion, a favour, and so on. Thus, the whole sentence might be used to mean *Let's ask Billy whether he would like to have Archie perform magic tricks at his birthday party.* This interpretation would make sense in the situation, and would be quite compatible with Grice's maxims of conversation, or with standard theories of discourse coherence. Still, in a context where the first part of the utterance ('Archie is a magician') implicates that Archie could perform magic tricks at Billy's party, the first interpretation found by following a path of least effort will be that Peter and Mary should ask Archie to perform. Since this would satisfy Peter's expectations of relevance, he should accept it as the intended interpretation, without looking any further for alternative interpretations that might also be relevant. (None of these other potential interpretations could be optimally relevant, because extra processing effort would be required to retrieve them. They are therefore not worth considering unless there is some reason to think that Mary has failed to express herself in an optimally relevant way.)

In this example, Mary is speaking literally (which shows how far even the interpretation of an utterance that is literally understood can go beyond its linguistic meaning and is not just a simple matter of decoding). Our claim is that the very same procedure that yields a literal interpretation in this case would yield a non-literal interpretation in others.

5.4   Meaning construction

The decoded senses of a word or other linguistic expression in an utterance provide a point of departure for an inferential process of meaning construction. The meaning constructed may be narrower than the decoded meaning, as in (8) or (9):

(8)   I have a temperature.

(9)   PETER: Does Gérard like eating?
        MARY: He's French!

In (8), 'temperature' would be understood as meaning a temperature above normal.[4] What the speaker is communicating would be false if her temperature were a regular 37°C/ 98.6°F. In (9), what Mary means is not just that Gérard is a French national, but that he is what she regards as a prototypical Frenchman, and therefore someone who likes eating.

On other occasions, the meaning constructed may be broader than the decoded meaning, as in (10)–(14):

(10)   Holland is flat.

(11)   The stones form a circle.

(12)   (*On a picnic, pointing to a flattish rock*): That's a table!

(13)   (*Handing someone a tissue*): Here's a Kleenex.

(14)   (*Handing someone a paper napkin*): Here's a Kleenex.

The uses of 'flat' in (10) and 'circle' in (11) are cases of approximation. Approximation is a variety of loose use or broadening in which a word with a relatively strict sense is extended to a penumbra of items (what Lasersohn 1999 calls a 'pragmatic halo') that strictly speaking fall outside its linguistically specified denotation. The uses of 'table' in (12) and 'Kleenex' in (13) and (14) are cases of category extension. Category extension, another variety of loose use or broadening, involves applying a word with a relatively precise sense to a range of items that clearly fall outside its linguistically specified denotation, but that share some contextually relevant properties with items inside the denotation. Thus, the flat rock referred to in (12) is definitely not a table, but has properties which make it a good substitute for a table on that occasion. The tissue referred to in (13) is not a Kleenex, but will do just as well. The paper napkin referred to in (14) is not even a tissue, but is the closest available thing to a tissue, and will do almost as well.

With narrowing, literalness is in some sense preserved: a high temperature is literally a temperature, and a Frenchman who likes eating is literally a Frenchman. With broadening, literalness is not preserved: Holland is not literally flat, the stones do not literally form a circle, the flattish rock is not literally a table, and neither the tissue nor the paper napkin is literally a Kleenex. However, narrowing and broadening are not two functionally distinct types of language use. They both involve the same process of meaning construction, which happens in some cases to lead to a narrowing of the encoded concept, and in other cases to a broadening.

How are these narrowed or broadened lexical meanings arrived at? By following the relevance-guided comprehension procedure outlined above. With (8) ('I have a temperature'), a literal interpretation based on the decoded meaning of 'temperature' would be an irrelevant truism, since anyone (or indeed anything) has a temperature, just as it has a mass or a location. In fact, there is no reason to think that the hearer constructs and entertains such a truism. Rather, what happens is that the concept TEMPERATURE is activated in the hearer's mind and points him towards a relevant interpretation. This concept is (or has) a parameter that can take a range of values, some of which would be relevant in the circumstances (by implying, for instance, that the speaker is ill and unable to work). In the process of arriving at a relevant overall interpretation of the utterance, the decoded concept TEMPERATURE provides a starting point for constructing a narrowed *ad hoc* concept TEMPERATURE* which ranges only over contextually relevant temperatures: that is, temperatures which depart from the human norm in a way that is easily brought to mind, with implications that are worth the hearer's processing effort.

Similarly, activation of the lexicalised concept FLAT in (10) ('Holland is flat') gives access to a range of implications that would follow from Holland's being strictly flat: that it is a good place for easy cycling or not a good place for mountaineering, for instance. These implications hold (to different degrees for different implications) even if Holland is only approximately flat. In a context where (10) is relevant, some of these implications will be immediately obvious to the hearer, and will fulfil his expectations of relevance. The resulting overall interpretation (including the presumption of relevance and the implications that make the utterance relevant) will be internally consistent on the assumption that 'flat' in (10) indicates the speaker's intention to convey that Holland is FLAT*, where the *ad hoc* concept FLAT* represents an approximation to flatness which is close enough to yield the implications that make the whole utterance contextually relevant (for a detailed discussion of this and related examples, see Wilson and Sperber 2002).

In these two examples, the words 'temperature' or 'flat' are used in an utterance to evoke (or, more technically, to activate to some degree) potential implications of the encoded concepts TEMPERATURE or FLAT. More generally, we claim that ideas evoked in comprehension stand in inferential relationships to the concepts that evoke them,[5] and are not mere associations based on past co-occurrence, with no inferential status. That is, the ideas evoked by the presence of a word in an utterance are likely to be true of items in the linguistically specified denotation of the word, or, equivalently, of items in the extension of the concept encoded by the word. In the case of narrowing, the implications hold across only part of the extension of the encoded concept (e.g. only some temperatures imply illness). In the case of broadening, the implications hold not only of items in the extension of the encoded concept but also of contextually salient items which fall outside the extension, but which share with items inside the extension properties that determine these implications (e.g. cycling is easy not only in flat, but also in flattish terrains).

Some of the implications evoked by the presence of a word are simultaneously evoked by the context. In (13) and (14) ('Here's a Kleenex,' said of a tissue or a paper napkin), implications of the form ... *can be used to blow one's nose* are activated in the hearer's mind not only by the word 'Kleenex' but by the fact that he has just been sneezing. Implications activated by both the utterance and the context are the first to come to mind, and are tentatively added to the interpretation until the hearer's expectations of relevance are satisfied. At that point, the explicit content of the utterance (in the case of an assertion, the propositions whose truth the speaker is committing herself to) is retroactively determined by mutually adjusting the implicit and explicit components of the interpretation. The explicit content of an utterance must be such that it contextually implies the implicit content. More technically, and in relevance-theoretic terms, the explicatures of an utterance must be such that, together with the implicit premises of the utterance, they warrant the derivation of its implicit conclusions (where both implicit premises and implicit conclusions are kinds of implicature). (On the mutual adjustment process, see Sperber and Wilson 1998a, 2005; Carston 2002a; Wilson and Sperber 2002, 2004; Wilson and Carston 2007.)

In the case of (8) ('I have a temperature'), the result of the mutual adjustment process is a contextual construal of 'temperature' as TEMPERATURE*, which is narrower than the lexicalised concept TEMPERATURE. In the case of (10) ('Holland is flat'), the result is a contextual construal of 'flat' as FLAT*, which is broader than the lexicalised concept FLAT. Narrowings and broadenings of meaning are thus arrived at by exactly the same procedure of online concept construction, and for the same reasons. In fact, as noted by Carston (1997), they may be combined in a single construal. Suppose that Mary in (9) says of Gérard, 'He's French!', intending to implicate that he likes eating, when, in fact, she knows that Gérard happens to be a citizen of Monaco. She would then be using neither the concept FRENCH, which denotes French nationals and is encoded (let us assume) by the word 'French', nor an appropriate narrowing, FRENCH*, but a concept FRENCH** which is narrower in some respects and broader in others, denoting people who fit some prototype of a French person without French nationality being either a sufficient condition or an absolutely necessary one for inclusion in its extension.

Strictly literal interpretations – those that involve neither narrowing nor broadening of the lexicalised concept – are arrived at by exactly the same process of mutually adjusting explicit content with implicit content. A literal interpretation results when the implications that make the utterance relevant in the expected way depend on the presence in the explicit content of the lexicalised concept itself (rather than some broadened or narrowed version).[6] Literal interpretations are not default interpretations: they are not the first to be considered, and they are not necessarily easier to construct than non-literal ones. In fact, some literal interpretations are fairly hard to get, as in (15):

(15)   If Holland were flat, water would flow from the borders towards the centre.

In describing a stretch of land as 'flat', we broaden the concept by ignoring not only the various types of unevenness present in any terrain, but also the curvature of the earth.[7] This second departure from the literal meaning of 'flat' is not so easily corrected.

There is a continuum of cases between approximations such as (10) and (11) and hyperboles. In fact, the same utterance can be properly understood hyperbolically, loosely, or literally, depending on the facts of the matter, with no sharp dividing line between the different interpretations. Consider (16):

(16)   MARY TO PETER: The soup is boiling.

If Peter is too far away to observe the state of the soup directly, how is he to select one of these possible interpretations? Via considerations of relevance. Suppose he is working upstairs; when he smells the soup Mary is making and says he is coming down to taste it, Mary answers as in (16). Then her utterance would be relevant as a warning not to bother: 'boiling' would function as a hyperbole, conveying *too hot to taste*. Or suppose instead that Peter is making the soup but has left the room, and Mary knows that the soup should not be allowed to boil at this stage. Then her utterance would be relevant enough if the soup were *almost* boiling: a loose, approximate use rather than a hyperbole. Suppose, finally, that Peter is making the soup but has left the room, and Mary knows that he wanted to skim it once it was properly boiling. Then in order to be relevant enough, her utterance would have to be interpreted literally.

5.5   The literal–loose–metaphorical continuum

There is a continuum of cases between limited category extensions such as (12)–(14) above and more creative ones such as (17) and (18):

(17)   Žižek is another Derrida.

(18)   For luggage, pink is the new black. (*New York Times*, 4 September 2005)

In (17) 'Derrida' is used as a common noun to denote a category of flamboyant and obscure philosophers à la Derrida. In (18), 'black' is used to denote a category of fashionable colours. In both cases, a category is extended to include items that share with its members some properties which may or may not be essential, but are at least salient. These examples of category extension, unlike the use of 'Kleenex' to refer to any tissue, are not analysable as mere loose uses. The claim in (17) is not that the differences between Žižek and Derrida are inconsequential, but that Žižek belongs to a broader category of which Derrida is the most salient member. The claim in (18) is not that pink is pretty much the same as black, but that it occupies, in the category of colours for luggage, the place previously occupied by black. Still, (17) and (18) are interpreted by the usual process: the presence of the words 'Derrida' or 'black' helps to activate implications about Žižek, on the one hand, and the colour pink, on the other, that make the utterance relevant in the expected way. By mutual adjustment of explicit content and implicatures, the explicit content is construed as containing an *ad hoc* concept (DERRIDA* or BLACK*) that contextually carries these implications.

There is a continuum of cases between hyperbole and metaphor. It might seem at first blush that hyperbole involves only a quantitative difference between the concept encoded and the concept contextually constructed, as in (19) below, while metaphor also involves a qualitative difference, as in (20):[8]

(19)   Joan is the kindest person on earth.

(20)   Joan is an angel.

However, the quantitative–qualitative distinction is not sharp. For instance, (21) and (22) would generally be classified as hyperboles rather than metaphors, although there is both a quantitative and a qualitative difference between something that is credible and something that is not, or between a saint and an ordinary kind person:

(21)   Joan is incredibly kind.

(22)   Joan is a saint.

In any case, whether they are classified as hyperboles or metaphors, (21) and (22) would be interpreted in the same way: the encoded concept helps to activate contextual implications that make the utterance relevant as expected, and the concept conveyed by the hyperbole/metaphor is one of an outstanding type of kindness characterised by these implications.

There is also a continuum of cases between category extension and metaphor. It might be argued that category extension involves the projection of defining, or at least characteristic, properties of the encoded concept onto a broader category, as in (12)–(14) and (17)–(18) above, whereas the type of broadening involved in metaphor is based on relatively peripheral, or at least contingent, properties, as in (23) or (24):

(23)   'Man is but a reed, the weakest in nature.' (Blaise Pascal)

(24)   My mind is cloudy.

Weakness is not a defining property of reeds (and it is only a property relative to some arbitrary comparison class); similarly, the difficulty of discerning parts is not a defining property of clouds.

However, some metaphors are based on fairly central properties of the lexicalised category. For instance, when the term for an animal body part is extended to a human body part, as in (25), the result would generally be classified as a metaphor:

(25)   Henry was proud of his mane.

A category may undergo successive broadenings, with more peripheral extensions necessarily losing some of the most central features of the lexicalised category. Thus, compare (17) ('Žižek is another Derrida') with (26) and (27):

(26)   Rebecca Horn is the Derrida of contemporary art.

(27)   Ferran Adria is more Derrida than Danko. (attested: www.egullet.org/tdg.cgi?
         pg=ARTICLE-tabledancingadria – Adria is the world famous chef of El Bulli,
         Danko is a famous San Francisco chef)

In each case, a different concept (DERRIDA*, DERRIDA**, DERRIDA***) is constructed, each marginally further away from the original concept (if we accept that there are concepts of individuals) or representation of Jacques Derrida.

Central and peripheral properties may combine, as in (28), a comment on a clip of George W. Bush allegedly wiping his glasses on an unsuspecting woman's shirt during an appearance on Jay Leno's TV show:

(28)   We're all human Kleenex to him (attested: www.iflipflop.com/2004/10/meta-
         phor-george-bush-uses-woman-as.html).

Here, the woman is implicitly described as a Kleenex, since she (or at least her clothes) can be used as one, and this carries the suggestion that Bush sees people as disposable artefacts of little value.

Most hyperboles involve only broadening of the encoded concept, with no narrowing. In (19), for instance, 'the kindest person on earth' (despite its singular form) is broadened to cover all very kind people, including Joan. By contrast, most metaphors involve both narrowing and broadening, and so cannot be seen simply as cases of category extension. In the metaphorical (20), 'angel' is interpreted as ANGEL*, which is narrowed, on the one hand, to cover only prototypical kind, caring angels (excluding avenging angels, angels of wrath or fallen angels) and broadened, on the other, to cover all very kind, caring people. However, this combination of narrowing and broadening is not a defining feature of metaphor. In the metaphorical (28), for instance, 'Kleenex' is broadened to something like the category of DISPOSABLE ITEMS, and this includes not only prototypical Kleenex but all Kleenex.

5.6   Inferential steps

We see this continuity of cases, and the absence of any criterion for distinguishing literal, loose, and metaphorical utterances, as evidence not just that there is

Table 5.1. *Interpretation of Mary's utterance, 'Archie is a magician'*

(a) Mary has said to Peter 'Archie is a magician'.	*Decoding of Mary's utterance.*
(b) Mary's utterance is optimally relevant to Peter.	*Expectation raised by the recognition of Mary's utterance as a communicative act.*
(c) Mary's utterance will achieve relevance by addressing Peter's suggestion that they have a show for Billy's birthday party.	*Expectation raised by (b), given that Mary is responding to Peter's suggestion.*
(d) Magicians (in one lexicalised sense of the term, MAGICIAN$_2$) put on magic shows that children enjoy.	*Assumption activated both by use of the word 'magician' and by Peter's wish to have a show for Billy's birthday party. Tentatively accepted as an implicit premise of Mary's utterance.*
(e) Archie could put on a magic show for Billy's birthday party.	*Implicit conclusion derivable from (d), together with an appropriate interpretation of Mary's utterance, which would make her utterance relevant-as-expected. Tentatively accepted as an implicit conclusion of the utterance.*
(f) Archie is a MAGICIAN$_2$.	*Interpretation of the explicit content of Mary's utterance as decoded in (a) which, together with (d), would imply (e). Interpretation accepted as Mary's explicit meaning.*
(g) Archie is a MAGICIAN$_2$ who could put on a magic show for Billy's birthday party that the children would enjoy.	*First overall interpretation of Mary's utterance (explicit content plus implicatures) to occur to Peter which would satisfy the expectation of relevance in (b). Accepted as Mary's meaning.*

some degree of fuzziness or overlap among distinct categories, but that there are no genuinely distinct categories, at least from a descriptive, psycholinguistic or pragmatic point of view.[9] Even more important than the lack of clear boundaries is the fact that the same inferential procedure is used in interpreting all these different types of utterance. Let us look in more detail at how this procedure applies to the interpretation of two examples, one at the literal end of the continuum, and the other at the metaphorical end.

At the literal end, we return to example (7):

(7)   PETER: For Billy's birthday party, it would be nice to have some kind of show.
        MARY: Archie is a magician. Let's ask him.

Table 5.1 shows the inferential steps that Peter goes through in interpreting the first part of Mary's utterance ('Archie is a magician'), with Peter's interpretive hypotheses on the left, and his basis for arriving at them on the right.

At the metaphorical end of the continuum, consider (29):

(29)   PETER: I've had this bad back for a while now, but nobody has been able to help.
        MARY: My chiropractor is a magician. You should go and see her.

Table 5.2. *Interpretation of Mary's utterance, 'My chiropractor is a magician'*

(a) Mary has said to Peter 'My chiropractor is a magician'.	*Decoding of Mary's utterance.*
(b) Mary's utterance is optimally relevant to Peter.	*Expectation raised by the recognition of Mary's utterance as a communicative act.*
(c) Mary's utterance will achieve relevance by addressing Peter's expressed concern about his back pain.	*Expectation raised by (b), given that Mary is responding to Peter's complaint.*
(d) Chiropractors are in the business of healing back pain.	*Assumption activated both by use of the word 'chiropractor' and by Peter's worry about his back pain. Tentatively accepted as an implicit premise of Mary's utterance.*
(e) Magicians (in one lexicalised sense of the term, MAGICIAN₁) can achieve extraordinary things.	*Assumption activated both by the use of the word 'magician' and by Peter's worry that no ordinary treatments work for him. Tentatively accepted as an implicit premise of Mary's utterance.*
(f) Mary's chiropractor, being in the business of healing back pain and able to achieve extraordinary things, would be able to help Peter better than others.	*Implicit conclusion derivable from (d) and (e), together with an appropriate interpretation of Mary's utterance, which would make her utterance relevant-as-expected. Tentatively accepted as an implicit conclusion of the utterance.*
(g) Mary's chiropractor is a MAGICIAN* (where MAGICIAN* is a meaning suggested by the use of the word 'magician' in the sense of MAGICIAN₁ and enabling the derivation of (e)).	*Interpretation of the explicit content of Mary's utterance as decoded in (a) which, together with (d) and (e), would imply (f). Interpretation accepted as Mary's explicit meaning.*
(h) Mary's chiropractor is a MAGICIAN*, who would be able to help Peter better than others by achieving extraordinary things.	*First overall interpretation of Mary's utterance (explicit content plus implicatures) to occur to Peter which would satisfy the expectation of relevance in (b). Accepted as Mary's meaning.*

Table 5.2 shows, again in simplified form, the inferential steps that Peter goes through in interpreting the first part of Mary's utterance ('My chiropractor is a magician').

In both cases, of course, interpretation is carried out 'online', and starts while the utterance is still in progress. We assume, then, that interpretive hypotheses about explicit content and implicatures are developed partly in parallel rather than in sequence, and stabilise when they are mutually adjusted so as to jointly confirm the hearer's expectations of relevance. And we are not suggesting that the hearer consciously goes through just the steps shown in the tables, with exactly those premises and conclusions. We are not making claims about exact sequences, consciousness, or the representational format of thought. We are making claims about the factors that cause hearers to converge on an interpretation which – when communication is successful – coincides with the one intended by the speaker.

Although 'magician' is interpreted literally in (7) and metaphorically in (29), the same kind of process is involved in both cases. With (7), the fact that one of the lexicalised senses of 'magician' is MAGICIAN$_2$, *someone who performs magic tricks to amuse an audience*, makes it particularly easy to access implications associated to this interpretation. Since these implications end up satisfying the hearer's expectations of relevance and are carried only by this precise meaning, one of the lexicalised senses of 'magician' is selected by the comprehension process as the contextually indicated meaning. With (29), 'magician' provides easy access to the information that if someone is a magician, they have extraordinary capacities, and this is enough to ground an optimally relevant overall interpretation. The concept used in this interpretation is substantially broader than MAGICIAN$_1$, so in this case, as a rhetorician would say, 'magician' is a metaphor. However, the hearer pays no more attention to the fact that 'magician' is used metaphorically in (29) than he does to the fact that it is used literally in (7).

For that matter, some people may have only a single encoded sense for 'magician': *someone with supernatural powers who performs magic*. They would still have no difficulty arriving at an appropriate interpretation of (7) by extending the category of 'real' magicians to include make-believe ones. For other people, the metaphorical sense may have become lexicalised, so that 'magician' now has the additional encoded sense *someone who achieves extraordinary things*. They would obviously have no trouble arriving at an appropriate interpretation of (29). Mary did not intend her utterance to be understood literally in (7) and metaphorically in (29); her communicative intentions – like those of all speakers – are about content and propositional attitude, not rhetorical classification.

Relevance theory's resolutely inferential approach to comprehension suggests a solution to the 'emergent property' issue raised in recent work on metaphor.[10] Consider (30):

(30)   This surgeon is a butcher.

Clearly, what this utterance evokes is the idea that the surgeon in question is grossly incompetent, dangerous, and so on. The problem, at least for theories of metaphor based on associations or 'connotations', is that being incompetent, dangerous, and so on are not properties particularly associated with either butchers or surgeons, so how do these properties emerge when the two categories are associated as in (30)?

If we treat the relationship between an utterance and its interpretation as inferential, then the issue is whether the properties that seem to 'emerge' in the metaphorical interpretation can in fact be inferred. It should be obvious that the answer is 'yes'. Surgeons and butchers both characteristically cut flesh, but in quite different ways. Surgeons cut live flesh; they cut as little as possible, and with the utmost care to avoid unnecessarily severing blood vessels, nerves or tendons, thus causing irreparable damage. Butchers cut dead flesh to produce pieces of meat for cooking; this places no principled restriction on how much should be cut (or minced, broken, pounded, etc.), and puts a premium on severing nerves, tendons, and other hard tissues. So a surgeon who treats flesh as a butcher does would indeed be grossly incompetent and dangerous. The inferential path to an adequate understanding of (30) involves an evocation of the way butchers treat flesh, and the construction on that basis of an *ad hoc* concept BUTCHER*, denoting people who treat flesh in the way butchers do. Practically all butchers and (one hopes) very few surgeons fall within the extension of this concept. For a butcher, being a BUTCHER* is a quasi-pleonastic property. For a surgeon, on the other hand, it does imply gross incompetence – such an inconceivable degree of incompetence, in fact, that (30) must be seen not just as a metaphor but also as a hyperbole.

A meat lover who cares about precise, careful cuts might praise a butcher by saying:

(31)   This butcher is a surgeon.

The interpretation of (31) is symmetrical with the one sketched above for (30), and involves the construction of an *ad hoc* concept SURGEON*, denoting people who cut flesh with extreme care. A butcher who is also a SURGEON* is outstandingly competent and trustworthy. The predicates BUTCHER* and SURGEON*, along with the implication of incompetence for a surgeon who is a BUTCHER* and of competence for a butcher who is a SURGEON*, emerge unproblematically in the course of an inferential comprehension process guided by the search for relevance.

Of course, examples (30)–(31) involve emergent properties that are particularly easy to analyse in inferential terms, and it remains to be seen how far the full range of cases can be dealt with along these lines. However, this account seems promising, and helps to bring out the contrast between inferential approaches to metaphor and more traditional associationist approaches. All inferential relationships are associations, but not all associations are inferential. In claiming that interpretation depends only on inferential relationships, we might have seemed to be depriving ourselves of some explanatory power. As this example suggests, just the opposite is true.[11]

5.7   Strength of contextual implications, strength of implicatures

We maintain that metaphors are not a distinct category of language use, let alone a discrete one. Are we then denying the obvious truth that metaphors often stand out as particularly creative and powerful uses of language? If not – and indeed we are not – how are these uses of language to be explained?

Utterances achieve relevance by producing cognitive effects. An utterance may have many cognitive effects or only a few, and these effects may be stronger or weaker. To illustrate, suppose you get to the airport in time for a flight scheduled to arrive in Atlanta at 2 p.m. Hearing an announcement that the flight may be delayed, you say to an airline employee:

(32)   I have to be in Atlanta no later than 5 p.m. Will I make it?

She replies as in either (33) or (34):

(33)   Your flight will be delayed by at least twenty minutes.

(34)   Your flight will be delayed by at least two hours.

Both (33) and (34) imply (35), but only (34) also implies (36):

(35)   You have at least twenty minutes to do as you please before boarding.

(36)   You have at least two hours to do as you please before boarding.

(35) in turn implies (37), while (36) implies both (37) and (38):

(37)   You have time for a drink before boarding.

(38)   You have time for a meal before boarding.

Clearly, (34) has more contextual implications than (33).

Both (33) and (34) also provide some evidence for the conclusion in (39):

(39)   You will get to Atlanta later than 5 p.m.

Another way of putting this is to say that (33) and (34) *weakly imply* (39). Such weak implications (or probabilifications) are also cognitive effects, and contribute to the relevance of a cognitive input.[12] Since the probability of your arriving late is increased more by (34) than by (33), (39) is a stronger implication (and hence a stronger cognitive effect) of (34) than it is of (33). But still, if you were to assume on the basis of either utterance that you will indeed get to Atlanta later than 5 p.m., this assumption would depend to a considerable extent on your own background beliefs (even more so in the case of (33) than (34)), although it would of course have been encouraged by what the airline employee told you. Overall, this example shows how the contextual implications of an utterance can vary in both quantity and strength.

A competent speaker must have good reason to suppose that what she says will be relevant to the hearer. The hearer himself may provide such a reason: for instance, by asking her a question, thereby letting her know that an answer would be relevant to him. Thus, if a stranger comes up to you in the street and asks what time it is, you can feel confident that it would be relevant to tell him the time, even if you neither know nor care exactly how it would be relevant, and are implicating nothing more than the presumption of relevance that any utterance conveys about itself.[13]

In most conversations or discourses, the speaker cannot have good reason to think that her utterances will be relevant enough without having some positive idea of the cognitive effects they will achieve. From the hearer's perspective, it is quite often safe to assume that the speaker both expected and intended him to derive some of the implications that he actually does derive, for otherwise she could not reasonably have thought her utterance would be optimally relevant to him. These intended implications are *implicatures* of the utterance. An implicature can be more or less strongly implicated. The speaker may have in mind a specific implication on which the relevance of her utterance depends, and a strong intention that the hearer should derive it; in that case it is strongly implicated. At the other extreme, she may have in mind a vague range of possible implications with roughly similar import, any subset of which would contribute to the relevance of her utterance, and a weak intention, for any of the implications in that range, that the hearer should derive it; these are weak implicatures. Her intentions about the implicatures of her utterance may fall anywhere between these two extremes. The strength of an implicature is determined by the manifest strength of the speaker's intention that a specific implication should be derived. It is important to distinguish the strength of an implicature from the strength of a contextual implication (whether or not it is also implicated), which is the probability that it is true, given that the premise from which it is contextually derived is true.

When the airline employee replies to your question in (32) (about whether you will get to Atlanta by 5 o'clock) as in (33) or (34), she must feel confident that, in telling you how long the delay is likely to be, she is giving you grounds for deriving a weak implication about the risk of your arriving late, thus indirectly answering your question. In other words, you can take her to be implicating that you might indeed be late, leaving it up to you to decide on the seriousness of the risk. The implication is weak – even weaker with (33) than with (34) – but it is fairly strongly implicated.

Does the airline employee also implicate (35) or (36) (viz. that you have at least twenty minutes / two hours to do as you please before boarding)? Although these implications go beyond simply providing an answer to your question, they might help to make the utterance optimally relevant to you in a way the speaker might have both foreseen and intended. When a plane is delayed, people generally want to know how much time they will have to wait before boarding. To that extent, the airline employee may be seen as implicating (35) or (36). These are strong implications of her utterance – they are very probably true – but they are only weakly implicated, because they only marginally increase the relevance of the utterance, and so the speaker's intention to convey them is not strongly manifest. After all, she may have felt that her utterance was relevant enough without even considering these further implications.

What about (37) (that you have time for a drink), or (38) (that you have time for a meal)? Does the airline employee also implicate these by replying as in (33) or (34)? Again, they are strong implications, which might contribute to the relevance of her utterance in a way the speaker could perhaps have foreseen, but they are even weaker implicatures, because they are among a range of implications with similar import (that you have enough time to buy a magazine, or buy and read one, that you have enough time to do your e-mail, and so on), some of which are likely to be relevant to you although the speaker is not in a position to know which. So she may be encouraging you to consider any of these implications that might be relevant to you, but not any specific one. These are very weak implicatures, if they are implicated at all. By contrast, if your question had been 'Do I have time for a drink?' the reply in (33) would strongly implicate (37), and the reply in (34) would strongly implicate (37) and weakly implicate (38), whereas both replies would only weakly implicate (39) (that you will get to Atlanta later than 5 p.m.), if they implicated it at all.

5.8   Poetic effects

Optimal relevance may be achieved by an utterance with a few strong implications, many weak implications, or any combination of weak and strong implications. A speaker aiming at relevance may implicate (that is, anticipate and intend) a few strong implicatures or a wide range of weak implicatures (which may themselves be strong or weak implications). There are many ways of achieving relevance, which differ in both the strength of the implications conveyed and the strength with which they are implicated.[14] Here we are particularly concerned with the case where relevance is achieved through a wide array of weak implications which are themselves weakly implicated. The speaker – or writer, since this method of achieving relevance is particularly well developed in literature – has good reason to suppose that enough of a wide array of potential implications with similar import are true or probably true, although she does not know which these are (hence they are weak implications) and is neither able to anticipate nor particularly concerned about which of them will be considered and accepted by the audience (hence they are weakly implicated). We have argued that the cognitive effects achieved by conveying such a wide range of weak implicatures are identifiable as *poetic effects* (Sperber and Wilson 1995: chapter 4, section 6; Pilkington 2000).

The production of genuinely relevant poetic effects can be a powerfully creative form of language use (creative on the part of both communicator and audience). Such effects can be created by literal, loose, or metaphorical forms of expression. Thus, classical Japanese haikus, which are among the most effective forms of poetry in world literature, typically involve a literal use of language. Consider Bashō's famous haiku (written in 1680):

> On a leafless bough
> A crow is perched –
> The autumn dusk.   (Translated by Joan Giroux, 1974)

This simple, literal description weakly implicates a wide array of implications which combine to depict a landscape, a season, a moment of the day, a mood, and so on, thereby achieving a powerful overall effect which varies to some extent from reader to reader.

By contrast, many metaphors are not particularly poetic. We are thinking here not so much of conventional metaphors which may have lost their poetic appeal, if they ever had one (was the phrase 'legs of a table' ever poetic?) as of less conventional but not particularly creative metaphors used to highlight a simple idea rather than suggest a complex one. Consider (40), a political comment on the Bush administration's handling of the 2005 Katrina hurricane, compared to its handling of the 2001 terrorist attack on the US:

(40)   Well, if 9/11 is one bookend of the Bush administration, Katrina may be the other. If 9/11 put the wind at President Bush's back, Katrina's put the wind in his face. If the Bush–Cheney team seemed to be the right guys to deal with Osama, they seem exactly the wrong guys to deal with Katrina. (Thomas Friedman, *New York Times*, 7 September 2005)

Here, the use of the metaphors 'bookend' and 'wind' to suggest opposing forces at two ends of a continuum (a case of force dynamics à la Talmy) is so flat that most readers are likely to bypass the obvious relationship between the wind and an explosion, on the one hand, and still more obviously, between the wind and a hurricane, on the other: the cognitive effects derivable from this relationship are unlikely to have been intended, and are hardly worth the effort. Nonetheless, these metaphors serve to make the author's point, which is definitely not of a poetic nature.

Although metaphors are neither necessary nor sufficient for the creation of genuine poetic effects, they are particularly well suited to this purpose, for several reasons. Consider, first, a trivial case of metaphor such as (41):

(41)   WOMAN TO UNCOUTH SUITOR: Keep your paws off me!

Here, 'your paws' refers unproblematically to the hearer's hands. Use of the word 'paws' also activates related notions, conceptions, and images having to do with animal paws, clumsiness, bestiality, and so on. From a relevance theory perspective, the fact that these ideas have been activated suggests that they may be relevant, and the effort spent in activating them, however marginal, suggests that they *should* be relevant (otherwise, the effort would have been wasted, contrary to the presumption of optimal relevance). While there is a wide range of possible implicatures which might contribute to the relevance of the utterance (that the addressee is clumsy, gross, lusting like a beast, and so on), none of them is strongly implicated by the speaker. We claim that they are weakly implicated: the hearer is indeed encouraged to consider at least some of them and see them as part of the speaker's meaning. It is these vague effects that make the use of 'paws' marginally more relevant than the use of 'hands'.

According to classical rhetoric, the literal meaning of the word 'paw' is replaced in (41) by the figurative meaning HAND. In more recent approaches based on category extension, the literal meaning of 'paw' is extended to include any EXTREMITY OF A LIMB (whether animal or human). In both analyses – substitution of a figurative meaning disjoint from the literal one, or inclusion of the linguistically specified denotation in a broader 'figurative' denotation – suggestions of clumsiness and bestiality are added to the figurative meaning as 'connotations' of the word 'paw'. Here, 'connotations' are associations in a strictly associationist sense: they are grounded in past co-occurrence and can go in any direction.

In fact, the word 'paw' has many associations other than clumsiness and bestiality which might be activated in a metaphor, from the softness of a cat's paw to the strength of a lion's. Association of the type appealed to in associationist psychology is a process which is too vague, on the one hand, and too powerful, on the other, to account for the subtlety and directionality of weak implicatures. As noted above, we would rather appeal only to associations based on properly inferential relationships, and, more generally, stick to an inferential rather than associationist account of comprehension. In (41), the alleged connotations are associated to the literal meaning of 'paw' (i.e. PAW), and not to its figurative meaning HAND or EXTREMITY OF A LIMB. From an inferential point of view, the idea that the literal meaning of 'paw' is discarded while its connotations remain is even more puzzling than the smile of the Cheshire cat: the cat's smile lingers at an empty location, whereas the connotations of the literal meaning of 'paw' are supposed to adorn the figurative meaning that has replaced it.

The alternative analysis we favour is the one we have been defending throughout this chapter. In processing (41), the hearer develops (in parallel) tentative interpretations of the explicit and implicit components of the speaker's meaning, and stops when they fit together in the sense that the explicit content contextually implies the implicated conclusions, and the explicit content and implicit content jointly satisfy the hearer's expectations of relevance. Given that the relationship between explicit content and implicit content is properly inferential, and given the nature of the mutual adjustment process used to determine these contents, the implications evoked by the decoded senses of the words used in the utterance must be genuine implications: that is, they must hold of at least part of the extension of the decoded senses. The *ad hoc* concepts constructed to carry these implications will then at least overlap with the concepts encoded by the utterance (otherwise we would be dealing with purely associationist rather than inferential relations). Since the concepts PAW and HAND have disjoint extensions, we claim that 'paw' in (41) could not be used to convey the meaning HAND. Nor can it be used to convey EXTREMITY OF A LIMB, since this broadened concept is not specific enough to contextually imply clumsiness, bestiality, and so on.

We assume that the *ad hoc* concepts built on the basis of most metaphorical uses of terms are genuinely *ad hoc*: that is, they are adjusted to the precise circumstances of their use, and are therefore unlikely to be paraphrasable by an ordinary language expression. This is why we resort to the '*' notation, and represent the concept pragmatically conveyed by 'paw' in (41) as PAW*. PAW* is the most easily constructed concept whose extension includes the hearer's hands, and which carries the weak contextual implications generally true of prototypical paws: that they are used clumsily, grossly, and so on. These weak implications are themselves weakly implicated: that is, they are weakly intended by the speaker. The utterance on this interpretation achieves optimal relevance by making a strong explicit request that the hearer remove his PAWS*, and weakly implicating that he is behaving clumsily and grossly. Note that PAW*, so construed, involves both a broadening and a narrowing of PAW, as do most *ad hoc* meanings conveyed by metaphorical uses.

So even a common metaphor such as 'Keep your paws off me!' achieves some of its relevance through an array of weak implicatures: a poetic touch, however modest. In more creative metaphors, relevance may depend to a much greater extent (or even entirely) on such weak implicatures, in a way that makes it quite appropriate to talk of 'poetic effects'. Consider the full version of Carl Sandburg's poem 'Fog', whose first two lines are one of the most widely quoted examples of creative metaphor:

> The fog comes
> on little cat feet.
> It sits looking
> over harbor and city
> on silent haunches
> and then moves on.

'On little cat feet' evokes an array of implications having to do with silence, smoothness, stealth. Taken together with the following four lines, the phrase evokes a movement which appears both arbitrary and yet composed, so that it is tempting to see it not as random but rather as guided by mysterious dispositions. Poems are read and re-read. On a second reading, the interpretation of the whole poem provides part of the context in which the first two lines are understood. Not unlike Bashō's literal haiku quoted above, Sandburg's extended metaphor weakly implicates an ever-widening array of implications which combine to depict a place, an atmosphere, a mood, achieving a powerful overall effect that varies from reader to reader and reading to reading. It is not part of the explicit content of the poem that the fog comes silently, or smoothly, or stealthily. Rather, what is part of the explicit content is that the fog comes ON-LITTLE-CAT-FEET*. And what is this concept? It is the concept of a property that is difficult or impossible to define, a property possessed in particular by some typical movements of cats (though not all of them – little cat feet can also move in violent or playful ways) and, according to the poem, by the movement of fog. How is this *ad hoc* concept ON-LITTLE-CAT-FEET* arrived at? By taking the poet to be attributing to the coming of the fog that property which contextually implies the very ideas suggested by the phrase 'little cat feet'.

The example of Sandburg's poem should help to clarify how and why metaphors are indeed particularly likely to achieve optimal relevance through the creation of poetic effects: the effort required for *ad hoc* concept construction calls for matching effects, and given the freedom left to the interpreter in the construction process, these effects are unlikely to consist in just a few strongly implicated strong implications. It is not that concept construction systematically demands more effort in the case of metaphors (see Gibbs 1994a, Noveck, Bianco and Castry 2001). Many metaphors are very easy to process, while, as any science student knows, arriving at an adequate literal understanding of a statement may take much more effort than a loose or even a metaphorical construal. Nor is it that literal expression is intrinsically less capable than metaphor of achieving poetic effects, as the comparison between Bashō's haiku and Sandburg's haiku-like poem shows. It is just that, on the whole, the closer one gets to the metaphor end of the literal–loose–metaphorical continuum, the greater the freedom of interpretation left to hearers or readers, and the more likely it is that relevance will be achieved through a wide array of weak implicatures, i.e. through poetic effects. So when you compare metaphors to other uses of words, you find a bit more of this and a bit less of that, but nothing deserving of a special theory, let alone a grand one.

6   Explaining irony

Deirdre Wilson and Dan Sperber

6.1   Traditional approaches to irony

Here are some typical examples of verbal irony:

(1)   MARY (AFTER A BORING PARTY): That was fun.

(2)   I left my bag in the restaurant, and someone kindly walked off with it.

(3)   SUE (TO SOMEONE WHO HAS DONE HER A DISSERVICE): I can't thank you enough.

In each case, the point of the irony is to indicate that a proposition the speaker might otherwise be taken to endorse (that the party was fun, the person who took her bag behaved kindly, or Sue is more grateful than she can say) is ludicrously inadequate (here, because of its falsity).[1] A hearer who fails to recognise this will have misunderstood the speaker's ironical intention. A speaker who doubts her hearer's ability to recognise this intention using background knowledge alone can provide additional cues (e.g. an ironical tone of voice, a wry facial expression, a resigned shrug, a weary shake of the head). The ability to understand simple forms of irony is thought to be present from around the age of six or seven,[2] and to be impaired in a variety of conditions including autism, Asperger's syndrome, schizophrenia and certain forms of right hemisphere damage.[3] One of the goals of pragmatics is to describe this ability and thus explain how irony is understood.

In classical rhetoric, verbal irony is analysed as a trope: an utterance with a figurative meaning that departs from its literal meaning in one of several standard ways. In metaphor, as in (4), the figurative meaning is a related simile or comparison; in hyperbole, as in (5), it is a weakening of the literal meaning; in meiosis (understatement), as in (6), it is a weakening of the literal meaning; and in irony, as in (7), it is the contrary or contradictory of the literal meaning:

(4)   a. Susan is a wild rose.
       b. Susan is like a wild rose.

(5)   a. The road is so hot you could fry an egg on it.
       b. The road is very hot.

(6)   a. He was a little intoxicated.
        b. He was very drunk.

(7)   a. You're a fine friend.
        b. You're not a fine friend / You're a terrible friend.

These definitions have become part of Western scholarly and folk linguistics and can be found in any dictionary. To turn them into an explanatory theory, one would need an account of the function fulfilled by using a literal meaning to convey a figurative meaning and a cognitively plausible procedure for deriving figurative meanings from literal ones. Classical rhetoric did not provide either of these, but then its aim was to provide an informal user's manual, not an explanatory theory of tropes.

Grice's brief discussion of tropes (Grice 1967/1989: 34) reanalyses the figurative meanings in (4b)–(7b) as conversational implicatures triggered by blatant violation of his first Quality maxim ('Do not say what you believe to be false'). On this account, the ironical utterances in (1)–(3) above might implicate (8)–(10):

(8)   That party was no fun.

(9)   Someone unkindly stole my bag.

(10)   I can't thank you at all.

Grice's account of tropes shares with the classical account the assumption that metaphor and irony, hyperbole and meiosis are cut to the same pattern. Both accounts treat (4)–(7) as violating a maxim, norm or convention of literal truthfulness, and both see their figurative meanings (or implicatures) as regular departures from their literal meanings, derivable from these literal meanings by some procedures for meaning substitution. To the extent that these accounts have implications for the processing of figurative utterances, they suggest that metaphor and irony should involve similar processes, show similar developmental patterns and break down in similar ways.

This traditional approach to figurative utterances is now increasingly questioned. On the descriptive level, Grice's account is generally taken to imply a two-stage processing model in which the literal meaning of an utterance has to be tested and rejected before a figurative interpretation is considered. And indeed, it is hard to see how the hearer could recognise an utterance as a *blatant* violation of Grice's maxim of truthfulness without first constructing and rejecting a literal interpretation. However, experimental studies of both metaphor and irony suggest that some figurative interpretations take no more effort to construct than literal interpretations, contrary to the predictions of the 'literal-first' model.[4]

On the theoretical level, the most fundamental drawback of the traditional approach is that it offers no clear explanation of why metaphor and irony should exist at all. In Grice's framework, figurative utterances such as (4a)–(7a) convey no more than could have been conveyed by uttering their strictly literal counterparts (4b)–(7b). Yet their interpretation necessarily involves rejection of the literal meaning (in Grice's terms, what the speaker has 'said or made as if to say') and construction of an appropriate implicature. On this account, metaphor and irony should cost more to process than their literal counterparts, but yield no extra benefit, which makes their use irrational and a waste of effort. In later work, Grice acknowledges that his account of irony is insufficiently explanatory (although he does not seem to have had similar worries about his parallel accounts of other tropes), and mentions some further features of irony which may be seen as intended to supplement his account or to point in the direction of an alternative account.

From Classical antiquity to Gricean pragmatics, there has been a rich literature in linguistics, rhetoric and literary studies on the nature and uses of irony. With the exception of the Romantics (whose important contribution has been on the critical rather than the descriptive side), all this literature accepts the basic tenet of the Classical approach, that irony consists first and foremost in a reversal of meaning, merely elaborating on this tenet by adding subtle observations, apt illustrations and interesting questions.

Our paper 'Les ironies comme mentions' (1978), published in English as 'Irony and the use–mention distinction' (1981), proposed a radical departure from this basic tenet. We argued that irony consists in echoing a thought (e.g. a belief, an intention, a norm-based expectation) attributed to an individual, a group, or to people in general, and expressing a mocking, sceptical or critical attitude to this thought. On this approach, an ironical utterance typically implies that the speaker believes the opposite of what was said, but this is neither the meaning nor the point of the utterance. When Mary in (1) says, after a boring party, 'That was fun', she is neither asserting literally that the party was fun nor asserting 'ironically' that the party was boring. Rather, she is expressing an attitude of scorn towards (say) the general expectation among the guests that the party would be fun. This approach was experimentally tested by Julia Jorgensen, George Miller and Dan Sperber in 'Test of the mention theory of irony' (1984), which provided a new paradigm for experimental research on irony.[5]

Under the direct or indirect influence of these two papers, much of the work now done on irony turns its back on the Classical approach and is based on the view that what irony essentially communicates is neither the proposition literally expressed nor the opposite of that proposition, but an attitude to this proposition and to those who might hold or have held it. For instance, with many interesting experiments and observations, Roger J. Kreuz and Sam Glucksberg (1989) proposed an 'echoic reminder theory of verbal irony' which adds to ours the idea that an ironical utterance has to *remind* the hearer of the thought it echoes (we would argue that this is indeed quite generally, although not necessarily, the case).

By far the most influential variation of our account, and also the most critical one, is the 'pretence theory of irony' proposed as an alternative to the echoic theory by Clark and Gerrig (1984) in a response to Jorgensen, Miller and Sperber.

Both echoic and pretence accounts reject the basic claim of the Classical and standard Gricean accounts, that the hallmark of irony is to communicate the opposite of the literal meaning. Both offer a rationale for irony, and both treat ironical utterances such as (1)–(3) as intended to draw attention to some discrepancy between a description of the world that the speaker is apparently putting forward and the way things actually are. Perhaps for this reason, the two approaches are sometimes seen as empirically or theoretically indistinguishable: several hybrid versions incorporating elements of both have been produced, and the boundaries between them have become increasingly blurred. We will argue, however, that the two accounts differ, and that the echoic account is preferable.

In rhetorical and literary studies as well as folk linguistics, the term 'irony' has been applied to a broad range of loosely related phenomena, not all of which fall squarely within the domain of pragmatics defined as a theory of overt communication and comprehension. Of those that do, some are clearly forms of echoic use, others do indeed involve pretence, while others have no more in common with (1)–(3) than the evocation of a discrepancy between representation and reality. It should not be taken for granted that all these phenomena work in the same way, or that in developing a theory of 'irony', we should aim to capture the very broad and vague extension of the common meaning of the term. Rather, we should aim to identify mechanisms and see what phenomena they explain. The existence of pretence in speech is uncontroversial, and so is the fact that it can be put to ironical use. We want to argue that echoing is also a common mechanism, distinct from pretence, and that not only can it be put to ironical use, but that it also explains typical properties of verbal irony such as the ironical tone of voice or the normative aspect of much irony. In particular, we will argue that typical cases of verbal irony such as (1)–(3) are best analysed as cases of echoic allusion, and not of pretence.

6.2   Three puzzling features of irony

From the Classical point of view, irony presents three puzzling features that have often been noted and that an adequate theory should explain:

Attitude in irony and metaphor

In Lecture 3 of the William James Lectures, Grice discusses a possible counter-example to the brief analysis of irony introduced in Lecture 2:

A and B are walking down the street, and they both see a car with a shattered window. B says, *Look, that car has all its windows intact.* A is baffled. B says, *You didn't catch on; I was in an ironical way drawing your attention to the broken window.* (Grice 1967/1989: 53)

B's utterance meets all of Grice's conditions for irony – the speaker 'says or makes as if to say' something blatantly false, intending to implicate the opposite – but it would not normally be understood as ironical. What is missing from the Gricean account? Grice suggests that what is missing may be the fact that irony involves the expression of a 'hostile or derogatory judgment or a feeling such as indignation or contempt' (p. 53). However, he makes no attempt to integrate this suggestion into his earlier account.

Grice was not, of course, the first to note that irony expresses a characteristic attitude. By contrast, metaphor does not. Neither the role of attitude in irony nor the fact that irony and metaphor differ in this respect has a straightforward explanation in the Classical or Gricean accounts, which treat both metaphor and irony as departures from a convention, norm or maxim of literal truthfulness. Why should one departure involve the expression of a characteristic attitude and the other not?

Normative bias

There is a widely noted normative bias in the uses of irony. The most common use of irony is to point out that situations, events or performances do not live up to some norm-based expectation. Its main use is to criticise or to complain. Only in special circumstances is irony used to praise, or to point out that some proposition lacking in normative content is false. This bias is unexplained on the Classical or Gricean accounts.

To illustrate: when someone is being clumsy, it is always possible to say ironically, 'How graceful', but when someone is being graceful, it takes special circumstances to be able to say ironically, 'How clumsy'. Such negative ironical comments are only appropriate when some prior doubt about the performance has been entertained or expressed. To say ironically of an odd number 'This is an even number' is appropriate only when an even number had been expected.

This normative bias was experimentally confirmed by Kreuz and Glucksberg (1989) using alternative versions of stories such as the following, with the italicised sentence either present or absent:

Nancy and her friend Jane were planning a trip to the beach.
'It's probably going to rain tomorrow', said Jane, who worked for a local TV station as a meteorologist.
The next day was a warm and sunny one.
As she looked out of the window, Nancy said, 'This certainly is awful weather.'

The results showed that participants were more likely to judge the ironical comment appropriate when it was preceded by the explicit prediction that the weather would be awful. By contrast, in positive versions such as the following, the ironical comment was judged equally appropriate whether or not the italicised sentence was present:

Nancy and her friend Jane were planning a trip to the beach.
 'The weather should be nice tomorrow', said Jane, who worked for a local TV station as a meteorologist.
 The next day was a cold and stormy one.
 As she looked out of the window, Nancy said, 'This certainly is beautiful weather.'

The ironical tone of voice

A further difference which is unexplained on the classical or Gricean accounts is that irony, but not metaphor, has a characteristic tone of voice. Not all ironical utterances use this tone of voice, but those that do help the audience recognise their ironical intent (see Bryant and Fox-Tree 2005). The 'ironical tone of voice' is characterised by a flat or deadpan intonation, slower tempo, lower pitch level and greater intensity than are found in the corresponding literal utterances (Ackerman 1983; Rockwell 2000; Bryant and Fox-Tree 2005), and is generally seen as a cue to the speaker's mocking, sneering or contemptuous attitude. Thus, Rockwell (2000: 485) treats the vocal cues to sarcasm – a subtype of irony which she defines as 'a sharply mocking or contemptuous ironic remark intended to wound another' – as closely related to those for contempt or disgust, and suggests that they may be the prosodic counterparts of facial expressions such as 'a sneer, rolling eyes, or deadpan expression'. Since not all vocal or facial expressions of mockery, contempt or disgust are perceived as ironical, the challenge for pragmatics is to explain what makes some such expressions of attitude ironical, while others are not.

   It might be thought that the negative tenor of the ironical tone of voice merely reflects the fact that irony is more often used to blame than to praise, but this cannot be the case. The ironical tone of voice has a negative tenor whether irony is used to blame or to praise (or so it seems: the issue has not been properly investigated). Thus, if in appropriate circumstances one were to praise a graceful performance by saying in an ironical tone of voice, 'How clumsy!' the tone used would not be substantially different from the one used in criticising a clumsy performance by saying, 'How graceful!'

6.3   The echoic account of irony

In any genuinely linguistic act of communication,[6] an utterance is used to represent a thought of the speaker's that it resembles in content (Sperber and Wilson 1995: chapter 4, section 7). In ordinary *descriptive* uses of language, this thought is about an actual or possible state of affairs. In *attributive* uses, it is not directly about a state of affairs, but about another thought that it resembles in content, which the speaker attributes to some source other than herself at the current time.[7] Different varieties of attributive use achieve relevance in different ways. We define *echoic use* as a subtype of attributive use in which the speaker's primary intention is not to provide information about the content of an attributed thought, but to convey her own attitude or reaction to that thought. Thus, to claim that verbal irony is a subtype of echoic use is to claim, on the one hand, that it is necessarily attributive, and, on the other, that it necessarily involves the expression of a certain type of attitude to the attributed thought.

The best-studied cases of attributive use are indirect reports of speech and thought, illustrated by the italicised expressions in (11)–(13):

(11)   a. John phoned his wife and told her that *the train was about to leave.*
       b. He was hoping that *they would have a quiet evening alone.*

(12)   a. An announcement came over the loudspeaker. *All the trains were delayed.*
       b. The passengers were angry. *When would they ever get home?*

(13)   a. *Would the trains ever run on time*, the passengers were wondering.
       b. *His evening was now ruined*, John feared.

In (11a), use of the verb 'told' unambiguously indicates that the following clause is an indirect report of speech; in (11b), use of the verb 'hope' unambiguously indicates that the following clause is an indirect report of thought. By contrast, utterances such as (12a)–(12b) are *tacitly* attributive: the audience is left to infer that the thoughts they represent are being attributed to some source other than the speaker (e.g. the railway authorities in (12a), the passengers in (12b)). The examples in (13a)–(13b) are intermediate cases, which are similar in style to the tacit reports in (12), but with a parenthetical indication that the reported information is being attributed to some other source.[8]

Indirect reports such as (11)–(13) are primarily intended to inform the audience about the content of an attributed thought. Although the speaker may incidentally indicate her own reaction to that thought, this is not the main point of the utterance, on which most of its relevance depends. By contrast, some attributive uses of language are primarily intended to achieve relevance by showing that the speaker has in mind a certain thought held by others (or by herself at another time) and wants to convey her attitude or reaction to it. These are what we call *echoic uses* of language.

The most easily recognisable cases of echoic use are those that convey the speaker's attitude or reaction to a thought overtly expressed in an immediately preceding utterance. Consider Sue's possible responses in (15) to Jack's announcement in (14) that he has finished a paper he's been working on all year:

(14)   JACK: I've finally finished my paper.

(15)   a. SUE (HAPPILY): You've finished your paper! Let's celebrate!
       b. SUE (CAUTIOUSLY): You've finished your paper. Really completely finished?
       c. SUE (DISMISSIVELY): You've finished your paper. How often have I heard you say that?

Here it is easy to see that Sue is not intending to inform Jack about the content of a thought he has only just expressed,[9] but to convey her own attitude or reaction to it. In (15a), she indicates that she accepts it as true and is thinking about its consequences; in (15b), she reserves judgement about whether it is true, and in (15c), she indicates that she does not believe it at all.

In other cases, echoic utterances convey the speaker's attitude not to immediately preceding utterances but to more distant utterances, or to tacitly attributed but unexpressed thoughts. And indeed, Sue could utter (15a)–(15c) echoically when Jack arrives home after e-mailing the good news from the office, or walks in saying nothing but waving a sheaf of papers and carrying a bottle of champagne.

The attitudes which can be conveyed in an echoic utterance range from acceptance and endorsement of the attributed thought, as in (15a), through various shades of doubt or scepticism, as in (15b), to outright rejection, as in (15c). The central claim of the echoic account is that what distinguishes verbal irony from other varieties of echoic use is that the attitudes conveyed are drawn from the *dissociative* range: the speaker rejects a tacitly attributed thought as ludicrously false (or blatantly inadequate in other ways). Dissociative attitudes themselves vary quite widely, falling anywhere on a spectrum from amused tolerance through various shades of resignation or disappointment to contempt, disgust, outrage or scorn. The attitudes prototypical of verbal irony are generally seen as coming from the milder, or more controlled, part of the range. However, there is no cut-off point between dissociative attitudes that are prototypically ironical and those that are not.[10]

Before applying this account to some examples, it is worth pointing out two features of attributive utterances in general which are also found in echoic utterances. First, attributive utterances (including tacit indirect reports) can be used to inform the hearer about the content not only of thoughts or utterances attributed to a particular individual on a particular occasion, but of those attributed to certain types of people, or to people in general. These may have their roots in culturally defined social, moral or aesthetic norms, or general human hopes or aspirations. For instance, (16) attributes a thought to common wisdom:

(16)   They say a glass of wine is good for you.

We should therefore expect to find echoic utterances (including ironical utterances) conveying the speaker's attitude or reaction to thoughts of this kind, and we do:

(17)   a. SUE (*pointing to Jack, who is more cheerful after drinking some wine*): As they say, a glass of wine is good for you!
         b. SUE (*pointing to Jack, who is rather boisterous after drinking some wine*): As they say, a glass of wine is good for you!
         c. SUE (*pointing to Jack, who has become a total nuisance after drinking some wine*): As they say, a glass of wine is good for you!

In (17a)–(17c), the same widely shared view is echoed – approvingly in (17a), sceptically in (17b) and ironically in (17c).

Second, an indirect report need not be identical in content to the attributed utterance or thought, but should merely resemble it closely enough (i.e. preserve enough of its logical or contextual implications) to inform the hearer about relevant aspects of its content. In different circumstances, the most appropriate indirect report may be a summary, paraphrase or elaboration of the original, or may merely pick out an implication or implicature which the speaker regards as particularly worthy of the hearer's attention. We should therefore expect to find echoic utterances (including ironical utterances) which are not identical in content to the original utterance or thought, but merely resemble it to some degree, and we do. Suppose, for instance, that Bill has made a long speech about himself. Sue might report what he said as in (18), giving only its gist, and she might do so ironically, indicating by her tone of voice that she dissociates herself from what Bill was trying to convey.

(18)   JACK: What did Bill say?
         SUE: He is a genius!

There is one respect in which an echoic utterance can depart even further from the content of the original than the corresponding indirect report. A thought can be analysed as consisting of a proposition entertained with a certain propositional attitude. In reporting a thought, the speaker must provide the audience with enough information not only about its propositional content, but also about the associated attitude (was it a *belief,* a *wish,* a *fantasy,* a *hope,* a *suspicion,* a norm-based expectation about how people *ought* to behave, etc.?). In tacit indirect reports such as (12a)–(12b), if the hearer is not in a position to infer this attitudinal information for himself, it is typically provided in a parenthetical comment, as in (13a)–(13b). In an echoic utterance, by contrast, since the main aim is not to provide information about the attributed thought, the speaker may be able to convey her reaction to it by endorsing or dissociating herself from a proposition that was only a constituent of the original. Thus, if Peter had been *hoping* for lovely weather and it turns out to be pouring with rain, Mary might say, echoically, 'The weather is lovely', in either an approving or a contemptuous tone of voice, in order to show how well- or ill-founded his hopes have turned out to be. Similarly, if our aesthetic norms imply that any given performance *ought* to be graceful, we can say, echoically, 'How graceful', in either an approving or a contemptuous tone of voice, in order to show how well or badly that particular performance lived up to the norm. In these cases, the assertive propositional attitude expressed in the ironical utterance differs from the optative or normative propositional attitude of the people whose thought is being echoed.

Here is how the typical examples of irony in (1)–(3) might be analysed on this account. In (1) ('That was fun') Mary might be dissociating herself from the propositional content of specific thoughts or utterances about the party (predictions or reassurances from her friends that it would be worth going to, or her own hopes, desires, expectations or fantasies about how the party would go). In that case, her utterance might communicate that the predictions or reassurances of her friends, and her own hopes, desires, expectations or fantasies, were ridiculously ill-founded. Alternatively, she might be dissociating herself from an application (to this particular party) of a widely shared normative representation of how parties are *supposed* to go. In that case, her utterance might communicate that this particular party has fallen ridiculously short of acceptable standards. In other circumstances, she could have used (1) echoically to endorse the propositional content of the same attributed utterances or thoughts, communicating that her friends' reassurances were true, her hopes, desires, expectations or fantasies about the party were fulfilled, or that the party lived up to the normative expectation that it *ought* to be fun.

While the whole utterance in (1) is echoic, only the word 'kindly' is echoically used in (2) ('I left my bag in the restaurant, and someone kindly walked off with it'). The speaker is asserting that she left her bag in the restaurant and that someone took it, but dissociating herself from the proposition that this person behaved kindly. Here, there is a clear divergence between the echoic and Gricean accounts. On the Gricean account, the speaker of (2) is expressing the blatant falsehood that someone kindly stole her bag, and implicating the opposite (i.e. that someone unkindly stole her bag). On the echoic account, the speaker of (2) cannot be seen as ironically dissociating herself from the thought that someone kindly stole her bag, because no rational person would entertain such a thought in the first place. By contrast, it is quite reasonable to *hope* or *wish* that whoever finds a lost bag will behave kindly, and the idea that we should treat each other kindly is part of a widely shared normative representation of how people *ought* to behave. By echoing this widely shared representation, the speaker of (2) might communicate that her hopes or desires were ridiculously unrealistic, or that the person who found her bag fell laughably short of acceptable standards of behaviour.

Similarly, Sue's utterance in (3) ('I can't thank you enough') might be understood as ironically echoing a specific hope or wish of Sue's that the addressee's behaviour would be worthy of gratitude, or a particular application (to the addressee's behaviour) of a widely shared normative representation of how people ought to behave.

A distinctive prediction of the echoic theory of irony is that it cannot work unless the audience can attribute to specific people, or to people in general, a thought that the ironical utterance can be taken to echo. The earliest experiments on irony based on the relevance theory approach (Jorgensen, Miller and Sperber 1984) were designed to test precisely this prediction of the echoic account – and they did confirm it, as did several later studies. For instance, participants in an experiment by Keenan and Quigley (1999) were divided into two groups, each of which heard a version of stories such as the following, containing one or other of the two italicised sentences:

One night, Lucy was going to a party. Lucy was all dressed up in her new party dress, ready to go, but she didn't have her party shoes on. Lucy didn't want to run upstairs with her nice dress on, so she called to her brother Linus who was upstairs reading. She yelled, 'Linus, please bring me my nice red party shoes! [*I want to look pretty for the party / I have to hurry or I'll be late*.]' So Linus, who was still reading his book, went to Lucy's closet and by mistake, he picked up Lucy's dirty old running shoes. When he went downstairs to hand them to Lucy, she looked at them and said, 'Oh great. Now I'll really look pretty.'

The two groups were then tested on their understanding of Lucy's final comment 'Now I'll really look pretty'. The results showed that participants who heard the version containing the earlier related utterance 'I want to look pretty for the party' understood Lucy's final comment as ironical significantly more often than those who heard the version containing the earlier unrelated utterance 'I have to hurry or I'll be late'. In other words, irony is easier to recognise when the echoic nature of the utterance is made more salient.

In a different kind of test of the echoic account, Happé (1993) investigated metaphor and irony comprehension in typically developing children and young people with autism, using stories such as the following:

David is helping his mother make a cake. She leaves him to add the eggs to the flour and sugar. But silly David doesn't break the eggs first – he just puts them in the bowl, shells and all. What a silly thing to do! When mother comes back and sees what David has done, she says:

'Your head is made out of wood!'

Q1: *What does David's mother mean? Does she mean that David is clever or silly?*

Just then father comes in. He sees what David has done and he says:
'What a clever boy you are, David!'

Q2: *What does David's father mean? Does he mean David is clever or silly?*

The stories were interrupted at two points with comprehension questions: Question 1 tests the comprehension of metaphor and Question 2 tests the comprehension of irony. Participants also took standard first- and second-order false-belief tests, and a significant correlation emerged: participants who passed no false-belief tests understood neither metaphorical nor ironical utterances; those who passed only first-order false belief tests understood some metaphorical but no ironical utterances, and those who passed both first-order and second-order false-belief tests understood both metaphorical and ironical utterances. Thus, metaphor comprehension correlates with success in first-order false-belief tasks and irony comprehension with success in second-order false-belief tasks.

Happé's interpretation of her results relied on the assumption that standard false-belief tasks reveal orders of mindreading ability, from which it would follow that irony requires a higher order of mindreading ability than metaphor. However, recent work with versions of the false-belief task adapted to infants has shown that infants are already able to attribute false beliefs.[11] This suggests that the standard false-belief task (which children pass only at around the age of four) does not provide adequate evidence on the developmental origins of this ability. Still, the relative complexity of different standard false-belief tasks (whether they are first-order or second-order) remains a good indicator of participants' metarepresentational proficiency. Hence Happé's results do confirm the relevance theory account of figurative utterances, which treats metaphor as expressing a thought about a state of affairs and irony as expressing a thought about another thought, and hence as requiring a higher-order of metarepresentational abilities.[12]

6.4   Pretence accounts of irony

In their discussion of Jorgensen, Miller and Sperber (1984), Clark and Gerrig (1984) did not try to defend the Classical view of irony.[13] Instead, they offered a novel account which in fact had much in common with the echoic account. The main idea behind Clark and Gerrig's account, and most current pretence accounts of irony, is that the speaker of an ironical utterance is not herself performing a speech act (e.g. making an assertion or asking a question) but pretending to perform one, in order to convey a mocking, sceptical or contemptuous attitude to the speech act itself, or to anyone who would perform it or take it seriously. This idea has been fleshed out in various ways, often within broader theories of mimesis or simulation (see e.g. Clark and Gerrig 1990; Walton 1990; Recanati 2000, 2004a; Currie 2002). Our concern here is not with these broader theories, which provide valuable insights into the nature of pretence, but only with the claim that irony necessarily involves pretence, or that the ability to understand pretence is the key to understanding typical cases of irony such as (1)–(3) above.

Although Grice's account of irony is very much in line with the Classical approach, he is sometimes credited, in particular by Clark and Gerrig (1984), with an early version of the pretence account. On the one hand, he treated all figurative utterances as cases of 'saying or making as if to say', where 'making as if to say' has obvious connections with pretence. On the other hand, he suggested that an otherwise unexplained difference between metaphor and irony – that whereas a metaphorical utterance can be prefaced with the phrase *To speak metaphorically*, an ironical utterance cannot be prefaced with the phrase *To speak ironically* – might be explained on the assumption that irony is a type of pretence:

To be ironical is, among other things, to pretend (as the etymology suggests), and while one wants the pretence to be recognised as such, to announce it as a pretence would spoil the effect. (Grice 1967/1989: 54)

Grice's two points could be reconciled on the assumption that he thought there were several different varieties of 'making as if to say', with irony – but not metaphor – belonging to a sub-variety that amounted to pretence (Grice 1967/ 1989: 34, 53–54, 120). Recanati (2004a: 71) interprets Grice along these lines, and appears to endorse a similar version of the pretence account:

Suppose the speaker says *Paul really is a fine friend* in a situation in which just the opposite is known to be the case. The speaker does not really say, or at least she does not assert, what she 'makes as if to say' (Grice's phrase). Something is lacking here, namely the force of a serious assertion. . . . What the speaker does in the ironical case is merely to *pretend* to assert the content of her utterance. . . . By pretending to say of Paul that he is a fine friend in a situation in which just the opposite is obviously true, the speaker manages to communicate that Paul is everything but a fine friend. She shows, by her utterance, how inappropriate it would be to ascribe to Paul the property of being a fine friend.

In discussing the following example from Jorgensen, Miller and Sperber (1984), Clark and Gerrig (1984) put forward a more elaborate version of the pretence account:

(19)   Trust the Weather Bureau! See what lovely weather it is: rain, rain, rain.

Jorgensen *et al.* had treated 'See what lovely weather it is' in (19) as an ironical echo of the weather forecaster's prediction. Clark and Gerrig (1984: 122) treat it as a type of pretence:

With *See what lovely weather it is*, the speaker is pretending to be an unseeing person, perhaps a weather forecaster, exclaiming to an unknowing audience how beautiful the weather is. She intends the addressee to see through the pretense – in such rain she obviously could not be making the exclamation on her own behalf – and to see that she is thereby ridiculing the sort of person who would make such an exclamation (e.g. the weather forecaster), the sort of person who would accept it, and the exclamation itself.

According to this version of the pretence account, understanding irony involves the ability to recognise that the speaker is pretending to perform a speech act and simultaneously expressing a certain type of (mocking, sceptical, contemptuous) attitude to the speech act itself, or to anyone who would perform it or take it seriously.

As it stands, however, this version of the pretence account does not solve the problem raised by Grice's counterexample (see section 6.2) in which the speaker points to a car with a broken window and says, 'Look, that car has all its windows intact'. As noted above, Grice's comment that irony involves the expression of a hostile or derogatory attitude does not really solve the problem. In the first place, not all expressions of a hostile or derogatory attitude are ironical, and in the second place, someone who seriously asserted that a car with an obviously broken window had all its windows intact would be no less worthy of ridicule or contempt than someone who seriously asserted that the weather is lovely when it's pouring with rain, or that Paul is a fine friend when he's patently not. So why does the irony fall flat in one case and not in the others?

According to the echoic account, what is missing from both the Gricean account and simpler versions of the pretence account is the idea that for irony to succeed, the object of the characteristic attitude must be a thought that the speaker is tacitly *attributing* to some actual person or type of person (or to people in general). As Sperber (1984: 131) stressed in his reply to Clark and Gerrig,

> Absurdity of propositions per se is irrelevant. The absurdity, or even the mere inappropriateness, of human thoughts, on the other hand, is often worth remarking on, making fun of, being ironic about. In other words, in order to be successfully ironic, the meaning mentioned must recognisably echo a thought that has been, is being, or might be entertained or expressed by someone.

On this view, what makes 'See what lovely weather it is' in (19) above a successful case of verbal irony is not the fact that it would be ridiculous or inappropriate to assert it in the pouring rain, but the fact that some recognisable person or type of person (or people in general) has entertained (as a prediction or as a mere hope) the thought that the weather would be good, and, with hindsight, the inappropriateness of that thought is worth remarking on. Similarly, what would make the utterance 'Look, that car has all its windows intact' a successful case of verbal irony would be the fact that some recognisable person or type of person has entertained, is entertaining or might entertain or express a thought with a similar content whose inappropriateness or inadequacy would be worth remarking on. This is the main idea behind the echoic account. Unless the pretence account is extended to include the idea that irony is tacitly attributive, it is hard to see how it can handle counterexamples such as Grice's at all.

6.5   Hybrid attributive–pretence accounts

In fact, the general idea behind the echoic account – that irony is necessarily attributive – has been quite widely accepted, even if particular aspects of it have been criticised (and occasionally misconstrued).[14] Several pretence theorists share the intuition that irony is tacitly attributive, but also maintain that irony involves the simulation or imitation of a (real or imagined) speech act, and is therefore a case of pretence. Attributive–pretence accounts differ from the versions of the pretence account discussed in the last section by claiming that irony is necessarily attributive, and from the echoic accounts discussed in this section by claiming that irony also necessarily involves pretence. We now outline the main features of some of these accounts and highlight their differences from the echoic account.

Kumon-Nakamura, Glucksberg and Brown (1995) propose an 'allusional pretence' account of irony which involves elements of both attribution and pretence. The attributive element is introduced through the requirement that an ironical utterance must 'allude to some prior expectation, norm or convention that has been violated in one way or another' (p. 61).[15] The pretence element is introduced to deal with a variety of ironical utterances which Kumon-Nakamura *et al.* see as allusive but not properly echoic. These include ironical assertions such as (20), questions such as (21), offers such as (22), and requests, such as (23):

(20)   *To someone arrogantly showing off their knowledge*: You sure know a lot.

(21)   *To someone acting inappropriately for their age*: How old did you say you were?

(22)   *To someone who has just gobbled the whole pie*: How about another small slice of pizza?

(23)   *To an inconsiderate and slovenly housemate*: Would you mind very much if I asked you to consider cleaning up your room some time this year?

For Kumon-Nakamura *et al.*, a crucial feature of these utterances is their *pragmatic insincerity*: the speaker 'makes as if' to perform a certain speech act while intentionally violating one of its sincerity conditions (e.g. the condition on questions that one should want to know the answer, or on offers that the offer is being made in good faith). While acknowledging that (20) might be seen as echoing the arrogant person's conception of himself, Kumon-Nakamura *et al.* claim that no such treatment is possible for (21)–(23).[16]

Kendall Walton (1990: 222–23) also treats irony as involving both attribution and pretence. After noting some of the parallels between verbal irony and free indirect discourse (see note 8), he comments that the speaker of an ironical utterance is not simply reporting the tacitly attributed beliefs or assertions, but is 'pretending to endorse the ideas she attributes'. Thus,

To speak ironically is to mimic or mock those one disagrees with, fictionally to assert what they do or might assert. Irony is sarcasm. One shows what it is like to make certain claims, hoping thereby to demonstrate how absurd or ridiculous it is to do so.

Recanati (2007: 223–27) treats both irony and free indirect speech as tacitly attributive varieties of mimicry or pretence:

The act of assertion is precisely what the speaker does *not* perform when she says that *p* ironically: rather, she plays someone else's part and mimics an act of assertion accomplished by that person. She does so not by pretending that that person is speaking[17] ... but by herself endorsing the function of speaker and saying that *p*, while (i) not taking responsibility for what is being said, and (ii) implicitly ascribing that responsibility to someone else, namely the person whose act of assertion is being mimicked. (Recanati 2007: 226)

Currie's (2006: 116) version of the pretence account can also be understood as incorporating a tacitly attributive element. According to Currie, in irony, 'one pretends to be doing something which one is not doing: speaking seriously and assertively, seriously asking a question, seriously expressing distaste', in order to target 'a restrictive or otherwise defective view of the world':

... what matters is that the ironist's utterance be an indication that he or she is pretending to have a limited or otherwise defective perspective, point of view or stance, F, and in doing so puts us in mind of some perspective, point of view or stance, G (which may be identical to F or merely resemble it) which is the target of the ironic comment. (Currie 2006: 118)

Assuming that the 'restrictive or otherwise defective view of the world' is tacitly attributed to some person or type of person (or people in general), Currie's version of the pretence account can be seen as incorporating the claim that irony is tacitly attributive. And indeed, he comments in a footnote:

Perhaps it would be more strictly true to say that the target is some one person's really having that perspective, or some tendency on the part of a group of persons, or persons in general, to have or be attracted to having that perspective. These are refinements that do not, in themselves, divide me from the echoic theorists, and so I do not emphasise them.[18] (Currie 2006: 118)

According to the pretence accounts discussed in this section, the speaker of an ironical utterance is pretending to perform a speech act while simultaneously expressing a mocking, sceptical or contemptuous attitude to an attributed utterance or thought. This approach to irony raises three immediate questions: what is the object of the speaker's mocking, sceptical or contemptuous attitude, what actual or imagined speech act is being simulated, and how is the attribution achieved?

It is tempting to assume that a pretence theorist could answer all three questions, and simultaneously account for the parallels between irony and free indirect reports, by treating irony as involving the imitation of an actual (or at least a plausibly attributable) speech act, which would also be the object of the characteristic attitude expressed in irony. On this approach, if the weather forecaster makes the announcement in (24), Mary might be seen as imitating this speech act in order to report it, as in (25), or to express her own mocking, sceptical or critical attitude to it, as in (26):

(24)   WEATHER FORECASTER: It will be lovely weather today.

(25)   MARY: Guess what I've just heard. *The weather is going to be lovely today.*

(26)   MARY [*in the pouring rain*]: *The weather is really lovely today.*

A pretence account of this type would not only explain the attributive nature of (25) and (26), but also capture the intuition that the object of the ironical attitude conveyed in (26) is the speech act the weather forecaster performed; it would thus appear to offer a genuine alternative to the echoic account.

However, there are several problems with this assumption. In the first place – as most pretence theorists recognise – the object of the ironical attitude need not be a speech act, but may be merely a thought that has not been overtly expressed in an utterance. While it makes sense to talk of mimicking, imitating or pretending to perform a public speech act, it makes no clear sense to talk of mimicking, imitating or pretending to perform a private thought. Pretence accounts of free indirect reports of thought run into a similar problem. According to Recanati (2007), these might be handled by broadening the notion of assertion to cover both public speech acts and private judgements, so that a speaker who reports either can be described as mimicking an 'act of assertion'. But this is a purely terminological proposal, and does not solve the problem of how a piece of public behaviour can mimic a private thought. By contrast, the notion of echoic attributive use outlined in section 6.3 above, which is based on resemblances in content rather than in behaviour and which therefore need not involve imitation, applies straightforwardly to any representation with a conceptual content, whether this is a public representation that can indeed be imitated or a mental representation that cannot.

A second problem with the claim that ironical utterances are imitations of actual (or plausibly attributable) speech acts is that even when there is an actual prior speech act that the ironical speaker can be seen as echoing, the ironical utterance need not preserve the illocutionary force of the original. Thus, Mary might ironically echo the weather forecaster's announcement in (24) ('It will be lovely weather today') by saying to her companion,

(27)   a. Isn't it lovely weather?
         b. What lovely weather we're having today!
         c. Let's enjoy this lovely weather.

These utterances resemble the original in propositional content, but not in illocutionary force, and it is hard to see how Mary could be seen as imitating the speech act that the weather forecaster performed; if she is pretending to perform any speech act in (27a), it is a question rather than an assertion. Or recall the experimental scenario in section 6.3 above, where Lucy asks Linus to bring her nice red party shoes. According to the pretence account, when Lucy says, ironically, 'Now I'll really look pretty', she is pretending to assert that she will really look pretty. However, the actual utterance that she is ironically echoing was 'I want to look pretty for the party', and this expresses a desire or wish, rather than a belief or judgement, that she will look pretty. The point is quite general, and shows that even when the object of the speaker's ironical attitude is an actual speech act (e.g. the weather forecaster's assertion in (24)), this speech act cannot be identified with the one the speaker is pretending to perform.

A pretence theorist might propose to handle these cases by claiming that ironical utterances are imitations, if not of actual speech acts, at least of speech acts that some actual person or type of person had envisaged. For instance, when Lucy says, ironically, 'Now I'll really look pretty', she might be seen as pretending to make an assertion that she had hoped to be able to make herself, or imagined others making about her, and expressing a mocking or contemptuous attitude to the thoughts in which its performance was anticipated. And indeed, as mentioned earlier (note 16), ironical utterances such as the over-polite request in (23) above ('Would you mind very much if I asked you to consider cleaning up your room some time this year?') are plausibly seen as echoing thoughts about future utterances. However, the claim that *all* ironical utterances which attribute thoughts (as opposed to actual or plausibly attributable speech acts) should be analysed on similar lines has two counterintuitive consequences. In the first place, it excludes ironical reflections on the failure of private hopes, wishes or fantasies that no-one would have dreamed of expressing. In the second place, it predicts that, when the primary object of irony is the inadequacy of some thought, it has to be a thought about future speech acts. Both consequences are quite implausible.

All this suggests that an adequate attributive–pretence account of irony should incorporate two distinct mechanisms, which can operate independently of each other. The first is a pretence mechanism, based on resemblances in public behaviour, which enables the speaker to perform an imaginary speech act without being committed to its illocutionary force. The second is an attributive mechanism of the type proposed in the echoic account, based on resemblances in conceptual content. In ironical utterances, the two mechanisms would combine, allowing the speaker to attribute to some actual person or type of person (or people in general) a thought similar in content to the imaginary speech act that she is pretending to perform, and to express a mocking, sceptical or contemptuous attitude to this attributed thought. The resulting predictions would coincide with those of the echoic account, but would involve two distinct mechanisms where the echoic account has only one. Which raises the following question: If the attributive–pretence account makes the same predictions as the echoic account, wouldn't it be more parsimonious to bypass the pretence element entirely and go directly to the echoic account?

6.6   Explaining the puzzling features of irony

To conclude, let us see how the echoic and pretence accounts of irony explain the three features of irony which are puzzling from the perspective of traditional theories.

The ironical attitude

From the Classical point of view, the fact that irony expresses an attitude while metaphor does not is puzzling. Why should the use of an expression to convey a figurative rather than a literal meaning come with an attitude in one case and not the other? From the relevance theory point of view, what irony conveys is not a figurative meaning but an attitude, the speaker's attitude to an attributed thought. Ironical attitudes are drawn from the dissociative range: the speaker distances herself from the attributed thought as ludicrously false, under-informative or irrelevant. Notice that mockery and contempt are attitudes which can be expressed not only to thoughts, but also to people, objects, events, and so on. On the echoic account, what distinguishes the ironical attitude is its object. Irony is directly targeted at attributed thoughts, and may be indirectly targeted, particularly in sarcasm, at the people, or type of people, who entertain such thoughts or take them seriously. On the echoic account, the ironical attitude is not a puzzling feature added to a specific kind of trope, it is constitutive of irony.

The echoic account suggests that what is missing from Grice's scenario of the car with a broken window is some evidence that the utterance *Look, that car has all its windows intact* is being echoically used to dissociate the speaker from an attributed thought. In the absence of such a thought, there is no object to which the speaker could be expressing an ironical attitude, and hence no irony. Now add to the scenario the assumption that as we walk down the street, I have been worrying about whether it is safe to leave my car there overnight and you have been trying to reassure me that cars are perfectly safe in the area. At that point, we come across a car with a broken window. Then my utterance, *Look, that car has all its windows intact* could be seen as ironically echoing your assurances in order to indicate how ill-founded they have turned out to be. No irony without an ironical attitude, no ironical attitude without an echoed attributed thought as its object.

How do pretence accounts of irony handle the ironical attitude? In general, pretending goes quite naturally with the expression of an attitude towards the kind of act one is pretending to perform or the kind of people who would perform such acts. One can pretend to be Superman and, in doing so, express one's admiration for Superman. One can also pretend to be a drunkard and, in doing so, make fun of drunkards. However, this is parody, not irony. Can the actions imitated in pretence be proper objects of a specifically ironical attitude? In non-attributive versions of the pretence account of irony, the object of the mocking, sceptical or contemptuous attitude must be either a speech act that the speaker is pretending to perform or the type of person who would perform it. When this pretend speech act imitates an actual speech act, then there is a target for irony. 'What a lovely day!', says Peter one morning.

'What a *lovely* day!', says Mary when the rain starts, both parodying Peter and expressing an ironical attitude to the content of his utterance. In many cases, however, the pretend speech act does not have a real-life counterpart, and is unlikely ever to have one. Most utterances of 'What a lovely day!' said in the pouring rain do not parody any actual utterance. If they are pretences, it is not at all obvious what is the point of the pretence, what its target is, and hence what makes it ironical. What is the point of expressing a mocking, sceptical or contemptuous attitude to a speech act that no-one has performed and that, in many cases, no reasonable person would perform? On this version of the pretence account, many typical cases of irony have no real target.

Hybrid attributive–pretence accounts may of course borrow the echoic explanation of the ironical attitude, but they do not add anything to it.

Normative bias

Why should irony be most commonly used to blame or complain? This puzzling fact was described and discussed at length in classical rhetoric, but never properly explained. From the perspective of the echoic account, it has a simple and compelling explanation. Norms, in the sense of socially shared ideas about how things should be, are always available to be ironically echoed when they are not satisfied. People should be polite, smart, handsome, actions should achieve their goal, the weather should be good, the prices should be low, and so on. So, when these norms are not satisfied, utterances such as 'She is so polite!', 'That was smart!', 'What a handsome man!', 'Well done!', 'Nice weather!', 'This is cheap!', and so on are readily understood as ironical because they echo a norm-based expectation that should have been met.

On the other hand, it takes special circumstances to be able to say ironically 'She is so impolite!' when someone is being polite, 'Horrible weather!' when the sun is shining, or 'This is an even number' when talking about an odd number. For irony to succeed in these cases, the thought that the person in question might behave impolitely, that the weather would be horrible, or that the number was odd must have been entertained or, even better, expressed. Only then is there some identifiable thought that can be ironically echoed.

It is quite possible, on the other hand, to pretend to perform a speech act without imitating and targeting any actual speech act. If irony were achievable simply by performing such a pretend speech act with a mocking attitude, as claimed by non-attributive versions of the pretence account, nothing in the mechanism of irony so understood would explain this normative bias. Hybrid attributive–pretence accounts may again borrow the echoic explanation of the normative bias, but it is the echoic element, not the pretence element of such accounts that is doing the explanatory work.

The ironical tone of voice

The echoic account offers a straightforward explanation of why there is an ironical tone of voice but no corresponding metaphorical tone of voice. The ironical tone of voice, we suggest, is a natural cue to the particular type of mocking, sceptical or contemptuous attitude that the speaker intends to convey to the thought being echoed. Since metaphor is not echoic and does not involve the expression of a characteristic attitude, there is no reason why we should expect to find a corresponding metaphorical tone of voice.

The pretence account also makes a clear prediction about the tone of voice used in irony. If the speaker is pretending to make an assertion, we would expect her to maintain the pretence by mimicking the tone of voice that someone actually making the assertion did, or would, use. This is just what Clark and Gerrig (1984: 122) propose:

> In pretense or make-believe, people generally leave their own voices behind for new ones. An actor playing Othello assumes a voice appropriate to Othello. An ironist pretending to be S′ might assume a voice appropriate to S′. To convey an attitude about S′, however, the ironist will generally exaggerate, or caricature, S′'s voice, as when an ironist affects a heavily conspiratorial tone of voice in telling a well-known piece of gossip. . . . With pretense, there is a natural account of the ironic tone of voice.

Notice, though, that this is not the 'ironical tone of voice' discussed in much of the literature, which takes for granted that the ironical speaker does not leave her own voice behind, but may instead use a tone of voice designed to reflect her own mocking, sceptical or contemptuous attitude. Rockwell's (2000: 485) comment that the vocal cues to sarcasm are closely related to those for contempt or disgust fits well with the claim of the echoic account that the 'ironical tone of voice' is simply the tone of voice optionally used to convey the attitudes characteristic of irony. This tone directly expresses the speaker's own ironical attitude, and is therefore quite incompatible with exaggeratedly imitating or caricaturing the tone of the person the ironist is pretending to be.

Although what Clark and Gerrig describe is not what is commonly recognised as the 'ironical tone of voice', and is indeed incompatible with it, they are right to point out that many examples discussed in the literature on irony could be uttered in an exaggerated imitation of the tone that someone genuinely performing the associated speech act might use. In fact, the tone of voice Clark and Gerrig describe is parodic rather than ironic, where parody is related to direct quotation as irony is related to indirect quotation. Parody does indeed exploit resemblances in behaviour: the speaker simulates a speech act, mimicking the tone of voice, form of words, etc. that someone genuinely performing that speech act might use. Moreover, parody can be used to express an ironical attitude to the thought expressed by the utterance being imitated. So, yes, there are cases where pretence and irony are combined, but far from being proto-typical cases of irony, they are characterised by a tone of voice quite distinct from the ironical tone of voice (which itself, as noted above, is only an optional feature of irony).

There is an easily perceptible difference between ironical and parodic tones of voice. Suppose that Bill keeps saying, 'Sally is such a nice person', whereas Judy totally disagrees. Judy might express a derogatory attitude to Bill's judgement of Sally in two superficially similar, but quite perceptibly different, ways. She might imitate Bill and repeat, 'Sally is such a nice person!' with an exaggerated tone of enthusiasm. Or she might utter the same sentence, but with a tone of contempt, so that there is a contradiction between the literal content of what she says and the tone in which she says it. The first tone of voice is indeed one of pretence and mockery. The second is the true ironical tone of voice (Sperber 1984).

As noted above, a puzzling feature of the ironical tone of voice is that its tenor is always negative, irrespective of whether the literal content of the utterance is positive or negative or whether the irony is used to praise or to blame. Thus, the tone of voice is the same when someone says, ironically, 'How graceful' in order to criticise a clumsy performance or 'How clumsy' in order to praise a graceful performance that the addressee had said would be clumsy. Indeed, the same negative tone of voice can be used when the literal content of an ironical utterance entirely lacks normative content, as when someone says, ironically, 'This is an even number' about an odd number that the addressee had said would be even. From a pretence point of view, this constancy of tone, whatever the literal tenor of the utterance, whatever the speaker's critical or laudatory intent, would be quite hard to explain. The echoic account, on the other hand, straightforwardly predicts this feature: the tone of voice expresses the relation-ship of the ironist to the thought she is echoing. In all cases, whether the literal content was positive or negative, and whether the intention is to praise or to blame, the ironist is adopting a negative attitude to the thought she echoes.

As before, hybrid attributive–pretence accounts can borrow from the echoic account explanations for features that are puzzling on a purely pretence account. Thus, Currie (2006) suggests that both parodic and regular ironical tones of voice can be accommodated within a pretence account using a notion of *scope of pretence*. In both cases, he claims, the ironical speaker is pretending to perform a speech act; in parodic irony, however, the accompanying (exaggeratedly sincere) tone of voice falls within the scope of the pretence, whereas in regular irony, the derogatory tone of voice falls outside the scope of the pretence, and is intended to reflect the actual speaker's views. Indeed, but what is explained by such a diluted pretence account that is not already explained in the echoic account? It seems to us that the pretence element in attributive–pretence accounts of irony adds to the complexity of the theory without yielding any corresponding benefit.

6.7   Conclusion

Sometimes a scholarly problem does get resolved. We believe that the echoic account of irony which we proposed some thirty years ago explains, at least in broad outline, what irony is and how it functions, and resolves the puzzles that Classical approaches could only describe. Much work has been inspired or otherwise stimulated by our proposal, many subtle observations have been made, many interesting experiments performed. We believe that this work has been successful in explaining aspects of irony when it has drawn from the echoic account and enriched it, but not otherwise. Aren't we modest?

Part II

Explicit and Implicit Communication

7   Linguistic form and relevance

Deirdre Wilson and Dan Sperber

7.1   Introduction

Our book *Relevance* (Sperber and Wilson 1986a) treats utterance interpretation as a two-phase process: a modular decoding phase is seen as providing input to a central inferential phase in which a linguistically encoded logical form is contextually enriched and used to construct a hypothesis about the speaker's informative intention. *Relevance* was mainly concerned with the inferential phase of comprehension: we had to answer Fodor's challenge that while decoding processes are quite well understood, inferential processes are not only not understood, but perhaps not even understandable (see Fodor 1983). Here we will look more closely at the decoding phase and consider what types of information may be linguistically encoded, and how the borderline between decoding and inference can be drawn.

It might be that all linguistically encoded information is cut to a single pattern: all truth conditions, say, or all instructions for use. However, there is a robust intuition that two basic types of meaning can be found. This intuition surfaces in a variety of distinctions: between *describing* and *indicating*, *stating* and *showing*, *saying* and *conventionally implicating*, or between *truth-conditional* and *non-truth-conditional*, *conceptual* and *procedural*, or *representational* and *computational* meaning. In the literature, justifications for these distinctions have been developed in both strictly linguistic and more broadly cognitive terms.

The linguistic justification goes as follows (see e.g. Recanati 1987). Utterances express propositions; propositions have truth conditions; but the meaning of an utterance is not exhausted by its truth conditions (i.e. the truth conditions of the proposition expressed). An utterance not only expresses a proposition but is used to perform a variety of speech acts. It can thus be expected to encode two basic types of information: truth-conditional and non-truth-conditional, or propositional and illocutionary – that is, information about the state of affairs it describes, and information indicating the various speech acts it is intended to perform.

The cognitive justification goes as follows (see e.g. Sperber and Wilson 1986a; Blakemore 1987, 1992). Linguistic decoding provides input to the inferential phase of comprehension; inferential comprehension involves the construction and manipulation of conceptual representations. An utterance can thus be expected to encode two basic types of information: representational and computational, or conceptual and procedural – that is, information about the representations to be manipulated, and information about how to manipulate them.

It is tempting to assume that these two approaches are equivalent, and classify the data in identical ways. This would be so, for example, if any construction which contributed to the truth conditions of an utterance did so by encoding concepts, while all non-truth-conditional constructions encoded procedural information. We want to argue that this assumption is false. The two distinctions cross-cut each other: some truth-conditional constructions encode concepts, others encode procedures; some non-truth-conditional constructions encode procedures, others encode concepts. This raises a more general question. What is the relation between the two approaches? Is the set of distinctions drawn by one approach somehow more basic than those drawn by the other? For example, is it possible to predict whether a given construction is truth-conditional or non-truth-conditional on the basis of some systematic interaction between the type of information it encodes and other linguistic or cognitive factors? We will touch briefly on these issues towards the end.

These internal questions about the decoding phase of comprehension are mainly of interest to linguistic semantics. Pragmatic theorists are more interested in an external question: How is the borderline between decoding and inference to be drawn? Linguistic decoding is not the only source of input to inferential comprehension. When Peter notices Mary's accent and decides that she is Scottish, this information is not *encoded* in her utterance, any more than it is encoded by the fact that she is drinking malt whisky or wearing a Black Watch tartan kilt. These are facts about her which Peter may notice, and from which he may draw inferences. How do these inferences interact with linguistically encoded information? How do we decide, as theorists, which information was decoded and which was inferred?

In *Relevance* we tried to answer some of these questions; answers to others will be attempted here. In Figure 7.1, we have tried to draw the threads together and give a general picture of the various types of information, decoded and inferred, that an utterance can convey.

This chapter is organised around the distinctions drawn in the diagram. We will start at the top, with the inferential phase of comprehension, and work down through external questions about the borderline between decoding and inference, to end with internal questions about the decoding phase.

7.2   Conveying and ostensively communicating

An utterance makes manifest a variety of assumptions: the hearer attends to as many of these as seem relevant to him. All these assumptions are conveyed by

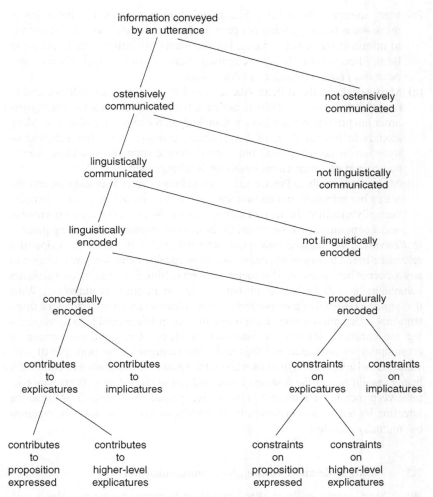

Figure 7.1 Types of information conveyed by an utterance

the utterance. Not all of them are *ostensively communicated*, as the following examples will show:

(a) Mary speaks to Peter: something in her voice or manner makes him think that she is sad. As she speaks, he is wondering about the reasons for her sadness. This is not what Mary wanted: she was trying to hide her feelings from him. In the terms of *Relevance*, Mary had neither an informative nor a communicative intention. The case is one of accidental information transmission.

(b) Mary speaks sadly to Peter. She intends him to notice her sadness, but to think she is bravely hiding her pain. In the terms of *Relevance*, she intends to inform Peter of her sadness, but she wants her informative intention to be fulfilled without being recognised. Some form of covert (hence non-ostensive) communication is taking place.

(c) Mary speaks sadly to Peter. She intends him to notice her sadness, and to realise that she intended him to notice it, but to think she wanted this higher-order intention to remain hidden from him. In the terms of *Relevance*, Mary intends to inform Peter of her sadness, and she wants her informative intention to be recognised but not to become mutually manifest. Again, some form of covert communication is taking place.

(d) Mary speaks sadly to Peter. She intends to inform him of her sadness, and she wants her informative intention not merely to be recognised, but to become mutually manifest. In the terms of *Relevance*, Mary has both an informative and a communicative intention. Ostensive communication is taking place.

In *Relevance*, we showed how examples (a)–(d) all fall within the scope of a relevance-based theory of cognition. As Mary speaks, Peter will pay attention to any aspect of her behaviour that seems relevant to him. Sometimes, to explain her behaviour, he will be led to attribute to her an informative intention. What distinguishes ostensive communication from other forms of intentional or unintentional information transmission is that the hearer has special help in recognising the speaker's informative intention. Ostensive communication creates a presumption of relevance and falls under the communicative principle of relevance. Of all accessible hypotheses about the speaker's informative intention, the hearer should accept the first one tested and found consistent with the communicative principle of relevance. Having recognised the speaker's informative intention by use of this criterion, he is entitled to treat it as not only manifest but mutually manifest.

7.3   Linguistic and non-linguistic communication

When Mary speaks sadly to Peter, intending to communicate that she is sad, his knowledge of language does not help him to recognise this aspect of her informative intention. Mary communicates her sadness to Peter, but she does not *linguistically* communicate it. For an assumption to be linguistically communicated, the linguistic properties of the utterance must help with its recovery. In this example, they do not.

This is not to say that paralinguistic clues such as tone of voice or manner play no role at all in linguistic communication. Consider the exchange in (1):

(1)   a. PETER: Can you help me?
       b. MARY (*sadly*): I can't.

Suppose that in saying (1b), Mary expected Peter not only to notice that she is sad, but to ask himself why she is sad, and to come to the conclusion in (2):

(2)   Mary is sad that she can't help Peter.

Suppose, moreover, that Mary intended not merely to inform Peter of (2) but to communicate it ostensively. Then in the terms of *Relevance*, (2) would be an explicature of (1b).

An utterance typically has several explicatures. Mary's utterance in (1b) might include those in (3):

(3)   a. Mary can't help Peter to find a job.
           b. Mary says she can't help Peter to find a job.
           c. Mary believes she can't help Peter to find a job.
           d. Mary regrets that she can't help Peter to find a job.

The explicatures of an utterance are constructed by enriching a linguistically encoded logical form to a point where it expresses a determinate proposition, such as (3a), and optionally embedding it under a higher-level description: for example, a speech-act description such as (3b), or a propositional-attitude description such as (3c) or (3d). Let us call (3a) the *proposition expressed* by the utterance and (3b)–(3d) its *higher-level explicatures*. Then not only the proposition expressed by the utterance but also all its higher-level explicatures are linguistically communicated. We will return to this point below.

Explicatures, like implicatures, have their own truth conditions, and are capable of being true or false in their own right. However, only the proposition expressed is normally seen as contributing to the truth conditions of the associated utterance. Here we will follow the standard semantic practice of calling a construction truth-conditional if and only if it contributes to the proposition expressed. This point will be important in later sections.

7.4   Linguistic communication and encoding

Not everything that is linguistically communicated is linguistically *encoded*. An interpretation is encoded when it is stipulated in the grammar. Since Grice's William James Lectures (Grice 1967, published in Grice 1989), a sustained and largely successful attack on unreflective appeals to encoding, the borderline between linguistic communication and linguistic encoding has been a major focus of pragmatic research. To illustrate recent developments in this area, we will consider some post-Gricean analyses of 'and'.

Grice showed that differences in the interpretation of conjoined utterances such as (4a) and (4b) can be explained without appeal to lexical encoding:

(4)   a. Peter got angry and Mary left.
           b. Mary left and Peter got angry.

The temporal connotations of (4a) and (4b) arise not, he said, from an extra, temporal sense of 'and', but from an interaction between the regular non-temporal sense and a pragmatic maxim of orderliness which instructs speakers to recount events in the order in which they happened. In other words, the temporal connotations of (4a) and (4b) are linguistically communicated without being linguistically encoded.

There are problems with Grice's account. In the first place, (4a) and (4b) have not only temporal but causal connotations: (4a) suggests that Mary left because Peter got angry and (4b) suggests the reverse. These suggestions do not follow from a maxim of orderliness alone. Or consider (5a)–(5d):

(5)   a. Peter went into the kitchen and found Mary.
        b. Peter took out his key and opened the door.
        c. Mary injured her leg and sued Peter.
        d. Mary is English and cooks well.

(5a) suggests that Peter found Mary in the kitchen, (5b) that Peter used his key to open the door, (5c) that Mary sued Peter for the injury to her leg, and (5d) that she cooks well despite the fact that she is English. None of these suggestions is linguistically encoded, as witness the fact that all are cancellable without contradiction. The problem raised by such suggestions is this. Either new maxims are needed to explain them – in which case Grice's framework is incomplete. Or they are explainable in terms of existing maxims such as the maxim of relevance – in which case the temporal connotations of (4a) and (4b) should be similarly explainable, and the maxim of orderliness is redundant.[1]

Relevance theory suggests the latter response. In processing (5b), for example, the hearer is looking for an interpretation consistent with the communicative principle of relevance: typically, an interpretation which yields adequate effects for the minimum justifiable effort in a way the speaker could manifestly have foreseen. A speaker who conjoins the two pieces of information in (5b) must intend an interpretation on which the effort of processing them jointly is justified by extra effects. Such an interpretation would be achieved if, for example, it was relevant to know why Peter took out his key, or how he opened the door.

The criterion of consistency with the communicative principle of relevance provides a means of bridging the gap between what is linguistically encoded and what is ostensively communicated. Of a range of possible hypotheses about the intended interpretation, all of which would yield enough effects to make the utterance worth his attention, the hearer should choose the most accessible one, the one that is easiest to construct. Although other hypotheses might yield adequate effects, this is the only one to yield adequate effects *for the minimum justifiable effort*, and thus satisfy the criterion of consistency with the communicative principle of relevance.

So why did Peter take out his key? How did he open the door? Well, we all have an easily accessible encyclopaedic schema for taking out a key and using it to unlock a door. On hearing (5b), it is natural to interpret it in accordance with this schema, as communicating that he used the key to open the door. No other hypothesis comes more readily to mind. If, on this basis, the hearer can achieve an overall interpretation consistent with the communicative principle of relevance, his hypothesis will automatically be confirmed. A maxim of orderliness is neither necessary nor sufficient to account for this interpretation. Similar arguments apply to the other examples in (4) and (5) above, making the invention of further maxims unnecessary.

Regina Blass (1989a, 1990) has used the criterion of consistency with the communicative principle of relevance to argue against an encoding account of a rather different type. Sissala, a Niger–Congo language, has two words for 'and', *a* and *ka*. These words are intersubstitutable in certain contexts, but carry different implications: *a* suggests that the event described in the second conjunct happened in the normal or obvious way, while *ka* suggests that it was somehow special, abnormal or unexpected. Thus, the Sissala equivalent of (6a) would suggest that Peter lit the fire in the normal way – say in the hearth – while (6b) would suggest that either the fact that Peter lit a fire, or the way he lit it, was unexpected (in ways that the context should help to narrow down):

(6)   a. Peter entered the room *a* lit a fire.
        b. Peter entered the room *ka* lit a fire.

These differences could be accounted for by lexical stipulation: treating *ka* as encoding a conventional implicature of unexpectedness, for example. Blass suggests a more interesting approach.

She notes, first, that (6a) and (6b) are not syntactically equivalent. *Ka* is a sentence conjunction, *a* a VP conjunction: thus (6b) contains an extra phonetically unrealised *S* node and subject *NP*, making it costlier to process. A speaker aiming at optimal relevance, who can achieve her intended effects by use of (6a), should therefore prefer (6a) to (6b). It follows that the only legitimate interpretation of (6b) is one not achievable by use of (6a). What could such an interpretation be?

By the arguments given above for (5b), (6a) should be understood, where possible, in terms of an encyclopaedic schema for entering a room and lighting a fire. In these circumstances, a speaker who intends something other than the interpretation that would be achieved by use of this schema will not be able to achieve it by (6a). Here the costlier (6b) comes into its own as a vehicle for the less stereotypical interpretation. In this way, Blass shows how the differences between (6a) and (6b) can arise without being linguistically encoded.

Her analysis is confirmed by the cancellability test. If an encoding account were correct, conjoined sentences with *ka* should always carry connotations of unexpectedness; on Blass's relevance-theoretic account, these connotations should only arise where a less costly alternative, such as (6a), is manifestly available. The crucial examples are thus sentences such as (7), where the two conjuncts have different subjects and conjunction-reduction is impossible, so that no manifestly less costly alternative exists:

(7)   Today Peter played football *ka* Mary played golf.

Since the Sissala equivalents of (7) need carry no connotations of unexpectedness, the relevance-theoretic analysis is confirmed.[2]

From the first, Grice's analysis of 'and' ran into a more serious problem, which could not be solved merely by modifying or replacing the maxims: it seemed to undercut the very possibility of a pragmatic account. According to Grice, pragmatic principles make little or no contribution to the truth conditions of utterances. He regarded (4a) and (4b) above as not only semantically but also truth-conditionally equivalent: their temporal and causal connotations were not part of the proposition expressed, but arose only at the level of implicature. But if this is so, as Cohen (1971) points out, the proposition expressed by (8a) is of the form *P or P*, and the utterance should be redundant; and the proposition expressed by (8b) is of the form *P and not P*, and the utterance should be contradictory:

(8)   a. I'm not quite sure what happened: either Peter got angry and Mary left, or Mary left and Peter got angry.
        b. What happened was not that Peter got angry and Mary left, but that Mary left and Peter got angry.

The fact that these utterances are perfectly acceptable creates a serious problem for Grice's account.

Using the relevance-theoretic framework, Robyn Carston (1988) has shown how the problem might be solved by abandoning one of Grice's assumptions while preserving the insights of the pragmatic approach. Grice assumed that the proposition expressed by an utterance is, essentially, recovered by decoding, and that the only contribution made by the maxims came almost entirely at the level of what was implicated rather than what was said. In *Relevance*, we challenged this assumption. We argued that although the logical form of an utterance is recovered by decoding, its fully propositional form is obtained by inferential enrichment of the linguistically encoded logical form, constrained by the criterion of consistency with the communicative principle of relevance. It is the propositional form of an utterance, not its logical form, that determines the proposition expressed. Carston has shown that Grice's problems disappear if the temporal and causal connotations of utterances such as (4a) and (4b) are treated not as implicatures, but as pragmatically determined aspects of the proposition expressed, which contribute to truth conditions and fall under the scope of logical operators and connectives.[3] Her analysis thus confirms the view that the inferential phase of comprehension is not restricted to the recovery of implicatures. We will return to this point below.

7.5   Conceptual and non-conceptual encoding

The distinction between conceptual and non-conceptual encoding has been explored in a series of publications by Diane Blakemore (1987, 1988, 1992; see also Blass 1990; Gutt 1991; Luscher 1989; Moeschler 1989a, 1989b). The idea behind it is this. Inferential comprehension involves the construction and manipulation of conceptual representations; linguistic decoding feeds inferential comprehension; linguistic constructions might therefore be expected to encode two basic types of information: concepts or conceptual representations on the one hand, and procedures for manipulating them on the other.

In the course of comprehension, an utterance is assigned a series of representations, phonetic, phonological, syntactic and conceptual. A *conceptual* representation differs from a phonetic, phonological or syntactic representation in two main respects. First, it has logical properties: it enters into entailment or contradiction relations, and can act as the input to logical inference rules. Second, it has truth-conditional properties: it can describe or partially characterise a certain state of affairs.

Consider (9):

(9)   Peter told Mary that he was tired.

Let us suppose that the logical form of (9) looks something like (10a), which is completed into the fully propositional form (10b) by an inferential process of reference assignment:

(10)   a. x told y at t_i that z was tired at t_j.
          b. Peter Brown told Mary Green at 3.00 p.m. on June 23 1992 that Peter Brown was tired at 3.00 p.m. on June 23 1992.

Then both the logical form (10a) and the fully propositional form (10b) are conceptual representations, the first recovered purely by decoding and the second by a combination of decoding and inference. The higher-level explicatures derived by embedding (10b) under various propositional-attitude or speech-act descriptions are further examples of conceptual representations recovered from (9) by a combination of decoding and inference.

The idea that there are expressions whose function is not so much to encode a concept as to indicate how to 'take' the sentence or phrase in which they occur has played an important role in pragmatics: in particular, in the work of Ducrot and his associates (Ducrot 1972, 1973, 1980, 1984; Anscombre and Ducrot 1983). In speech-act theory, such expressions are treated as illocutionary-force indicators; in the Gricean framework, they are treated as carrying conventional implicatures (for discussion of Grice's treatment, see below).

Within relevance theory, the idea that an expression may encode procedural constraints on the inferential phase of comprehension was first put forward by Diane Blakemore (Brockway 1981; Blakemore 1987, 1992). Consider (11), which we have divided into sub-parts (a) and (b):

(11)   a. Peter's not stupid. b. He can find his own way home.

This utterance has two possible interpretations, which would be encouraged, respectively, by the formulations in (12a) and (12b):

(12)   a. Peter's not stupid; so he can find his own way home.
         b. Peter's not stupid; after all, he can find his own way home.

On the first interpretation, (11a) provides evidence for a conclusion drawn in (11b); on the second, (11a) is confirmed by evidence provided in (11b). Blakemore argues that discourse connectives such as 'so' and 'after all' should not be seen as encoding concepts. They do not contribute to the truth conditions of utterances, but constrain the inferential phase of comprehension by indicating the type of inference process that the hearer is expected to go through. As Blakemore points out, such expressions contribute to relevance by guiding the hearer towards the intended contextual effects, thus reducing the overall effort required.

In terms of the distinctions drawn in section 7.1, Blakemore's semantic constraints on relevance are both procedural and non-truth-conditional. On her approach, 'so' and 'after all' do not encode concepts, and do not contribute to the truth conditions of utterances; instead, they guide the inferential phase of comprehension. Blakemore's analysis of discourse connectives raises an interesting theoretical question: Are the truth-conditional and the conceptual, the non-truth-conditional and the procedural necessarily linked? Does the fact that an expression is truth-conditional entail that it encodes a concept, and the fact that an expression is procedural entail that it encodes a procedure? In later sections, we will argue that it does not. In the next section we will compare Blakemore's account of discourse connectives with Grice's.

7.6   Explicit and implicit conceptual encoding

Blakemore's work on discourse connectives amounts to a reanalysis in procedural terms of Grice's notion of conventional implicature. Grice does not talk in terms of a conceptual–procedural distinction. Nonetheless, he seems to have thought of the conventional implicatures carried by discourse connectives such as 'but', 'moreover', 'so' and 'on the other hand' in conceptual rather than procedural terms. For one thing, his choice of the term 'implicature' suggests that he thought of conventional implicatures, like conversational implicatures, as distinct propositions with their own truth conditions and truth values. Moreover, he talks in almost identical terms of what was conventionally implicated and what was said, noting, for instance, that items or situations are 'picked out by', or 'fall under', both what was conventionally implicated and what was said.

The difference between conventional and conversational implicatures was, of course, that conventional implicatures were semantically decoded, whereas conversational implicatures were not decoded but inferred. The difference between saying and conventionally implicating was that the truth conditions of the utterance were determined by what was said, whereas conventional implicatures were non-truth-conditional. In terms of the distinctions drawn in section 7.1, then, Grice appears to treat conventional implicatures as linguistically encoded conceptual representations which make no contribution to the truth conditions of the utterances that carry them, but contribute rather to implicatures. His analysis shows how a linguistic expression which is non-truth-conditional might nonetheless encode conceptual rather than procedural information.

At various points in his writings, Grice analyses 'but', 'moreover', 'on the other hand' and 'so' in terms of his notion of conventional implicature. To illustrate his approach, we will look at his treatment of 'on the other hand' in his 'Retrospective Epilogue' (Grice 1989: 362). Consider (13):

(13)   My brother-in-law lives on a peak in Darien; his great aunt, on the other hand, was a nurse in World War I.

Grice saw the speaker of (13) as asserting that her brother-in-law lived on a peak in Darien and that his great aunt was a nurse in World War I, and conventionally implicating that she has in mind some contrast between these two assertions:

What was asserted by (13):
(a) The speaker's brother-in-law lives on a peak in Darien.
(b) The brother-in-law's great aunt was a nurse in World War I.
What was conventionally implicated by (13):
(a) and (b) contrast in some way.

Grice seems to have thought of conventional implicatures in standard speech-act terms, as indicating the type of speech act performed. Thus, he says of (13):

Speakers may be at one and the same time engaged in performing speech acts at different but related levels. One part of what [the speaker of (13)] is doing is making what might be called ground floor statements about the brother-in-law and the great aunt, but at the same time as he is performing these speech acts he is also performing a higher-order speech act of commenting in a certain way on the lower-order speech acts. He is contrasting in some way the performance of some of these lower-order speech-acts with others, and he signals his performance of this higher-order speech act in his use of the embedded enclitic phrase 'on the other hand'. The truth or falsity ... of his words is determined by the relation of his ground-floor speech acts to the world; consequently, while a certain kind of misperformance of the higher-order speech-act may constitute a semantic offense, it will not touch the truth-value ... of the speaker's words. (Grice 1989: 362)

Notice here the striking similarity between Grice's talk of 'higher-order speech acts' performed by discourse connectives and relevance theory's notion of a 'higher-level explicature'. This raises an interesting question about where the borderline between explicit and implicit communication should be drawn. Grice, like Blakemore, treats the discourse connectives as contributing to implicit rather than explicit communication. Roughly speaking, he equates what is explicitly communicated with what is said (i.e. the proposition literally expressed by an utterance), so that all non-truth-conditional constructions are automatically seen as falling on the implicit side.

We do not follow him on this. In *Relevance* (1986a: 182) we offered a definition of explicitness and degrees of explicitness:

Explicitness:
An assumption communicated by an utterance *U* is explicit if and only if it is a development of a logical form encoded by *U*.

On the analogy of 'implicature', we call an explicitly communicated assumption an *explicature*. Logical forms are 'developed' into explicatures by inferential enrichment. Every explicature, then, is recovered by a combination of decoding and inference, and the greater the element of decoding, the more explicit it will be.

As noted above, our category of explicatures includes not only the proposition expressed by the utterance, but a range of higher-level explicatures obtained by embedding the proposition expressed under an appropriate speech-act or propositional-attitude description. If Grice is right to claim that discourse connectives convey linguistically encoded information about 'higher-order speech acts', they would in our framework be analysed as contributing to explicit rather than implicit communication. In general, relevance theorists see the explicit side of communication as much richer, and involving a much greater element of pragmatic inference, than Griceans have thought.

Leaving this issue aside for the moment, let us return to semantics proper, and consider whether discourse connectives such as 'so', 'after all', 'on the other hand', etc., are best analysed in conceptual or procedural terms. Grice's conceptual analysis can be directly compared with Blakemore's, since both offer analyses of 'so'. Consider (14):

(14)   a. It's raining.
        b. So the grass is wet.

According to Grice, the use of 'so' in (14) indicates that the speaker is 'performing the speech-act of explaining', with (14a) being put forward as an explanation of (14b):

What was said by (14):
(a) It's raining.
(b) The grass is wet.
What was conventionally implicated by use of 'so':
(a) explains (b).

According to Blakemore, 'so' is an inferential connective indicating that the assumption which follows it is a conclusion. On her account, (14b) is put forward as a conclusion drawn from (14a):

Propositions expressed by (14)
(a) It's raining.
(b) The grass is wet.
Procedural information encoded by 'so':
Process (14b) as a conclusion.

Notice first that there are purely descriptive reasons for preferring Blakemore's account: Grice's analysis does not work for all uses of 'so'. (15) is one of Blakemore's examples. The speaker sees someone arrive home laden with parcels and says:

(15)   So you've spent all your money.

Here, there is no explanatory clause corresponding to (14a). The speaker is not explaining the fact that the hearer has spent all her money, but drawing a conclusion from an observation she has made. Blakemore's account fits (15) better than Grice's.

In fact there are uses of 'so' which look like counterexamples to any speech-act account. Consider (16a), understood as an indirect speech report of (16b):

(16)   a. Peter thought that Mary had a holiday, so he should have one too.
        b. Peter thinks, 'Mary had a holiday, so I should have one too'.

(16a) is compatible with Blakemore's inferential account. Though not drawing an inference herself, the speaker of (16a) is attributing a certain inference to Peter. By contrast, she is neither performing a speech act of explanation herself, nor attributing any speech act to Peter: she is reporting thoughts, not words. This suggests that what is needed is not a better speech-act analysis of 'so', but a cognitive analysis such as the one Blakemore has proposed.

Leaving this objection aside, let us recast Grice's analysis so that it avoids the descriptive problem in (15). This could be done by treating (17a) as encoding the conventional implicature in (17b):

(17)   a. P, so Q.
        b. Q is a consequence of P.

This modified Gricean account is directly comparable with Blakemore's: the only difference between them is that one is conceptual and the other is procedural. Is there any way of choosing between the two accounts?

There is one piece of direct evidence in favour of Blakemore's approach and against the Gricean treatment. Most 'conventional implicatures' are carried by so-called discourse connectives: 'so', 'now', 'well', 'moreover', 'however', and so on. Discourse connectives are notoriously hard to pin down in conceptual terms. If 'now' or 'well' encodes a proposition, why can it not be brought to consciousness? Why is it so hard for non-native speakers of German to grasp the meaning of *ja* and *doch*? How can the results of Ducrot's complex analyses of 'but' and other connectives be at once so simple and so insightful? The procedural account suggests an answer to these questions. Conceptual representations can be brought to consciousness: procedures can not. We have direct access neither to grammatical computations nor to the inferential computations used in comprehension. A procedural analysis of discourse connectives would explain our lack of direct access to the information they encode.

There are two further types of construction whose analysis provides indirect evidence for Blakemore's procedural account of discourse connectives and against a Gricean conceptual account. In the next section, we will look at some non-truth-conditional expressions which, unlike the discourse connectives, clearly call for conceptual treatment. In the following section, we will look at some non-truth-conditional constructions which clearly call for procedural treatment. Indirect evidence for Blakemore's account of discourse connectives is that they seem to have more in common with constructions in the procedural than the conceptual class.

7.7   Proposition expressed versus higher-level explicatures

In section 7.3, we distinguished the proposition expressed by an utterance from its higher-level explicatures. In section 7.5, we argued that from a cognitive point of view, these higher-level explicatures are conceptual representations, capable of entailing and contradicting each other and representing determinate states of affairs. Though true or false in their own right, they do not generally contribute to the truth conditions of their associated utterances. Mary's utterance in (1b) above (in which Mary says sadly that she can't help Peter) is true or false depending on whether she can or can't help Peter find a job, not on whether she does or doesn't say, or believe, or regret that she can't help him.

Now consider the utterances in (18):

(18)   a. Seriously, I can't help you.
        b. Frankly, I can't help you.
        c. Confidentially, I can't help you.
        d. Unfortunately, I can't help you.

Illocutionary adverbials such as 'seriously', 'frankly' and 'confidentially', and attitudinal adverbials such as 'unfortunately', are standardly treated as making no contribution to the truth conditions of utterances in which they occur. Recanati (1987: 50) says of the attitudinal adverb 'happily':

Deleting the adverb would not change the proposition expressed by the sentence ... because the modification introduced by the adverb is external to the proposition and concerns the speaker's emotional attitude to the latter. This attitude is neither 'stated' nor 'described', but only 'indicated'.

Here we will consider only illocutionary adverbials, and we will take for granted their non-truth-conditional status (for more detailed discussion, see Ifantidou 1993). The main point we want to make is that, even though illocutionary adverbials are clearly non-truth-conditional, there are good reasons to treat them as encoding concepts.

Notice, first, that even if the illocutionary adverbials in (18) are non-truth-conditional, their synonymous manner-adverbial counterparts in (19) must clearly be treated as encoding concepts which contribute to the truth conditions of the associated utterances in the regular way:

(19)   a. Mary told Peter seriously that she couldn't help him.
         b. Mary said frankly to Peter that she couldn't help him.
         c. Mary informed Peter confidentially that she couldn't help him.

Given this, the simplest hypothesis is that in (18) they encode exactly the same concepts. The only difference is that in interpreting (18), the hearer must incorporate these concepts into a higher-level explicature some elements of which are not encoded but inferred. The fact that the illocutionary adverbials make no contribution to the truth conditions of (18) would then follow from the more general fact that the higher-level explicatures with which they are associated make no contribution to truth conditions either. This analysis fits well with standard speech-act accounts of illocutionary adverbials, on which an illocutionary adverb such as 'seriously' is seen not as contributing to the proposition expressed by the utterance, but as modifying the type of speech-act performed (Bach and Harnish 1979: chapter 10, section 3; Nølke 1990).

By contrast, a procedural analysis of illocutionary adverbials would run into serious difficulties. First, as has often been pointed out, an utterance like (20) is ambiguous, with the two possible interpretations in (21):

(20)   Seriously, are you leaving?

(21)   a. I ask you seriously whether you are leaving.
         b. I ask you to tell me seriously whether you are leaving.

This is not surprising on the explicature account. Whenever (20) is interpretable as a request to tell, the illocutionary adverb should be interpretable as modifying either the requesting or the telling. It is not obvious how this ambiguity could be handled in procedural terms.

Second, many sentence adverbials are semantically complex. Consider (22a)–(22d):

(22)   a. Frankly speaking, he has negative charisma.
        b. Speaking frankly, though not as frankly as I'd like to, he isn't much good.
        c. In total, absolute confidence, how are you getting on with Maria?
        d. While he's out getting the coffee, what did you think of Bill's talk?

Such compositionality is unsurprising if illocutionary adverbials encode conceptual representations, which can undergo semantic interpretation rules in the regular way. It is not obvious what compositionality would mean in procedural terms.

Third, in some cases at least, the speaker who uses an illocutionary adverbial can lay herself open to charges of untruthfulness in its use. Consider (23)–(25):

(23)   a. MARY: Frankly, this steak is less than perfect.
        b. PETER: That's not true. You're not being frank.

(24)   a. MARY: Seriously, what a gorgeous tie.
        b. PETER: That's not true. You're never serious.

(25)   a. MARY: Now I've brought you your fourth whisky, what did you think of the play?
        b. PETER: That's not true. It's only my third.

If illocutionary adverbials encode elements of conceptual representations which can be true or false in their own right, such exchanges are not surprising.

In fact, in some cases an illocutionary adverbial seems to contribute directly to the truth conditions of the associated utterance. Consider (26):

(26)   a. PETER: What can I tell our readers about your private life?
        b. MARY: On the record, I'm happily married; off the record, I'm about to divorce.

If the illocutionary adverbials 'on the record' and 'off the record' made no contribution to the truth conditions of (26b), then Mary's utterance should be perceived as contradictory; yet intuitively it is not. But if these adverbials contribute to truth conditions, then *a fortiori* they encode conceptual representations, and the procedural analysis is disconfirmed.

It seems, then, that there is good reason to treat illocutionary adverbials as both non-truth-conditional and conceptual, thus abandoning the idea that all non-truth-conditional meaning is necessarily procedural and cut to a single pattern.

7.8   Constraints on explicatures and constraints on implicatures

We have now illustrated three of the four logically possible types of meaning distinguished in section 7.1:

(a) Most regular 'content' words, including the manner adverbials 'seriously', 'frankly', etc., are *conceptual and truth-conditional*: they encode concepts which are constituents of the proposition expressed by the utterance, and hence contribute to the utterance's truth conditions.

(b) Various types of sentence adverbial, including the illocutionary adverbials 'seriously', 'frankly', etc., are *conceptual and non-truth-conditional*: they encode concepts which are constituents not of the proposition expressed but of higher-level explicatures.

(c) Discourse connectives such as 'so' and 'after all' are *procedural and non-truth-conditional*: they encode procedural constraints on implicatures.

In this section, we will argue that personal pronouns such as 'I' and 'you' illustrate the fourth category of meaning: they are both *procedural and truth-conditional*.

The idea that there are procedural constraints on truth-conditional content was suggested (in different terms) by Jakobson and Benveniste in their discussion of 'shifters'. However, when Benveniste (1966: 252) says that the pronoun 'I' means 'the speaker of the utterance in which the token of "I" occurs', his proposal is seriously ambiguous. Kaplan (1989) points out (again in different terms) that the claim that 'I' means 'the speaker' has different consequences depending on whether it is conceptually or procedurally understood.

Suppose that David Kaplan says (27):

(27)   I do not exist.

Then if 'I' is treated as encoding the *concept* THE SPEAKER, (27) will express the proposition in (28):

(28)   The speaker of (27) does not exist.

But if 'I' is treated merely as encoding an instruction to identify its referent by first identifying the speaker, then (27) will express the proposition in (29):

(29)   David Kaplan does not exist.

These two propositions differ in their truth conditions. (29) is true in any state of affairs in which David Kaplan does not exist. (28) is true in any state of affairs in which (27) is uttered and its speaker does not exist. Since such a state of affairs is impossible, if (27) expressed the proposition in (28), it would be necessarily false. Kaplan argues that though (27) is false whenever it is uttered, it is not necessarily false. The proposition it expresses is true in any state of affairs in which David Kaplan does not exist. In other words, (27) must be understood as expressing (29), not (28).

Accordingly, Kaplan proposes to distinguish the *content* of an expression from its *character*. The content of 'I' in (27) is the individual David Kaplan; the character of 'I' is a rule for identifying its content in any given context. Such rules, Kaplan comments,

> tell us for any possible occurrence of the indexical what the referent would be, but they do not constitute the content of such an occurrence. Indexicals are directly referential. The rules tell us what it is that is referred to. Thus, they determine the content (the propositional constituent) for a particular occurrence of an indexical. But they are not a part of the content (they constitute no part of the propositional constituent). (Kaplan 1989: 523)

In terms of the distinctions drawn in section 7.1, this amounts to the claim that 'I' and other pronouns are both truth-conditional and procedural, thus illustrating the fourth logically possible type of encoded meaning, and refuting the assumption that there is a necessary linkage between the truth-conditional and the conceptual.[4]

We have now looked at two quite different types of procedural expression: discourse connectives and pronouns. Both constrain the inferential phase of comprehension by reducing the hypothesis space that has to be searched in arriving at the intended interpretation. Discourse connectives impose constraints on *implicatures*: they guide the search for intended contexts and contextual effects. Pronouns impose constraints on *explicatures*: they guide the search for the intended referent, which is part of the proposition expressed. This raises the possibility that there might be a still further type of procedural expression, which constrains not the proposition expressed by an utterance but its *higher-level explicatures*.

At the end of *Relevance*, we drew attention to a range of constructions which seem to us to be best analysed in these terms. The idea that declarative sentences and their non-declarative counterparts express the same propositions but perform different speech acts is familiar from speech-act theory. While there are serious problems with the speech-act approach to non-declarative sentences (see Wilson and Sperber 1988a), we believe that the semantic differences between declarative sentences and their non-declarative counterparts can be successfully analysed as differences not in the propositions they express but in the higher-level explicatures they communicate: for example, a declarative utterance should be treated as a case of *saying that*, and an imperative utterance as a case of *telling to*.[5] Notice that this proposal, like the one for 'I' above, can be understood in two different ways. On one interpretation, Mary's utterance in (1b) above would be treated as conceptually encoding the higher-level explicature 'the speaker says that she can't help Peter':

(1)		a.	PETER: Can you help me?
		b.	MARY (*sadly*): I can't.

Understood in this way, our proposal would be a variant of the performative hypothesis abandoned for excellent reasons many years ago (on the history of the performative hypothesis, see Levinson 1983). On the other interpretation – the one proposed in *Relevance* – what is encoded is not a conceptual representation but a set of hints for constructing one. The content of this higher-level representation will be partially determined by contextual information, and will specify the illocutionary force of the utterance in terms of much richer concepts than the abstractions 'saying that' or 'telling to'. As we said in *Relevance*:

Illocutionary-force indicators such as declarative or imperative mood or interrogative word order merely have to make manifest a rather abstract property of the speaker's informative intention: the direction in which relevance is to be sought. (Sperber and Wilson 1986a: 254)

That is, illocutionary-force indicators should be seen as encoding procedural constraints on the inferential construction of higher-level explicatures. It seems clear that this interpretation is to be preferred. (For details of this approach to non-declaratives, see Wilson and Sperber 1988a; Clark 1993.)

As is well known, the functions performed in English by mood and word order are performed in many other languages by so-called discourse or illocutionary particles. Certain dialects of French, for example, have an interrogative particle *ti*, which appears to perform the same functions as word-order inversion does in other dialects. If word-order inversion is correctly analysed as encoding not a concept but a constraint on higher-level explicatures, then by the same arguments, illocutionary particles such as *ti* (at least such particles as are fully integrated into the syntax, i.e. are genuine parts of the language) should be analysed in similar terms. Perhaps the question particle 'eh' in English might be a candidate for similar treatment.

In the framework of relevance theory, Regina Blass (1990) has analysed the 'hearsay' particle *rɛ* in Sissala as encoding a constraint on explicatures. Perhaps some 'attitudinal' discourse particles (again, to the extent that they are fully integrated into the language) might be analysed on similar lines. When Mary uses the dissociative particle 'huh!' in (30), for example, she might be seen as encouraging the construction of the higher-level explicature in (31):

(30)	Peter's a genius, huh!

(31)	Mary doesn't think that Peter's a genius.

Within this category of procedural constraints on explicatures, there is thus a rich variety of data to explore.

For discourse particles such as *ti*, the failure of the performative hypothesis provides direct evidence against an analysis in terms of conceptual encoding and for a procedural account. Returning to the analysis of discourse connectives such as 'so' and 'after all', their obvious similarities to discourse particles provide indirect evidence against an account in terms of conceptual encoding and for a procedural account.

In this section, we have proposed that certain pronouns, illocutionary-force indicators and discourse particles should all be analysed as encoding procedural constraints on explicatures. The pronouns are truth-conditional and contribute to the proposition expressed; illocutionary-force indicators and discourse particles are non-truth-conditional and contribute to higher-level explicatures. These differences between them should not, we feel, be allowed to obscure the important similarities between the types of meaning they encode.

7.9   Conclusion

In section 7.1, we outlined two contrasting approaches to linguistic semantics, one focusing on utterances, their truth conditions and the speech acts they are used to perform, the other locating utterances within a broader cognitive framework. Throughout this chapter we have taken a resolutely cognitive approach. We assume, in fact, that the primary bearers of truth conditions are not utterances but conceptual representations; to the extent that utterances have truth conditions, we see these as inherited from the propositions those utterances express. We have tried to show that an approach along these lines can yield genuine insight into the varieties of linguistically encoded meaning.

What, then, of the more traditional linguistic approach? Surely there is still a consistent, coherent set of intuitions about the truth conditions of utterances that any adequate theory of linguistic semantics needs to explain? There may be, though we know of no systematic effort to show that this is so. Most semanticists simply assume (as we have throughout this chapter) that every utterance encodes a single logical form, expresses a single proposition and has a single set of truth conditions. We do not know how far this assumption can be maintained. In utterances with illocutionary adverbials, or parentheticals of the type discussed by Ifantidou (1993), Itani (1990) and Blakemore (1991), it might be argued, à la Grice, that the speaker is simultaneously making two assertions, each with its own truth conditions; one might then investigate the possibility that intuitions about the truth conditions of the utterance as a whole are based on the assertion which makes the major contribution to overall relevance. Clearly, much research remains to be done in this area. What we hope to have shown is that such research can be usefully conducted within the broader cognitive and communicative framework outlined here.

8   Pragmatics and time

Deirdre Wilson and Dan Sperber

8.1   Introduction

In interpreting utterances such as (1) and (2), the hearer generally treats the events described as temporally or causally related:

(1)   a. I took out my key and opened the door.
        b. John dropped the glass and it broke.
        c. They planted an acorn and it grew.
        d. Peter left and Mary got angry.

(2)   a. I took out my key. I opened the door.
        b. John dropped the glass. It broke.
        c. They planted an acorn. It grew.
        d. Peter left. Mary got angry.

Such relations are not encoded in the meanings of the sentences uttered. This chapter is concerned with how they arise. We will look in particular at the following problems:

(a) *The sequencing problem.* Why does the hearer generally take the events to have happened in a certain order, so that in (1d), for example, he would assume that Peter left before Mary got angry?

(b) *The interval problem.* Why does the hearer generally take the events described to be separated by different intervals, so that in (1b), for example, he would assume that the glass broke as soon as it was dropped, whereas in (1c) he would not expect the acorn to have sprouted as soon as it touched the ground?

(c) *The cause–consequence problem.* Why does the hearer often take the events to stand in a causal or consequential relation, so that in (1b), for example, he would assume that the glass broke *because* it was dropped?

In the recent linguistic literature, these problems have been approached from two rather different perspectives. Within the Gricean pragmatic tradition, a sharp line is drawn between decoding and inference, and the temporal and causal connotations of (1) and (2) are seen as purely inferential. Within this tradition, the aim is to find a few very general pragmatic principles which will

169

interact with sentence meaning and contextual assumptions to yield the desired interpretations. In the framework of 'discourse semantics', by contrast, the dividing line between decoding and inference is less clear-cut, and a variety of special-purpose rules have been proposed to generate temporal and causal connotations.[1] In this chapter, we will look mainly at issues that arise within the Gricean pragmatic framework. A fuller account would deal with the many interesting questions raised by the 'discourse semantic' approach.

The chapter is organised as follows. We will argue, first, that while Grice was right to treat the temporal and causal connotations of (1) and (2) as properly pragmatic, they are best analysed not as implicatures but as pragmatically determined aspects of truth-conditional content, or 'what is said'. We will then look at some attempts to deal with the sequencing problem using principles such as Grice's maxim 'Be orderly', and suggest a more general approach. Finally, we will show how all three problems might be tackled within the framework of relevance theory, and point out some implications of this approach.

8.2   Temporal and causal connotations: implicatures or pragmatically determined aspects of what is said?

Ordinary-language philosophers (e.g. Strawson 1952) used to argue, on the basis of examples like (1), that 'and' in natural language differs in meaning from truth-functional '&' in logic. In these examples, so the argument went, natural-language 'and' was equivalent in meaning to 'and then', or 'and so'; hence, a change in the order of conjuncts would lead to a change of meaning. In logic, by contrast, 'P & Q' was invariably equivalent to 'Q & P'.

Grice, in his William James Lectures (1967, published in Grice 1989), defended the view that natural-language 'and' was equivalent in meaning to '&' in logic. He pointed out that the temporal and causal connotations of utterances such as (1) were not best analysed as part of the meaning of 'and', since the non-conjoined utterances in (2) have the same temporal and causal connotations. On his view, these connotations were best derived via the operation of his Cooperative Principle (CP) and maxims. In other words, he rejected a decoding account of these connotations in favour of an inferential approach.

In Grice's framework, the temporal and causal connotations of (1) and (2) were analysed as conversational implicatures: that is, beliefs that had to be attributed to the speaker to preserve the assumption that she was obeying the CP and maxims (or at least the CP). More generally, Grice seems to have assumed that any aspect of utterance interpretation governed by the CP and maxims must be analysed as an implicature, and Gricean pragmaticists have generally followed him on this.[2] Grice drew a sharp dividing line between what was conversationally implicated and what was strictly said. Conversational implicatures made no contribution to the truth conditions of utterances, which were determined solely by what was said. It should follow from Grice's account that the temporal and causal connotations of (1) and (2), which he treats as conversational implicatures, make no contribution to the truth conditions of utterances in which they occur. But there are problems with this approach.

On Grice's account, natural-language 'and' is semantically equivalent to truth-functional '&' in logic. As Cohen (1971) pointed out, if Grice is right, then reversing the order of the conjuncts in (1) should make no difference to truth conditions: 'P and Q' should always be truth-conditionally equivalent to 'Q and P'. But consider (3) and (4):

(3)   It's always the same at parties: either I get drunk and no-one will talk to me or no-one will talk to me and I get drunk.

(4)   a. What happened was not that Peter left and Mary got angry but that Mary got angry and Peter left.
        b. A: So Peter left and Mary got angry?
           B: No. Mary got angry and Peter left.

The disjunction in (3) is not redundant: the assumption that the events happened in a different order in each disjunct makes a genuine contribution to the truth conditions of the utterance. Similarly, the conjunction in (4a) is not a contradiction, and the two utterances in (4b) are not truth-conditionally equivalent. Such examples create a serious problem for Grice. Something which according to him is an implicature appears to be falling within the scope of logical operators and connectives. That is, it appears to be contributing to the truth conditions of the utterance as a whole – in Grice's terms, not to what was implicated but to what was said.

The causal connotations of (1) create similar problems. Consider (5):

(5)   Someone left a manhole uncovered and I broke my leg.

(5) would generally be understood as communicating that the speaker broke her leg not only *after* the manhole was left open but *as a result* of the manhole being left open. That these causal connotations can contribute to truth conditions is shown by (6) and (7):

(6)   If someone leaves a manhole uncovered and you break your leg, sue.

(7)   a. PETER: If you leave that manhole uncovered, someone's going to break their leg.
        b. MARY: No they won't.

In (6), the hearer is not being told to sue if he breaks his leg at some point after someone leaves a manhole open. In (7), Mary's denial is equivalent not to (8a) but to (8b):

(8)   a. No-one's going to break their leg.
        b. No-one's going to break their leg on that manhole.

These examples show that the sequencing problem and the cause–consequence problem cannot be solved at the level of implicature. Grice himself was aware of this. In a part of the William James Lectures that was only published much later (Grice 1989), he considered a similar counterexample to his analysis of 'if': an example in which, quite clearly, something he wanted to treat as an implicature was falling under the scope of logical connectives and contributing to truth conditions. Grice took pains to emphasise that this should not happen, and added 'I am afraid I do not yet see what defense, if any, can be put up against this objection' (Grice 1989: 83).

In our book *Relevance* (1986a: 183), we suggested a possible defence. Grice's problem, we argued, arose from his assumption that the only way pragmatic principles can contribute to utterance interpretation is by giving rise to implicatures. Grice assumed that the truth-conditional content of an utterance is recovered largely by decoding, and it seems not to have occurred to him that his CP and maxims could play a role in determining what is said. Robyn Carston (1988) showed how a variety of Gricean 'implicatures', including the temporal and causal connotations of (1) and (2), could be reanalysed as pragmatically determined aspects of what is said. On her account, pragmatic principles make a much greater contribution to truth-conditional content than has generally been assumed. In what follows, we will adopt her approach, and treat the temporal and causal connotations of (1) and (2) as inferentially determined aspects of what is said.[3]

8.3   The sequencing problem and the maxim 'Be orderly'

Grice's solution to the sequencing problem was based on his maxim 'Be orderly', which instructs speakers to recount events in the order in which they happened. Several of the special-purpose sequencing principles proposed by discourse semanticists look like attempts to implement this maxim in the form of code-like rules. Dowty's Temporal Discourse Interpretation Principle (1986) is a case in point:

Temporal Discourse Interpretation Principle
   Given a sequence of sentences $S_1 \ldots S_n$ to be interpreted as a narrative discourse, the reference time of each sentence Si is interpreted to be:
(a) a time consistent with the definite time adverbials in Si, if there are any;
(b) otherwise, a time which immediately follows the reference time of the previous sentence S_{i-1}.

In this section, we will consider the implications of approaches along these lines.

Notice, first, that neither Grice's maxim of orderliness nor Dowty's code-like variant yields any insight into the interval problem or the cause–consequence problem. For example, (1b) would be compatible with Grice's maxim of order-liness if ten years had elapsed between the dropping and the breaking of the glass, yet this is not normally an appropriate interval for the interpretation of (1b). The maxim of orderliness leaves the interval problem untouched.

Defenders of sequencing principles generally acknowledge that further machinery is needed to solve the interval problem. We all know that if a glass is dropped it typically breaks upon impact, whereas if an acorn is planted it takes some time to grow. The idea would be that these contextual assumptions interact with further pragmatic principles to determine the correct intervals between events in (1b) and (1c). Here, an obvious point is that if such principles are good enough to solve the interval problem, then *a fortiori* they will solve the sequencing problem, and sequencing principles are redundant.

Similar remarks apply to the cause–consequence problem. In order to make the correct predictions about the truth conditions of (6) and (7), some pragmatic principles are needed that will interact with contextual assumptions to assign the appropriate causal relations between the events described. But, since causal relations are typically sequential, such principles would *a fortiori* solve the sequencing problem and make sequencing principles redundant.

A further problem with sequencing principles of the type proposed above is that the constraints they impose on utterance interpretation seem to be too strong. Take an utterance that describes two events or states without explicitly stipulating any temporal ordering between them. Then there are four logically possible ways in which the events or states might be temporally related:
(a) the first mentioned state/event happened before the second;
(b) the two were simultaneous;
(c) the second happened before the first;
(d) no ordering, or some subtler ordering, is pragmatically understood.
Contrary to what is suggested by Grice's maxim of orderliness or Dowty's Temporal Discourse Interpretation Principle, all four logically possible order-ings are realised.

As we have seen, (1) and (2) illustrate possibility (a), with the first mentioned event happening before the second. Possibility (b) is illustrated in (9):

(9)   a. Susan is underage and can't drink.
         b. The home crowd cheered and the away crowd booed.
         c. Bill smiled. He smiled sadly.

As (9a) shows, the fact that two states are fully overlapping does not preclude the possibility that one is a consequence of the other. This looks like a counter-example to Levinson's (1983: 146) account of how temporal and causal con-notations are derived:

Levinson's proposal
Given *p and q*, try interpreting it as:
  (i) *p and then q*; if successful, try:
  (ii) *p and therefore q*; if successful try also:
  (iii) *p, and p is the cause of q*.

On Levinson's account, the temporal sequencing principle in (i) seems intended to function as a filter, saving the hearer the effort of looking for cause–consequence relations if the sequencing principle does not apply. On this account, since (9a), for example, cannot be interpreted by clause (i) as saying 'Susan is underage and then she can't drink', the hearer should never even test whether the cause–consequence clauses in (ii) and (iii) apply. Clearly, this prediction is false.

   Possibility (c) is illustrated by (10):

(10)   a. The glass broke. John dropped it.
         b. I hit Bill. He insulted me.
         c. I got caught. My best friend betrayed me.

In these examples, the speaker first states a fact and then explains it. The natural interpretation of (10a) is that the glass broke both after John dropped it and because John dropped it. In (10b) the temporal and causal order could run either way, and in many circumstances would be taken to run contrary to the predictions of Grice's maxim of orderliness. (These examples have been dealt with in the framework of discourse semantics by Lascarides, Asher and Oberlander 1992; Lascarides 1992; and in the framework of relevance theory by Carston 1993a.)

   Notice, by the way, that this is one of the few cases where an interpretation possible for a non-conjoined utterance is generally not available for its conjoined counterpart. An adequate account of temporal and causal connotations should explain why the reverse-causal interpretations of (10) are not available for (11):

(11)   a. The glass broke and John dropped it.
         b. I hit Bill and he insulted me.
         c. I got caught and my best friend betrayed me.

Finally, as has often been noted, no ordering is necessarily imposed in examples like (12):

(12)   a. That night, our hero consumed half a bottle of whisky and wrote a letter to
            Lady Anne.
         b. Today I signed a contract with a publisher and had tea with an old friend.

There are also some more interesting cases, first noted by Sue Schmerling (1975), where it is not clear what the various sequencing principles would predict. These are cases where, intuitively at least, there is both a temporal and a consequential relation, but the temporal relation is not adequately paraphrased by the addition of 'then'. Schmerling's example was (13); a simpler example without the quantified NP would be (14):

(13)   a. We investigated all of the cases and discovered that the problem was more complex than we had thought.

        b. We investigated all of the cases and then discovered that the problem was more complex than we had thought.

(14)   a. I spoke to John and discovered that he was charming.

        b. I spoke to John and then discovered that he was charming.

What the addition of 'then' does to (14a) is to convert it from an interpretation on which I spoke to John and *in* doing so discovered that he was charming into one on which I spoke to John and *after* doing so discovered that he was charming. In both cases there is an intuitive temporal relation, but the temporal relations are not the same. It appears that many sequencing principles would wrongly interpret (14a) as meaning (14b) (and Levinson's principles mentioned above, having failed at clause (i), would not assign a consequential relation at all).

Towards the end of his 1986 article, David Dowty lists some of the problems with sequencing principles that have been mentioned here. He suggests that his Temporal Discourse Interpretation Principle might perhaps be treated as a default rule, 'to be followed when neither time adverbials nor entailments and implicatures of the discourse itself give clues to the ordering of events', and adds:

At this point, in fact, one is entitled to ask whether the Temporal Discourse Interpretation Principle is to be regarded as an independent principle of discourse interpretation per se, or merely as a description of the typical outcome of the interaction of various conversational principles and the speakers'/hearers' knowledge of typical events and typical goals of narratives, any one clause of which may be overridden in various ways in exceptional cases. But this is not a question which can be profitably addressed here. (Dowty 1986: 58–59)

Dowty's comments raise an issue of principle. Clearly, Grice's maxim 'Be orderly' is inadequate to deal with the full range of cases discussed in this section. At this point, a choice must be made. One can either go in the direction of discourse semantics, and try to develop a set of special-purpose interpretation rules which will deal with the full range of cases; or one can take seriously the distinction between decoding and inference, and go in the direction of a more general inferential account. In the rest of this chapter, we will explore the second option by sketching the lines along which we think a general inferential solution might be found.

8.4   Understanding and relevance

In our book *Relevance* (1986a), we developed an account of inferential communication designed to explain how hearers recognise the overtly intended interpretation of an utterance: the one the speaker wants the hearer to recover, is actively helping the hearer to recover, and would acknowledge if asked. Our account was based on the following assumptions. First, every utterance has a variety of possible interpretations, all compatible with the information that is linguistically encoded. Second, not all these interpretations occur to the hearer simultaneously: for example, some disambiguations, some contextual assumptions, some implicatures require more effort to recover. Third, hearers are equipped with a single, very general criterion for evaluating interpretations as they occur to them. And, fourth, this criterion is powerful enough to enable the hearer to recognise the intended interpretation as soon as it is encountered, without having to construct and evaluate a range of alternative interpretations.

The criterion proposed in *Relevance* is based on a fundamental assumption about human cognition: that human cognition is relevance-oriented; we pay attention to information that seems relevant to us. Now every utterance starts out as a request for the hearer's attention. As a result, it creates an expectation of relevance. It is around this expectation of relevance that our criterion for evaluating possible interpretations is built.

Relevance is defined in terms of cognitive effects and processing effort. Cognitive effects are achieved when newly presented information interacts with a context of existing assumptions by strengthening an existing assumption, by contradicting and eliminating an existing assumption, or by combining with an existing assumption to yield a contextual implication (that is, a conclusion deducible from new information and existing assumptions together, but from neither new information nor existing assumptions alone). The greater the cognitive effects, the greater the relevance will be.

Cognitive effects, however, do not come free: they cost some mental effort to derive, and the greater the effort needed to derive them, the lower the relevance will be. The processing effort required to understand an utterance depends on two main factors: the form in which it is presented (audibility, legibility, dialect, register, syntactic complexity and familiarity of constructions all affect processing effort); and the effort of memory and imagination needed to construct a suitable context. The greater the processing effort required, the lower will be the relevance, and the greater the risk of losing the hearer's attention.

Relevance theory assumes that every aspect of communication and cognition is governed by the search for relevance. Cognition is governed by the search for maximal relevance (i.e. the greatest possible effects for the smallest possible effort). This is expressed in the First, or Cognitive, Principle of Relevance (Sperber and Wilson 1995: 260–78):

Cognitive Principle of Relevance
Human cognition tends to be geared to the maximisation of relevance.

What is unique to overt communication is that, approaching an utterance addressed to us, we are entitled to have not just hopes but steady expectations of relevance. The Second, or Communicative, Principle of Relevance is the principle that every utterance (or other act of ostensive communication) creates a presumption of relevance in the hearer. Relevance, we have seen, is defined in terms of cognitive effect and processing effort; but what exactly does the hearer's presumption of relevance amount to, in terms of effort and effect?

It is clear that the presumption is not one of maximal relevance. Communicators are not always expected to give the most relevant possible information, or to present it in the least effort-demanding way, as a presumption of maximal relevance would suggest. On the content side, the speaker may not have the information that the hearer would find most relevant; she may be unwilling to give it, or unable to think of it at the time. On the formal side, lack of time, lack of ability or stylistic preferences may prevent her expressing herself in the most economical way. Moreover, the most relevant utterance the speaker can think of may still not be relevant enough to be worth the hearer's attention; we need to set a lower limit on the expected degree of relevance, to explain why such an utterance would generally not be produced.

In *Relevance* (1995: 260–78), we define a notion of optimal relevance, designed to take these various factors into account:

Optimal relevance
An utterance, on a given interpretation, is optimally relevant iff:
(a) It is relevant enough for it to be worth the addressee's effort to process it;
(b) It is the most relevant one compatible with the communicator's abilities and preferences.

Clause (a) of the definition of optimal relevance sets a lower limit on the expected degree of relevance. Clause (b) takes into account the fact that the speaker may be unwilling or unable to produce the most relevant possible utterance, or to formulate it in the least effort-demanding way. More positively, clause (b) incorporates the idea that if the speaker can see a way of increasing the relevance of the utterance at no cost to herself, it is in her interest to do so: the more relevant the utterance, the more likely the hearer will be to attend to it and understand it correctly. These ideas may be illustrated by applying them to an example.

According to clause (a) of the definition of optimal relevance, the hearer is entitled to expect the utterance to be relevant enough to be worth his attention. In general, this means that he is entitled to expect it to be more relevant than any other information that he could have been processing at the time. How relevant that is depends on what is going on elsewhere in his cognitive environment. Thus, suppose that someone walks into an important lecture and says (15):

(15)   Ladies and gentlemen, the building is on fire.

'The building' is a referential expression, and different assignments of reference lead to different levels of cognitive effect. In the circumstances, the first hypothesis to come to the audience's mind would be that 'the building' means the building where the lecture is taking place. Clearly, the utterance, on this interpretation, would be relevant enough to be worth the audience's attention: their minds would be immediately filled with thoughts of how to get out. In the circumstances, it is hard to see what other interpretation would be relevant enough to justify the interruption, and the interpretation just suggested is basically the only possible one.

It might be thought that in other circumstances the intended interpretation would be harder to pin down. Surely there might be several radically different combinations of content and context, each of which would yield enough cognitive effects to make the utterance worth the audience's attention? This is where clause (b) of the definition of optimal relevance comes in. Recall that we are talking about overt communication, where the speaker is anxious to avoid misunderstanding, and is actively helping the hearer to recognise the intended interpretation. Clearly, it is in such a speaker's interest to make sure that there is no alternative line of interpretation which is both more accessible to the hearer than the intended one, and is relevant enough to be worth his attention, since such an interpretation is likely to lead him astray.

Clause (b) of the definition of optimal relevance, which excludes gratuitous calls on the hearer's processing effort, covers this type of case: that is, it excludes the possibility that the hearer will be expected to recover, process and accept the wrong interpretation before lighting on the intended one. From clause (b), it follows that a speaker aiming at optimal relevance should try to formulate her utterance in such a way that the first acceptable line of interpretation to occur to the hearer is the intended one. From the hearer's point of view, this clause has an immediate practical consequence. Having found a line of interpretation which satisfies his expectation of relevance in a way the speaker might manifestly have foreseen, he need look no further. The first such line of interpretation is the only one; all alternative lines of interpretation are disallowed.

The Communicative Principle of Relevance, then, is a principle of optimal rather than maximal relevance (*Relevance* 1995: 266–78):

Communicative Principle of Relevance
Every act of overt communication communicates a presumption of its own optimal relevance.

It is worth noting, though, that in order to be acceptable and comprehensible, an utterance does not actually have to be optimally relevant, but merely such that the speaker might reasonably have expected it to be so. In the first place, hearers are capable of correctly interpreting cases of accidental irrelevance, where an utterance is irrelevant to the hearer for reasons the speaker manifestly could not have foreseen. In the second place, hearers are capable of correctly interpreting cases of accidental relevance, where an utterance is optimally relevant to the hearer in a way the speaker manifestly could not have foreseen. To allow for these two types of case, we claim in *Relevance* that interpretations are accepted or rejected according to the following criterion of *consistency with the communicative principle of relevance*:[4]

Criterion of consistency with the communicative principle of relevance
An utterance, on a given interpretation, is consistent with the communicative principle of relevance if and only if the speaker might reasonably have expected it to be optimally relevant to the hearer on that interpretation.

This criterion, and the definition of optimal relevance which underlies it, provide the key to the relevance-theoretic account of comprehension. In the remainder of this chapter, we will apply them to a range of examples including those in (1) and (2) above.

8.5   The interval problem

The interval problem illustrated in (1) and (2) is a special case of a much more general problem. There are many other types of case where temporal intervals are left open by the semantics and narrowed down in the pragmatics. Compare (16a) and (16b):

(16)   a. I have had breakfast.
         b. I have been to Tibet.

The speaker of (16a) would generally be understood as saying that she had had breakfast that morning, whereas the speaker of (16b) might be understood as saying merely that she had visited Tibet at some time in her life. An adequate treatment of the interval problem should explain why this is so.

Let us assume that what is linguistically encoded in both cases is that the event described took place at some point within an interval stretching back from the moment of utterance. Then the speaker of (16a) can be understood as saying that she has had breakfast *within the last few minutes, within the last few hours, within the last few days, weeks, or months*, and so on, and the hearer's task is to decide which interval she had in mind. Notice that the possible interpretations are logically related: the cases in which the speaker has had breakfast *within the last few minutes* are a subset of those in which she has had breakfast *within the last few hours, days, weeks*, and so on. Notice, too, that the hearer's choice will affect the truth conditions of the utterance: the claim that I have not had breakfast may be true if the chosen interval is the last few hours but false if it is the last few weeks.

There are several variants of the interval problem, each with a similar logical structure. Suppose we meet in the University library, and I say to you:

(17)   I've been here all day.

The interpretation of 'here' involves spatial rather than temporal intervals: I might mean that I have been *in this room, in this library, in this building, in this town, in this country*, etc., all day. Again, the possible interpretations are logically related: the cases in which I have been *in this room* all day are a subset of those in which I have been *in this library, this building, this town*, etc., all day. Again, the hearer's choice of interval will affect the truth conditions of the utterance: (17) has different truth conditions depending on whether it is taken to mean *in this room, this town, this country*, etc.

The interpretation of many comparative adjectives has a similar subset structure. Thus, consider (18):

(18)   a. John is rich.
         b. Susan is tall.
         c. We are happy to see you.
         d. Bill has a fast car.

(18d), for example, might mean *fast enough to overtake some/many/most/all other cars; fast enough to cause envy among some/many/most/all of Bill's friends*, etc., with the set of cars that are fast enough to overtake *all* other cars being a subset of those that are fast enough to overtake some/many/most other cars, and so on.

Or consider (19):

(19)   Mary is a working mother.

As Lakoff (1987: 80–82) points out, (19) would generally be understood as communicating more about Mary than that she is a female parent who works: it might suggest, for example, that Mary's children are not grown up and living away from home, that she did not give them up for adoption at birth, and so on; that she not only works but works for money, for more than an hour or two a week, and so on. In other words, (19) is typically understood as applying to some subset of the set of people who satisfy the definition *female parent who works*. As the literature on prototype effects shows, similar cases of concept narrowing occur in the interpretation of virtually every utterance.

The interval problem raised by examples (1) and (2), then, is a special case of a much more general problem, which seems to demand a general solution. We will argue that relevance theory is particularly well suited to resolving indeterminacies with a subset structure of the type just illustrated.

Notice first that the hearer's choice of interval in (16) will affect not only the truth-conditional content of the utterance but also its cognitive effects. Narrower intervals are associated with greater cognitive effects: thus, if you tell me that you have had breakfast *within the last few minutes*, I will be able to derive all the cognitive effects I could have derived from knowing that you have had breakfast *within the last few days*, and more besides.

We claim that these differences in logical structure explain the differences in interpretation of (16a) and (16b). According to clause (a) of the definition of optimal relevance, the hearer should look for an interpretation which is relevant enough to be worth his attention. The difference between (16a) and (16b) is that in (16a), the interval must be narrowed much more drastically to achieve even minimally adequate effects.

In normal circumstances, unless the speaker of (16a) is understood as saying that she has had breakfast within the last few hours, her utterance will have no cognitive effects at all. Most of us would take for granted that she had had breakfast at some point in her life; moreover, it is hard to see what effects she might have hoped to achieve by telling us that she had had breakfast, say, three weeks ago. One can, of course, imagine special circumstances in which the fact that someone has become a breakfast-eater would be highly relevant; but in normal circumstances, the only way for (16a) to achieve adequate effects is by conveying that the speaker has had breakfast on the very day of utterance. With

(16b), by contrast, the information that the speaker has visited Tibet at some point in her life would generally be quite relevant enough.

To generalise: the semantics of (16a) and (16b) tells us that the event described happened at some point in an interval stretching back from the time of utterance to the beginning of the universe; the pragmatics tells us that it happened recently enough for the fact to be worth mentioning. In the search for optimal relevance, we will narrow the interval to a point where we have an interpretation consistent with the communicative principle of relevance. Similar remarks apply to the other examples mentioned above. Thus, when I say that Bill has a fast car, I must be understood as meaning that it is fast enough for the fact to be worth mentioning: how fast that is will vary from occasion to occasion. When I say that Mary is a working mother, I must be understood as meaning that she belongs to some subset of working mothers whose properties are such that the fact that Mary belongs to it is worth mentioning; and so on.

Relevance theory, then, suggests the following general strategy for solving the interval problem: look for an interval narrow enough to yield an interpretation consistent with the communicative principle of relevance. Which raises a further general question: How is the appropriate interval to be found? Here, it is reasonable to assume that hearers have a range of more specific strategies for finding the appropriate interval. It is to these that we now turn.

8.6   The role of contextual assumptions

Let us return to our original examples and look more carefully at the role of contextual assumptions in the interpretation of (1) and (2). Different utterances make different assumptions accessible. Differences in the accessibility of contextual assumptions will affect not only the order in which interpretations are tested, but the acceptability of the results. In this section, we will try to show how the assumptions of relevance theory interact with some widely accepted views on accessibility of contextual information to yield some explanatory insight into the sequencing problem, the interval problem and the cause–consequence problem.

We assume, as do most other people working in the area, that the hearer of (1a), for example, is given immediate access to his encyclopaedic assumptions about keys and doors. We also assume that encyclopaedic entries may contain ready-made chunks or schemas describing often-encountered sequences of actions or events. If such schemas exist, it is clear that we all have one for taking out a key and using it to unlock a door; moreover, by virtue of frequent use, such a schema would be highly accessible to a hearer interpreting (1a). Using this schema, it should be possible to infer that the interval between the events described is very small – a few seconds, a few minutes at most.

So far, so obvious. Everyone who has ever looked at the interval problem says that somehow it is solved by an interaction of contextual assumptions and pragmatic principles. But no-one, so far as we know, has a pragmatic principle which would explain why the hearer is *entitled* to use normal assumptions in interpreting (1a). After all, there would be nothing to stop someone taking out her key, falling asleep on the doorstep and opening the door next morning; or indeed being arrested and serving a life sentence between taking out her key and finally opening the door. What entitles the hearer to assume that the speaker did not have some such non-standard situation in mind?

As far as we can see, on most other approaches, an unargued appeal is made to statistical likelihood of events. The speaker *could* have meant something else, but because the event described is statistically unlikely, the associated interpretation is statistically unlikely too. No such appeal is needed in relevance theory: the appropriate interpretation falls out automatically from the criterion of consistency with the communicative principle of relevance.

Because, at least in normal circumstances, normal assumptions are the easiest to access, the hearer is entitled to use them as long as they give rise to an interpretation consistent with the communicative principle of relevance. And as long as they do, by clause (b) of the definition of optimal relevance, other, less accessible lines of interpretation are disallowed. From which there follows a further prediction: in the circumstances just described, a speaker who wants to communicate that some non-standard interval elapsed between taking out the key and opening the door would be unable to communicate it by means of (1a).

By the same token, the interpretation of (1b) and (1c) will depend on accessible contextual schemas. The standard assumption is that a dropped glass breaks on impact, whereas a planted acorn takes days or weeks to grow. Encyclopaedic knowledge about these events makes certain assumptions highly accessible; if these lead on to interpretations consistent with the communicative principle of relevance, all other lines of interpretation are disallowed.

Consider now another aspect of the interpretation of (1a). Though the speaker does not explicitly say so, in normal circumstances she would be taken to communicate that she opened the door with the key, and that she did so in the normal way, by inserting the key in the lock. These facts are explained by the relevance-theoretic account. By saying that she took out her key, the speaker causes her hearer some processing effort; if this is not to be gratuitous, it must make some contribution to cognitive effects. Again, the existence of an encyclopaedic schema points to an obvious hypothesis: that she used the key in the normal way to open the door. In normal circumstances, the resulting interpretation would be consistent with the communicative principle of relevance, and all other lines of interpretation would be disallowed.

What happens when there is no ready-made schema to guide the interpretation process? Consider (20):

(20)   John took out his handkerchief and opened the door.

This utterance does not describe a regular and frequently encountered sequence of events, and it is unlikely that the hearer has an appropriate schema waiting to be used. In fact, there are at least two lines of interpretation that he might pursue. In the context of a detective story, one way to exploit the information that John took out his handkerchief might be to assume that he used it to cover the door handle as he opened it, to avoid leaving fingerprints. This interpretation would yield both a sequencing effect and a definite hypothesis about the interval between the two events. In other circumstances, the best hypothesis might simply be that these are two unrelated events that happened at about the same time. Notice, though, that by the arguments given above, the fact that John took out his handkerchief must contribute in some way to overall relevance, and the reader of a planned text will be left with a strong expectation that the fact that John took out his handkerchief will prove relevant later on.

Talk of instruments leads naturally to talk of causes. Consider (1d):

(1)   d. Peter left and Mary got angry.

Why would this be naturally understood as communicating not only that Mary got angry after Peter left, but that she got angry *because* he left? Here we must speculate a little further about the type of mental schemas that humans are likely to construct. A large part of our cognitive life is taken up with consideration of causes and effects.[5] On the assumptions of relevance theory, this is no accident: causal stories are highly relevant, because they enable us to predict the consequences of our own actions and those of others. It is not surprising, then, that causal schemas come readily to mind for the interpretation of utterances such as (1d). As we have seen, if (1d) is to yield an interpretation consistent with the communicative principle of relevance, the information that Peter left must make some contribution to overall cognitive effects. Just as it is easy to see the key as an instrument in (1a), so it is easy to see Peter's departure as a cause in (1d). If this highly accessible line of interpretation proves consistent with the communicative principle of relevance, all other interpretations will be disallowed.

As Posner (1980) has shown, there is a huge variety of ways in which conjoined utterances such as (1) and (2) may be enriched with instrumental, causal, locative, durative, etc. material. It should be clear how all these cases would be handled in relevance-theoretic terms. If the linguistically encoded information is too vague, or too incomplete, to yield an interpretation consistent with the communicative principle of relevance, it will be enriched using immediately accessible contextual assumptions, to a point where it is relevant enough.

What we have tried to develop in the last few sections are general answers to two very general questions: why is it that, in interpreting an utterance, the hearer often enriches its truth-conditional content beyond what is strictly encoded; and how does the enrichment process go? We have argued that the enrichment process is triggered by expectations of relevance, which warrant the selection of the most accessible enrichment that yields an acceptable overall result. This account makes no appeal to special-purpose sequencing principles such as Grice's maxim of orderliness or Dowty's Temporal Discourse Interpretation Principle; the temporal and causal connotations of (1) and (2) arise from an interaction between sentence meaning, general cognitive factors and the criterion of consistency with the communicative principle of relevance.

8.7   Reverse-causal interpretations

In this final section, we will look at some examples that have been claimed to cast doubt on the feasibility of a general inferential account of the type just sketched. We will draw heavily on the work of Robyn Carston (see in particular Carston 1993a; 1998b), who has discussed these issues in some detail.

Recall examples (10)–(11) above, in which the reverse-causal interpretations available for non-conjoined utterances are apparently not available for the corresponding conjoined utterances:

(10)   a. The glass broke. John dropped it.
        b. I hit Bill. He insulted me.
        c. I got caught. My best friend betrayed me.

(11)   a. The glass broke and John dropped it.
        b. I hit Bill and he insulted me.
        c. I got caught and my best friend betrayed me.

Bar-Lev and Palacas (1980) have argued on the basis of these examples that 'and' must encode some additional information that blocks the reverse-causal interpretations. If so, then our inferential approach must be supplemented by an additional element of decoding.

According to Bar-Lev and Palacas (1980: 141) the differences between (10) and (11) result from the fact that 'and' encodes the following constraint:

Bar-Lev and Palacas: Semantic command constraint
The second conjunct is not prior to the first (chronologically or causally).

This would allow for the 'forward' temporal and causal interpretations of the utterances in (1), for the overlapping interpretations of utterances such as (9) and (13), and for the non-temporal and non-causal interpretations of utterances such as (12). However, it would rule out the reverse-causal interpretations of (11), which violate the semantic command constraint.

There are several problems with this account. In the first place, there are counterexamples. Larry Horn (p.c.) has pointed out that in cases such as (21b) a reverse-causal interpretation is possible with 'and':

(21) a. PETER: Did John break the glass?
      b. MARY: Well, the glass broke, and John dropped it.

Here, Mary clearly implicates that the glass broke because John dropped it. Or consider (11c) above, with additional 'comma' intonation:

(11) c'. I got caught, and my best friend betrayed me.

(11c') might well convey that the speaker got caught *because* her best friend betrayed her. Notice that in these cases the inference is relatively indirect: the temporal and causal connotations appear to be part of what is implicated rather than what is said. In any case, (21b) and (11c') are counterexamples to the semantic command constraint, which excludes both reverse-causal and reverse-temporal interpretations.

In the second place, there are differences in the interpretations of conjoined and non-conjoined utterances which are not explained by the semantic command constraint. Compare (22) and (23):

(22) a. I met someone famous last night. I met Chomsky.
      b. I met someone famous last night, and I met Chomsky.

(23) a. I ate somewhere nice yesterday. I ate at Macdonald's.
      b. I ate somewhere nice yesterday, and I ate at Macdonald's.

The events described in the non-conjoined utterances in (22a) can be understood as simultaneous (or identical); corresponding interpretations are not available for the conjoined utterances in (22b). Similar remarks apply to (23a) and (23b). There is nothing in Bar-Lev and Palacas's constraint to explain why this is so.

Bar-Lev and Palacas themselves cite a range of conjoined examples which are not explained by their constraint. These involve a variety of rhetorical relations which they call exemplification, as in (24), conclusivity, as in (25), and explanation, as in (26):

(24) a. Wars are breaking out all over: Champaign and Urbana have begun having border disputes.
      b. Wars are breaking out all over, and Champaign and Urbana have begun having border disputes.

(25) a. There are his footprints: he's been here recently.
      b. There are his footprints, and he's been here recently.

(26) a. Language is rule-governed: it follows regular patterns.
      b. Language is rule-governed, and it follows regular patterns.

In each case, an interpretation which is possible for the non-conjoined (a) sentence is ruled out for the conjoined (b) sentence. Bar-Lev and Palacas comment that in these non-temporal, non-causal utterances with 'and', neither 'forward' nor 'backward' relations between the conjuncts are possible. Notice that their semantic command constraint does not exclude these cases, and any constraint which excludes them would be likely to run into counterexamples with utterances such as (27):

(27)   a. Wars are breaking out all over, and Champaign and Urbana in particular have begun having border disputes.
        b. There are his footprints, and so he's been here recently.
        c. Language is rule-governed, and the reason is that it follows regular patterns.

Here, though the 'excluded' relations are explicitly encoded, the results are quite acceptable.

Rather than pursue the decoding approach to these examples, we would suggest the following inferential account. In each of (22a)–(26a), the speaker raises a question in the first part of the utterance, which is answered in the second part. In (22a), for instance, she expects the hearer to start wondering who she met; in (24a) she expects him to start wondering where wars are breaking out; in (26a) she anticipates the question 'What does it mean to say that language is rule-governed?'

Conjoined utterances with 'and' exclude interpretations along these lines: that is, interpretations on which the second conjunct achieves relevance primarily by answering a question raised by the first. Why is this so? One possible explanation (suggested by Blakemore 1987) is that a conjoined utterance is presented as a unit, encouraging the hearer to process the two conjuncts jointly and in parallel, looking for implications derivable from both. Question–answer pairs are not normally suited to joint processing, as witness the unacceptability of (28):

(28)   a. ?You'll never guess what time I finished, and I finished at 6.00.
        b. ?What time do you think I finished, and I finished at 6.00.
        c. ?You'll be amazed when you hear what time I finished, and I finished at 6.00.

Inferential approaches along these lines have been explored by Carston (1993a; 1998b). If successful, they would eliminate the need for a decoding account.[6]

8.8   Conclusion

In this chapter, we have sketched an inferential account of the causal and temporal connotations of utterances (1) and (2). This account is very general, and deals with a wide range of phenomena that are neither temporal nor causal in nature. By contrast, the various special-purpose principles proposed by discourse semanticists have limited application, and are themselves in need of further explanation. We believe that these principles are best seen as implementations of a more general inferential account such as the one developed here. Unless backed by such an account, their appeal will remain more descriptive than explanatory.

9   Recent approaches to bridging: truth, coherence, relevance

Deirdre Wilson and Tomoko Matsui

9.1   Introduction

Some classic examples of bridging reference are given in (1):

(1)   a. Jane has a new house. *The front door* is blue.
       b. Susan sent her meal back. *The steak* was underdone.

In interpreting the italicised NPs *the front door, the steak,* the hearer has to supply a referent which is not explicitly mentioned in the preceding discourse, but whose existence can be inferred from what has gone before. One way of doing this would be to add the following assumptions to the context in which the italicised NPs are interpreted:

(2)   a. Jane's new house has a front door.
       b. Susan's meal included steak.

Such assumptions may be seen as 'bridging the gap' between what has been explicitly stated in the first part of the utterance and what is needed for reference assignment in the second. The need for such assumptions is what mainly distinguishes bridging reference from other types of reference. We will call them *bridging assumptions*, and the italicised NPs *bridging NPs*.

Early analyses of bridging (e.g. Clark and Haviland 1977; Sanford and Garrod 1981) were conducted in a largely Gricean pragmatic framework, with its machinery of Cooperative Principle and maxims, maxim-violation, inferential intention-recognition, and so on. Bridging assumptions such as those in (2) were treated as Gricean implicatures: beliefs that had to be attributed to the speaker in order to preserve the assumption that she was obeying the Cooperative Principle and maxims in saying what she said. In developing their account of bridging, Clark and Haviland added further maxims to the framework, stating felicity conditions on the use of specific linguistic constructions, whose violation (real or apparent) would trigger the bridging process. For example, the bridging implicatures in (2) would be triggered by violation of a Maxim of Antecedence governing the use of definite NPs.

Early analyses of bridging thus raised pragmatic questions on two quite different levels. On the one hand, there were *general* pragmatic questions having to do with the justification of an overall pragmatic framework and its consequences for the analysis of various pragmatic processes. On the other, there were *specific* pragmatic questions having to do with the felicity conditions on the use of particular constructions (e.g. definite descriptions, referential expressions), and the particular effects they achieve. In this chapter, our concern is mainly with general pragmatic questions. We have focused on the analysis of bridging more for the light it can shed on pragmatic processes in general than for the particular problems raised by the analysis of definite NPs.

Most recent approaches to pragmatics start from the Gricean assumption that the hearer, in interpreting an utterance, is looking not just for some arbitrary interpretation but for the one overtly intended by the speaker. Many of them also share the following assumptions about the general form that pragmatic processes such as disambiguation, reference resolution, identification of implicatures, and so on, should take:

(3)   a. Candidate interpretations (e.g. disambiguations, reference assignments, implicatures, and so on) differ in their accessibility to the hearer, and are therefore evaluated in a certain order.
        b. They are evaluated in terms of some criterion of pragmatic acceptability that the resulting overall interpretation should meet.
        c. The first interpretation that satisfies the pragmatic criterion is the one the hearer should choose.

Here, assumption (3a) concerns *accessibility*, or *effort*, (3b) concerns *acceptability*, or *effect*, and (3c) concerns the relation between the two. In practice, psycholinguists tend to focus more on questions of effort, and pragmaticists (or discourse analysts, or text linguists) on questions of effect. However, an adequate pragmatic framework should integrate the two.

On the effort side, it is clear that a hearer who is looking for the overtly intended interpretation is not always justified in simply choosing the first interpretation that comes to mind; so a pragmatic criterion based on considerations of accessibility alone is unlikely to work. On the effect side, two main types of criterion are currently on offer: (a) those based on Grice's maxims of Quality and/or Quantity, which assume that hearers expect utterances (or discourses) to be true, or true and informative, or true and informative and evidenced; and (b) those based on Grice's maxim of Relation, which assume that hearers also expect utterances (or discourses) to be relevant, or coherent. We will argue that theories of type (a) are insufficient, and that we should be trying to construct theories of type (b). We will then compare two type (b) theories – coherence theory and relevance theory – and try to show that relevance theory offers the best way of integrating not only the effort and effect factors, but also the intuitions that underlie the truth-based and coherence-based approaches.

9.2   Pragmatic approaches to bridging

Let us start with a brief survey of approaches to bridging, organised around the twin factors of accessibility, or effort, and acceptability, or effect. Many of our examples are drawn from a questionnaire on bridging developed by Tomoko Matsui (and discussed in more detail in Matsui 1995, 1998, 2000). While the numbers involved in this questionnaire were small, the results are quite suggestive, and we will use them to illustrate the type of problems that an adequate analysis of bridging would have to solve.

9.2.1   Accessibility

In the case of bridging, two main types of factor affect the accessibility of candidate referents:

(4)   a. The accessibility of the linguistic antecedent, e.g. *the house* in (1a);
         b. The accessibility of the bridging assumption.

We will say a word about each – briefly, since it seems clear that hearers do not simply choose the first interpretation that occurs to them, and it's the pragmatic criterion used in evaluating this interpretation that mainly concerns us here.

9.2.1.1 Accessibility of linguistic antecedents   In the general literature on reference resolution, a lot of work has been done on factors affecting accessibility of linguistic antecedents. These include order of mention, syntactic position, recency of mention, manner of mention, thematic role, semantics of the main verb, parallel function, choice of conjunction, and overall salience in discourse (for survey and discussion, see Matsui 1995, 2000). The focus-based (or 'centering') approaches developed by Grosz (1981), Sidner (1983) and Grosz and Sidner (1986), and adopted both in psycholinguistics (Sanford, Moar and Garrod 1988) and formal semantics (Asher and Wada 1988), have been particularly fruitful: the constituent claimed to be 'in focus' is precisely the most accessible linguistic antecedent for reference assignment.[1]

Most work on bridging assumes that what would be the most accessible antecedent for direct reference would also be the most accessible antecedent for bridging. This is explicitly argued in Erku and Gundel (1987), who consider examples like the following:

(5)   We went to a Thai restaurant. *The waitress* was from Bangkok.

(6)   We stopped for drinks at the New York Hilton before going to the Thai restaurant. *The waitress* was from Bangkok.

In (5), *the waitress* would typically be understood as the one in the Thai restaurant. In (6), there are two possible antecedents, *the Hilton* and *the Thai restaurant*, and the question is how *the waitress* in (6) would be understood. According to Erku and Gundel, she would be understood as the one in the Hilton, despite the strong encyclopaedic association between *Thai* and *Bangkok*. They explain this by appeal to the relative accessibility of the two antecedents, as predicted by Sidner's 'Expected Focus Algorithm', which picks out the focus on the basis of syntactic position and thematic role. In (6), the Expected Focus Algorithm would pick out the main clause NP *the Hilton* rather than the subordinate clause NP *the Thai restaurant*; this focused constituent would then be the expected antecedent for the bridging NP *the waitress*. By the same token, the expected antecedent for *the baby orang-utan* in (7) would be *the Hilton*, not *the zoo*.

(7)   ?We stopped for drinks at the Hilton before going to the zoo. *The baby orang-utan* was really cute.

According to Erku and Gundel, (7) would be perceived as unacceptable or stylistically infelicitous because the most accessible antecedent has to be rejected on the basis of encyclopaedic knowledge about where baby orang-utans are to be found. Their analysis thus makes the following two claims: (a) if at all possible, the hearer chooses the most accessible antecedent; and (b) if the most accessible interpretation has to be rejected, as in (7), the utterance will be considered stylistically infelicitous.

Matsui's questionnaire contains some examples designed to test these claims. In each case, the bridging NP is *the humidity*, and there are two possible antecedents: *England* and *Hong Kong*. Participants were asked to answer the question, 'Where did the humidity (not) bother John?', and to note any utterance they regarded as stylistically infelicitous. Percentage responses are shown in brackets after each example:

(8)   a. John worked in England before moving to Hong Kong 5 years ago. *The humidity* didn't bother him. [40% England; 60% Hong Kong]
        b. John worked in Hong Kong before moving to England 5 years ago. *The humidity* didn't bother him. [60% Hong Kong; 40% England]
        c. John worked in England before moving to Hong Kong 5 years ago. *The humidity* really bothered him. [40% England; 60% Hong Kong]
        d. John worked in Hong Kong before moving to England 5 years ago. *The humidity* really bothered him. [100% Hong Kong]

These responses show that participants did not always choose the most accessible antecedent as predicted by the Expected Focus Algorithm. Their preferences were split in all cases except (8d), which is the only one to behave as expected. Participants were also asked to note any utterance they regarded as stylistically infelicitous. Only one person noted an infelicity in (8), and that went counter to Erku and Gundel's predictions: it was in (8b), with the interpretation 'Hong Kong', which according to the Expected Focus Algorithm is the more accessible antecedent.

In fact most work on reference resolution, including Sidner's, recognises, first, that the accessibility of referents is affected by a variety of factors other than thematic role; and second, that the most accessible candidate can be rejected and another selected on pragmatic grounds. The differences in interpretation of the examples in (8) provide obvious confirmation of this point. Although we will continue to use the Expected Focus Algorithm as a rough guide to the accessibility of antecedents, our main concern will be with the pragmatic criterion used to accept or reject interpretations. As we will show, this criterion itself sheds some light on questions of accessibility, since one of the factors affecting the accessibility of interpretations is likely to be the hearer's expectation about the effects the speaker is aiming to achieve.

9.2.1.2 Accessibility of bridging assumptions   A second factor affecting the accessibility of candidate referents is the accessibility of bridging assumptions such as (2a)–(2b) above. Early experimental work showed that bridging in standard examples like (1a)–(1b) is extremely fast. Sanford and Garrod (1981) explained this in terms of frame-based or scenario-based associations between the linguistic antecedent (e.g. *the house* in (1a)) and the candidate referent. The idea is that processing of the linguistic antecedent in (1a)–(1b) would automatically activate encyclopaedic information containing the frame-based bridging assumptions in (2a)–(2b). An early version of this idea is found in Hawkins (1978):

(9)   The bridging assumption must belong to a frame associated with the antecedent. Otherwise the utterance will be unacceptable.

Matsui's questionnaire contained a range of examples which on the whole bore out this common-sense assumption that accessibility of encyclopaedic knowledge affects the acceptability of bridging. Participants were given sets of four examples and asked to rank their acceptability on a 7-point scale (with 7 being the most acceptable and 1 the least). Here is an illustration, with the mean ratings shown in brackets after each example:

(10)   a. I was looking at van Gogh's self-portrait. *The missing ear* made me feel sad. [6.54]
        b. I went to see some impressionist paintings. *The missing ear* made me feel sad. [4.08]
        c. I went to a gallery yesterday. *The missing ear* made me feel sad. [3.23]
        d. I spent all day in London. *The missing ear* made me feel sad. [1.46]

The research was done at a time when a van Gogh exhibition in London was receiving a lot of publicity. Even so, the interpretation of each successive example involves a little more creativity (hence, effort), and as predicted on frame-based accounts, the greater the creativity, the lower the acceptability.

However, Erku and Gundel (1987) show that the simplest version of the frame-based approach is inadequate to explain the acceptability or unacceptability of bridging. They compare examples such as (11a)–(11c):

(11)   a. ?A car went by. *The dog* was barking.
           b. Don't go near that house. *The dog* will bite you.
           c. Don't go near the car. *The dog* will bite you.

The frame-based criterion in (9) above would rule out (11a) as unacceptable, because dogs are not part of the frame for cars. However, as Erku and Gundel point out, (11b) would normally be acceptable, even though dogs are not normally part of the frame for houses; moreover, (11c) shows that an acceptable link can be made between car and dog. Indeed, even (11a) would be acceptable in certain circumstances, e.g. as a denial of (12):

(12)   Dogs never bark in cars.

Again the conclusion must be that while the accessibility of bridging assumptions is a factor affecting overall pragmatic acceptability, it is not the only one.

The arguments of this section confirm the view that, whatever the accessibility facts, they can be overridden if the resulting interpretation is not pragmatically acceptable. The question is, what constitutes pragmatic acceptability? Psycholinguists have rarely been seriously interested in this question; pragmatic theorists must be.

9.2.2   Acceptability

According to Grice, hearers can identify the intended interpretation of an utterance because utterances raise certain expectations. The Gricean expectation is, of course, that the speaker was obeying the Cooperative Principle and maxims (or at least the Cooperative Principle) in saying what she said. Most recent approaches to pragmatics have started out as attempts to develop one or more of Grice's maxims into an adequate pragmatic criterion. We will look first at type (a) theories, based on the maxims of Quality and/or Quantity (truthfulness and/or informativeness) and then at type (b) theories, based on the maxim of Relation, 'Be relevant'.

9.2.2.1   Truth-based approaches   What we are calling truth-based approaches are built around the Quality and/or Quantity maxims. A prototypical example is Lewis (1979), who suggests that the hearers should use something like the following pragmatic criterion in interpreting bridging cases:

(13)   Accept the first candidate referent that leads to an overall interpretation which
          is true, informative and evidenced.

On Lewis's view, reference is assigned to the most salient (hence accessible) candidate; if the resulting interpretation is pragmatically unacceptable, saliencies are reordered according to the following rule, until an acceptable interpretation is found:

(14)   *Rule of accommodation for comparative salience*
If at time t something is said that requires, if it is to be acceptable, that x be more salient than y; and if, just before t, x is no more salient than y; then – ceteris paribus and within certain limits – at t, x becomes more salient than y. (Lewis 1979/1983: 242)

In this case, the motivation for the reinterpretation process is the expectation that the utterance will be true, informative and evidenced.

Some of Matsui's questionnaire examples were designed to test the claim that the most accessible candidate may be rejected in favour of a less accessible one which leads to a more factually plausible interpretation. Here are some cases which seem to fit this view:

(15)   a. I prefer England to Italy. I hate *the pasta* there. [100% Italy]
        b. I prefer the country to the town. *The traffic* really bothers me. [100% town]
        c. I prefer London to Edinburgh. I hate *the snowy winters*. [100% Edinburgh]
        d. I prefer Italy to England. *The weather* is worse. [60% Italy; 40% England]

In these examples, the most accessible antecedent (according to the Expected Focus Algorithm) is the direct object of *prefer*, but this is rejected in favour of a less accessible candidate, and it could be argued that the reason is that the resulting interpretation is more likely to be true.

The question is how this argument could be worked out in detail. Several families of truth-based criteria could be proposed, each making different predictions. First, a truth-based criterion might be strong or weak. A strong criterion would compare competing interpretations and choose the most factually plausible (or plausible and informative, or plausible, informative and evidenced) one; a weak criterion would accept the first interpretation that reaches a certain threshold of factual plausibility (or plausibility and informativeness, etc.), without necessarily comparing it with alternative interpretations. Second, a truth-based criterion may be local or global. A local criterion would pick out the most factually plausible (or plausible and informative, etc.) interpretation of the utterance currently being processed; a global criterion would aim to maximise the factual plausibility of the discourse as a whole. Finally, the predictions of a criterion based on truth alone would differ from those of a criterion based on truth and informativeness, truth and evidencedness, or truth, informativeness and evidencedness. Without considering all these possibilities, we would like to suggest that none of them is likely to work unless some appeal to a notion of coherence or relevance is made.

Consider, first, a strong, local criterion, which compares alternative interpretations of the utterance currently being processed and chooses the one that is most likely to be true (with a minimal check for consistency with prior discourse, but no expectation of relevance or coherence). One consequence of such a strong criterion is that the accessibility factor in comprehension would have to be discounted: the fact that one interpretation was more accessible than others would no longer be any reason for accepting it. Another consequence is that all possible interpretations would have to be computed and compared, which in many cases would lead to a combinatorial explosion. Moreover, some of the questionnaire results do not seem to fit this criterion. Consider (16):

(16)   I prefer the restaurant on the corner to the student canteen. *The cappuccino* is less expensive.

The most accessible antecedent for *the cappuccino* (according to the Expected Focus Algorithm) is the direct object *the restaurant*. However, it is part of encyclopaedic knowledge that cappuccino in a student canteen is likely to be less expensive than cappuccino in an ordinary restaurant. If the hearer simply chooses the most factually plausible interpretation of the utterance currently being processed, we might therefore expect the most accessible candidate to be rejected, and *the cappuccino* in (16) to be understood as referring to the cappuccino in the student canteen. In the questionnaire, this hypothesis was tested by asking the following questions:

(17)   a. Where is the cappuccino less expensive? [Restaurant: 100%]
         b. In general, where do you get less expensive cappuccino, a student canteen or a restaurant? [Canteen: 100%]

Here, the results were unequivocal: 100 per cent of participants said that *the cappuccino* in (16) referred to the cappuccino in the restaurant; and 100 per cent of participants said that the cappuccino in a student canteen is generally less expensive than the cappuccino in a restaurant. So the hypothesis that the hearer chooses the most factually plausible interpretation of the utterance currently being processed is not borne out.

Consider now a weak local criterion, which simply accepts (again with a minimal check for consistency with prior discourse but no expectation of coherence or relevance) the first interpretation to reach a certain threshold of factual plausibility, which, as in this example, may be rather low. Weak criteria are preferable to strong criteria from the processing-effort point of view. However, while this criterion would explain the results in (16), it no longer explains the interpretation of the examples in (15). In (15a), for instance, the most accessible interpretation of the second part of the utterance (according to the Expected Focus Algorithm) is the one on which the speaker is saying she hates the pasta in England. This interpretation is both factually plausible and consistent with the prior discourse, and the revised pragmatic criterion no longer explains why it is rejected when a much less factually plausible interpretation of (16) is retained.

Consider now a strong global criterion designed to pick out the interpretation on which the discourse as a whole is most likely to be true (or true and informative, or true, informative and evidenced). It might be thought that this would explain the results in both (15) and (16). For example, it might be suggested that in (15a), the speaker's claim that she prefers England to Italy somehow makes it more plausible that she hates the pasta in Italy; and in (16), her claim that she prefers the restaurant on the corner somehow makes it more plausible that the cappuccino there is less expensive. But – even leaving aside the processing-effort disadvantages of strong criteria – it is not easy to see how this idea could be worked out. After all, it is quite possible to like a country without liking its food, or to like a restaurant despite the fact that it serves expensive coffee. Moreover, someone who says she prefers England to Italy would not normally be taken to implicate that she prefers the food in England; and someone who says she prefers one restaurant to another would not normally be taken to implicate that the coffee in her preferred restaurant is less expensive. So it is hard to see how the first part of these utterances could be seen as providing evidence for the second.

We all feel, of course, that the only *pragmatically* plausible interpretation of (15a) is the one on which the speaker prefers England to Italy *because* she hates the pasta in Italy, and that the only pragmatically plausible interpretation of (16) is the one on which the speaker prefers the restaurant on the corner *because* it serves less expensive coffee. It might be argued that these interpretations can be dealt with in a truth-based framework by treating the second part of these utterances as providing evidence for the first. But there are several problems with this approach.

One problem is that hearers may be able to choose between two interpretations, both of which provide evidence for an earlier statement. Consider (18):

(18)   I ran from the classroom to the playground. *The children* were making too much noise.

This utterance has two interpretations: the speaker may have run out of the classroom to escape the noisy children; or she may have run into the playground to rebuke the noisy children. A hearer assigning reference according to the strong truth-based criterion would now have to consider not only the intrinsic plausibility of the two possible interpretations of the second part of the utterance, but also the amount of evidence that each of them would provide for the first part of the utterance (or perhaps for the implicitly communicated information that the speaker ran from one place to the other because the children there were making too much noise). More generally, every possible combination of disambiguations, reference assignments and enrichments would have to be compared, not only for its own intrinsic plausibility but for the amount of evidence it provides for earlier statements (or implicatures) in the discourse. The resulting combinatorial explosion would dramatically increase the processing effort required. (For empirical arguments against this version of the criterion, see section 9.4.)

Matsui's questionnaire contains another type of example which is hard to explain in terms of this approach. These examples were in fact designed to test the hypothesis that encyclopaedic associations between the bridging NP and one of two roughly equally accessible antecedents might affect the hearer's choice. The idea was that a hearer motivated by considerations of factual plausibility should assign reference to the more strongly associated antecedent. Consider (19):

(19)   a. Kevin moved from England to New Zealand. He loves *the sheep*. [100% New Zealand]
         b. Kevin moved from New Zealand to England. He loves *the sheep*. [100% England]
         c. Kevin moved from England to New Zealand. He hates *the sheep*. [100% New Zealand]
         d. Kevin moved from New Zealand to England. He hates *the sheep*. [60% England; 40% New Zealand]

According to the Expected Focus Algorithm, the prepositional phrases *from England* and *to New Zealand* are roughly equally accessible as antecedents for the bridging NP *the sheep*, with a marginal preference, if anything, for the goal phrase (e.g. *to New Zealand* in (19a)). At the same time, for British participants, at least, there is a strong association between New Zealand and sheep, and on this basis one might expect a hearer guided by local expectations of truth to interpret *the sheep* in all four examples as being in New Zealand. As the questionnaire results show, this expectation is not borne out in the case of (19b), where 100 per cent of participants preferred the antecedent *England*, or (19d), where preferences were split.

These results present further problems for the strong global criterion envisaged above. Consider (19a) and (19b), with the interpretations shown. How were these interpretations arrived at? According to the strong global criterion, they would be arrived at by treating the second part of the utterance as providing evidence for the statement made in the first part. On this approach, (19a) would be understood as saying that Kevin moved from England to New Zealand *because* he loved the sheep in New Zealand, and (19b) would be understood as saying that Kevin moved from New Zealand to England *because* he loved the sheep in England. This may be so, but there is another equally plausible interpretation on which the second part of the utterance describes not the reason for Kevin's move, but merely a result. In these examples, it is not easy to be sure which interpretations participants were getting, since they converge on the same antecedent. However, in (19c) they come apart, and it is clear that the Result rather than the Reason interpretation was preferred. This presents a further problem for the strong global criterion, since the Result interpretation does not stand in any obvious evidential relation to the first part of the utterance. To put it more generally, utterances in discourse may be related in various ways.

According to the truth-based approach, all these relations must be analysable in terms of the notions of truth, informativeness and evidence. The above examples suggest that things are not as simple as that.

We have attributed to Lewis the view that a pragmatically acceptable interpretation must be true, informative and evidenced. In fact, he adds that other considerations, of relevance, for example, may be involved. The results discussed in this section tend to confirm the view that, as far as pragmatic acceptability is concerned, being true, informative and evidenced is not enough. We now turn to two rival attempts to supply the missing ingredient: coherence-based and relevance-based approaches.

9.2.2.2 Coherence-based approaches   Perhaps the most popular current view in both the psycholinguistic and the computational literature is that the missing ingredient is one of discourse coherence. A prototypical example is Hobbs (1979), who says, essentially:

(20)   Accept the first candidate referent that yields an overall interpretation which is coherent with prior discourse.

Here the challenge is to develop a theoretically adequate notion of coherence. Attempts have been made to analyse this in terms of theoretical notions such as discourse topic or discourse plan (e.g. Reinhart 1981; Grosz and Sidner 1986; Giora 1997). However, by far the most popular view in both the computational and the psycholinguistic literature is that an appropriate notion of coherence can be defined in terms of a set of coherence relations that hold between successive utterances in a discourse: for instance, Elaboration, Temporal Sequence, Cause–Consequence, and so on. It is this relation-based notion of coherence that we will look at here.[2]

The assumption behind coherence-based approaches to comprehension is that hearers expect utterances to be coherent with prior discourse; when an utterance has two possible interpretations, they will choose the one that satisfies their expectation of coherence. Here is a classic example from Jerry Hobbs, showing how the search for coherence can guide reference resolution:

(21)   John can open Bill's safe. *He* knows the combination.

According to Hobbs, *he* should be interpreted as referring to John rather than Bill because, on this interpretation, the second part of the utterance would count as an Elaboration (or Explanation) of the first. Approaches along these lines have been developed by Hobbs (1979), Samet and Schank (1984), Mann and Thompson (1988) and Asher and Lascarides (1995).

The coherence-based approach seems to shed some light on our questionnaire examples. Returning to the examples in (15), where participants unanimously rejected the most accessible antecedent in favour of an alternative, less accessible one, it might be argued that they were guided by considerations of coherence. In (15a), for instance, by taking *Italy* as the antecedent for *the pasta*, they could interpret the second part of the utterance as giving a Reason, or an Explanation, for why the speaker prefers England to Italy. Similarly, in (16), it might be argued that hearers chose *the restaurant* as antecedent for *the cappuccino* because the resulting interpretation would provide a Reason, or Explanation, for why the speaker preferred the restaurant, and that this was enough to outweigh considerations of factual plausibility.

Although it seems intuitively obvious that something like this is going on, there are many descriptive and theoretical problems with the coherence-based approach outlined above. Here, we will mention just two. In the first place, the hearer may be able to choose between two interpretations, both of which would make the discourse coherent. Consider (22):

(22)   a. Jane moved from California to Manchester. She hates *the warm winters*. [100% California]
        b. Sara left Australia for England. She hates *the sandy beaches*. [100% Australia]

Each of these examples has two possible interpretations, each involving a different coherence relation. In (22a), for instance, Jane may have moved from California to Manchester *because* she hates the warm winters in California (Explanation); or she may have moved from California to Manchester and *as a result* hate the warm winters in Manchester (Result). Both interpretations are causal: in the Result case the causal relation runs forwards (from the event described in the first part of the utterance to the one described in the second), and in the Explanation case, it runs backwards (from the event described in the second part of the utterance to the one described in the first). As the questionnaire results show, participants unanimously chose the Explanation interpretation, in which the causal relation runs backwards. The same point applies to (22b), where participants again chose the Explanation interpretation. The question is why this is so.

An obvious answer is that coherence relations may themselves be more or less accessible. One attempt to deal with the accessibility of coherence relations in a psychologically motivated way is by Sanders, Spooren and Noordman (1992, 1993). They analyse the coherence relations in terms of a set of features, e.g. Causal versus Additive, Basic versus Non-Basic Order, which may be used to predict their accessibility. In fact, the proposed analysis makes the wrong predictions about the interpretation of (22a) and (22b). According to Sanders *et al.*, relations involving Basic (forwards) Order should be more accessible than those involving Non-Basic (backwards) Order, and on this approach, interpretations based on Result rather than Explanation should be preferred. More generally, this approach predicts that the accessibility of coherence relations depends on their intrinsic features, so that whatever relation is most accessible in one situation will be most accessible in all others. Yet it is clear that the preferred interpretations of participants vary from situation to situation. For example, in (19c), as noted above, 100 per cent of participants favoured a Result interpretation, even though an Explanation interpretation would have been quite plausible. This suggests that the accessibility of coherence relations cannot be accounted for solely in terms of intrinsic features, as Sanders *et al.* imply.

A second problem for coherence theories is that an utterance may have two alternative interpretations, both of which satisfy the *same* coherence relation. An example was given in (18) above:

(18)   I ran from the classroom to the playground. *The children* were making too much noise.

Here, as noted above, the bridging NP *the children* has two possible antecedents. Whichever is chosen, the second part of the utterance will provide an Explanation of the event described in the first part. In this case, knowing the intended coherence relation will not solve the problem of reference resolution; yet it is easy to see that there are circumstances in which one or other interpretation would be preferred.

More generally, coherence-based approaches raise descriptive questions about which coherence relations exist, and explanatory questions about why they exist and how they are acquired. We will return to these questions after sketching an alternative attempt to supply the missing ingredient, this time by developing a notion of relevance.

9.2.2.3 *Relevance-based approaches*

Erku and Gundel (1987) argue that in the interpretation of bridging examples, considerations of relevance are decisive:

What we would like to suggest here is that the only thing which makes it possible for [bridging] expressions to be recognised as anaphoric is the maxim of relation, i.e. the expectation that the speech act performed in the use of some sentence be relevant to the context in which it occurs. (Erku and Gundel 1987: 542).

In their view, what makes the difference between the acceptable and unacceptable examples in (11) above is not discourse coherence but relevance. Similarly, they argue that the stylistic unacceptability of example (7) above is due to some connection between relevance and topic, or expected focus. Their criterion for pragmatic interpretation would therefore be something like the following:

(23)   Accept the first candidate referent that yields an overall interpretation which is relevant.

However, they make no attempt to provide a theoretical definition of relevance, commenting merely that:

The importance of this notion [relevance] in the pragmatics of natural language has been noted in a number of works ... There has, however, been relatively little progress in making the notion explicit. (Erku and Gundel 1987: 543)

For several years, relevance theorists have been trying to develop a notion of relevance which might form the basis for a psychologically plausible account of comprehension. This is what we will turn to now.

9.3   Relevance theory and bridging

Relevance theory shares the Gricean assumption that hearers are looking for the overtly intended interpretation of an utterance. It differs from the Gricean approach in two main respects. First, it is not maxim-based: it contains no general communicative principles that speakers and hearers have to know and use. Second, it does not assume that communication is necessarily cooperative in Grice's sense: that speaker and hearer have to share a common purpose over and above that of understanding and being understood. Its basic claim is that what is fundamental to communication – because it is fundamental to cognition – is the pursuit of relevance.

On the cognitive level, relevance theory claims that human attention and processing resources go to information that seems relevant. This is expressed as the First, or Cognitive, Principle of Relevance:

(24)   *Cognitive Principle of Relevance*
         Human cognition tends to be geared to the maximisation of relevance.

Relevance is defined in terms of cognitive effects and processing effort:

(25)   *Relevance*
         a. The greater the cognitive effects, the greater the relevance;
         b. The smaller the effort needed to achieve those effects, the greater the
            relevance.

Cognitive effects are achieved when new information interacts with existing contextual assumptions in one of three ways:

(26)   *Cognitive effects*
         a. Strengthening an existing assumption;
         b. Contradicting and eliminating an existing assumption;
         c. Combining with an existing assumption to yield contextual implications.

Processing effort is affected by two main factors: the form in which the information is presented, and the accessibility of the context. The accessibility factors discussed above in section 9.2 would fit in here.

To illustrate these ideas, suppose that Peter wants to get to Boston by plane as soon as possible, and doesn't know when the next plane is. He asks Mary, who may (truly) tell him one of three things:

(27)   a. The next plane to Boston is at 5.30.
          b. The next plane to Boston is sometime after 4.00.
          c. The next plane to Boston leaves 7,500 seconds after 3.25.

Which information would be most relevant to Peter? Answer: (27a). This is more relevant than (27b) for reasons of effect: it implies everything that (27b) does, and more besides. It is also more relevant than (27c), this time for reasons of effort. Since 7,500 seconds after 3.25 is in fact 5.30, (27c) has the same cognitive effects as (27a), but more processing effort is needed to derive them.

Moving now to the level of communication, relevance theory proposes a Second, or Communicative, Principle of Relevance, which is justified as follows. To communicate with someone is to offer them information. Offers raise expectations. If I offer you food, you expect it to be edible. If human cognition is relevance-oriented, then offers of information should raise expectations of relevance; and by standard Gricean arguments, if there is an interpretation that the speaker might reasonably have intended to satisfy these expectations, that is the one the addressee should choose.

We define a notion of optimal relevance which is meant to spell out what the addressee is entitled to look for in terms of effort and effect:

(28)   *Optimal relevance*
          An utterance is optimally relevant to an addressee iff:
          a. It is relevant enough to be worth the addressee's processing effort;
          b. It is the most relevant one compatible with the speaker's abilities and preferences.

This entitlement is spelled out in the Second, or Communicative, Principle of Relevance:

(29)   *Communicative Principle of Relevance*
          Every utterance communicates a presumption of its own optimal relevance.

The communicative principle of relevance and the definition of optimal relevance in turn suggest a comprehension procedure which we claim is spontaneously followed in utterance interpretation:

(30)   *Relevance-theoretic comprehension procedure*
          Follow a path of least effort in computing cognitive effects:
          a. Consider interpretations (disambiguations, reference assignments, etc.) in their order of accessibility;
          b. Stop when the expected level of relevance is achieved.

This procedure integrates effort and effect in the following way. It claims that the hearer is entitled to expect at least enough cognitive effects to make the utterance worth his attention, that the processing effort involved in comprehension is the effort needed to achieve these effects, and that the hearer is entitled to accept the first interpretation that satisfies the particular expectation of relevance that the utterance, in that context, has raised.

To illustrate how these ideas might apply to a straightforward case of bridging, consider one of the questionnaire examples which received a unanimous response:

(22)   b. Sara left Australia for England. She hates *the sandy beaches*. [100% Australia]

Here, the comprehension procedure works smoothly. On the effort side, *Australia* is the most accessible antecedent: first, because it is picked out by the Expected Focus algorithm as the direct object of *left*; and second, because of the encyclopaedic association between *Australia* and *sandy beaches*. Moreover, the second part of the utterance, on this interpretation, could be expected to achieve at least adequate cognitive effects by answering a question implicitly raised by the interpretation of the first part: why did Sara leave Australia for England? To say that the first part of the utterance implicitly raises a question amounts to no more than saying that it provides easy access to a context in which an answer to this question would be relevant enough to be worth the hearer's attention. There is no need to appeal to a coherence relation of Explanation. From the relevance-theoretic point of view, computation of coherence relations is a waste of effort unless it gives rise to otherwise inaccessible effects. The expectation of optimal relevance is enough on its own to account for the interpretation of this example.

One advantage of the relevance-based approach over the coherence-based approach is that it allows for greater flexibility in the relations between utterances in discourse. There is no need to assume that there is a finite set of discrete coherence relations which must be recognised as part of the comprehension process. Part of the appeal of the coherence-based approach rests on its use of relations such as Explanation, Temporal Sequence, Cause–Consequence, and so on, which everyone would intuitively recognise as holding between utterances in discourse. But theoretical accounts of coherence relations have repeatedly encountered two problems. First, there are questions about how fine-grained the relations should be. The number of relations proposed has varied between 3 and 300, with no obvious way of deciding between them (see e.g. Hovy 1990). There are also questions about how many of the relations a pair of utterances can enter into simultaneously. The more fine-grained the relations, and the more of them can be simultaneously recognised, the greater the flexibility in interpretation. But by analysing comprehension in terms of cognitive effects, relevance theory achieves the same flexibility with no additional machinery, and no awkward questions about where to draw the line.

The second problem is that many pairs of utterances do not stand in any of the intuitively obvious coherence relations, and to account for their interpretation in coherence-based terms, apparently arbitrary new relations have to be invented. Consider (31), for instance, another example on which participants responded unanimously:

(31)   I prefer the town to the country. *The traffic* doesn't bother me. [town 100%]

Here the most accessible antecedent is *the town*, picked out by both the Expected Focus Algorithm and the encyclopaedic association between *town* and *traffic*. On this interpretation, the second part of the utterance might be expected to achieve at least adequate cognitive effects by answering questions of the following sort, in a context easily accessible from the interpretation of the first part:

(32) a. Isn't the town too noisy?
      b. Wouldn't she rather have the quiet of the country?
      c. Isn't there anything she dislikes about the town?

Yet none of the intuitively obvious coherence relations is involved in this interpretation. One could, of course, invent a relation such as Anticipated Objection and claim that it must be identified as part of the process of identifying the intended effects. But this would add a pointless extra element of effort, which could be eliminated by bypassing the coherence relation and going directly to the effects. In this way, relevance theory accounts for the intuitions behind the coherence-based approach, but without the machinery of coherence relations.[3]

Relevance theory thus provides a relatively developed framework in which the results of detailed studies of specific aspects of comprehension might be integrated and explained. In the rest of this section, we will briefly sketch relevance-theoretic analyses of some of the bridging cases that were problematic for the truth-based and coherence-based approaches.

A unique feature of the relevance-theoretic comprehension process is that it involves a mutual adjustment of content, context and cognitive effects. The hearer may approach an utterance with more or less specific expectations of cognitive effects (Sperber and Wilson 1998a), which may alter the prior saliencies of contents and contexts. A hearer expecting a specific type of cognitive effects should pay attention to interpretations (disambiguations, reference assignments, etc.) which are likely to yield these effects, whether or not these interpretations were intrinsically salient. Similarly, retrieval mechanisms may search for background assumptions that were not immediately accessible, but which may allow the derivation of the expected effects. In this way, prior orderings of accessibility may be overturned. Since the accessibility of an interpretation affects its acceptability, it follows that an utterance judged unacceptable in isolation may be made more acceptable by manipulation of expected effects.

Consider from this perspective the problems raised by Erku and Gundel in connection with the examples in (11):

(11) a. ?A car went by. *The dog* was barking.
      b. Don't go near that house. *The dog* will bite you.
      c. Don't go near the car. *The dog* will bite you.

Erku and Gundel note that while (11a) is generally perceived as unacceptable in isolation, it would become more acceptable if understood as a denial of the prior utterance in (12):

(12)   Dogs never bark in cars.

Relevance theory sheds some light on this example. Recall that one way of achieving cognitive effects is by contradicting and eliminating existing assumptions. When (11) is produced in response to (12), this line of interpretation becomes highly salient. In order to achieve the expected cognitive effects, the hearer must use the assumption that there was a dog in the car, which in turn becomes salient as an implicated contextual assumption. Similar points apply to (11b) and (11c). In (11b), for instance, the first part of the utterance raises the question of why the hearer should not go near the house. The second part of the utterance can be interpreted as an answer to this question on the assumption that the dog is near the house; this in turn becomes salient as an implicated contextual assumption. More generally, the more specific the expected cognitive effects, the more the interpretation process will be effect-driven, and the less the bridging assumptions will need to be independently accessible in advance of the interpretation process, e.g. as part of a frame. Conversely, the more accessible the intended bridging assumptions, the more the interpretation process will be effort-driven, and the less the hearer will need to have specific expectations about intended cognitive effects.

Discourse connectives provide another way of manipulating expectations about intended cognitive effects. The presence of a discourse connective can dramatically alter the interpretation of bridging examples, as the questionnaire results show. Thus, consider (33)–(36), where a discourse connective is added in the second member of the pair:

(33)   a. I prefer Edinburgh to London. I hate the snowy winters. [London 100%]
         b. I prefer Edinburgh to London. *However*, I hate the snowy winters. [Edinburgh 100%]

(34)   a. I prefer Italy to England. I hate the pasta there. [England 80%]
         b. I prefer Italy to England. *However*, I hate the pasta there. [Italy 100%]

(35)   a. I prefer the town to the country. The traffic really bothers me. [country 80%]
         b. I prefer the town to the country. *However*, the traffic really bothers me. [town 100%]

(36)   a. Kevin moved from New Zealand to England. He loves the sheep. [England 100%]
         b. Kevin moved from New Zealand to England. *However*, he loves the sheep. [New Zealand 80%]

In the relevance-based framework, discourse connectives are seen as guiding the search for relevance by constraining the choice of contexts and cognitive effects. Connectives like *but* and *however* encourage a 'denial of expectation' understanding (see e.g. Blakemore 1987; Moeschler 1989a; Luscher 1994), in which the second part of the utterance is understood as contradicting and eliminating a potential implication of the first part. The addition of such a discourse connective thus encourages specific expectations of cognitive effects, in turn increasing the accessibility of any background assumptions needed to obtain these effects. In this way, the relevance-theoretic framework integrates the effort and effect factors, and shows how they interact.

According to Erku and Gundel, a relevance-based approach should shed some light on the stylistic unacceptability of examples like (7) above, in which a highly accessible interpretation had to be rejected on grounds of factual implausibility. In fact, the questionnaire results suggest that participants are not particularly worried by these examples, and do not usually mark them as unacceptable. Relevance theory suggests that an utterance should be found unacceptable if the speaker manifestly could not have intended it to satisfy the addressee's expectation of relevance. This may be for reasons of effort, as in (10c)–(10d) above, where the obvious reformulations in (10a)–(10b) would manifestly have spared the addressee some gratuitous processing effort. Or it may be for reasons of effect, as in (33a) above, where although 100 per cent of participants chose *London* as antecedent, 60 per cent of them found the utterance unacceptable: presumably because it is hard to see how the speaker could reasonably have expected to convince them that she preferred Edinburgh to London on the ground that *London* had snowy winters. There should also be interesting interactions between effort and effect. For instance, consider (37), with the acceptability ratings shown in brackets:

(37)   a. Peter went to a Japanese restaurant. *The waitress* was from Osaka. [5.77]
        b. Peter went to a Japanese restaurant. *The cashier* was very friendly. [5.69]
        c. Peter went to a Japanese restaurant. *The poison* was in the fish. [4.23]
        d. Peter went to a Japanese restaurant. *The ambulance* came in 10 minutes. [2.46]

In the questionnaire, (37d) received a very low acceptability rating, presumably because the bridging assumption was considered too inaccessible given normal expectations of effect. Relevance theory predicts that this example could be made more acceptable either by increasing the accessibility of the bridging assumption, or by manipulating the audience's expectation of effect – for example, by producing the utterance as a one-liner in a Woody Allen stand-up routine. Results of this type would confirm the relevance-theoretic linkage between effort and effect.

Having sketched the assumptions of relevance theory and their application to some of the questionnaire examples, we would like to end by making some more direct comparisons between relevance-based and coherence-based approaches.

9.4   Comparing coherence theory and relevance theory

Let us start with an example that we have used several times, as presenting problems for both truth-based and coherence-based approaches:

(18)   I ran from the classroom to the playground. *The children* were making too much noise.

This utterance has two interpretations, on both of which the second part of the utterance can be seen as giving an Explanation for the event described in the first part. This presents a problem for the coherence-based approach, since knowing the intended coherence relation is not sufficient for reference resolution.

A paper on disambiguation by Asher and Lascarides (1995) suggests a possible solution: that where an evidential relation is involved, the hearer should choose the interpretation which provides most evidence for the expected conclusion. Consider their example (38):

(38)   a. They put a plant there. It ruined the view. [prediction: *plant* = 'factory']
        b. They put a plant there. It improved the view. [prediction: *plant* = 'tree']

The word *plant* is ambiguous. In this case, knowing the intended coherence relation is not sufficient for disambiguation, because whichever interpretation is chosen, the second part of the utterance will present a Result of the event described in the first part. According to Asher and Lascarides, a hearer in this situation should choose the interpretation that 'reinforces coherence relations': that is, the one *most likely* to lead to the result described, or that provides *most evidence* for an expected conclusion. On this approach, Asher and Lascarides suggest that *plant* in (38a) should be taken to mean FACTORY because a factory is most likely to ruin the view, while in (38b) it should be taken to mean TREE because a tree is most likely to improve the view. By the same token, *children* in (18) should be taken to mean THE CHILDREN IN THE PLAYGROUND or THE CHILDREN IN THE CLASSROOM, depending on which interpretation is seen as providing most evidence for the claim that the speaker ran from the classroom to the playground.

This approach is very similar to the strong, global truth-based approach discussed at the end of section 9.2.2.1, and shares many of the problems listed there. It also raises empirical problems for both coherence-based and truth-based approaches. In the first place, it suggests that the hearer of (38) will be unable to disambiguate the word *plant* correctly until the end of the following utterance. All the psycholinguistic evidence shows that tentative disambiguations are made online, but neither the coherence-based approach nor the strong global truth-based approach sheds any light on how this process works. By contrast, the relevance-theoretic comprehension procedure described in (30) above is compatible with the psycholinguistic evidence that hearers follow a path of least effort in the course of online disambiguation. It also sheds some light on how expectations of specific cognitive effects may alter the accessibility of interpretations.

A second empirical problem with Asher and Lascarides's proposal is that hearers do not always choose the interpretation that 'reinforces coherence relations', i.e. that provides the *most* evidence for an expected conclusion. Consider (39):

(39)   a. Many young people nowadays are unemployable. They can't even write a letter.
        b. John wrote a letter. His wife was unimpressed.

The phrase *write a letter* can mean either WRITE A LETTER OF THE ALPHABET or ENGAGE IN CORRESPONDENCE. In (39a) and (39b), it would typically be understood to mean ENGAGE IN CORRESPONDENCE. However, this is not what Asher and Lascarides's disambiguation strategy predicts. Each of (39a) and (39b) has two interpretations which fit the same evidential coherence relation: Explanation in (39a) and Result in (39b). According to Asher and Lascarides, the hearer should choose the interpretation that provides the most evidence for the expected conclusion. In (39a), he should therefore ask himself which would provide more evidence for the claim that young people are unemployable: that they can't write a letter of the alphabet, or that they can't engage in correspondence? Similarly, in (39b) he should ask himself which would be more likely to leave John's wife unimpressed: the fact that he wrote a letter of the alphabet, or the fact that he engaged in correspondence? In both cases, Asher and Lascarides's strategy would pick out the LETTER OF THE ALPHABET interpretation, and in both cases, this prediction would be wrong.

Relevance theory explains why. According to the relevance-theoretic comprehension procedure, hearers should follow a path of least effort in computing cognitive effects, and stop when their expectation of relevance is satisfied. For a variety of reasons having to do with both effort and effect, the most accessible interpretation of the phrase *write a letter* is ENGAGE IN CORRESPONDENCE. In the first place, it would normally be taken for granted that someone can write a letter of the alphabet; as a result, it is hard to see how this interpretation could be intended to achieve adequate effects in normal circumstances. By contrast, it is easy to see how the information that someone had engaged in correspondence might be intended to achieve adequate effects, and hearers are likely to develop a ready-made encyclopaedic schema giving easy access to these standard effects. Frequent use of the phrase in this interpretation should further increase its accessibility. Thus, the relevance-theoretic comprehension procedure gives some insight into the interpretation of these examples.

A further problem with coherence-based approaches to pragmatics is that they provide no account of how isolated utterances are understood. Consider (40), for example:

(40)   John wrote a letter.

According to Asher and Lascarides, this example would be disambiguated using 'domain information'; when (40) is embedded in a longer discourse, this domain-based interpretation could be overridden by considerations of coherence. The reference to 'domain information' would presumably involve some version of the truth-based pragmatic criterion, and would be subject to the same criticisms. Notice, also, that the two senses of *write a letter* stand in an entailment relation (one cannot engage in correspondence without writing a letter of the alphabet) so that the interpretation on which (40) means that John wrote a letter of the alphabet is always the more likely to be true. A strong truth-based criterion would therefore run into particular problems with this example. By contrast, the relevance-theoretic comprehension procedure works as well for (40) as it does for the longer discourses in (39).

Notice, too, that the coherence-based approach would have to provide some account of how to draw the line between truth-based and coherence-based processes. This is by no means straightforward, as is shown by the examples in (41):

(41)   a. John's a very very clever man.
          b. John's a very clever man, very.
          c. John's a very clever man, a very clever man.
          d. John's a very clever man. He's a very clever man.

All these utterances involve repetition: of a word in (41a) and (41b), a phrase in (41c), and a sentence in (41d). It would be nice to be able to offer a unitary account of how repetitions achieve their effects, but this is not possible on a coherence-based approach. On this approach, repetition of full sentences, as in (41d), is generally seen as involving a coherence relation of Elaboration, or Restatement. However, on the accounts outlined above, coherence relations are seen as holding only between units of discourse, and the question arises of how many units of discourse there are in (41a)–(41c). It seems implausible that mere repetition of a word, as in (41a), would introduce a separate unit of discourse. Hence, coherence-based approaches must provide separate accounts of repetition in single units and pairs of units, and must furthermore provide a cut-off point between (41a) and (41d).[4]

By contrast, the relevance-theoretic approach provides a straightforward account of all such cases. Repetition involves additional processing effort. On relevance-theoretic assumptions, this extra effort must be offset by extra effects, and according to the relevance-theoretic comprehension procedure, the hearer should follow a path of least effort in deriving these extra effects. Thus, the hearer of (41a)–(41d) would probably assume that John is cleverer than he would otherwise have thought (and since each successive utterance in the series demands greater effort, it would be interesting to investigate whether the level of expected effect increases accordingly). In this case, as in previous ones, the relevance-theoretic framework seems to explain a wider range of examples, more accurately and with less machinery, than the coherence-based approach.

9.5   Conclusion

This chapter had two main aims: first, to shed some light on the analysis of bridging, and second, to compare three recent approaches to pragmatics, based on notions of truth, coherence and relevance. We have tried to show that truth-based approaches are inadequate on their own, and that coherence-based approaches must generally be supplemented by some form of truth-based approach. Coherence-based approaches thus suffer from all the problems of truth-based approaches, and more besides. We have tried to show that the relevance-theoretic approach is preferable to the coherence-based approach on both descriptive and theoretical grounds: it applies as well to isolated utterances as to longer stretches of discourse; it provides a comprehension procedure which does not involve computing all possible interpretations and choosing the best one; it shows how expectations of relevance can affect the accessibility of candidate interpretations, and how accessibility can in turn affect acceptability; and it explains most of the intuitions of acceptability that coherence-based approaches were designed to explain. We would like to end by commenting briefly on the relations between the truth-based and relevance-based approaches.

Relevance theory, unlike most other approaches to pragmatics, has no independent maxim or convention of truthfulness. It does, however, assume that the assumptions entertained by an individual may vary in their strength (i.e. degree of evidence), and that the strength of input assumptions affects the strength of any cognitive effects. The stronger the cognitive effects, the greater the relevance. It follows that expectations of relevance may lead to expectations about the strength of input assumptions: that is, the factual plausibility of the proposition expressed by the utterance, and of the contextual assumptions needed to derive the expected cognitive effects. Since we have seen that expectations of relevance may affect the accessibility of candidate interpretations, it also follows that considerations of factual plausibility may affect the accessibility of bridging assumptions and candidate reference resolutions. Thus, the relevance-theoretic framework should be able to explain the intuitions about factual plausibility that underpin the truth-based approach.[5]

10 Mood and the analysis of non-declarative sentences

Deirdre Wilson and Dan Sperber

How are non-declarative sentences understood? How do they differ semantically from their declarative counterparts? Answers to these questions once made direct appeal to the notion of illocutionary force. When they proved unsatisfactory, the fault was diagnosed as a failure to distinguish properly between mood and force. For some years now, efforts have been under way to develop a satisfactory account of the semantics of mood. In this chapter, we consider the current achievements and future prospects of the mood-based semantic programme.

10.1 Distinguishing mood and force

Early speech-act theorists regarded illocutionary force as a properly semantic category. Sentence meaning was identified with illocutionary-force potential: to give the meaning of a sentence was to specify the range of speech acts that an utterance of that sentence could be used to perform. Typically, declarative sentences were seen as linked to the performance of assertive speech acts (committing the speaker to the truth of the proposition expressed), while imperative and interrogative sentences were linked to the performance of directive speech acts (requesting action and information, respectively). Within this framework, pragmatics, the theory of utterance interpretation, had at most the supplementary role of explaining how hearers, in context, choose an actual illocutionary force from among the potential illocutionary forces semantically assigned to the sentence uttered.

The speech-act semantic programme foundered on cases where sentence meaning and illocutionary-force potential come apart. For instance, declarative sentences are not always used to perform assertive speech acts. They 'occur unasserted' – and without change of meaning – in metaphor and irony, acting and impersonation, fiction and fantasy, jokes and example sentences, loose talk and rough approximations, and free indirect speech and thought; and as constituents of complex sentences: for example, in conditionals and disjunctions, or as subject or object complements. The fact that a sentence can retain its meaning although used without any of the potential forces semantically assigned to it is an argument against identifying meaning with force.

This suggests that illocutionary force is a pragmatic rather than a semantic category, a property not of sentences but only of utterances. What is it, then, that distinguishes declarative, imperative, and interrogative sentences on the purely semantic level? An answer increasingly proposed in the literature is that it is not force but mood.

Here, 'mood' should be taken not in its traditional syntactic sense, as referring to verbal inflection (e.g. indicative, imperative, optative), but in a semantic sense, as referring to the semantic or logical properties that distinguish, say, declarative sentences from imperative, interrogative and exclamative sentences. In the narrow syntactic sense, English has no interrogative or exclamative mood; in the semantic sense, at least if the mood-based semantic programme is to go through, it must. On this approach, each syntactic sentence type must be seen as determining a proprietary semantic mood common to literal and non-literal, serious and non-serious, embedded and non-embedded utterances of tokens of that type.[1] And, at least in non-literal, non-serious cases, determining the force of an utterance is no longer a simple matter of choosing among a range of potential forces semantically assigned to the sentence uttered.

The new mood-based programme has two interdependent tasks: to character-ise the semantic moods, and to describe the relation between mood and force. A crucial constraint on the overall account is that it should help to explain why utterances have the forces they do. As Donald Davidson (1979b) puts it,

> [A satisfactory theory of mood] must assign an element of meaning to utterances in a given mood that is not present in utterances in other moods. And this element should connect with the difference in force between assertions, questions and commands in such a way as to explain our intuition of a conventional relation between mood and use. (Davidson 1979b/1984: 116)

Thus, sentence meaning, and in particular the meaning of mood, must interact with contextual assumptions and pragmatic principles to yield a satisfactory account of how utterances are understood.

The new, mood-based programme, then, is really a combined semantic and pragmatic programme. Differences in the semantic characterisation of mood often result from differences in assumptions about the nature and role of prag-matics. Is pragmatic interpretation carried out by code-like rules or conventions, or by inferential enrichment based on contextual assumptions and general prag-matic principles? We want to propose an inferential treatment of the relation between mood and force.

We will argue that most existing mood-based proposals are in fact empirically inadequate, and will briefly sketch an alternative account. This alternative account, however, casts doubt on a fundamental, though implicit, assumption of the mood-based programme, and thus on this programme's general feasibility.

10.2   Characterising imperative mood

Given a powerful enough pragmatic theory, the moods themselves might be treated as semantically primitive, mere notational inputs to code-like rules or conventions of pragmatic interpretation. This is how we propose to understand the claim that mood is a conventional indicator of force. On this account, although mood is distinct from force, there is nothing more to understanding a mood than simply knowing the range of speech acts it is conventionally, or standardly, used to perform. As R. M. Hare (1970) puts it,

When we say that 'The cat is on the mat' is a typical indicative (when we mention its mood, that is), we identify the type of speech act which it is standardly used to perform. Thus mood signs ... classify sentences according to the speech acts to which they are assigned by the conventions which give meanings to those signs. (Hare 1970/ 1971: 91)

Here, the whole burden of interpretation is left to pragmatics, which must describe not only the range of 'standard' forces and how the appropriate member of this range is chosen in context, but also how, in 'non-standard' cases, the conventional correlation between mood and force can break down, and what the effects of the breakdown will be.

The conventional correlation between mood and force is generally seen as breaking down in two main ways: in non-literal or non-serious utterances, and under embedding. For the moment, we will leave these two types of case aside, and consider various proposals about the standard or conventional force of imperative mood.[2]

Take the claim that imperative utterances are standardly used with directive force, where a directive act is defined as an attempt to get the hearer to perform the action described by the proposition expressed. The following look like clear counterexamples, in that a main-clause imperative is literally and seriously used without the predicted directive force:

Advice

(1)   a. PETER: Excuse me, I want to get to the station.
        b. MARY: Take a number 3 bus.

Here, Mary is advising Peter what to do. There is no reason to think she cares whether Peter follows her advice, and hence no reason to analyse her utterance as an attempt to get Peter to take a number 3 bus.

Permission

(2)   a. PETER: Can I open the window?
        b. MARY: Oh, open it, then.

Here, Mary is giving Peter permission to open the window. There is no reason to think she cares whether Peter performs the permitted action, and hence no reason to analyse her utterances as an attempt to get him to open the window.

Threats and dares

Mary, seeing Peter about to throw a snowball, says threateningly:

(3)   Go on. Throw it. Just you dare.

Mary's utterance is not an attempt to get Peter to throw the snowball – on the contrary.

Good wishes

Mary, visiting Peter in hospital, says:

(4)   Get well soon.

Since the 'action' described is not under Peter's control, there is no reason to analyse Mary's utterance as an attempt to get Peter to perform it.

Audienceless cases

Imperatives can be used in the absence of an agent or hearer, as when Mary looks at the sky and says:

(5)   Please don't rain,

or gets into her car and mutters:

(6)   Start, damn you.

The absence of both hearer and agent makes it hard to see these utterances as attempts to get someone to perform the action described.

Predetermined cases

Imagine a child, sent to apologise to someone, thinking to herself as she reluctantly approaches his door:

(7)   Please be out.

Or a mother, whose notoriously ill-tempered child has been sent to apologise to someone, thinking to herself as the child arrives home:

(8)   Please don't have made things worse.

Here, not only is there no hearer, but the events described have already happened (or failed to happen), and cannot be affected by what is said. Again, the predictions made by the directive analysis of imperatives are not borne out.

We know of no analysis of imperative mood as a conventional indicator of force that deals satisfactorily with the full range of examples listed above. For instance, Susan Schmerling (1982), who discusses many of them, offers the following alternative: a serious, literal imperative counts as an attempt by the speaker to bring about the state of affairs described by the proposition expressed (but not necessarily an attempt by the speaker to get the *hearer* to bring about this state of affairs). While this proposal would deal with good wishes, audienceless cases and predetermined cases, it does not handle advice, permission, threats or dares.

John Searle (1975a) defines directive speech acts as attempts by the speaker to get the hearer to perform some action (but not necessarily the action described by the proposition expressed). While this proposal would deal with threats and dares, it sheds no light on our other categories of example. It also creates a new problem: how does the hearer decide which action the speaker wants him to perform?

One could, of course, abandon the search for a unitary analysis, and say simply, as Jennifer Hornsby (1988) seems to do, that the imperative mood in English can be used with the force of a request, command, advice, permission, threat, dare, good wish, and so on. This squares with the description of mood as a conventional indicator of force. However, it also means abandoning any attempt at an explanatory account of the relation between mood and force. Why, in language after language, do imperative sentences have just this cluster of uses? We should surely be looking for a characterisation of mood that enables us not merely to describe but to explain these facts.

All this suggests that mood cannot be satisfactorily analysed as a conventional indicator of force. However, this is not the end of the mood-based programme. It might be possible to assign the moods some intrinsic semantic content that would lay a satisfactory foundation for an explanatory pragmatic account of force. Truth-conditional semanticists typically look for some analogue of truth conditions to assign to non-declarative sentences. For example, Colin McGinn (1977) treats imperatives as having not truth conditions but fulfilment conditions, which are satisfied if and only if the state of affairs described by the imperative is 'made the case'.[3]

Could this semantic characterisation interact with contextual assumptions and pragmatic principles to yield an explanatory account of the full range of forces with which imperative sentences can be uttered? It is hard to tell, since little is said about the pragmatic principles with which the semantic characterisation is supposed to interact. Standardly, a connection is made, via a pragmatic maxim of truthfulness (e.g. 'Do not say what you believe to be false'), between declarative utterances and expressions of belief. Let us suppose there is an analogous maxim connecting imperative utterances with expressions of desire, so that the speaker of an imperative utterance would be understood as communicating a desire that the state of affairs described should be 'made the case'.

Then advice, permission, threats and dares – which, as we have seen, need communicate no such desires – are counterexamples to this analysis. But then again, if there is no connection between imperative utterances and expressions of some attitude at least akin to desire, it is hard to see why the hearer of an imperative utterance should ever recognise that the speaker wants him to bring about the state of affairs described.

Even assuming that this problem could be solved, some of our examples (1)–(8) would still be troublesome for a framework such as McGinn's. With good wishes such as 'Get well soon', audienceless cases such as 'Please don't rain', and predetermined cases such as 'Please don't have made things worse', the state of affairs described is under no-one's control, and so nothing is 'made the case'. Nor is there any obvious reason to regard these utterances as non-serious or non-literal. This suggests that McGinn's analysis, and any analysis that replaces truth conditions with fulfilment, obedience or compliance conditions, is empirically inadequate.

Martin Huntley (1984) makes a more radical semantic proposal. The distinction between declarative and imperative sentences, he argues, is a special case of a more general semantic distinction between indicative and non-indicative mood. Semantically, indicatives 'involve indexical reference to the actual world', whereas non-indicatives (i.e. imperatives, infinitival clauses and non-finite 'that'-clauses) do not. As a result, non-indicatives, and imperatives in particular, can 'represent a situation as being merely envisaged as a possibility, with no commitment as to whether it obtains, in past, present or future, in this world' (1984: 122). This proposal is a radical departure from those considered so far, in that it makes no reference, even indirectly, to notions from the theory of force. The question is, as Huntley acknowledges, whether it lays an adequate semantic foundation for the prediction of illocutionary force.

It seems to us that it does not. It is hard to see why a hearer should conclude, from the mere fact that the speaker is envisaging a certain situation as a possibility, that he is being requested, advised, permitted, etc., to bring it about. There is a crucial difference between imperatives and infinitival clauses in this respect. As Huntley predicts, the speaker of the infinitival utterances (9a) and (9b) can envisage a certain state of affairs without necessarily representing it as either achievable or desirable:

(9)   a. To spend all one's life in the same room. Imagine.
        b. To meet the president of the United States. Hmm!

Thus, as one might expect, (9a) and (9b), and infinitival clauses in general, can be seriously and literally uttered without imperatival force (that is, without being intended or understood as orders, requests, advice, permission, good wishes, or any of the other speech acts standardly performed by imperative utterances). By the same token, Huntley's analysis predicts that imperatives can be seriously and literally uttered without imperatival force. But of course, they can't. We conclude that imperatives and infinitival clauses cannot be treated as semantically equivalent.

We want to suggest that the crucial semantic and pragmatic differences between imperatives and infinitival clauses are linked to the notions of achievability and desirability: the semantic analysis of imperatives must make reference to these notions, while the semantic analysis of infinitival clauses need not. This is not to say that infinitival clauses can never be used with imperatival force. When can they be so used? When it is clear in the context that the state of affairs 'envisaged as a possibility' is also regarded by the speaker as both achievable and desirable. Why do serious, literal imperatives have the imperatival forces they do? Because the notions of achievability and desirability are there from the start, as part of the meaning of imperative sentences themselves. We believe that this semantic characterisation can interact with additional contextual assumptions and general pragmatic principles to yield an explanatory account of the full range of imperative utterances, including those in (1)–(8). Here is a sketch of how an account along these lines might go.

We start from the fairly standard assumption that thoughts can be entertained, and the utterances that express them can be used, as descriptions (i.e. truth-conditional representations) of states of affairs in different types of world. In particular, they can be entertained or used as descriptions of states of affairs in the actual world, or in alternative possible worlds, some of which may be not only possible but *desirable*, while others may be not only possible but *potential*, where a potential world is compatible with the individual's assumptions about the actual world, and may therefore be, or become, actual. Different linguistic constructions might then be semantically specialised for use with descriptions of states of affairs in different types of world. For instance, imperative sentences may be specialised for describing states of affairs in worlds which are regarded as both *potential* and *desirable*.

In the simplest types of case, an imperative is used to describe a state of affairs which is regarded as both potential and desirable by the speaker herself. Notice that desirability is a three-place relation: x regards y as desirable from the point of view of z. Normally, in using an imperative, the speaker has some specific person z (typically, either herself or her hearer) in mind, and expects the hearer to recognise who this is and interpret the utterance accordingly. This semantic characterisation of imperatives is thus compatible with a number of different, more specific, pragmatic interpretations. We will argue that serious, literal imperatives fall into two broad pragmatic categories, depending on how this semantic indeterminacy is pragmatically resolved.

With requests, commands, orders, good wishes, audienceless and predetermined cases, the indeterminacy is resolved in favour of the speaker, who is understood as indicating that the state of affairs described is desirable from her own point of view. Within this broad category of cases, additional contextual assumptions are needed to distinguish the subcategories familiar from the work of speech-act theorists.

For example, if the hearer is manifestly in a position to bring about the state of affairs described, the utterance will have the force of something like a request, command, order or plea. These subcategories are distinguishable from each other by manifest assumptions about the social and physical relations between speaker and hearer, and about the degree of desirability of the state of affairs described.

Good wishes fall into the same broad category as requests, but require two additional assumptions: first, the speaker manifestly believes that neither she nor her hearer is in a position to bring about the state of affairs described, and second, she manifestly regards this state of affairs as beneficial to the hearer. Audienceless and predetermined cases are also types of wish, though here the assumption is that the state of affairs described will be beneficial to the speaker, and there need be no hearer present at all.

Advice and permission belong to the other broad category of imperative utterances, in which the semantic indeterminacy is resolved in favour of the hearer: the speaker communicates that the state of affairs described is desirable not from her own point of view but from her hearer's. When Mary advises Peter to take a number 3 bus, she indicates that from his point of view it would be desirable to take that particular bus, given that he wants to get to the station. With permission, the indeterminacy is again resolved in favour of the hearer, but what is at issue is the potentiality rather than the desirability of the state of affairs described. When Peter asks Mary if he can open the window, he represents a certain state of affairs as desirable from his own point of view, but expresses doubts about its potentiality, given that Mary can refuse to let him open it. By saying 'Oh, open it, then', Mary incidentally concedes the desirability (to Peter) of this state of affairs, but more importantly, she guarantees its potentiality, thus removing the only obstacle to Peter's opening the window.

On the account just sketched, the relation between linguistic form and force (or, more generally, pragmatic interpretation) is mediated by a direct semantic link between linguistic form and representations of propositional attitude. The intrinsic semantic properties of imperative form are characterisable in terms of a complex propositional attitude, itself analysable into two more elementary attitudes: the belief that a certain state of affairs is potential, and the belief that it is desirable from someone's point of view. These elementary attitudes recur in the analysis of other linguistic constructions. For instance, the difference between hortatives and optatives seems to be that while both involve assumptions about desirability, only hortatives involve assumptions about potentiality: one can wish for, but not exhort someone to bring about, states of affairs that one knows to be unachievable. The proposed treatment of imperatives might thus form the basis for a rather more general account.

Notice that the semantic characterisation we have proposed makes no reference to terms from the theory of force. However, we have shown that, unlike Huntley's characterisation, it does lay an adequate foundation for an explanatory account of force. The force of an imperative utterance is determined, on the one hand, by the fact that the speaker has represented a certain state of affairs as both potential and desirable, and on the other hand, by manifest contextual assumptions. So far, we have said nothing about the general pragmatic principles by which contextual assumptions are selected and semantic indeterminacies resolved. Answers to these questions will be sketched below.

10.3   Explaining non-literal, non-serious cases

Most work on the semantics of non-declarative sentences treats the interpretation of non-literal, non-serious cases – for example, metaphor, irony, impersonations, jokes and example sentences – as a purely pragmatic matter: it is assumed that, semantically, there is nothing to distinguish them from literal, serious cases. Since we think these non-literal cases hold the key to the analysis of interrogative sentences, we will discuss them briefly here.

In our book *Relevance* (1986a: chapter 4, section 7), we argued that there are two fundamentally different types of representation, and therefore two fundamentally different uses to which thoughts or utterances can be put. On the one hand, there is *descriptive* representation, which is a relation between thoughts or utterances and possible or actual states of affairs which make (or would make) them true. On the other hand, there is *interpretive* representation, which is a relation between thoughts or utterances and other thoughts or utterances that they resemble in content. While the notion of descriptive representation is quite familiar, the notion of interpretive representation is less so. We see interpretive representation as playing a fundamental role in the analysis of both non-literal utterances and interrogatives.

In appropriate conditions, any object in the world can be used to represent another object that it resembles. You ask me what is the shape of Brazil, and I point to an appropriately shaped cloud in the sky; I encourage you to buy me another drink by imitating the act of drinking; I make fun of someone by mimicking his walk. It follows that any utterance can be used to represent another object that it resembles. In direct quotation, an utterance is used to represent another utterance that it resembles in linguistic form, while in indirect quotation, an utterance is used to represent another utterance or thought that it resembles in propositional content. Indirect quotation of speech or thought is a typical example of *interpretive representation*, based on *interpretive* resemblances between two items with a propositional content.

In *Relevance* (1986a: chapter 4, section 7), we analyse interpretive resemblance in terms of shared analytic and contextual implications. The *analytic implications* of a proposition P are its non-trivial logical implications; these remain invariant from context to context. The *contextual implications* of a proposition P, by contrast, are determined by the context (i.e. the set of mentally represented background assumptions) in which it is processed. The contextual implications of a proposition P in a context C are those propositions logically implied by the union of P and C, but by neither P nor C alone. On this approach, any thought or utterance can be used to represent another thought or utterance that it interpretively resembles – that is, with which it shares analytic or contextual implications.

Interpretive resemblance is a matter of degree. At one extreme, two utterances or thoughts may share no analytic or contextual implications when processed in a given context, and thus not resemble each other interpretively at all. At the other extreme lies full identity of analytic and contextual implications. When a thought or utterance P is used to represent another thought or utterance Q that it resembles in content, P is a *literal* interpretation of Q if and only if P and Q share all their analytic and contextual implications. Literalness, so defined, is a special case of interpretive resemblance.

In a framework with a maxim, norm or convention of literal truthfulness, utterances are expected to be fully literal interpretations of the speaker's thoughts. We reject the maxim of truthfulness and the assumption that non-literalness involves a departure from the norms of communication. We have argued instead that the expectation crucial to communication is one not of literal truthfulness but of optimal relevance, where in order to be optimally relevant, an utterance must convey enough contextual implications to be worth the hearer's attention, and put the hearer to no unjustifiable effort in obtaining them (Sperber and Wilson 1987a, 1987b).

In this framework, loose talk and metaphor arise naturally in the search for optimal relevance. Suppose that a speaker has a complex thought P, with many implications, which it would not be economical to spell out explicitly. Still, these implications are easily derivable from utterance Q when it is processed in an appropriate context. Q also has further implications which do not form part of the speaker's thought, and which she does not want to convey. For a hearer with an expectation of optimal relevance rather than literal truthfulness, Q may well be the most economical way of conveying the speaker's meaning (Sperber and Wilson 1986a, 1986b).

To illustrate, consider the following metaphorical imperative:

(10)   Build your own road through life.

In interpreting this utterance, the hearer's task is to identify a subset of its analytic and contextual implications which the speaker might reasonably have expected to make it relevant enough to be worth his attention, and which could not have been more economically conveyed by some other easily available utterance. By processing (10) in the context of his encyclopaedic knowledge of road building, he might derive such implications as: 'Do not follow the lead of others', 'Make up your own mind what to do and where to go', 'Plan your life', 'Aim at consistency and continuity', 'Be creative', and so on. These are all implications that a speaker aiming at optimal relevance might have intended to convey. Other implications, for instance, 'Buy a steamroller', 'Take a course in engineering', and 'Submit your plans to the Department of Transport', are inconsistent with information given elsewhere in the utterance (e.g. the instruction to build a road through *life*), or with manifest assumptions about what the speaker might reasonably have intended to communicate in the circumstances.

In *Relevance*, we argued that a given utterance has no more than a single interpretation (or a small range of roughly equivalent interpretations) that a given hearer can take a rational speaker to have intended to convey. To be optimally relevant, an utterance must yield enough implications to be worth the hearer's attention, and put the hearer to no gratuitous effort. Although many interpretations might yield enough implications to be worth the hearer's attention, only the most accessible of these will yield these implications for no gratuitous effort. In deciding which implications the speaker intended to convey, the hearer should thus select the minimal (because most easily accessible) subset. In other words, he should take the utterance to be fully literal only if nothing less than full literalness will do. Thus, if a rational speaker aiming at optimal relevance could have intended to convey some, but not all, of the implications obtainable by processing (10) in an appropriate context, then that is how she should be understood.

In the first instance, then, every utterance is presented as a more or less literal interpretation of the thought of the speaker. But a thought itself may be descriptively or interpretively used: it may be entertained as a description of a state of affairs in an actual, possible, potential or desirable world, or as an interpretive representation of other thoughts that it resembles in content. For example, Mary may entertain the thought that Peter is unhappy, not as a description of the actual world, but as an interpretive representation of what he said or implied. She may indicate this explicitly by saying 'Peter says he is unhappy'; or (in appropriate circumstances) she may say, simply, 'Peter is unhappy', expecting the hearer to understand that she is representing not what she takes to be Peter's actual mental state, but what she takes him to have said or implied. In that case, her utterance would be *tacitly interpretive*.

Tacitly interpretive utterances can be used not only to report someone else's utterances or thoughts, but also to express the speaker's attitude – positive or negative, approving or disapproving – to the attributed thoughts. In *Relevance* (chapter 4, section 9), we described such utterances as *echoic*, and analysed verbal irony as a case of echoic interpretive use: the speaker echoes a thought which she attributes to some other person or group of people, while tacitly dissociating herself from it as ludicrously false or inappropriate.

To illustrate, consider the following exchange:

(11)   a. PETER: Can I open the window?
        b. MARY: Go ahead and let in some nice Arctic air.

Here, Mary's utterance would plausibly be understood as ironical. On that interpretation, she is not giving Peter permission to open the window. On the contrary, she is suggesting that it was ridiculous of him even to think of asking her permission. He could only have done so, she implies, if he thought she liked to be freezing cold. By caricaturing this attributed thought (that is, by offering a less-than-literal interpretation of it), Mary makes it clear that she dissociates herself from it and finds it ridiculous.

So far, we have considered two main types of interpretive utterance. An utterance may be a more or less literal interpretation of the speaker's thought, which may itself be an interpretation of a thought attributed to someone other than the speaker (or the speaker herself at another time). Utterances of example sentences in linguistic or philosophical discussion might be seen as illustrating a third type of interpretive use. The example token may be interpretively used to represent an utterance or thought type that it resembles in content. For instance, we used example (10) above to represent a certain type of imperative utterance or thought. This example, though interpretively used, was not used to attribute a thought or utterance to any actual person or type of person: it was used to represent a possible, or potential, but non-attributed, utterance or thought. In the next section, we will argue that interrogative sentences belong to yet another category of interpretive use: they are specialised for representing not descriptive thoughts, nor attributed thoughts, nor possible or potential thoughts, but *desirable* thoughts.

10.4   Characterising interrogative mood

The literature on interrogatives parallels the literature on imperatives: some people treat interrogative mood as a conventional indicator of force; others try to assign it some intrinsic semantic content that would interact with contextual assumptions and pragmatic principles to yield a more explanatory account. We will argue that most existing analyses are empirically inadequate.

Take the claim that interrogatives standardly or conventionally have the force of questions, where a question is defined as a request for information. As Bach and Harnish (1979: 40) put it,

Questions are special cases of requests, special in that what is requested is that the speaker provide the hearer with certain information.

This is perhaps the standard speech-act account of interrogatives. Let us assume that a speaker cannot appropriately request information that she already has, or that she knows the hearer is unable to provide. Then even when non-serious, non-literal and embedded cases are left aside, the following look like clear counterexamples, in that a main-clause interrogative is literally and seriously used without the predicted force:

Rhetorical questions

Peter has made a New Year's resolution to give up smoking. As he lights up on New Year's Day, Mary says to him:

(12)   What was your New Year's resolution?

It is clear in the circumstances that Mary already knows the answer, and that her utterance is not a request for information. Intuitively, rhetorical questions of this type function as reminders, and do not call for any overt response.

Exam questions

Examiners usually know more about the subject than examinees, and it would be odd to treat exam questions as requests for information.

Guess questions

Mary hides a sweet in her hand, puts both hands behind her back, and says to Peter:

(13)   Which hand is it in?

Her utterance doubly fails to fit the standard speech-act account: the questioner already knows the answer, whereas the hearer doesn't and can at best make a guess. These cases bear obvious similarities to exam questions.

Surprise questions

Consider the following exchange:

(14)   a. PETER: The president has resigned.
         b. MARY: Good heavens. Has he?

It seems inappropriate to describe Mary's utterance as a request for information which she was given only a few seconds ago. Intuitively, (14b) expresses Mary's surprise or incredulity at the information she has been given. As such, it is a counterexample to the standard speech-act account.

Expository questions

Often, a writer or speaker asks a question in order to arouse the audience's interest in an answer that she plans to give herself. At the beginning of this chapter we asked two such expository questions. They are better seen as offers of information than as requests for information.

Self-addressed questions

When Mary says to herself 'Now why did I say that?' she is better seen as wondering why she said what she did than requesting information – which she could appropriately request from herself only if she simultaneously possessed and lacked it.

Speculative questions

When Mary thinks to herself, or asks Peter idly, 'What is the best analysis of interrogative sentences?' there is even less reason to analyse her utterance as a request for information. Mary may know that she does not know the answer; she may know that Peter does not know the answer; she may know that no-one knows the answer. On the speech-act account, there is no point in asking a question unless you think your hearer may be able to provide the answer. This rules out all speculative questions: that is, all questions which are of more than passing interest.

Martin Bell (1975), who discusses many of these examples, proposes a weakened speech-act account on which 'standard' questions are treated as requests to tell rather than to inform: the assumption being that one can appropriately request a hearer to tell one something one already knows. While this would deal with exam questions and guess questions, it does not handle rhetorical questions, surprise questions, expository questions, self-addressed questions or speculative questions.

John Lyons, in a more radical departure from the standard speech-act account, argues that interrogatives are conventionally used not to ask questions but to 'pose' them:

When we pose a question, we merely give expression to, or externalise, our doubt; and we can pose questions which we do not merely expect to remain unanswered, but which we know, or believe, to be unanswerable. (Lyons 1977: 755)

The problem with this proposal is that not all interrogative utterances are expressions of doubt (at least doubt about the correct answer). In exam questions, guess questions, surprise questions, expository questions, and many types of rhetorical question (e.g. (12) above), the speaker is in no doubt about the correct answer, and a different type of analysis is required.

All this suggests that interrogative mood cannot be satisfactorily analysed as a conventional indicator of force: interrogative sentences must instead be assigned some intrinsic semantic content that will lay an adequate foundation for an explanatory account of force.

Within truth-conditional frameworks, some analogue of truth conditions has been sought for interrogatives, as for imperatives. Hamblin (1973), for example, treats interrogatives as denoting their sets of possible answers, and Karttunen (1977) treats them as denoting their sets of true answers. The main problem with this approach is that it provides no obvious explanation of the pragmatic differences among positive questions such as (15), negative questions such as (16) and alternative questions such as (17):

(15)   Did you see Susan?

(16)   Didn't you see Susan?

(17)   Did you or did you not see Susan?

Each of these questions has the possible answers 'Yes' and 'No', and a true answer to any one is a true answer to all. For Hamblin and Karttunen, (15)–(17) should thus be synonymous. Why is it, then, that while utterances of (15) are generally neutral in tone, the speaker of (16) suggests that she had expected the hearer to see Susan, and (17) sounds impatient or hectoring?[4]

Bolinger (1978) develops this point at length, with a wealth of convincing examples. He goes on to argue that indirect questions introduced by 'if' are not synonymous with those introduced by 'whether': the former are embedded versions of *yes–no* questions such as (15) and (16), while the latter are embedded versions of alternative questions such as (17). This indirectly supports the claim that *yes–no* questions are not synonymous with their alternative counterparts.

Bolinger concludes that *yes–no* questions such as (15) and (16) are semantically very similar to conditionals:

Both conditionals and YNQs [*yes–no* questions] are hypotheses. A conditional hypothesises that something is true and draws a conclusion from it. A YNQ hypothesises that something is true and confirmed, amended or disconfirmed by a hearer. (Bolinger 1978: 102)

While Bolinger's criticisms of existing approaches seem to us well founded, his own account is empirically inadequate. In the first place, if interrogatives are a type of hypothesis, they should have the illocutionary force of hypotheses. Yet typically, to make a hypothesis is to commit oneself, however tentatively or temporarily, to its truth, whereas to ask a *yes–no* question is not. Bolinger's account offers no explanation of why this might be so. Moreover, there are *yes–no* versions of rhetorical questions, guess questions, exam questions, expository questions and audienceless cases, and contrary to what Bolinger predicts, none of these is a request for confirmation, disconfirmation or amendment by a hearer. Nor is it obvious that Bolinger's account of *yes–no* questions can be generalised to handle *wh*-questions.

It seems, then, that there is no satisfactory existing analysis of interrogative mood. We believe there is a reason for this failure. Interrogatives do have some intrinsic semantic content in virtue of their interrogative form, but this content is not analysable in anything approaching truth-conditional terms. In the terms outlined in the last section, interrogatives are semantically specialised not for descriptive but for interpretive use. In the simplest, most intuitive terms, interrogatives are interpretively used to represent what the speaker regards as relevant answers.

On this account, interrogative utterances, like echoic utterances, are doubly interpretive: they interpretively represent a thought of the speaker's, which itself interpretively represents another utterance or thought. However, while echoic utterances are used to represent *attributed* thoughts, interrogative utterances are used to represent *desirable* thoughts.[5]

What makes a thought desirable? In *Relevance*, we argued that a thought is desirable only if it is relevant – that is, only if it is rich enough in cognitive effects (e.g. contextual implications) to be worth the individual's attention. To regard a certain thought as desirable to someone is thus to regard it as relevant enough to be worthy of his attention. The claim that interrogatives represent desirable thoughts thus amounts to the claim that they represent not possible answers, nor true answers, but *relevant* answers.

How does the hearer decide what answer the speaker would regard as relevant? In the case of *yes–no* questions, the solution is straightforward. A positive question expresses a positive proposition, a negative question expresses a negative proposition, and an alternative question expresses both a positive and a negative proposition. The easiest assumption for the hearer to make, and thus the assumption favoured by considerations of relevance, is that the speaker has chosen to express the very proposition she would regard as relevant if true. That is, a positive question such as (15) indicates that a positive answer would be, if anything, more relevant than a negative one, a negative question such as (16) suggests that a negative answer would be, if anything, more relevant than a positive one, and an alternative question such as (17) indicates that a positive and a negative answer would be equally relevant. Although we have not the space to show it here, this analysis should interact with considerations of relevance, and in particular with considerations of effort, to account for the pragmatic differences among utterances of (15)–(17).

Although *wh*-questions do not express complete propositions but merely incomplete logical forms, we claim that they are interpretively used to represent complete propositions that they resemble. Which complete propositions? The natural assumption, and hence the assumption favoured by considerations of relevance, is that they represent completions of the incomplete logical forms they express. In other words, the speaker of a *wh*-question expresses an incomplete logical form, and indicates that she would regard some completion of it as relevant if true.

On this account, interrogatives are the interpretive counterpart of imperatives, which are used to represent desirable states of affairs. As with imperatives, desirability introduces an element of indeterminacy, which must be pragmatically resolved by making some assumption about who it is that, according to the speaker, would regard the thought in question as desirable. As always, the first assumption that yields an acceptable interpretation is the only such assumption, and is the one the hearer should choose.

Like imperatives, interrogatives fall into two broad pragmatic types, depending on how the semantic indeterminacy is resolved. With requests for information, exam questions, guess questions, surprise questions, self-addressed questions and speculative questions, the indeterminacy is resolved in favour of the speaker, who indicates that she would regard the answer as relevant to herself. Further contextual assumptions are needed to distinguish among the various subtypes of this broad type.

Consider the following exchange:

(18)   a. MARY: Where did I leave my keys?
          b. PETER: In the kitchen drawer.

Suppose that Mary manifestly regards an answer to her question as desirable to herself, manifestly expects Peter to know the answer, and manifestly expects him to supply it. Then (18a) would have the force of a request for information. Suppose that while Mary manifestly regards an answer as desirable to herself, she is manifestly not addressing Peter. Then (18a) would have the force of a self-addressed question or speculation.

Still within the same broad pragmatic category of questions, suppose that Mary manifestly expects Peter to answer her question; but suppose, moreover, that she is manifestly in a better position than he is to know the answer – say, because she has just hidden the keys herself. Then (18a) would have the force of a request for an answer, but not a request for information. How can this be? Peter's answer (18b), like any utterance, expresses both a proposition and an attitude, and may be relevant in a variety of ways: for example, by providing evidence about the state of affairs it describes, or by providing evidence about Peter's beliefs about this state of affairs. If Mary's utterance had been a request for information, Peter's response would have been relevant in the first of these two ways; if, as we are imagining, Mary's utterance is a guess question, Peter's response might be relevant in the second way: by providing information about Peter's beliefs, his ability to predict Mary's actions, his willingness to cooperate with her, and so on. Exam questions might be dealt with along similar lines.[6]

With rhetorical and expository questions, the semantic indeterminacy is resolved in the hearer's favour: the speaker indicates that she regards the answer as relevant to him. Consider the following exchange:

(19)   a. PETER: Will they keep their promises?
          b. MARY: Have politicians ever kept their promises?

Here, Mary's utterance could be a genuine request for information. Suppose, though, that Mary manifestly regards the answer as relevant to Peter rather than to herself, manifestly knows the answer herself, and is manifestly prepared to give it. Then (19b) would have the force of an expository question or offer of information. Suppose, instead, that though she manifestly regards the answer as relevant to Peter, she also manifestly expects him to know it already, or to be in a position to work it out for himself without being told. Then (19b) would be a rhetorical question with the force of a reminder. Expository questions and rhetorical questions thus fit naturally into the framework.

In this section, we have tried to show that existing analyses of interrogative mood are empirically inadequate, and to present an alternative account that lays an adequate semantic foundation for the prediction of illocutionary force. Fundamental to our account have been the notions of interpretive representation and of a desirable (i.e. relevant) thought. Notice that our semantic analysis of interrogatives parallels our semantic analysis of imperatives in two important respects: first, it makes no direct reference to terms from the theory of force; and second, it relies heavily on semantic indeterminacy and the claim that such indeterminacy is resolved during the process of pragmatic interpretation.

On this account, the pragmatic force of an interrogative utterance is determined, on the one hand, by the fact that the speaker has represented a certain thought as desirable to someone, and on the other, by manifest contextual assumptions. How are contextual assumptions selected and semantic indeterminacies resolved? Here we have appealed to a single, general pragmatic principle, based on a notion of optimal relevance, and argued that in resolving semantic and contextual indeterminacies, a rational hearer should select the first interpretation (if any) that a rational speaker aiming at optimal relevance might have intended to convey. This completes our sketch of the semantics and pragmatics of imperatives and interrogatives.

10.5   Conclusion

The account just sketched is far from complete: we have ignored embedded cases, jokes, fantasies and fictions, threats and pseudo-imperatives, surprise questions and other types of echoic question, and 'minor sentence types' (e.g. exclamative, optative, hortative). However, we hope to have shown that an approach along these lines is both feasible and generalisable. In this last section, we consider its implications for analyses based on mood.

We have argued for a direct semantic link between linguistic form and representations of propositional attitude. Imperative sentences (or rather, such characteristic features as imperative verb inflection, negative marking and imperative particles such as 'please') are linked to representations of potentiality and desirability. Interrogative sentences (or rather such characteristic features as interrogative word order, intonation and interrogative particles) are also linked to representations of desirability, in this case desirability of a thought rather than a state of affairs. Are we claiming, then, to have a satisfactory analysis of the semantic moods?

Not really – because we see no reason to assume that semantic moods exist. As we understand it, there is an implicit assumption behind mood-based approaches that we would want to question. The assumption is that the moods are unanalysable and mutually exclusive semantic categories: that every sentence belongs to one and only one mood, which is not itself decomposable into more elementary moods.

It is easy to think of grounds for questioning this assumption. For instance, many languages have two types of interrogative sentence: those with an indicative verb, which expect an indicative answer, and those with a subjunctive verb, which expect a subjunctive answer. The Omotic languages of Southern Ethiopia have both indicative and imperative interrogatives – that is, interrogatives with an imperative verb, which expect an imperative answer. In each case, the meaning of the interrogative is a function of the meaning of the interrogative marker, on the one hand, and of indicative, subjunctive or imperative verb form, on the other. On the assumption that every syntactic sentence type determines a distinct and unanalysable mood, it would be surprising if a hearer encountering, say, an imperative interrogative for the first time was able to understand it. On our account, a hearer who already understood imperatives, on the one hand, and indicative interrogatives, on the other, should automatically understand imperative questions. This claim could be easily tested.

More seriously, what we see as the fundamental distinction between interpretive and descriptive use cross-cuts any distinction among sentence types, and hence any distinction among semantic moods. As we have shown, every utterance – whatever its syntactic or semantic type – is in the first instance a more or less literal interpretation of a thought of the speaker's. This fact is not linguistically encoded in any way. Nor is the distinction between literal and less-than-literal interpretation. Although there are one or two linguistic indicators of loose use (e.g. hedges, or the use of 'oh' in 'There were, oh, a thousand people there'), it is in general left to the hearer, on the basis of considerations of relevance, to decide how faithful a representation has been attempted.

Similarly, any utterance, of any syntactic or semantic type, can be used as a second-order interpretation, and the fact is not normally linguistically encoded. Though there are linguistic indicators of echoic use (e.g. the 'hearsay' particles used in many languages, or the French reportative conditional), it is in general left to the hearer, on the basis of considerations of relevance, to decide whether a second-order interpretation is involved and if so, of what type.

Interrogatives, we have argued, do encode the fact that they are second-order interpretations of a certain type. But this does not prevent them from being used echoically too. Consider (20):

(20)   John sighed. Would she never speak?

The question in (20) is a case of free indirect speech. As such, it is triply interpretive: it is a more or less literal interpretation of a thought of the speaker's or writer's, which is itself an echoic interpretation of a thought attributed to John, which is in turn an interpretation of a desirable thought, namely, the answer to the question. Of these facts, only the last is linguistically encoded, and as this example makes clear, the encoding is indeterminate in two important respects: as to who regards the answer as desirable, and to whom.

The picture that emerges is both more complex and more highly structured than standard mood-based analyses would suggest. The echoic question in (20) is used to represent not a single propositional attitude but a stack of attitudes, each embedding or being embedded in another. An echoic imperative or declarative may involve a comparable array: it can, for example, be used in the appropriate circumstances to represent the speaker's view of what Bill suggested that Jenny regarded as an actual, potential or desirable state of affairs. Moreover, the elementary attitudes that make up these complex arrays are not tied to any single sentence type: any sentence may be used as a faithful representation of the speaker's thought, or of an attributed thought, or of a possible but non-attributed thought. In *Relevance*, we argued that even the subtype of attitude encoded by interrogatives is shared in essential respects by exclamatives (Sperber and Wilson 1986a: 253–54).

If we are right, then the linguistic form of a non-declarative utterance vastly underdetermines the way it is understood. In this, as in every other aspect of interpretation, considerations of relevance play a vital constraining and enriching role. The greater the contribution of pragmatics, the less has to be attributed to linguistic semantics. Our claim is that the characteristic linguistic features of declarative, imperative or interrogative form merely encode a rather abstract property of the intended interpretation: the direction in which the relevance of the utterance is to be sought.

11   Metarepresentation in linguistic communication

Deirdre Wilson

11.1   Introduction

Several strands of research on metarepresentation have a bearing on the study of linguistic communication. On the whole, there has been little interaction among them, and the possibility of integrating them with an empirically plausible pragmatic theory has not been much explored. This chapter has two main aims: to illustrate the depth and variety of metarepresentational abilities deployed in linguistic communication, and to argue that a pragmatic account of these abilities can both benefit from and provide useful evidence for the study of more general metarepresentational abilities.

A metarepresentation is a representation of a representation: a higher-order representation with a lower-order representation embedded within it. The different strands of research on metarepresentation that have a bearing on the study of linguistic communication vary in the type of metarepresentations involved and the use to which they are put. First, there is the philosophical and psychological literature on mindreading (or 'theory of mind'), which deals with the ability to form *thoughts* about *attributed thoughts* (Whiten 1991; Davies and Stone 1995a, 1995b; Carruthers and Smith 1996). Suppose a child sees a ball being put into a box. Having formed the thought in (1), he might go on, by observing his companions, to form thoughts of the type in (2):

(1)   The ball is in the box.

(2)   a. John thinks the ball is in the box.
        b. John thinks the ball is not in the box.
        c. John thinks Sue thinks the ball is in the box.
        d. John thinks Sue thinks the ball is not in the box.

There is a now a substantial body of work on how this metapsychological ability develops and how it can break down. It may be present to varying degrees. People may differ, for example, in their ability to attribute to others beliefs incompatible with their own. A child who believes (1) and lacks this ability would be limited to the metarepresentations in (2a) and (2c). A child with first-order 'theory of mind' could attribute to others beliefs that differ from his own (as in (2b)); and one with second-order 'theory of mind' could attribute to others beliefs about the beliefs of others which differ from his own (as in (2d)) (Leslie 1987; Astington, Harris and Olson 1988; Frye and Moore 1991; Fodor 1992; Gopnik and Wellman 1992; Lewis and Mitchell 1994; Smith and Tsimpli 1995; Scholl and Leslie 1999). People with autism are typically said to be lacking in first- or second-order metapsychological abilities of this type (Baron-Cohen, Leslie and Frith 1985; Leslie 1991; Baron-Cohen, Tager-Flusberg and Cohen 1993; Happé 1993, 1994; Baron-Cohen 1995).

Second, there is the Gricean pragmatic literature on the attribution of speakers' meanings. Grice shifted attention away from a code model of communication and towards an inferential account in which the formation and recognition of communicators' intentions was central. Thanks to his work, the idea that verbal comprehension is a form of mindreading has been relatively uncontroversial in pragmatics for more than thirty years (Grice 1967, 1989; Bach and Harnish 1979; Levinson 1983; Davis 1991; Neale 1992; Sperber and Wilson 1995; Kasher 1998). Grice treats the comprehension process as starting from a metarepresentation of an *attributed utterance* and ending with a metarepresentation of an *attributed thought*. Suppose Mary says (3) to Peter:

(3)   You are neglecting your job.

In understanding her utterance, Peter might entertain a series of metarepresentations of the type in (4):

(4)   a. Mary said, 'You are neglecting your job'.
        b. Mary said that I am neglecting my job.
        c. Mary believes that I am neglecting my job.
        d. Mary intends me to believe that I am neglecting my job.
        e. Mary intends me to believe that she intends me to believe that I am neglecting my job.

Unlike the literature on mindreading, the Gricean pragmatic literature deals with the specific metacommunicative ability to attribute speaker meanings on the basis of utterances. It might thus be seen as forming a bridge between the literature on mindreading and the philosophical, literary and linguistic literature on quotation, which is the third strand of research on metarepresentation that I will look at here.

The literature on quotation is mainly concerned with *utterances* about *attributed utterances*. Unlike the Gricean pragmatic literature, it deals with a type of metarepresentation used not in *identifying* the speaker's meaning but as *part of* the speaker's meaning. For example, Peter might report Mary's utterance in (3) in one of the following ways:

(5)   a. Mary said to me, 'You are neglecting your job'.
        b. Mary told me I was not working hard enough.

    c. According to Mary, I am 'neglecting' my work.
    d. Mary was pretty rude to me. I am neglecting my job!

The examples in (5) illustrate the four main types of quotation discussed in the literature: direct quotation, as in (5a), indirect quotation, as in (5b), mixed direct and indirect quotation, as in (5c), and free indirect quotation, as in (5d). Here, both the higher-order representation and the lower-order representations are utterances, and both are components of the speaker's meaning: they are part of what Peter intends to communicate by uttering (5a)–(5d) (Davidson 1968, 1979a; Partee 1973; McHale 1978; Coulmas 1986; Cappelen and Lepore 1997a; Noh 1998b, 2000; Saka 1998).

So far, all the lower-order representations I have looked at have been attributed utterances or thoughts. There is a further, more disparate literature on non-attributive representations of a more abstract nature, linguistic, logical or conceptual. Consider the examples in (6):

(6)   a. 'Dragonflies are beautiful' is a sentence of English.
        b. 'Shut up' is rude.
        c. It's true that tulips are flowers.
        d. ROSES AND DAISIES ARE FLOWERS entails that roses are flowers.
        e. I like the name 'Petronella'.
        f. 'Abeille' is not a word of English.
        g. TULIP implies FLOWER.

Here the higher-order representation is an *utterance* or *thought* and the lower-order representation is an *abstract representation*: for example, a sentence type, as in (6a), an utterance type, as in (6b), a proposition, as in (6c)–(6d), a name, as in (6e), a word, as in (6f), or a concept, as in (6g). Such cases have been approached from a variety of perspectives: for example, the philosophical literature on quotation includes some discussion of non-attributive *mentions* of words or concepts (see also Garver 1965); and the ability to make grammaticality judgements, to think about sentence or utterance types, or to consider evidential or entailment relations among propositions or thought-types, has given rise to a substantial experimental and developmental literature (Gombert 1990; Overton 1990; Morris and Sloutsky 1998).

Metarepresentation, then, involves a higher-order representation with a lower-order representation embedded inside it. The higher-order representation is generally an utterance or a thought. Three main types of lower-order representation have been investigated: *public representations* (e.g. utterances); *mental representations* (e.g. thoughts); and *abstract representations* (e.g. sentences, propositions). How do these metarepresentational abilities fit together, with each other and with the architecture of the mind? I will argue that it is worth considering them together and attempting to integrate them with an empirically plausible pragmatic theory. In section 11.2, I will consider how the Gricean metacommunicative ability used in attributing speakers' meanings might fit with the more general metapsychological abilities studied in the literature on mindreading, and argue that some of Grice's assumptions about pragmatics must be modified if a serious attempt at integration is to be made. In section 11.3, I will sketch a pragmatic theory which might fit better with existing research on mindreading. In section 11.4, I will show how this theory might help with the analysis of quotation and other types of linguistic metarepresentation.

11.2   Gricean pragmatics and mindreading

Grice sees both communicator and audience as deeply involved in metarepresentation: the communicator in metarepresenting the thoughts she wants to convey, the audience in metarepresenting the communicator's intentions. Clearly, this metacommunicative ability has a lot in common with the more general mindreading ability illustrated in (2). It is conceivable that there is no difference between them, and that the ability to identify speakers' meanings is nothing but the general mindreading ability applied to a particular, communicative domain. Arguably, this is the approach that Grice himself would have favoured (see Sperber 2000a). An alternative hypothesis is that the metacommunicative ability is a specialisation of the more general mindreading ability, adapted for use in the communicative domain. This hypothesis is currently being explored in work on relevance theory, and is the one I will develop here (Sperber 1996, 2000a; Origgi and Sperber 2000).

If either of these possibilities is to be seriously investigated, however, some of Grice's pragmatic assumptions will have to be dropped. His framework does not fit straightforwardly with existing research on mindreading, for several reasons. In the first place, his conception of communication involves, if anything, not too little metarepresentation but too much. For a Gricean speaker's meaning to be conveyed, the speaker's intentions must be not merely recognised but transparent, in a sense that seems to be definable only in terms of an infinite series of metarepresentations. One way of spelling out the required notion of transparency is to claim that the speaker must not only (a) intend to inform the hearer of something, and (b) intend the hearer to recognise this informative intention, but (c) intend the hearer to recognise the higher-order intention in (b), and so on ad infinitum. On this approach, for a speaker's meaning to be conveyed, the speaker's informative intention – and every contextual assumption needed to identify it – must become *mutually known* (Searle 1969; Schiffer 1972; Grice 1982; Smith 1982; Recanati 1986; Sperber and Wilson 1995). However theoretically justified this conclusion, it creates a practical problem: it is hard to see how an infinite series of metarepresentations could ever be mentally represented. The search for a definition of speaker's meaning that would simultaneously satisfy the theoretical requirement of transparency and the practical requirement of psychological plausibility was a major preoccupation of early inferential accounts (Clark and Carlson 1981; Clark and Marshall 1981; Sperber and Wilson 1982, 1987a, 1990b; Gibbs 1987; Garnham and Perner 1990).

A second problem is that Grice's rational reconstruction of how hearers attribute speakers' meanings takes the form of a conscious, discursive reasoning process quite unlike the spontaneous inferences deployed in other forms of mindreading. Here is his 'working out schema' for the identification of conversational implicatures (Grice 1967/1989: 50):

Grice's working out schema for conversational implicatures
(a) He has said that p.
(b) There is no reason to suppose that he is not observing the maxims, or at least the CP [= Cooperative Principle].
(c) He could not be doing this unless he thought that q.
(d) He knows (and knows that I know that he knows) that I can see that the supposition that he thinks that q is required.
(e) He has done nothing to stop me thinking that q.
(f) He intends me to think, or is at least willing to allow me to think, that q.
(g) And so he has implicated that q.

It is hard to imagine even adults going through such lengthy chains of inference in the attribution of speaker meanings. Yet preverbal infants seem to be heavily involved in inferential communication, as the following example (from a description by Andrew Lock of an encounter with a 14-month-old infant) shows:

Mother enters the room holding a cup of tea. Paul turns from his playpen in her direction and obviously sees it. (i) He cries vestigially and so attracts his mother's attention; immediately he points toward her and smacks his lips concurrently. [Paul's way of asking for food or drink.]
    Mother: No, you can't have this one, it's Andy's.
    Mother gives me [i.e. Andy Lock, the observer of the incident] the cup of tea, and I put it on the mantelpiece to cool. Paul crawls across to me and grasps my knees. (ii) I turn to look at him; he looks toward the mantelpiece and points, turns back to me, continues to point, and smacks his lips. (Lock 1980: 95–96)

Surveying a range of examples of this type, and noting the presence of such typical features of inferential communication as attracting the audience's attention, pointing, gaze alternation, and ritualised gestures such as lipsmacking and vestigial crying, Bretherton (1991: 57) concludes:

I suggest that the most parsimonious explanation of these phenomena is that, by the end of the first year, infants have acquired a rudimentary ability to impute mental states to self and other ... and, further, that they have begun to understand that one mind can be interfaced with another through conventional or mutually comprehensible signals.

While it is easy to accept that preverbal infants engage in inferential communication, it is hard to imagine them going through the sort of conscious, discursive reasoning described in Grice's working out schema.

In fact, the problem is more serious, since Gricean pragmatics substantially underestimates the amount of inference involved in linguistic communication. As his working out schema shows, Grice saw the starting point for inferential comprehension as the recovery of a literal meaning (or 'what is said'), which was supposed to be determined independently of the speaker's intentions. Yet there is good evidence that speakers' intentions help to determine not only what is implicated but also 'what is said'. This is most obvious in disambiguation and reference resolution, but (as I will show in later sections) there is a very wide range of further cases in which sentence meaning substantially underdetermines 'what is said' (Carston 1988, 1998b, 2002a; Recanati 1989, 2000; Sperber and Wilson 1995, 1998a; Wilson and Sperber 1998b, 2002). To accommodate these, Grice's working out schema for implicatures would have to be supplemented with further schemas designed to deal with disambiguation, reference resolution, and other linguistically underspecified aspects of 'what is said': for example, resolution of lexically vague expressions, and interpretation of semantically incomplete expressions like 'too big'. While reflective inferences of the Gricean type do occur (for example in repairing misunderstandings or reading the later work of Henry James), disambiguation and reference resolution are in general intuitive processes which take place below the level of consciousness, and an adequate pragmatic theory should recognise this.

There is experimental evidence that the ability for inferential intention recognition plays a role in language acquisition, and in particular in the acquisition of lexical meanings. In one study (Tomasello and Kruger 1992), the experimenter used a novel verb in telling a child what she was about to do. She then performed an apparently accidental action (marked by saying 'Whoops'), and an apparently intended action (marked by saying 'There!' and looking pleased). The child assumed that the verb described the apparently satisfactory action rather than the apparently accidental one. Paul Bloom (1997: 10), who surveys a variety of examples of this type, concludes that 'even very young children infer the referential intention of the speaker (through attention to cues that include line-of-regard and emotional indications of satisfaction) when determining the meaning of a new word'. As with inferential communication in preverbal infants, it is easier to think of this as an intuitive rather than a reflective process.

If lexical comprehension involves an element of mindreading, the ability of people with autism to grasp an intended lexical meaning should also be impaired. Here is an illustration from the autobiography of someone with Asperger's syndrome:

[During my first year at school], we were required to take naps each day. I vividly remember my teacher announcing, 'Children, find your mats and take your nap.' I refused. Again the teacher called my parents. Again my parents made their way to the school.

> 'Liane, why won't you take your nap?' my parents wondered of me.
> 'Because I can't.'
> 'You see!' the teacher said smugly.
> 'Why can't you take your nap?' my parents continued.
> 'Because I don't have a mat.'
> 'You most certainly do have a mat. There it is in your cubby,' the teacher replied.
> 'I do not have a mat.'
> 'You see what I mean?' the teacher asked my parents. 'She is an obstinate child.'
> 'Why do you say you don't have a mat?' the folks asked, not giving up on me.
> 'That is not a mat. That is a rug,' I honestly and accurately replied.
> 'So it is,' said my father. 'Will you take a nap on your rug?'
> 'If she asks me to,' I said matter-of-factly ...

I wasn't trying to be difficult, I was trying to do the right thing. The trouble was, the teacher assumed I understood language like other children. I did not. (Willey 1999: 19–20)

But the difficulty in Asperger's syndrome seems to lie at the intuitive rather than the reflective level. If anything, failures at the intuitive level are compensated by an increase in the sort of reflective reasoning envisaged in Grice's working out schema, as the following comment (from the same writer) suggests:

If [my husband] were to tell me he was disappointed he had missed me at lunch, I would wonder if he meant to say he was sad – which is simply regretfully sorry; unhappy – which is somewhere between mad and sad; disheartened – which is a lonely sad; mad – which makes you want to argue with someone over what they had done; angry – which makes you want to ignore the person you are feeling this way towards; furious – which makes you want to spit; or none of the above. In order for me really to understand what people are saying I need much more than a few words mechanically placed together. (Willey 1999: 63)

Here the author describes a conscious attempt to resolve a lexical vagueness that most people would deal with spontaneously and unreflectively. This again suggests that the basic metacommunicative capacity is an intuitive rather than a reflective one.

Grice himself might not have been opposed to the idea of an intuitive metacommunicative capacity. What mattered to him was that this capacity – whether intuitive or reflective – was not code-based but inferential:

The presence of a conversational implicature must be capable of being worked out; for even if it can in fact be intuitively grasped, unless the intuition is replaceable by an argument, the implicature (if present at all) will not count as a conversational implicature; it will be a conventional implicature. (Grice 1989: 31)

Grice's fundamental contribution to pragmatics was to show that much of verbal comprehension is inferential; but an empirically plausible pragmatic theory should also be concerned with how the inference processes go. Here, it is not the intuitions but the working out schema that ought to be replaced.

A third problem is that, despite the elaborate-looking working out schema, Grice's framework suggests no explicit procedure for identifying the content of particular speaker's meanings. Grice showed that hearers have certain very general expectations – which he analysed in terms of a Cooperative Principle and maxims of truthfulness, informativeness, relevance and clarity – and that they look for meanings that satisfy those expectations. But how exactly is this done? How does the hearer decide, for instance, that someone who uses the word 'mat' intends to refer to a rug, or that someone who says 'I was disappointed not to see you' is angry and expects an apology? If we look for guidance to the working out schema for implicatures, we find that the content of the implicature is introduced at step (c), but no explanation is given of how it is derived. In fact, the function of the working out schema is not to help the hearer construct a hypothesis about the content of the implicature, but merely to show how, once constructed, it might be confirmed as part of the speaker's meaning. But until we have some idea of how hypotheses about the speaker's meaning are constructed, we will be unable to see how the metacommunicative and metapsychological abilities might fit together.

My main concern in this chapter is with empirical questions about the role of metarepresentation in identifying the content of speakers' meanings. In section 11.3, I will outline a pragmatic theory – relevance theory – which suggests a comprehension procedure that might replace Grice's working out schema and form the basis of a metacommunicative module. As to the theoretical problem of how to define speaker's meaning without getting into an infinite regress, Grice himself proposed a possible way out. He suggested that although full transparency in communication is not in practice achievable (because of the infinity of metarepresentations required), communicators might simply *deem* it to be achieved (Grice 1982). This has the unfortunate consequence of making speaker's meaning an idealisation that is never achieved in real life. At the end of section 11.3, I will suggest an alternative solution which avoids this unfortunate consequence and shows how the theoretical goal of transparency and the practical goal of psychological plausibility might be reconciled.

11.3   Relevance theory and communication

Relevance theory (Sperber and Wilson 1987a, 1995) is based on a definition of relevance and two general principles: the *Cognitive Principle* that human cognition tends to be geared to the maximisation of relevance; and the *Communicative Principle* that utterances create expectations of relevance.

Cognitive principle of relevance:
Human cognition tends to be geared to the maximisation of relevance.

Communicative principle of relevance:
Every utterance (or other act of inferential communication) communicates a presumption of its own optimal relevance. (Sperber and Wilson 1995: 260)

Relevance is treated as a property of inputs to cognitive processes and analysed in terms of cognitive effect and processing effort. When an input (e.g. an utterance) is processed in a context of available assumptions, it may yield some cognitive effect (e.g. by modifying or reorganising these assumptions). Other things being equal, the greater the cognitive effects achieved, the greater the relevance of the input. However, the processing of the input, and the derivation of these effects, involves some mental effort. Other things being equal, the smaller the processing effort required, the greater the relevance of the input.

It follows from the cognitive principle of relevance that human attention and processing resources tend to be allocated to the inputs that seem most relevant. It follows from the communicative principle of relevance (and the definition of optimal relevance, cf. Sperber and Wilson 1995: 266–78) that the speaker, by the very act of addressing someone, communicates that her utterance is the most relevant one compatible with her abilities and preferences, and is at least relevant enough to be worth his processing effort. This in turn suggests a comprehension procedure which might form the basis for a modularised metacommunicative ability.

Inferential comprehension starts from the recovery of a linguistically encoded sentence meaning, which is typically quite fragmentary and incomplete. The goal of pragmatic theory is to explain how the hearer, using available contextual information, develops this into a full-fledged hypothesis about the speaker's meaning. The communicative principle of relevance motivates the following comprehension procedure which, according to relevance theory, is automatically applied to the online processing of attended verbal inputs. The hearer takes the linguistically decoded sentence meaning; following a path of least effort in the accessing of contextual information, he enriches this sentence meaning at the explicit level and complements it at the implicit level, until the resulting interpretation meets his expectation of relevance; at which point, he stops:

Relevance-theoretic comprehension procedure
Follow a path of least effort in computing cognitive effects.
(a) Consider interpretations in order of accessibility.
(b) Stop when your expectation of relevance is satisfied.

The mutual adjustment of explicit content and implicatures, constrained by expectations of relevance, is the central feature of relevance-theoretic pragmatics (Carston 1998b, 2002a; Sperber and Wilson 1998a; Wilson and Sperber 1998b, 2002).

The expectations of relevance created (and adjusted) in the course of the comprehension process may be more or less sophisticated. Sperber (1994a) discusses three increasingly sophisticated strategies, each requiring an extra layer of metarepresentation, which might correspond to stages in pragmatic development. The simplest strategy is one of Naive Optimism. A Naively Optimistic hearer expects the speaker to succeed in being optimally relevant. In other words, he looks for an interpretation on which the utterance would satisfy his expectations of relevance: if he finds one, he assumes that it was the intended one and attributes it as a speaker's meaning; if he does not, he has no further resources, and communication will fail. In Sperber's terms, a Naively Optimistic hearer assumes that the speaker is both competent and benevolent: competent enough to avoid misunderstanding, and benevolent enough not to lead him astray. Thus, suppose a mother tells her child:

(7)   I'll write you a letter.

'Write you a letter' may mean *write a letter of the alphabet for you, write a message for you*, or *write a message to you*. The mother has spoken competently if the first satisfactory interpretation to occur to her child (i.e. the first to satisfy the expectations of relevance raised by this particular utterance) is the intended one; she has spoken benevolently if the utterance on this interpretation not only seems relevant enough but is genuinely so. A Naively Optimistic hearer has no need to think about the speaker's thoughts in identifying her meaning: the only time he needs to metarepresent the speaker's thoughts is when, having found a satisfactory interpretation, he attributes it as the speaker's meaning.

A more complex strategy, which requires an extra degree of metarepresentation, is one of Cautious Optimism. A Cautiously Optimistic hearer assumes that the speaker is benevolent, but not necessarily competent. Instead of taking the first interpretation that makes the utterance seem relevant enough and attributing it as the speaker's meaning, he can ask himself on what interpretation the speaker *might have thought* her utterance would be relevant enough. This extra layer of metarepresentation allows him to avoid misunderstanding in two types of case where a Naively Optimistic hearer would fail.

The first is the case of *accidental relevance*. An utterance is accidentally relevant when the first satisfactory interpretation (i.e. the first interpretation that makes the utterance seem relevant enough) is not the intended one. Suppose that – for reasons his mother could not reasonably have foreseen – the first interpretation of (7) that the child finds satisfactory is one on which his mother is offering to help him practise his handwriting. A Naively Optimistic hearer would accept this as the intended interpretation. A Cautiously Optimistic hearer should be able to consider whether his mother could have expected her utterance, on this interpretation, to be relevant enough.

An utterance may also be *accidentally irrelevant*. An obvious case is when someone mistakenly tells you something you already know. Another arises with slips of the tongue. Suppose Mary tells Peter:

(8)   I've been feeding the penguins in Trafalgar Square.

A Naively Optimistic hearer would restrict himself to the linguistically encoded meaning of 'penguins', would be unable to find a satisfactory interpretation, and communication would fail. By adopting a strategy of Cautious Optimism and asking himself on what interpretation Mary *might have thought* her utterance would be relevant enough to him, Peter may be able to infer that she was talking about pigeons, not penguins. Clearly, most ordinary hearers are capable of this.[1]

While a Cautiously Optimistic hearer can deal with speaker incompetence, his assumption of speaker benevolence may still lead him astray. The strategy of Sophisticated Understanding allows hearers to cope with the fact that speakers are not always benevolent: they may intend an utterance to *seem* relevant enough without in fact being so. For example, in saying (8), Mary may be lying about where she has been. A Cautiously Optimistic hearer might be able to cope with her slip of the tongue, but only if he does not realise she is lying: a benevolent communicator could not intend to inform him of something she knows to be false. Using the strategy of Sophisticated Understanding, Peter may be able to identify Mary's meaning even if he knows she is lying, by asking himself under what interpretation she *might have thought he would think* her utterance was relevant enough. In identifying the intended interpretation, he therefore has to metarepresent Mary's thoughts about his thoughts. Most adult speakers are capable of this.

To sum up. A Naively Optimistic hearer need not reflect on the speaker's thoughts at all in identifying the speaker's meaning: he simply takes the first interpretation that satisfies the expectations of relevance raised by the utterance, and treats it as the intended one. A Cautiously Optimistic hearer can consider what interpretation the speaker *might have thought* would make the utterance relevant enough: at the cost of an extra layer of metarepresentation, he can cope with cases where the speaker tries to be relevant enough, but fails. Finally, a hearer using the strategy of Sophisticated Understanding can consider on what interpretation the *speaker might have thought he would think* the utterance was relevant enough; at the cost of a further layer of metarepresentation, he can cope with deceptive cases in which nothing more than the appearance of relevance is attempted or achieved (see Sperber 2000a for discussion).

These strategies have implications for the development of pragmatic abilities. A child starting out as a Naive Optimist should make characteristic mistakes in comprehension (in disambiguation and reference resolution, for example), and there is some experimental evidence for this (Bezuidenhout and Sroda 1996, 1998). Roughly speaking, the move from Naive Optimism to Cautious Optimism coincides with the development of the ability to pass standard first-order false-belief tests, and there should also be implications for verbal comprehension in people with autism and Asperger's syndrome (Happé 1993; Leslie and Happé 1989; for general discussion of the relation between pragmatic abilities and mindreading, see Nuti 2003).

At the end of section 11.2, I pointed out an undesirable consequence of Grice's solution to the infinite-regress problem. On his account, transparency in communication, although *deemed* to be achieved, is never actually achievable, so that full-fledged communication never occurs. Relevance theory suggests an alternative definition of overt communication that avoids this unfortunate consequence. The first step is to replace the notion of mutual knowledge (or mutual belief) with a notion of *mutual manifestness* (Sperber and Wilson 1995: chapter 1, section 8). Manifestness is a dispositional notion which is weaker than knowledge (or belief) in just the required way:

Manifestness
An assumption is manifest to an individual at a given time iff he is capable at that time of mentally representing it and accepting its representation as true or probably true.

An assumption cannot be known or believed without being explicitly represented;[2] but it can be manifest to an individual if it is merely capable of being non-demonstratively inferred. By defining overt communication in terms of a notion of mutual manifestness, the theoretical requirement of transparency and the practical requirement of psychological plausibility can be reconciled. (On mutual knowledge versus mutual manifestness, see Garnham and Perner 1990; Sperber and Wilson 1990b.)

Relevance theory analyses inferential communication in terms of two layers of intention: (a) the *informative intention* to make a certain set of assumptions manifest (or more manifest) to the audience, and (b) the *communicative intention* to make the informative intention mutually manifest (Sperber and Wilson 1995: chapter 1, sections 9–12):

Ostensive-inferential communication
The communicator produces a stimulus which makes it mutually manifest to communicator and audience that the communicator intends, by means of this stimulus, to make manifest or more manifest to the audience a set of assumptions *I*.

When the stimulus is an utterance, the content of the speaker's meaning is the set of assumptions *I* embedded under the informative intention. As long as the informative intention is made mutually manifest, transparency is achieved. An infinite series of metarepresentations is available in principle; however, it does not follow that each assumption in the series must be mentally represented. Which metarepresentations are actually constructed and processed in the course of interpreting a given utterance is an empirical question. On this account, the attribution of a full-fledged speaker's meaning involves a fourth-order metarepresentation of the type shown in (4e) above: she intends me to believe that she intends me to believe. .... This is complex enough to suggest a modularised metacommunicative ability, but finite enough to be implemented.

In this section, I have described a comprehension procedure which might form the basis for a modularised metacommunicative ability, itself a sub-part of the more general metapsychological ability, or 'theory of mind'. The procedure is guided by an expectation of relevance (created and adjusted in the course of the comprehension process) which may be more or less sophisticated, with implications for development and breakdown. In the next section, I will turn to the content of the speaker's meaning (that is, the set of assumptions *I* embedded under the informative intention) and show that this may also contain a meta-representational element which is very rich and varied.

11.4   Relevance theory and linguistic metarepresentation

11.4.1   Resemblance in linguistic metarepresentation

As noted above, the literature on quotation is mainly concerned with utterances about attributed utterances, such as those in (5) (repeated below):

(5)   a. Mary said to me, 'You are neglecting your job'.
         b. Mary told me I was not working hard enough.
         c. According to Mary, I am 'neglecting' my work.
         d. Mary was pretty rude to me. I am neglecting my job!

Direct quotation, as in (5a), has been linked by different analysts to a variety of related phenomena: demonstrations, pretence, play-acting, mimesis, and non-serious actions (Sternberg 1982a; Clark and Gerrig 1990; Walton 1990; Recanati 2000). When a literary example such as (9) is read out on the radio, it is easy to see why direct quotation has been treated as belonging to 'a family of nonserious actions that includes practising, playing, acting and pretending' (Clark and Gerrig 1990: 766):

(9)   'Out of the question', says the coroner. 'You have heard the boy. "Can't exactly say" won't do, you know. We can't take that in a court of justice, gentlemen. It's terrible depravity. Put the boy aside.' (Dickens: *Bleak House*, Penguin Classic, 1996: 177)

Similar claims have been made for free indirect quotation, as in (5d).

However, if we are interested in a notion of metarepresentation that extends to the full range of cases, public, mental and abstract, these analyses will not do. It is hard to see how notions such as pretence, mimesis and play-acting, which apply to public representations, can help with cases where the lower-order representation is chosen for its content or abstract properties, as in the indirect speech report in (5b), the non-attributive mentions in (6), or indirect reports of thought such as (10):

(10)   What, reduced to their simplest reciprocal form, were Bloom's thoughts about
            Stephen's thoughts about Bloom and Bloom's thoughts about Stephen's thoughts
            about Bloom's thoughts about Stephen? He thought that he thought that he was a
            jew whereas he knew that he knew that he knew that he was not. (Joyce: *Ulysses*,
            Bodley Head, 1960: 797)

Nor do they help with cases where the higher-order representation is mental
rather than public, as in the mental attributions of utterances or thoughts that
underlie the metapsychological and metacommunicative abilities (cf. (2) and
(4) above). What is worth retaining from these analyses is the idea that
quotation involves the exploitation of resemblances. I will argue that all
varieties of metarepresentation, public, mental and abstract, can be analysed
in terms of a notion of *representation by resemblance*, opening the way to a
unified account.

It is assumed in some of the literature on quotation that identity rather than
resemblance is the normal or typical case. Direct quotations are treated as
verbatim reproductions of the original utterance, and indirect quotations as
reproductions of its content (for discussion, see Davidson 1968, 1979a;
Cappelen and Lepore 1997a, 1997b; Noh 1998c, 2000; Saka 1998). This
assumption is too strong. In many cases, indirect quotation involves paraphrase,
elaboration, or exaggeration rather than strict identity of content. For example,
(5b) is a paraphrase of the original in (3), and it might be used to report a more
remotely related utterance such as (11), which merely contextually implies or
implicates that Peter is neglecting his job:

(11)   You spend too much time at the theatre.

Particularly in academic circles, where even typographical errors are often repro-
duced verbatim, the idea that direct quotation is based on resemblance rather than
identity may be harder to accept. But the degree of accuracy required in verbatim
reporting depends on culture and circumstance (reproduction of phonetic features, hesitations, mispronunciations and repairs may or may not be relevant).
Moreover, not all direct quotation is verbatim, as the following examples show:

(12)   a. Descartes said, 'I think, therefore I am'.
        b. I looked at John and he's like, 'What are you saying?'
        c. And so the kid would say, 'Blah blah blah?' [tentative voice with rising
           intonation] and his father would say 'Blah blah blah' [in a strong blustery
           voice], and they would go on like that. (Clark and Gerrig 1990: 780)
        d. And I said, 'Well, it seemed to me to be an example of this this this this this
           this and this and this', which it was you know. (Clark and Gerrig 1990: 780)

(12a) is a translation; the expression 'he's like' in (12b) indicates that what
follows should not be taken as a verbatim reproduction; and in (12c) and (12d)
the expressions 'blah blah blah' and 'this this this' indicate very loose

approximations indeed (for discussion, see Coulmas 1986; Clark and Gerrig 1990; Gutt 1991; Wade and Clark 1993).

A quotation, then, must merely resemble the original to some degree. Resemblance involves shared properties. As the above examples suggest, the resemblances may be of just any type: perceptual, linguistic, logical, mathematical, conceptual, sociolinguistic, stylistic, typographical. Typically, direct quotation, as in (5a), increases the salience of formal or linguistic resemblances, and indirect quotation, as in (5b), of semantic or logical resemblances. We might call these *metalinguistic* and *interpretive* resemblances, respectively (Wilson and Sperber 1988b; Sperber and Wilson 1995: chapter 4, sections 7–9; Noh 1998b, 2000). Mixed quotation, as in (5c), exploits both metalinguistic and interpretive resemblances, while reports of thought, and metarepresentations of thought in general, are typically interpretive.

Interpretive resemblance is resemblance in content: that is, sharing of implications. Two representations resemble each other (in a context) to the extent that they share logical and contextual implications. The more implications they have in common, the more they resemble each other. Identity is a special case of resemblance, in which two representations share all their implications in every context. According to relevance theory, in interpreting a quotation, or more generally a linguistic metarepresentation, the hearer is not entitled to assume a strict identity between representation and original. Rather, following the relevance-theoretic comprehension procedure, he should start deriving implications that might plausibly be shared with the original, and stop when he has enough to satisfy his expectation of relevance. Thus, resemblance, rather than identity, is the normal or typical case (Sperber and Wilson 1990a, 1998a; Gibbs 1994a; Wilson and Sperber 1998b, 2002).

Developmental studies of quotation have provided useful data on the production side, showing, for instance, the order of appearance of propositional-attitude verbs such as 'think', 'want', 'hope', 'fear', etc. (Bretherton and Beeghly 1982; Wellman 1990; Bartsch and Wellman 1995). Here I will look mainly at the comprehension side, and argue that language contains a huge variety of metarepresentational devices whose comprehension might interact in interesting ways with the metapsychological and metacommunicative abilities. I will also try to show that the recognition and interpretation of linguistic metarepresentations involves a substantial amount of pragmatic inference, bearing out my claim in section 11.2 that Gricean pragmatics has considerably underestimated the inferential element in comprehension.

11.4.2   Decoding and inference in linguistic metarepresentation

The semantic and philosophical literature has been mainly concerned with overtly marked quotations such as (5a)–(5c), whose presence is linguistically indicated by use of higher-order conceptual representations (e.g. MARY SAID, PETER THOUGHT). Literary and stylistic research has been more concerned with free indirect cases such as (5d), where the presence, source and type of the metarepresentation is left to the reader to infer. Consider (13):

(13)   Frederick reproached Elizabeth. She had behaved inconsiderately.

The second part of (13) has three possible interpretations: it may be understood as an assertion by the narrator that Elizabeth had behaved inconsiderately, a tacit indirect report of what Frederick said, or a tacit indirect report of what he thought. The literature on 'point of view' in fiction provides a wealth of clues to the presence of various types of tacit indirect reporting, and critical procedures by which indeterminacies as to source and type of metarepresentation might be resolved (Walton 1976; Cohn 1978; Banfield 1982; Sternberg 1982b; Fludernik 1993).

To take just one example, consider (14), a passage from *Persuasion* which describes the reactions of the hero, Wentworth, on seeing the heroine, Anne Elliot, after a gap of many years. Anne's sister has just passed on Wentworth's overheard comment to a friend that Anne was 'so altered he would not have known her'. Anne is shocked and upset. Jane Austen continues:

(14)   Frederick Wentworth had used such words, or something like them, but without an idea that they would be carried round to her. He had thought her wretchedly altered, and, in the first moment of appeal, had spoken as he felt. *He had not forgiven Anne Elliot. She had used him ill; deserted and disappointed him; and worse, she had shewn a feebleness of character in doing so, which his own decided, confident temper could not endure. She had given him up to oblige others. It had been the effect of over-persuasion. It had been weakness and timidity.*

He had been most warmly attached to her, and had never seen a woman since whom he thought her equal; but, except from some natural sensation of curiosity, he had no desire of meeting her again. Her power with him was gone for ever. (Austen, *Persuasion*, World's Classics, 1990: 61–62)

As noted by Leech and Short (1981: 339) three different interpretations have been proposed for parts of the italicised passage in (14). Mary Lascelles (1939: 204) treats the first part as a straightforward authorial description, and the last part as a free indirect report of what Wentworth said. Wayne Booth (1961: 252) reads the whole passage as a free indirect report of Wentworth's thoughts. This disagreement has critical consequences. For Lascelles, the passage amounts to an 'oversight' on Austen's part, since it fails to present events from the point of view of Anne Elliot, which is consistently maintained in the rest of the novel. For Booth, it is not an oversight at all. By showing us Wentworth's thoughts at this one decisive point in the story, Austen creates a genuine doubt in our minds about what the outcome will be. 'It is deliberate manipulation of inside views in order to destroy our conventional security. We are thus made to go along with

Anne in her long and painful road to the discovery that Frederick loves her'
(Booth 1961: 252). Later critics have tended to prefer Booth's interpretation as
yielding a more 'coherent' reading.

In literary examples of this type, the interpretation process may be deliberate
and time-consuming, calling on evidence from sources beyond the immediate
context. In other cases, the presence of a tacit quotation can be more straightforwardly detected. Here are some examples from the 'Question and Answer'
column in a newspaper:

(15)   a. Why is it that we curry favour?
         b. Why is it that someone who tries to convert others proselytises?
         c. Why is it that we trip the light fantastic if we go out for a good evening?
         d. Why is it that we have to take off our shoes before entering a mosque?
         e. Why is it that gorillas beat their chests?
         f. Why is it that we get butterflies in our stomachs when we are nervous?

Although none of these questions contained quotation marks, some of them
were clearly metalinguistic ('Why is it that we *say* we "curry favour"?'), while
others were straightforwardly descriptive. In the published responses, (15a)–
(15c) were treated as metalinguistic, (15d)–(15e) were treated as descriptive,
and (15f) was treated as both. Intuitively, considerations of relevance help the
reader decide how these questions were intended: it is easier to see how (15a)–
(15c) would be relevant as metalinguistic rather than descriptive questions,
while the reverse is true for (15d)–(15e). The relevance-theoretic comprehension procedure should shed light on how these utterances are understood.

A hearer following the relevance-theoretic comprehension procedure should
consider interpretive hypotheses in order of accessibility. Having found an
interpretation that satisfies his expectation of relevance, he should stop. The
task of the speaker is to make the intended interpretation accessible enough to be
picked out by a hearer following a path of least effort in deriving implications.
Notice that the best way of doing this is not always to use overt linguistic means.
In appropriate circumstances, the hearer may be able to infer some aspect of the
intended interpretation with less effort than would be needed to decode it from a
linguistically unambiguous prompt. Returning to (10), for example, it is relatively easy for the reader to infer that the pronouns in the last sentence of the
passage must be understood as in (10'):

(10')   Bloom thought that Stephen thought that Bloom was a jew, whereas Bloom
          knew that Stephen knew that Bloom knew that Stephen was not.

This interpretation is the only one justifiable in terms of both effort and effect. It
is the most accessible (hence least effort-demanding) one, since it is exactly
patterned on the immediately preceding utterance, in which the intended referents are linguistically marked. It is acceptable on the effect side, since it answers

a question raised by the immediately preceding utterance, and satisfies the reader's expectation of relevance thereby. The less explicit formulation in (10) is thus stylistically preferable to the one in (10′), which would cost the hearer some gratuitous linguistic processing effort.

Linguistic metarepresentations range from the fully explicit and conceptually encoded, as in (5a)–(5b), to the fully tacit, as in (13). Most languages also have a range of quotative devices which are used to mark an utterance as attributive without the degree of foregrounding shown in (5a)–(5b). English has hearsay adverbs ('allegedly', 'reportedly'), adjectives ('self-confessed', 'so-called'), particles ('quote – unquote'), parentheticals ('as Chomsky says', 'according to Bill'), and noun-phrases ('Derrida's claim that', 'the suspect's allegation that'). French also has hearsay prepositions (*selon*), connectives (*puisque*) and morphology (the 'reportative conditional'); German has hearsay modals (*will*). Japanese has a hearsay particle (*tte*) which, if added to the second part of (13), would mark it unambiguously as an attributed utterance; Sissala has an interpretive particle (*rε*) which does not distinguish between attributed utterances and thoughts. Inverted commas, 'finger dancing' and intonation provide further orthographic and paralinguistic resources for indicating attributive use. These devices work in very varied ways, and their semantic properties and pragmatic effects deserve more attention than I can give them here (see Ducrot 1983; Blass 1989b, 1990; Ifantidou-Trouki 1993; Wilson and Sperber 1993; Ifantidou 1994, 2001; Itani 1996; Noh 1998b).

Most languages also have a range of what might be thought of as self-quotative or self-attributive expressions, which add a further layer of metarepresentation to the communicated content. Parallel to 'he thinks' and 'he says' are 'I think' and 'I say'; and most of the hearsay expressions mentioned above have epistemic or illocutionary counterparts. Consider (16)–(17):

(16)   a. Allegedly, the Health Service is on its last legs.
          b. Confidentially, the Health Service is on its last legs.
          c. Unfortunately, the Health Service is on its last legs.

(17)   a. There will be riots, the security forces warn us.
          b. There will be riots, I warn you.
          c. There will be riots, I fear.

In (16a) and (17a), the parenthetical comment is used to attribute an utterance to someone other than the speaker; in (16b)–(16c) and (17b)–(17c), it carries speech-act or propositional-attitude information about the speaker's own utterance (Urmson 1963; Recanati 1987; Blakemore 1991). Into this category of epistemic or illocutionary expressions fall mood indicators (declarative, imperative), evidentials ('doubtless'), attitudinal particles ('alas') and illocutionary-force indicators ('please'), which, by adding a higher-order metarepresentation to the basic layer of communicated content, might be seen as bridging the gap between the metacommunicative ability studied in Gricean pragmatics and the literature on quotation proper (Recanati 1987; Wilson and Sperber 1988a, 1993; Chafe and Nichols 1986; Clark 1991; Fillmore 1990; Ifantidou 1994, 2001; Papafragou 1998a, 1998b, 1998c, 2000).

As with freer forms of quotation, these higher-order metarepresentations need not be linguistically marked. Compare (18a) and (18b):

(18)   a. The grass is wet, because it's raining.
        b. It's raining, because the grass is wet.

Although syntactically similar, these utterances would normally be understood in different ways. (18a) would be understood as making the purely descriptive claim that the rain has caused the grass to get wet. The speaker of (18b) would normally be understood as communicating that the fact that the grass is wet has caused her to *say*, or *believe*, that it's raining. In (18a), the causal relation is between two states of affairs; in (18b), it is between a state of affairs and an utterance or thought. In interpreting (18b), the hearer must construct a higher-order representation of the type 'she says', or 'she thinks', and attribute it as part of the speaker's meaning (on epistemic or illocutionary interpretations, see Sweetser 1990; Blakemore 1997; Noh 1998c; Papafragou 1998a, 1998b, 2000).

In (18b), the inferred higher-order representation may be either epistemic or illocutionary. In other cases, this indeterminacy may be pragmatically resolved. Suppose someone comes up to me in the street and says (19):

(19)   Your name is Deirdre Wilson.

The information that my name is Deirdre Wilson is patently irrelevant to me. What the speaker must be intending to communicate is that she *knows*, or *believes*, that my name is Deirdre Wilson; only on this interpretation will (19) be relevant enough.

In still further cases, what has to be pragmatically resolved is whether some higher-order information made manifest by the utterance is part of the speaker's meaning or merely accidentally transmitted. Consider (20):

(20)   a. MARY [*whispering*]: I'm about to resign.
        b. MARY [*frowning*]: You're late.
        c. MARY [*puzzled*]: The radio's not working.

Here, paralinguistic features such as facial expression, gestures and intonation provide a clue to Mary's attitude to the proposition she is expressing, which may or may not be salient enough, and relevant enough, to be picked out by the relevance-theoretic comprehension procedure.[3] In the next section, I will look at a range of cases in which the speaker's attitude to an attributed utterance or thought makes a major contribution to relevance, and must be treated as part of the communicated content.

11.4.3   Reporting and echoing

The literature on quotation has been much concerned with reports of speech and thought, which achieve relevance mainly by informing the hearer about the content of the original. There is a wide range of further, *echoic*, cases which achieve relevance mainly by conveying the speaker's attitude to an attributed utterance or thought. Echoic utterances add an extra layer of metarepresentation to the communicated content, since not only the attribution but also the speaker's attitude must be represented.

The attitudes conveyed by echoic utterances are very rich and varied: the speaker may indicate that she agrees or disagrees with the original, is puzzled, angry, amused, intrigued, sceptical, etc., or any combination of these. Here I will limit myself to three broad types of attitude: endorsing, questioning and dissociative. Suppose Peter and Mary have been to see a film. As they come out, one of the following exchanges occurs:

(21)   PETER: That was a fantastic film.

(22)   MARY: a. [*happily*] Fantastic.
            b. [*puzzled*] Fantastic?
            c. [*scornfully*] Fantastic!

In (22a), Mary echoes Peter's utterance while indicating that she agrees with it; in (22b), she indicates that she is wondering about it; and in (22c) she indicates that she disagrees with it. The resulting interpretations might be as in (23):

(23)   a. She believes I was right to say/think *P*.
        b. She is wondering whether I was right to say/think *P*.
        c. She believes I was wrong to say/think *P*.

Like regular quotations, echoic utterances may be metalinguistic or interpretive: the attitude expressed may be to the form of the original (e.g. a word, an accent, a pronunciation) or to its content. In (22b), for example, Mary may be wondering whether Peter meant to say the word 'fantastic', or to pronounce it as he did; or she may be wondering whether he really believes the film was fantastic, and why.

As with regular quotations, the speaker's attitude may be overtly expressed ('I agree that', 'I doubt that', 'I wonder whether'), or left to the hearer to infer, as in (22). Intonation, facial expressions and other paralinguistic features may provide additional clues, and most languages also have various attitudinal devices, parallel to the hearsay devices above, which may be used to increase the salience of the intended interpretation. Endorsing attitudes to attributed contents are conveyed by factive verbs ('he knows', 'he admits', 'they point out') and parentheticals ('as Chomsky says', 'as these arguments have shown') (on factives and endorsing attitudes, see Kiparsky and Kiparsky 1971; Sperber 1997). Questioning attitudes can be conveyed by expressions such as 'eh?', 'right?', 'aren't you?', as in (24):

(24)   a. You're leaving, eh?
         b. You don't want that piece of cake, right?
         c. You're thinking of resigning, aren't you?

There is also a range of more or less colloquial dissociative expressions. Suppose Peter tells Mary that he's planning to enter the New York marathon, and she replies as in (25):

(25)   a. You're bound to win, *I don't think*.
         b. You're sure to win. *Not*.
         c. You're going to run the marathon, *huh*!

Here, the addition of the italicised expressions makes it clear that the main clause is attributive, and that Mary's attitude is a sceptical or dissociative one.

A central claim of relevance theory has been that verbal irony is tacitly dissociative: the speaker expresses a wry, or sceptical, or mocking attitude to an attributed utterance or thought (Sperber and Wilson 1981, 1990a, 1995, 1998b; Wilson and Sperber 1992). Consider Mary's utterance in (22c) above. This is clearly both ironical and echoic. Relevance theory claims that it is ironical partly *because* it is echoic: irony consists in echoing a tacitly attributed thought or utterance with a tacitly dissociative attitude. This analysis has been experimentally tested, and the theoretical claims behind it have been much discussed (Clark and Gerrig 1984; Curcó 1998; Jorgensen, Miller and Sperber 1984; Sperber 1984; Kreuz and Glucksberg 1989; Martin 1992; Gibbs 1994a; Kumon-Nakamura, Glucksberg and Brown 1995; Sperber and Wilson 1998b). There is experimental evidence that irony involves an extra layer of metarepresentation which makes it harder than metaphor to understand for people with autism who fail standard second-order false-belief tests and are therefore seen as lacking a second-order 'theory of mind' (Happé 1993; on the development of metaphor and irony, see Winner 1988).

On this account, verbal irony is interpretive: the speaker conveys a dissociative attitude to an attributed content. Parody might then be thought of as its metalinguistic counterpart: the speaker conveys a dissociative attitude not (only) to an attributed content but to the style or form of the original. Typically, the degree of resemblance involved in parody is quite loose. Consider (26a), a mocking inversion of the saying in (26b):

(26)   a. Our friends are always there when they need us.
         b. Our friends are always there when we need them.

(26a) is a case of echoic allusion, in which the speaker makes a serious assertion while simultaneously expressing a mocking attitude to the related utterance in (26b).[4] A further type of case which might be seen as involving an echoic allusion is (27b):

(27)   a. PRINCE CHARLES: Hello, I'm Prince Charles.
         b. TELEPHONE OPERATOR: And I'm the Queen of Sheba.

It has been suggested (I think by Dan Sperber) that the speaker of (27b) is echoing the utterance in (27a) in order to draw attention to a rather abstract property that the two utterances share: their obvious falsehood or absurdity (see Noh 1998b for discussion). In all these cases, the idea that attribution is based on resemblance rather than identity plays an important role.

Consider now the contrast between denial and negation. Negation is properly semantic; denial (typically conveyed by use of negative sentences) is a speech act, whose function is to reject some aspect of an attributed utterance or thought. In other words, denial is echoic. Here are some illustrations:

(28)   a. PETER: Oh, you're in a miserable foul mood tonight.
         b. MARY: I'm not in a miserable foul mood; I'm a little tired and would like to be left alone.

                                                        (Carston 1996: 322)

(29)   Around here we don't eat tom[eiDouz] and we don't get stressed out. We eat tom[a:touz] and we get a little tense now and then. (Carston 1996: 320)

(30)   Mozart's sonatas weren't for violin and piano, they were for piano and violin. (Horn 1989: 373)

(31)   I didn't manage to trap two mongeese: I managed to trap two mongooses. (Horn 1989: 373)

In (28b), Mary echoes and rejects Peter's description of her; in (29), the speaker objects to the American pronunciation of 'tomatoes' and the expression 'stressed out'; in (30), she rejects the description of Mozart's sonatas as 'for violin and piano'; and in (31), she rejects the claim that she managed to trap two 'mongeese' rather than two 'mongooses'. Such denials fit straightforwardly into the pattern of previous sections. Like regular quotations, they may be interpretive, as in (28), or metalinguistic, as in (29)–(31). As with irony and free indirect quotations, the presence of the attributive element is not overtly marked.

In fact, this picture of denial is not the standard one. Linguists generally define denial as involving the rejection of an attributed *utterance*, treating rejections of attributed thoughts as cases of regular negation. For example, van der Sandt (1991: 331) claims that the 'essential function' of echoic denials is 'to object to a previous utterance'. His category of denials would include (28)–(31), which all metarepresent attributed utterances, but would exclude rejections of attributed thoughts. Horn (1989, sections 3.2; 6) takes an even more restrictive view. He points out (correctly) that an utterance such as (28) may be used to reject not only previous utterances but also attributed thoughts or assumptions which are 'in the discourse model'; however, instead of concluding that all these cases are echoic denials, he decides to exclude all of them from his category of echoic utterances. For him, the only genuine cases of echoic denial are metalinguistic, based on resemblances in form. Carston (1996) offers what seems to me a more satisfactory account. She includes in the category of echoic denials the full set of cases involving both attributed utterances and attributed thoughts. On her account, (28)–(31) would all be treated as echoic, as would any utterance used to metarepresent and reject an attributed utterance or thought (for discussion, see Horn 1985, 1989; Burton-Roberts 1989; McCawley 1991; van der Sandt 1991; Carston 1996; Iwata 1998; Noh 1998b, 2000).

What linguists call 'echo questions' are formally distinguishable from regular interrogatives by their declarative syntax and rising intonation. Their treatment has generally run parallel to the treatment of metalinguistic negation. Consider (22b) above, or (32b)–(34b):

(32)   a. PETER: You finally managed to solve the problems.
        b. MARY: Managed? I solved them in two minutes.

(Noh 1998a: 611)

(33)   a. PETER: I need a holiday.
        b. MARY: You need a holiday? What about me?

(34)   a. TOURIST: Where can I find some tom[eiDouz]?
        b. LONDONER: You want tom[eiDouz]? Try New York.

All four questions are clearly echoic in the sense defined above: the speaker echoes and questions some aspect of the form or content of an attributed utterance. However, as with echoic denials, linguistic analyses of echoic questions have generally been over-restrictive. 'Echo questions' are generally treated as echoing prior utterances, not thoughts:

Echo questions are distinguished from other questions by their restricted context. An echo occurs in dialogue as a reaction to a prior utterance and is interpretable only with respect to it, while other questions may be the first or the only utterance in a discourse. (Banfield 1982: 124)

Echo questions generally require a linguistic context in which the original utterance ...
has been previously uttered within the discourse. (Horn 1989: 381)

Yet there seem to be clear cases of echoic questions used to metarepresent
attributed thoughts. Compare (35a)–(35c):

(35)   a. MARY [*seeing Peter walk towards the door*]: Just a minute. You're going
shopping?

           b. ?MARY [*seeing Peter walk towards the door*]: Just a minute. Henry VIII
had six wives?

           c. MARY [*seeing Peter walk towards the door*]: Just a minute. Did Henry VIII
have six wives?

Here, the echoic question in (35a) and the regular interrogative in (35c) are
pragmatically appropriate, but the echoic question in (35b) is not. The
obvious way of explaining this would be to treat the utterances in (35a) and
(35b) as echoing and questioning thoughts that Mary attributes to Peter. In
(35a), his behaviour gives her ground for inferring his thoughts even though
he hasn't spoken: in (35b), it does not. This would make it possible to
maintain the parallel between verbal irony, denials and echo questions: all
are tacitly attributive, and all may be used for the attribution of both utterances and thoughts (Blakemore 1994; Escandell-Vidal 1998, 2002; Noh
1998a, 1998c, 2000).

11.4.4   *Non-attributive cases*

So far, the only lower-order representations I have looked at have been
attributive. As noted in section 11.1, there are also non-attributive cases:
mentions of sentence types, utterance types or proposition types, as in (6)
(repeated below):

(6)   a. 'Dragonflies are beautiful' is a sentence of English.
        b. 'Shut up' is rude.
        c. It's true that tulips are flowers.
        d. ROSES AND DAISIES ARE FLOWERS entails that roses are flowers.
        e. I like the name 'Petronella'.
        f. 'Abeille' is not a word of English.
        g. TULIP implies FLOWER.

These are worth considering because they do not obviously fall within the scope
of the metapsychological or metacommunicative abilities, and might contrast in
interesting ways with attributions of utterances and thoughts.

To understand the cases of mention in (6), the hearer must be able to recognise
linguistic, logical or conceptual resemblances between representations

considered in the abstract rather than tied to a particular individual, place or time. Because no attribution is involved, this ability might be present even if the intuitive metapsychological or metacommunicative capacity is impaired. Indeed, there is evidence from the autobiographical writings of people with autism (several of whom have been students of linguistics) of a serious interest in linguistic form (Williams 1992; Frith and Happé 1999; Willey 1999). Here is how one of them describes her fascination with language:

> Linguistics and the act of speaking itself have always been among my keenest interests ... Words, and everything about them, hold my concentration like nothing else. On my overstuffed bookshelf sit several thesauruses, a half dozen dictionaries, famous quotations books, and a handful of personal reflection journals. Language appeals to me because it lends itself to rules and precision even more often than it does to subjectivity ... Some words can please my eyes, given that they have the symmetry of line and shape I favor. Other words can fascinate me by the melodies they sing when they are spoken. Properly handled ... words can work miracles on my sensibilities and my understanding of the world, because each one has its own personality and nuance and its own lesson to teach. (Willey 1999: 30)

This is in marked contrast to the comments of the same writer on her inability to discern the intentions behind other people's use of words.

Relevance theorists have argued that there are several further types of non-attributive metarepresentation which have been less widely recognised, and which clearly contrast with the attributive cases discussed above. For example, regular (non-attributive) interrogatives and exclamatives have been treated in relevance theory as representations of *desirable thoughts* (or desirable information); and regular (non-attributive) negations and disjunctions have been treated as representations of *possible thoughts* (possible information). Parallel to these, we might expect to find (non-attributive) representations of possible and desirable utterances. I will end this survey with a few illustrations of each.

In relevance theory, regular (non-echoic) interrogatives such as those in (36) have been analysed as the metarepresentational counterparts of imperatives:

(36)   a. Is today Tuesday?
        b. What day is it today?
        c. When are we leaving?

Imperatives are used to represent *desirable states of affairs*; interrogatives are used to represent *desirable thoughts*. Someone who utters an imperative indicates that she is thinking about a state of affairs which she regards as desirable from someone's point of view. Someone who utters an interrogative indicates that she is thinking about a possible thought (or a potential piece of information) which she regards as desirable from someone's point of view.

Since thoughts are desirable only because they are relevant, this amounts to claiming that interrogatives represent relevant thoughts, and since the thought metarepresented by an utterance must resemble the utterance in content, this amounts to claiming that questions metarepresent relevant answers (Wilson and Sperber 1988a; Clark 1991; Sperber and Wilson 1995: chapter 4, section 10).

This account of interrogatives has some advantages over alternative analyses. For example, in speech-act theory, interrogatives are generally treated as encoding requests for information (Bach and Harnish 1979; Harnish 1994; Searle 1969). One problem with this approach is that not all interrogative utterances are requests for information: they may be offers of information, rhetorical questions, exam questions, idle speculations, and so on. Relevance theory solves this problem in the following way. An interrogative utterance merely indicates that the speaker regards the answer as relevant to *someone*. It will only be understood as a request for information if two further contextual conditions are fulfilled: (a) it is manifest that the speaker regards the answer as relevant to herself; and (b) it is manifest that the hearer is in a position to provide it. In other conditions, it will be differently understood. For example, it will be understood as an offer of information if (a) it is manifest that the speaker regards the answer as relevant to the hearer, and (b) it is manifest that the speaker herself is in a position to provide it. Other types of interrogative speech act also fall out naturally from this account (Wilson and Sperber 1988a, 1988b; Clark 1991; Sperber and Wilson 1995: chapter 4, section 10).

The analysis of interrogatives as inherently metarepresentational brings them into interesting contact with the literature on mindreading. On the relevance-theoretic account, the production and interpretation of interrogatives necessarily involves a higher degree of metarepresentational ability than standard declaratives, but differs in two respects from the examples that have been central in the 'theory of mind' literature: first, the metarepresented proposition is not attributed to anyone, and second, it is not treated as either false (as in the false-belief task) or true (as in pretence). The fact that it is not attributed to anyone suggests that someone who fails second-order 'theory of mind' tasks might be expected to pass tasks involving regular interrogatives, but fail on echo questions, for example.

If interrogatives are used to metarepresent desirable thoughts, we might expect to find cases in which an utterance is used to metarepresent a desirable utterance. There is no shortage of candidates. Here are some possible examples:

(37)   a. VICAR [*to bride*]: I, Amanda, take you, Bertrand, to be my lawful wedded husband.
         BRIDE: I, Amanda, take you, Bertrand, to be my lawful, wedded husband.

(38)   MARY [*to Peter, as doorbell rings*]: If that's John, I'm not here.

(Noh 1998c)

(39)   a. QUIZ-SHOW HOST: The first man to walk on the moon was?
         b. CONTESTANT: Neil Diamond.

In (37a), the vicar metarepresents an utterance that he wants the bride to produce. In the 'speech-act conditional' in (38), the consequent is used to metarepresent an utterance that Mary wants Peter to produce; (38) expresses something equivalent to 'If that's John, *say* I'm not here' (van der Auwera 1986; Sweetser 1990; Noh 1998c). The quiz-show question in (39) might be analysed on similar lines: the host is not producing a regular interrogative, but meta-representing an utterance he wants the contestant to produce. Further illustrations include the utterances of prompters in a theatre, and solicitors whispering answers to their clients in court.

The literature on standard mentions contains many examples of utterances used to represent possible thoughts or utterances. For instance, mentions of propositions, as in (6c)–(6d) above, amount to metarepresentations of possible thought types, and mentions of utterances, as in (6b) above, amount to metarepresentations of possible utterance types. But there may be a much wider range of candidates than this. Consider the examples in (40):

(40)   a. Ducks don't bite.
         b. Maybe I'll leave.
         c. Either William will become a soldier or Harry will.

Regular (non-attributive) uses of negation, modals and disjunctions, as in (40a)–(40c), seem to presuppose the ability to think about possible thoughts and evaluate their truth or falsity, which suggests that there is some ground for treating all these examples as metarepresentational. The development of attributive uses of negatives, modals and interrogatives contrasts in interesting ways with the development of non-attributive uses, and this might shed some light on the interaction between metalogical, metacommunicative and metapsychological abilities (Overton 1990; Gombert 1990; Bloom 1991; Noveck, Ho and Sera 1996; Morris and Sloutsky 1998; Papafragou 1998c).

Apart from the standard mentions of utterance types illustrated in (6b) above, metarepresentations of possible but non-attributed utterances might include the following advertisements from a recent Glenfiddich whisky campaign in England:

(41)   [*Picture of a newspaper with the headline*]: French admit Britain is best.
         [*Caption*]: Till then, there's Glenfiddich to enjoy.

(42)   [*Picture of a newspaper with the headline*]: World's funniest man is a Belgian.
         [*Caption*]: Till then, there's Glenfiddich to enjoy.

Drafts, essay plans and rehearsals of future conversations might be seen as providing further examples. There is evidence, then, that all four categories of non-attributive representation are filled.

11.5   Conclusion

In this survey, I have tried to show something of the depth and variety of the metarepresentational abilities used in verbal comprehension. Language is full of metarepresentational devices, but the information they encode falls far short of determining the speaker's meaning: I have outlined a pragmatic comprehension procedure which might help to resolve such indeterminacies in meaning and form the basis for a modularised metacommunicative ability which is itself a sub-part of a more general metapsychological ability, or 'theory of mind'.

The comprehension of linguistic metarepresentations (i.e. those expressed as utterances) also interacts with the metapsychological ability in interesting ways. I have tried to show that linguistic metarepresentations vary not only in degree of explicitness but also in the type of original they are used to represent: utterances, thoughts or abstract representations. By comparing comprehension in these different types of case, it might be possible to gain new insight into the metapsychological and metacommunicative abilities. To take just one illustration, there are cases (such as (20) above) in which the mindreading ability directly feeds the comprehension process, by using paralinguistic information (gestures, facial expressions, intonation, and so on) as clues to the speaker's mood or epistemic state, which may in turn be picked out by the pragmatic comprehension procedure for attribution as part of a speaker's meaning. Inferring these aspects of speaker's meaning is likely to prove particularly difficult for people whose general mindreading ability is impaired. It would be interesting to investigate whether the use of overt linguistic devices would facilitate comprehension in these cases, and if so, in what way.[5] For instance, is it easier to attribute a false belief when it is expressed or implied by an utterance ('The ball is in the cupboard') than by inferring it on the basis of non-communicative behaviour alone?

From the linguist's point of view, there are also benefits to be gained by considering metarepresentational devices in the context of the more general metapsychological and metacommunicative abilities. As I have shown, in studying linguistic metarepresentations, linguists have tended to concentrate on cases involving the attribution of utterances, and many echoic utterances and 'hearsay' devices may have broader uses than existing research suggests. Studies of lexical acquisition are already being conducted within a broader metacommunicative and metapsychological framework; the acquisition of specifically metarepresentational devices within this framework should also yield interesting results.

Part III

Cross-Disciplinary Themes

12 Pragmatics, modularity and mindreading

Dan Sperber and Deirdre Wilson

12.1 Introduction

Pragmatic studies of verbal communication start from the assumption (first defended in detail by the philosopher Paul Grice) that an essential feature of most human communication, both verbal and non-verbal, is the expression and recognition of intentions (Grice 1957, 1969, 1982, 1989). On this approach, pragmatic interpretation is ultimately an exercise in metapsychology, in which the hearer infers the speaker's intended meaning from evidence she has provided for this purpose. An utterance is, of course, a linguistically coded piece of evidence, so that verbal comprehension involves an element of decoding. However, the decoded linguistic meaning is merely the starting point for an inferential process that results in the attribution of a speaker's meaning.

The central problem for pragmatics is that the linguistic meaning recovered by decoding vastly underdetermines the speaker's meaning. There may be ambiguities and referential ambivalences to resolve, ellipses to interpret, and other indeterminacies of explicit content to deal with. There may be implicatures to identify, illocutionary indeterminacies to resolve, metaphors and ironies to interpret. All this requires an appropriate set of contextual assumptions, which the hearer must also supply. To illustrate, consider the examples in (1) and (2):

(1)   a. They gave him life.
        b. Everyone left.
        c. The school is close to the hospital.
        d. The road is flat.
        e. Coffee will be served in the lounge.

(2)   a. The lecture was as you would expect.
        b. Some of the students did well in the exam.
        c. Someone's forgotten to take out the rubbish.
        d. TEACHER: Have you handed in your essay?
           STUDENT: I've had a lot to do recently.
        e. John is a soldier.

In order to decide what the speaker intended to assert, the hearer may have to disambiguate and assign reference, as in (1a), fix the scope of quantifiers, as in (1b), and assign appropriate interpretations to vague expressions or approximations, as in (1c)–(1d). In order to decide what speech act the speaker intended to perform, he may have to resolve illocutionary indeterminacies, as in (1e) (which may be interpreted as an assertion, a request or a guess). Many utterances also convey implicit meaning (*implicatures*): for example, (2a) may implicate that the lecture was good (or bad), (2b) may implicate that not all the students did well in the exam, (2c) may convey an indirect request and (2d) an indirect answer, while (2e) may be literally, metaphorically or ironically intended. Pragmatic interpretation involves the resolution of such linguistic indeterminacies on the basis of contextual information. The hearer's task is to find the meaning the speaker intended to convey, and the goal of pragmatic theory is to explain how this is done.

Most pragmaticists working today would agree with this characterisation of pragmatics. Most would also agree that pragmatic interpretation is ultimately a non-demonstrative inference process which takes place at a risk: there is no guarantee that the meaning constructed, even by a hearer correctly following the best possible procedure, is the one the speaker intended to convey. However, this picture may be fleshed out in several different ways, with different implications for the relation of pragmatics to other cognitive systems. On the one hand, there are those who argue that most, if not all, aspects of the process of constructing a hypothesis about the speaker's meaning are closely related to linguistic decoding. These code-like aspects of interpretation might be carried out within an extension of the language module, by non-metapsychological processes whose output might then be inferentially evaluated and attributed as a speaker's meaning. On the other hand, there are those who see pragmatic interpretation as metapsychological through and through. On this approach, both hypothesis construction and hypothesis evaluation are seen as rational processes geared to the recognition of speakers' intentions, carried out by Fodorian central processes (Fodor 1983), or by a 'theory of mind' module dedicated to the attribution of mental states on the basis of behaviour (Astington, Harris and Olson 1988; Davies and Stone 1995a, 1995b; Carruthers and Smith 1996). Both positions are being explored in current work on pragmatics.

We want to defend a view of pragmatic interpretation as metapsychological through and through. However, departing from our earlier views (Wilson and Sperber 1986; Sperber and Wilson 1995), we will argue that pragmatic interpretation is not simply a matter of applying Fodorian central systems or general mindreading abilities to a particular (communicative) domain. Verbal comprehension presents special challenges, and exhibits certain regularities, not found in other domains. It therefore lends itself to the development of a dedicated comprehension module with its own particular principles and mechanisms. We will show how such a metacommunicative module might have evolved as a specialisation of a more general mindreading module, and what principles and mechanisms it might contain; we will also indicate briefly how it might apply to the resolution of linguistic indeterminacies such as those in (1) and (2) (for fuller accounts, see Sperber and Wilson 1995; Carston 2002a; Wilson and Sperber 2004).

12.2   Two approaches to communication

Before Grice's pioneering work, the only available theoretical model of communication was what we have called the classical code model (Sperber and Wilson 1995: chapter 1, sections 1–5; Wilson 1998a), which treats communication as involving a sender, a receiver, a set of observable signals, a set of unobservable messages, and a code that relates the two. The sender selects a message and transmits the corresponding signal, which is received and decoded at the other end; when all goes well, the result is the reproduction in the receiver of the original message. Coded communication need involve no metapsychological abilities. It clearly exists in nature, in both pure and mixed forms (where coding and inference are combined). Much animal communication is purely coded: for example, the bee dance used to indicate the direction and distance of nectar (von Frisch 1967; Hauser 1996). It is arguable that some human non-verbal communication is purely coded: for example, the interpretation by neonates of facial expressions of emotion (Fridlund 1994; Sigman and Kasari 1995; Wharton 2003b). Human verbal communication, by contrast, involves a mixture of coding and inference. As we have seen, it contains an element of inferential intention-attribution; but it is also partly coded, since the grammar of a language just is a code which pairs phonetic representations of sentences with semantic representations of sentences.

In studying such a mixed form of communication, there is room for debate about where the borderline between coding and inference should be drawn. One way of limiting the role of metapsychological processes in verbal comprehension would be to argue for an extension in the domain of grammar, and hence in the scope of (non-metapsychological) linguistic decoding processes. This is sometimes done by postulating hidden linguistic constituents or multiple ambiguities; approaches along these lines are suggested by Millikan (1984, 1998) and Stanley (2002) (for discussion, see Origgi and Sperber 2000; Carston 2004; Breheny 2002). But however far the domain of grammar is expanded, there comes a point at which pragmatic choices – choices based on contextual information – must be made. An obvious example of a pragmatic process is reference resolution, where the hearer has to choose among a range of linguistically possible interpretations of a referential expression (e.g. 'I', 'now', 'this', 'they') on the basis of contextual information. Here, too, it is possible to argue that code-like procedures play a role in determining how pragmatic choices are made.

Many formal and computational approaches to linguistics suggest that certain aspects of pragmatic interpretation can be dealt with in code-like terms. One way of handling reference resolution along these lines is to set up contextual parameters for the speaker, hearer, time of utterance, place of utterance, and so on, and treat the interpretation of referential expressions such as 'I', 'you', 'here' and 'now' as initially determined by reference to these (e.g. Lewis 1970; Kaplan 1989). There are also code-like ('default-based') treatments of generalised conversational implicatures (e.g. the implicature regularly carried by (2b) above that not all the students did well in the exam) (see for example Gazdar 1979; Lascarides and Asher 1993; Levinson 2000). These formal accounts might be combined with an inferential approach by assuming that the output of these non-metapsychological pragmatic decoding processes is inferentially evaluated before being attributed as a speaker's meaning.

Grice himself seems to have seen explicit communication as largely a matter of linguistic and contextual decoding, and only implicit communication as properly inferential (Grice 1967/1989: 25), and many pragmaticists have followed him on this (see Searle 1969; Bach and Harnish 1979; Levinson 1983; Bach 1994a; for discussion, see the papers by Breheny, Carston, Recanati and Stanley in *Mind & Language* 17, 2002). However, the code-like pragmatic rules that have been proposed so far do not work particularly well. For example, even if 'now' refers to the time of utterance, it is still left to the hearer to decide whether the speaker, on a given occasion, meant *now this second, this minute, this hour, day, week, year*, etc. (Predelli 1998). For other referential expressions (e.g. 'he', 'they', 'this', 'that'), and for disambiguation and the other aspects of explicit communication illustrated in (1) above, it is hard to think of a code-like treatment at all. Similarly, default-based accounts of generalised conversational implicatures typically overgenerate (Carston 1998a), and it is widely acknowledged that particularised implicatures (which depend on special features of the context) are not amenable to code-like treatment at all (Levinson 2000).

What the available psycholinguistic evidence shows is that, other things being equal, from a range of contextually available interpretations, hearers tend to choose the most salient or accessible one, the one that costs the least processing effort to construct (Gernsbacher 1994). This is also what many theoretical accounts of pragmatic interpretation (e.g. Lewis 1979; Sperber and Wilson 1995) predict that hearers should do. The question is whether they do this because they are following a conventional, code-like procedure that children have to learn (as they have to learn that 'I' refers to the speaker, 'now' to the time of utterance, and so on), or because this is a sound way of inferring the speaker's intentions, independently of any convention. If it is such a rational procedure, then it falls outside the scope of a decoding model and inside an inferential account. We will argue that, within the specifically communicative domain, it is indeed rational for hearers to follow a path of least effort in constructing a hypothesis about the speaker's meaning, and that the pragmatic interpretation process is therefore genuinely inferential (for discussion, see Origgi and Sperber 2000; Carston 2002b; Recanati 2002b).

Inferential comprehension, then, is ultimately a metapsychological process involving the construction and evaluation of a hypothesis about the communicator's meaning on the basis of evidence she has provided for this purpose. It clearly exists in humans, in both pure and mixed forms. As we have seen, verbal communication involves a mixture of coding and inference, and there is room for debate about the relative contributions of each. By contrast, much non-verbal communication is purely inferential. For example, when I point to the clouds to indicate that I was right to predict that it would rain, or hold up my full glass to indicate that you need not open a new bottle on my account, there is no way for you to decode my behaviour, and no need for you to do so. You could work out what I intend to convey by a straightforward exercise in mindreading, by attributing to me the intention that would best explain my behaviour in the situation (though if we are right, you can actually do it even more directly, via a dedicated comprehension procedure). Thus, metapsychological inference plays a central role in human communication, both verbal and non-verbal.

These theoretical arguments are confirmed by a wealth of experimental evidence linking the development and breakdown of general mindreading abilities and communicative abilities, both verbal and non-verbal. In autism, both general mindreading and non-verbal communication are impaired (Baron-Cohen 1995; Perner, Frith, Leslie and Leekam 1989; Sigman and Kasari 1995; see also Langdon, Davies and Coltheart 2002). There are also links between the development and breakdown of general mindreading and verbal communication (Happé 1993; Wilson 2000; and the papers by Bloom, Happé and Loth, Langdon, Davies and Coltheart, and Papafragou in *Mind and Language* 17, 2002). For example, normal word learning involves the ability to track speakers' intentions, and correlates in interesting ways with the ability to pass the false-belief tests used in the study of general mindreading (Bloom 2000, 2002; Happé and Loth 2002). Reference resolution is another pragmatic ability that correlates in interesting ways with the ability to pass false-belief tests (Mitchell, Robinson and Thompson 1999); and there seems to be a well-established correlation between the interpretation of irony and second-order mindreading abilities (Happé 1993; Langdon, Davies and Coltheart 2002). However, there are different ways of analysing both general mindreading abilities and their links to specifically communicative abilities. In the next section, we will consider some of these.

12.3   Two approaches to inferential communication

Grice was rather non-committal on the source of pragmatic abilities and their place in the overall architecture of the mind. He wanted to be able to show that our communicative behaviour is rational:

> I am enough of a rationalist to want to find a basis that underlies these facts, undeniable though they may be; I would like to be able to think of the standard type of conversational practice not merely as something that all or most do *in fact* follow but as something that it is reasonable for us to follow, that we *should not* abandon. (Grice 1967/1989: 29)

However, he was prepared to retreat, if necessary, to the 'dull but, no doubt at a certain level, adequate answer' that 'it is just a well-recognised empirical fact that people do behave in these ways; they learned to do so in childhood and have not lost the habit of doing so' (pp. 28–29).

He was equally non-committal on the form of the comprehension process. What he clearly established was a link between pragmatic abilities and more general mindreading abilities. But mindreading itself can be analysed in rather different ways. It may be thought of as a conscious, reflective activity, involving Fodorian central processes, and many of Grice's remarks about the derivation of implicatures are consistent with this. For example, his rational reconstruction of the derivation of conversational implicatures is a straightforward exercise in 'belief–desire' psychology:

> He said that P; he could not have done this unless he thought that Q; he knows (and knows that I know that he knows) that I will realise that it is necessary to suppose that Q; he has done nothing to stop me thinking that Q; so he intends me to think, or is at least willing for me to think, that Q. (Grice 1967/1989: 30–31)

For Grice, calculability was an essential property of implicatures, and he gave several examples of how particular implicatures might be derived using a 'working-out schema' like the one given above. But there are several reasons for thinking that the actual comprehension process should not be modelled along these lines.

In the first place, it is hard to imagine even adults going through such lengthy chains of inference in the attribution of speaker meanings. Yet preverbal infants already appear to be heavily involved in inferential communication, and they are surely not using the form of conscious, discursive reasoning illustrated in Grice's 'working-out schema' (see the papers by Bloom, Happé and Loth, and Papafragou in *Mind and Language* 17, 2002). In the second place, we have argued above that Grice substantially underestimated the amount of metapsychological inference involved in comprehension. Given the failure of the non-metapsychological pragmatic decoding account, his working-out schema for implicatures would have to be supplemented with further schemas designed to deal with disambiguation, reference assignment and other inferential aspects of explicit communication. While reflective inferences of this type do occur when spontaneous inference fails to yield a satisfactory interpretation, inferential comprehension is in general an intuitive, unreflective process which takes place below the level of consciousness.

All this is more consistent with a view of inferential comprehension as falling within the domain of an intuitive 'theory of mind' module. This view is tacitly adopted in much of the literature on mindreading, and explicitly defended by Bloom (2000, 2002). Grice himself makes remarks indicating that he might not have been averse to a modularised implementation of his approach, in which the recovery of implicatures was treated as an intuitive rather than a reflective process:

The presence of a conversational implicature must be capable of being worked out; for even if it can in fact be intuitively grasped, unless the intuition is replaceable by an argument, the implicature (if present at all) will not count as a conversational implicature; it will be a conventional implicature. (Grice 1967/1989: 31)

There is thus no requirement in the Gricean framework that implicatures should actually be recovered by reflective reasoning. A modular view is also possible.

There has been a strong (though by no means unanimous) trend in the development of the cognitive sciences, and in particular in developmental and evolutionary psychology and in neuropsychology, towards a more modular view of the mind. (We use 'module' in a looser sense than the one suggested by Fodor 1983, to mean a domain- or task-specific autonomous computational mechanism; see Sperber 1996: chapter 6; 2001.) One reason for this trend is that a general-purpose inferential mechanism can only derive conclusions based on the formal (logical or statistical) properties of the input information it processes. By contrast, a dedicated inferential mechanism or module can take advantage of regularities in its specific domain, and use inferential procedures which are justified by these regularities, but only in this domain. Typically, dedicated modules exploit the relatively 'fast and frugal heuristic' (Gigerenzer, Todd *et al.* 1999) afforded by their special domain.

A cognitive ability may become modularised in the course of cognitive development, as in the case of reading or chess expertise. However, it is reasonable to assume that many modular structures have a strong genetic component. The selection pressures which lead to the emergence of cognitive systems over evolutionary time must also tend to make these systems more efficient, and in particular to attune them, via dedicated mechanisms, to the specific problems and opportunities it is their function to handle. Much developmental evidence also suggests that infants and young children come equipped with domain-specific cognitive mechanisms (Hirschfeld and Gelman 1994; Barkow, Cosmides and Tooby 1995). Mindreading is one of the best-evidenced cases in this respect.

Most theories of mindreading do assume that it is performed not by a general-purpose reasoning mechanism, which takes as premises a number of explicit hypotheses about the relationships between behaviour and mental states, but by a dedicated module. What is still open to debate is how this module exploits the regularities in intentional behaviour. According to the rationalisation (or 'theory-theory') account, the mindreading module carries out a form of belief–desire reasoning which differs from the 'folk-psychology' of philosophers not so much in its logic as in the fact that it is modularised: that is, performed automatically, unconsciously, and so on. On this approach, mindreading is a form of automatic inference to the best rationalisation of behaviour. It involves, in particular, the attribution to the agent of beliefs and desires that would make her observed behaviour rational given its actual or likely effects. Another possibility (proposed by the 'simulation theory') is that mindreading succeeds by exploiting similarities between the interpreter and the agent whose behaviour is being interpreted, and amounts to a form of simulation. However, while it is true that an utterance is a type of action, and a speaker's meaning is a type of intention, we want to argue that neither the rationalisation nor the simulation view of mindreading adequately accounts for the hearer's ability to retrieve the speaker's meaning.

According to the rationalisation account (e.g. Davies and Stone 1995b; Carruthers and Smith 1996), the procedure for inferring the intention behind an action should be as follows: first, decide what effect of the action the agent could have both predicted and desired; second, assume that this was the effect the agent intended to achieve. In most cases of utterance interpretation, this rationalisation procedure would not work, because the desired effect just *is* the recognition of the speaker's intention. As we have seen, the gap between sentence meaning and speaker's meaning is so great (going well beyond the standard ambiguities normally considered in the literature) that there may be no way of listing the possible speaker's meanings without some advance knowledge – however sketchy – of what she might want to convey. Moreover, the range of possible speaker's meanings that the hearer is able to reconstruct may include several candidates that, to the best of his knowledge, the speaker might have wanted to convey. In other words, only a hearer with some advance knowledge of at least the gist of what the speaker might have wanted to convey would find it relatively easy to reconstruct the intention behind her utterance using a rationalisation procedure. But we often say or write things that our hearers or readers did not anticipate, and we have no particular reason to doubt that we will be understood. In such cases, the standard procedures for inferring intentions do not help with identifying the speaker's meaning. Unlike what happens in regular cases of intention attribution, hearers cannot *first* identify a desirable effect of the utterance, and *then* infer that the speaker's intention was precisely to achieve this effect.

According to the simulation account (e.g. Davies and Stone 1995a), we attribute intentions by imaginatively simulating the action we are interpreting, thus discovering in ourselves the intention that underlies it. As an account of comprehension, this is not too promising either. Since the same sentence can be used to convey quite different meanings in different situations, a hearer who is simulating the speaker's linguistic action in order to retrieve her meaning must provide a considerable amount of contextualisation, based on particular hypotheses about the speaker's beliefs, preferences, and so on. Again, this would only work in cases where the hearer already has a fairly good idea of what the speaker is likely to mean. On this approach, the routine communication of genuinely unanticipated contents would be difficult or impossible to explain.

More generally, the problem of applying a unitary procedure for inferring intentions from actions to the special case of inferring speakers' meanings from utterances is that speakers' meanings typically carry a vastly greater amount of information than more ordinary intentions. This is true whether information is treated in quantitative probabilistic or qualitative semantic terms. In the repertoire of human actions, utterances are much more differentiated than other types of actions: many utterances are wholly new, whereas it is relatively rare to come across actions that are not reiterations of previous actions. While stereotypical utterances ('Nice day, isn't it?') make up a significant proportion of all uttered sentence *tokens*, they are only a minute proportion of all uttered sentence *types*. Leaving stereotypical utterances aside, the prior probability of most utterances ever occurring is close to zero, as Chomsky pointed out long ago. Semantically, the complexity of ordinary intentions is limited by the range of possible actions, which is in turn constrained by many practicalities. There are no such limitations on the semantic complexity of speakers' meanings. Quite simply, we can say so much more than we can do. Regular intention attribution, whether achieved via rationalisation or simulation, is greatly facilitated by the relatively narrow range of possible actions available to an agent at a time. There is no corresponding facilitation in the attribution of speakers' meanings. It is simply not clear how the standard procedures for intention attribution could yield attributions of speakers' meanings, except in easy and trivial cases.

Add to this the fact that, on both Gricean and relevance-theoretic accounts, there are always several levels of metarepresentation involved in inferential comprehension, while in regular mindreading a single level is generally enough (Grice 1989; Sperber and Wilson 1995: chapter 1; Wilson 2000). It is hard to believe that two-year-old children, who fail for instance on regular first-order false-belief tasks, can recognise and understand the peculiar multi-level representations involved in communication, using nothing more than a general ability to attribute intentions to agents in order to explain their behaviour.

All this makes it worth exploring the possibility that, within the overall 'theory of mind' module, there has evolved a specialised sub-module dedicated to comprehension, with its own proprietary concepts and mechanisms (Sperber 1996, 2000a).

Given the complexity of mindreading, the variety of tasks it has to perform, and the particular regularities exhibited by some of these tasks, it is quite plausible to assume that it involves a variety of sub-modules. A likely candidate for one sub-module of the mindreading mechanism is the ability, already present in infants, to infer what people are seeing or watching from the direction of their gaze. Presumably, the infant (or indeed the adult) who performs this sort of inference is not feeding a general-purpose inferential mechanism with, say, a conditional major premise of the form 'If the direction of gaze of a person P is towards an object O, then P is seeing O' and a minor premise of the form 'Mummy's direction of gaze is towards the cat' in order to derive the conclusion: 'Mummy is seeing the cat.' It is also unlikely that the infant (or the adult) rationalises or simulates the observed eye-movement behaviour. In other words, the inference involved is not just an application of a relatively general and internally undifferentiated mindreading module to the specific problem of inferring perceptual states from direction of gaze. It is much more plausible that humans are equipped from infancy with a dedicated module, an Eye Direction Detector (Baron-Cohen 1995), which exploits the de facto strong correlation between direction of gaze and visual perception, and directly attributes perceptual and attentional states on the basis of direction of gaze. This attribution may itself provide input for other dedicated devices, such as those involved in word learning (Bloom 2000, 2002). In infants at least, such attributions need not be available at all for domain-general inference or verbal expression.

Similarly, for reasons given above, we doubt that normal verbal comprehension is achieved either by wondering what beliefs and desires would make it rational for the speaker to have produced a given utterance, or by simulating the state of mind that might have led her to produce it. The question is: Are there regularities specific to the production of utterances (or of communicative behaviour more generally) which might ground a more effective dedicated procedure for inferring a speaker's meaning from her utterance? If there are, they are not immediately obvious, unlike the strong and simple correlation between gaze direction and visual attention. Nevertheless, we have argued (Sperber and Wilson 1995; Sperber 2000a; Wilson 2000) that human communication exploits a tendency of human cognition to seek relevance in a way that narrowly constrains the interpretation of utterances, thus providing inferential comprehension with a strong regularity in the data which justifies a dedicated procedure. In the next section, we will outline these claims, adopting an evolutionary perspective.

12.4 Relevance, cognition and communication

Two kinds of evolutionary transformation may be distinguished. Some are continuous, and involve the gradual increase or decrease of a variable such as body size or visual acuity. Others are discrete, and involve the gradual emergence of a new trait or property, such as eyes or wings. We claim that relevance has been involved in two evolutionary transformations in human cognition, one of which is continuous and the other discrete. The continuous transformation has been an increasing tendency of the human cognitive system to maximise the relevance of the information it processes. The discrete transformation has been the emergence of a relevance-based comprehension module.

Cognitive efficiency, like any other kind of efficiency, is a matter of striking the best possible balance between costs and benefits. In the case of cognition, the cost is the mental effort required to construct representations of actual or desired states of affairs, to retrieve stored information from memory, and to draw inferences. The benefits are cognitive effects: that is, enrichments, revisions and reorganisations of existing beliefs and plans, which improve the organism's knowledge and capacity for successful action (Sperber and Wilson 1995).

In most animal species, the function of cognition is to monitor quite specific features of the environment (or of the organism itself) which enable it to exploit opportunities (for feeding, mating, and so on) and avoid dangers (from predators, poisonous food, and so on). For these animals, cognitive efficiency is a matter of achieving these benefits at the lowest possible cost. When the environment of such a species has remained stable enough for long enough, there is likely to have been a continuous transformation in the direction of greater efficiency, involving, in particular, a reduction in the costs required to achieve the given range of benefits. In some cases, this increase in efficiency may also involve the emergence of cognitive mechanisms attuned to specific aspects of the environment, which provide new cognitive benefits: this would be an example of a discrete transformation.

In humans, a considerable amount of cognitive activity is spent in processing information which has no immediate relevance to improving the organism's condition. Instead, a massive investment is made in developing a rich, well-organised data-base of information about a great many diverse aspects of the world. Some – though not all – of these data will turn out to be of practical use, perhaps in unforeseen ways. As a result, humans have an outstanding degree of adaptability to varied and changing environmental conditions, at the cost of a uniquely high investment in cognition.

Human cognition has three notable characteristics: it involves the constant monitoring of a wide variety of environmental features, the permanent availability (with varying degrees of accessibility) of a huge amount of memorised data, and a capacity for effortful attentional processing which can handle only a rather limited amount of information at any given time. The result is an attentional bottleneck: only a fraction of the monitored environmental information can be attentionally processed, and only a fraction of the memorised information can be brought to bear on it. Not all the monitored features of the environment are equally worth attending to, and not all the memorised data are equally helpful in processing a given piece of environmental information. Cognitive efficiency in humans is primarily a matter of being able to select, from the environment on the one hand, and from memory on the other, information which it is worth bringing together for joint – and costly – attentional processing.

What makes information worth attending to? There may be no general answer to this question, but merely a long list of properties – practical usefulness, importance to the goals of the individual, evocative power, and so forth – that provide partial answers. We have argued instead that all these partial answers are special cases of a truly general answer, based on a theoretical notion of relevance. Relevance, as we see it, is a potential property of external stimuli (e.g. utterances, actions) or internal representations (e.g. thoughts, memories) which provide input to cognitive processes. The relevance of an input for an individual at a given time is a positive function of the cognitive benefits that he would gain from processing it, and a negative function of the processing effort needed to achieve these benefits.

With relevance characterised in this way, it is easy to see that cognitive efficiency in humans is a matter of allocating the available attentional resources to the processing of the most relevant available inputs. We claim that in hominid evolution there has been a continuous pressure towards greater cognitive efficiency, so that human cognition is geared to the maximisation of relevance (we call this claim the First, or Cognitive, Principle of Relevance). This pressure has affected both the general organisation of the mind/brain and each of its components involved in perception, memory and inference. The result is not that humans invariably succeed in picking out the most relevant information available, but that they manage their cognitive resources in ways that are on the whole efficient and predictable.

The universal cognitive tendency to maximise relevance makes it possible, at least to some extent, to predict and manipulate the mental states of others. In particular, an individual A can often predict:

(a) which stimulus in an individual B's environment is likely to attract B's attention (i.e. the most relevant stimulus in that environment);
(b) which background information from B's memory is likely to be retrieved and used in processing this stimulus (i.e. the background information most relevant to processing it);
(c) which inferences B is likely to draw (i.e. those inferences which yield enough cognitive benefits for B's attentional resources to remain on the stimulus rather than being diverted to alternative potential inputs competing for those resources).

To illustrate: suppose that Peter and Mary are walking in the park. They are engaged in conversation; there are trees, flowers, birds and people all around them. Still, when Peter sees their acquaintance John in a group of people coming towards them, he correctly predicts that Mary will notice John, remember that he moved to Australia three months earlier, infer that there must be some reason why he is back in London, and conclude that it would be appropriate to ask him about this. Peter predicts Mary's train of thought so easily, and in such a familiar way, that it is not always appreciated how remarkable this is from a cognitive point of view. After all, there were lots of other stimuli that Mary might have noticed and paid attention to. Even if she did pay attention to John, there were lots of other things she could have remembered about him. Even if she did remember that he had left for Australia, there were lots of other inferences she could have drawn (for example, that he had been on a plane at least twice in the past three months). So why should it be so easy for Peter to predict Mary's train of thought correctly? Our answer is that it is easy for two reasons: first, because attention, memory retrieval and inference are guided by considerations of relevance, and second, because this regularity in the data is built into our ability to read the minds of others.

Most studies of mindreading have focused on the attribution of beliefs and desires. There has also been a lot of interest in joint attention, and particularly its role in early language acquisition. However, the understanding that we have of others routinely extends to an awareness of what they are attending to and thinking about even in situations where we ourselves are attending to and thinking about other things. There is no rich body of evidence on the development of these aspects of mindreading. However, it would be possible to set up, as a counterpart to the famous false-belief task, a 'disjoint attention task' in which the participant has to infer what a certain character is paying attention to in a situation where there is a discrepancy between (a) what is relevant to the participant and (b) what is relevant to the character. We predict that children will succeed on well-designed tasks of this kind long before they succeed on standard false-belief tasks. After all, children try to manipulate the attention of others long before they try to manipulate their beliefs.

This ability to recognise what other people are attending to and thinking about, and to predict how their attention and train of thought are likely to shift when a new stimulus is presented, may be used in manipulating their mental states. An individual A may act on the mental states of another individual B by producing a stimulus which is likely:

(a) to attract B's attention;
(b) to prompt the retrieval of certain background information from B's memory;
(c) when jointly processed with the background information whose retrieval it has prompted, to lead B to draw certain inferences intended by A.

A great deal of human interaction takes this form. Individual *A* introduces into the environment of another individual *B* a stimulus which is relevant to *B*, and which provides evidence for certain intended conclusions. For example, Peter opens the current issue of *Time Out*, intending not only to see what films are on, but also to provide Mary with evidence that he would like to go out that evening. Mary chooses not to stifle a yawn, thereby providing Peter with evidence that she is tired. In this interaction, each participant produces a stimulus which is relevant to the other, but neither openly presents this stimulus as manifestly intended to attract the other's attention. These are covert – or at least not manifestly overt – attempts at influencing others.

However, many attempts to influence others are quite overtly made. For example, Peter may establish eye contact with Mary and tap the issue of *Time Out* before opening it, making it clear that he intends Mary to pay attention to what he is doing and draw some specific conclusion from it. Mary may not only choose not to stifle her yawn, she may openly and deliberately exaggerate it, with similar results. By engaging in such ostensive behaviour, a communicator provides evidence not only for the conclusion she intends the addressee to draw, but also of the fact that she intends him to draw this conclusion. This is *ostensive–inferential* communication proper: that is, communication achieved by ostensively providing an addressee with evidence which enables him to infer the communicator's meaning.

Ostensive–inferential communication is not the only form of information transmission. A great deal of information is unintentionally transmitted and sub-attentively received. Some is covertly transmitted, particularly when it would be self-defeating to be open about the fact that one intends the other participant to come to a certain conclusion, as when wearing a disguise. However, ostensive–inferential communication is the most important form of information transmission among humans. In a wide range of cases, being open about one's intention to inform someone of something is the best way – or indeed the only way – of fulfilling this intention. For example, if Peter wants to go out with Mary, Mary will want to know about it; similarly, if Mary is too tired to go out, Peter will want to know about it. By being open about their intention to inform each other of something – that is, by drawing attention to their behaviour in a manifestly intentional way – each elicits the other's cooperation, in the form of increased attention and a greater willingness to make the necessary effort to discover the intended conclusion.

Notice that ostensive–inferential communication may be achieved without the communicator providing any direct evidence for the intended conclusion. All she has to do is provide evidence of the fact that she intends the addressee to come to this conclusion. For example, Peter might just tap the cover of *Time Out* without even opening it. This is not normally part of the preparations for going out, and provides no direct evidence of his desire to go out.

Still, by ostensively tapping the magazine, he does provide Mary with direct evidence that he intends her to come to the conclusion that he wants to go out. Similarly, when Mary ostensively imitates a yawn, this is not direct evidence that she is tired, but it is direct evidence that she intends Peter to come to the conclusion that she is tired. The same would be true if Peter said, 'Let's go out tonight!' and Mary replied, 'I'm tired'. Utterances do not provide direct evidence of the state of affairs they describe (notwithstanding some famous philosophical exceptions).

The fact that ostensive–inferential communication may be achieved simply by providing evidence about the communicator's intentions makes it possible to use symbolic behaviours as stimuli. These may be improvised (as when Peter taps the cover of the magazine), standardised (as in a fake yawn), or coded (as in an utterance). In each case, the symbolic stimulus provides evidence which, combined with the context, enables the audience to infer the communicator's meaning. How is this evidence used? How can it help the hearer discover the communicator's meaning when it never fully encodes it, and need not encode it at all? What procedure takes this evidence as input and delivers an interpretation of the communicator's meaning as output? This is where considerations of relevance come in.

12.5   Relevance and pragmatics

When it is manifest that individual *A* is producing an ostensive stimulus (e.g. an utterance) in order to communicate with another individual *B*, it is manifest that *A* intends *B* to find this stimulus worth his attention (or else, manifestly, communication would fail). Humans are good at predicting what will attract the attention of others. We have suggested that their success is based on a dedicated inferential procedure geared to considerations of relevance. These considerations are not spelled out and used as explicit premises in the procedure, but are built into its functioning instead. So when *B* understands that *A* intends him to find her ostensive stimulus worth his attention, we can unpack his understanding in terms of the notion of relevance (terms which remain tacit in *B*'s own understanding): *A* intends *B* to find the stimulus *relevant enough* to secure his attention.

Thus, every utterance (or other type of ostensive stimulus, though we will talk only of utterances from now on) conveys a presumption of its own relevance. We call this claim the Second, or Communicative, Principle of Relevance, and argue that it is the key to inferential comprehension (Sperber and Wilson 1995: chapter 3). What exactly is the content of the presumption of relevance that every utterance conveys? In the first place, as we have already argued, the speaker manifestly intends the hearer to find the utterance at least relevant enough to be worth his attention. But the amount of attention paid to an utterance can vary: it may be light or concentrated, fleeting or lasting, and may be attracted away by alternative competing stimuli. It is therefore manifestly in the speaker's interest for the hearer to find her utterance as relevant as possible, so that he pays it due attention. However, in producing an utterance, the speaker is also manifestly limited by her abilities (to provide relevant information, and to formulate it in the best possible way) and her preferences (and in particular her goal of getting the hearer to draw not just some relevant conclusion, but a specifically intended one). So the exact content of the presumption of relevance is as follows:

Presumption of relevance
The utterance is presumed to be the most relevant one compatible with the speaker's abilities and preferences, and at least relevant enough to be worth the hearer's attention.   (Sperber and Wilson 1995: 266–78)

The content of this presumption of relevance can be rationally reconstructed along the lines just shown, but there is no need to assume that hearers go through such a rational reconstruction process in interpreting utterances. Our suggestion is, rather, that the presumption of relevance is built into their comprehension procedures.

The fact that every utterance conveys a presumption of its own relevance (i.e. the communicative principle of relevance) motivates the use of the following comprehension procedure in interpreting the speaker's meaning:

Relevance-theoretic comprehension procedure
(a) Follow a path of least effort in computing cognitive effects. In particular, test interpretive hypotheses (disambiguations, reference resolutions, implicatures, etc.) in order of accessibility.
(b) Stop when your expectations of relevance are satisfied.

The hearer is justified in following a path of least effort because the speaker is expected (within the limits of her abilities and preferences) to make her utterance as relevant as possible, and hence as easy as possible to understand (since relevance and processing effort vary inversely). It follows that the plausibility of a particular hypothesis about the speaker's meaning depends not only on its content but also on its accessibility. In the absence of other evidence, the very fact that an interpretation is the first to come to mind lends it an initial degree of plausibility. It is therefore rational for hearers to follow a path of least effort in the particular communicative domain (though not, of course, in other domains).

The hearer is also justified in stopping at the first interpretation that satisfies his expectations of relevance because, if the speaker has succeeded in producing an utterance that satisfies the presumption of relevance it conveys, there should never be more than one such interpretation. A speaker who wants to make her utterance as easy as possible to understand should formulate it (within the limits of her abilities and preferences) in such a way that the first interpretation to satisfy the hearer's expectations of relevance is the one she intended to convey. It is not compatible with the presumption of relevance for an utterance to have two alternative co-occurring interpretations, either of which would be individually satisfactory, since this would put the hearer to the unnecessary extra effort of trying to choose between them. Thus, when a hearer following the path of least effort arrives at an interpretation which satisfies his expectations of relevance and is compatible with what he knows of the speaker, this is the most plausible hypothesis about the speaker's meaning for him. Since comprehension is a non-demonstrative inference process, this hypothesis may well be false; but it is the best a rational hearer can produce. (Note, incidentally, that the hearer's expectations of relevance may be readjusted in the course of comprehension. For example, it may turn out that the effort of finding any interpretation at all would be too great: as a result, the hearer would disbelieve the presumption of relevance and terminate the process, with his now null expectation of relevance trivially satisfied.)

Here is a brief illustration of how the relevance-guided comprehension procedure applies to the resolution of linguistic indeterminacies such as those in (1) and (2) above. Consider the following dialogue, in which Mary's utterance 'John is a soldier' corresponds to (2e):

(3)   PETER: Can we trust John to do as we tell him and defend the interests of the Linguistics Department in the University Council?
         MARY: John is a soldier!

Peter's mentally represented concept of a soldier includes many attributes (e.g. patriotism, sense of duty, discipline) which are all activated to some extent by Mary's use of the word 'soldier'. However, they are not all activated to the same degree. Certain attributes also receive some activation from the context (and in particular from Peter's immediately preceding allusions to trust, doing as one is told, and defending interests), and these become the most accessible ones. These differences in accessibility of the various attributes of 'soldier' create corresponding differences in the accessibility of various possible implications of Mary's utterance, as shown in (4):

(4)   a. John is devoted to his duty
         b. John willingly follows orders
         c. John does not question authority
         d. John identifies with the goals of his team
         e. John is a patriot
         f. John earns a soldier's pay
         g. John is a member of the military

Following the relevance-theoretic comprehension procedure, Peter considers these implications in order of accessibility, arrives at an interpretation which satisfies his expectations of relevance at (4d), and stops there. He does not even consider further possible implications such as (4e)–(4g), let alone evaluate and reject them. In particular, he does not consider (4g), i.e. the literal interpretation of Mary's utterance (contrary to what is predicted by most pragmatic accounts, e.g. Grice 1967/1989: 34).

Now consider dialogue (5):

(5)   PETER: What does John do for a living?
        MARY: John is a soldier!

Again, Mary's use of the word 'soldier' adds some degree of activation to all the attributes of Peter's mental concept of a soldier, but in this context, the degree of activation, and the order of accessibility of the corresponding implications, may be the reverse of what we found in (3): that is, (g) may now be the most accessible implication and (a) the least accessible one. Again following the relevance-theoretic comprehension procedure, Peter now accesses implications (g) and (f) and, with his expectations of relevance satisfied, stops there. Thus, by applying exactly the same comprehension procedure (i.e. following a path of least effort and stopping when his expectations of relevance are satisfied), Peter arrives in the one case at a metaphorical interpretation, and in the other at a literal one. (For interesting experimental evidence on depth of processing in lexical comprehension, see Sanford 2002. For a fuller relevance-theoretic account of lexical comprehension, and in particular of the relation between literal, loose and metaphorical uses, see Carston 1997, 2002a; Sperber and Wilson 1998a; Wilson and Sperber 2002.)

12.6   Conclusion

We have considered two possibilities. First, comprehension might be an application of a general mindreading module to the problem of identifying the speaker's meaning (a neo-Gricean view). Second, it might involve a sub-module of the mindreading module, an automatic application of a relevance-based procedure to ostensive stimuli, and in particular to linguistic utterances. We have argued that, given the particular nature and difficulty of the task, the general mindreading hypothesis is implausible. We have also argued that the tendency of humans to seek relevance, and the exploitation of this tendency in communication, provide the justification for a dedicated comprehension procedure. This procedure, although simple to use, is neither trivial nor easy to discover. So how can it be that people, including young children, spontaneously use it in communication and comprehension, and expect their audience to use it as a matter of course? Our suggestion has been that relevance-guided inferential comprehension of ostensive stimuli is a human adaptation, an evolved sub-module of the human mindreading ability.

13 Testing the cognitive and communicative principles of relevance

Jean-Baptiste Van der Henst and Dan Sperber

13.1 Introduction

A general theory is testable not directly but through consequences it implies when taken together with auxiliary hypotheses. The test can be weaker or stronger depending in particular on the extent to which the consequences tested are specifically entailed by the theory (as opposed to following mostly from the auxiliary hypotheses and being equally compatible with other general theories). The earliest experimental work based on relevance theory (Jorgensen, Miller and Sperber 1984; Happé 1993) tested and confirmed Sperber and Wilson's (1981) echoic account of irony (and much experimental work on irony since then has broadly confirmed and refined it further). While this account of irony is part and parcel of relevance theory, it is nevertheless compatible with different pragmatic approaches. The experimental confirmation of this account therefore provides only weak support for relevance theory as a whole. More recent experimental work has explicitly formulated, tested and confirmed other, more specific and central consequences of relevance theory.[1] Here we review experiments that test consequences of the most central tenets of the theory: the cognitive and communicative principles of relevance.

13.2 The basic tenets of relevance theory

Relevance, as characterised in relevance theory, is a property of inputs to cognitive processes. These inputs include external stimuli (e.g. utterances) and internal representations (e.g. memories or conclusions of inferences, which may then be used as premises for further inferences). When is an input relevant? An input is relevant to an individual when processing it in a context of previously available assumptions yields positive cognitive effects: that is, improvements to the individual's knowledge that could not be achieved by processing either the context on its own or the new input on its own. These improvements may consist in the derivation of contextual implications, the confirmation of uncertain assumptions, the correction of errors, and also, arguably, the reorganisation of knowledge so as to make it more appropriate for future use.

Inputs are not just relevant or irrelevant; when relevant, they are more or less so. What makes some inputs worth processing is a relatively high degree of relevance. Many of the potential inputs competing for an individual's processing resources at a given time may offer a modicum of relevance, but few are likely to be relevant enough to deserve attention. What makes these inputs worth processing is, in the first place, that they yield comparatively greater cognitive effects. However, two inputs that yield the same amount of cognitive effect may differ in the amount of processing effort[2] required to produce this effect. Obviously, the less the effort, the better. If relevance is what makes an input worth processing, then the relevance of an input is not just a matter of the cognitive effect it yields, but also of the mental effort it requires. Hence the characterisation of relevance in terms of effect and effort:

(1)   *Relevance of an input to an individual*
        a. Other things being equal, the greater the positive cognitive effects achieved by processing an input, the greater the relevance of the input to the individual at that time.
        b. Other things being equal, the greater the processing effort expended, the lower the relevance of the input to the individual at that time.

Here is a simplified illustration of how the relevance of alternative inputs might be compared in terms of effort and effect. Suppose you want to take the next train to Bordeaux and are presented with one of the statements (2)–(4) (assumed to be uttered by a reliable informer):

(2)   The next train to Bordeaux is at 3.24 p.m.

(3)   The next train to Bordeaux is after 3 p.m.

(4)   The next train to Bordeaux is at 36 minutes before 4 p.m.

All three statements would be relevant to you, but (2) would be more relevant than either (3) or (4). Statement (2) would be more relevant than (3) for reasons of cognitive effect: (2) entails (3), and therefore yields all the conclusions derivable from (3) and more besides, and these extra conclusions themselves have practical consequences for the planning of your trip. Statement (2) would be more relevant than (4) for reasons of processing effort: although (2) and (4) are logically equivalent, and therefore yield exactly the same cognitive effects, these effects are easier to derive from (2) than from (4), which requires an additional effort of calculation with no additional benefit whatsoever (in the ordinary situation envisaged). More generally, when similar amounts of effort are required by two alternative inputs, the effect factor is decisive in determining degrees of relevance, and when similar amounts of effect are achievable, the effort factor is decisive. In experimental work, as we will illustrate, this makes it relatively easy to manipulate the relevance of stimuli across conditions by keeping the effort factor constant and modifying the effect factor or, conversely, by keeping the effect factor constant and modifying the effort factor.

Relevance theory claims that, because of the way our cognitive system has evolved, humans have an automatic tendency to maximise relevance. As a result of constant selection pressure towards increasing efficiency, our perceptual mechanisms tend automatically to pick out potentially relevant stimuli, our memory mechanisms tend automatically to store and, when appropriate, retrieve potentially relevant pieces of knowledge, and our inferential mechanisms tend spontaneously to process these inputs in the most productive way. This universal tendency is described in the First, or Cognitive, Principle of Relevance:

(5)   *Cognitive Principle of Relevance*
        Human cognition tends to be geared to the maximisation of relevance.

This spontaneous tendency to maximise relevance makes it possible to predict to some extent which available stimuli people will pay attention to and how they will process them.

There is a wealth of evidence from the experimental study of attention and memory that could be reanalysed in order to see how far it supports the cognitive principle of relevance. This is not our field of expertise, but we suspect that the challenge there would be not so much to find some support, but to find support that is specific enough to relevance theory: in other words, to find predictions that follow from the cognitive principle of relevance but not – or not as directly – from standard psychological approaches to attention and memory. In other areas, the study of inference and of communication in particular, the cognitive principle does have consequences that are far from trivial. Some of these consequences in the domain of category-based induction have been explored by Medin, Coley, Storms and Hayes (2003). In section 13.3 we will present experimental tests of consequences based on work on relational reasoning by Van der Henst and his collaborators.

Relevance theory has mostly been an exploration of the implications of the Second, Communicative Principle of Relevance for human verbal communication. The human tendency to maximise relevance makes it possible not only to predict some of the cognitive processes of others, but also to try to influence them – indeed, how could you aim at influencing others if you had no way to predict how your behaviour would affect their thoughts? Human intentional communication, and in particular verbal communication, involves the attribution of mental states to one another by the communicator and the addressee. This attribution is greatly facilitated by the relative predictability of relevance-guided cognitive processes. In particular, a speaker must intend and expect that the hearer will pay attention to the utterance produced. If attention tends automatically to go to inputs that seem relevant enough to be worth processing, then it follows that, to succeed, the speaker must intend and expect her utterance to be seen as relevant enough by the hearer she is addressing. By the very act of speaking to him, the communicator therefore encourages the hearer to presume that the utterance is so relevant. This is the basis for the Communicative Principle of Relevance:

(6)   *Communicative Principle of Relevance*

Every utterance conveys a presumption of its own optimal relevance.

According to the theory, an utterance conveys not just a vague expectation, but a precise presumption of relevance, which is captured by the notion of optimal relevance:

(7)   *Optimal relevance*
        An utterance is optimally relevant to the hearer just in case:
        a. It is relevant enough to be worth the hearer's processing effort;
        b. It is the most relevant one compatible with the speaker's abilities and preferences.

According to clause (7a) of this definition, the hearer is entitled to expect the utterance to be at least relevant enough to be worth processing, which means (given the cognitive principle of relevance) that the utterance should be more relevant than any alternative input available at the time.

Is the hearer entitled to expect more relevance than this (already high) minimum level spelled out in clause (7a)? The speaker wants to be understood. It is therefore in her interest to make her utterance as easy as possible to understand, and to provide evidence not just for the cognitive effects she aims to achieve in the hearer but for further cognitive effects which, by holding his attention, will help her achieve her goal. However, speakers are not omniscient, and they cannot be expected to go against their own interests and preferences in producing an utterance. There may be relevant information that they are unable or unwilling to provide, and wordings that would convey their meaning more economically, but that they are unable to think of at the time, or are unwilling to use (for reasons of propriety for instance). All this is spelled out in clause (7b) of the definition of optimal relevance, which states that the ostensive stimulus is the most relevant one (i.e. the one that yields the greatest effects, in return for the smallest processing effort) that the communicator is able and willing to produce.

The communicative principle of relevance justifies a specific inferential procedure for interpreting an utterance, that is, for discovering what the speaker meant by uttering it:

(8)   *Relevance-guided comprehension procedure*
        a. Follow a path of least effort in constructing and testing interpretive hypotheses (regarding disambiguation, reference resolutions, implicatures, etc.).
        b. Stop when your expectations of relevance are satisfied.

Given clause (7b) of the definition of optimal relevance, it is reasonable for the hearer to follow a path of least effort, because the speaker is expected (within the limits of her abilities and preferences) to make her utterance as easy as possible to understand. Since relevance varies inversely with effort, the very fact that an interpretation is easily accessible gives it an initial degree of plausibility. It is also reasonable for the hearer to stop at the first interpretation that satisfies his expectations of relevance, because there should never be more than one. A speaker who wants her utterance to be as easy as possible to understand should formulate it (within the limits of her abilities and preferences) so that the first interpretation to satisfy the hearer's expectation of relevance is the one she intended to convey. An utterance with two apparently satisfactory competing interpretations would cause the hearer the unnecessary extra effort of choosing between them, and, because of this extra effort, the resulting interpretation (if there were one) could never satisfy clause (7b) of the definition of optimal relevance. Thus, when a hearer following the path of least effort arrives at an interpretation that satisfies his expectations of relevance, he should, in the absence of contrary evidence, adopt it. Since comprehension is a non-demonstrative inference process, this interpretation of the speaker's meaning may be erroneous. Still, it is the most plausible interpretation in the circumstances.

The hypothesis that hearers spontaneously follow the relevance-guided comprehension procedure spelled out in (8) can be experimentally tested by manipulating the effort factor, and in particular by changing the order of accessibility of various interpretations. It can also be tested by manipulating the effect factor, and thereby making a specific interpretation more or less likely to satisfy the hearer's expectations of relevance. As we will illustrate in section 13.4, this is what Girotto, Sperber and their collaborators have done in a series of experiments with the Wason Selection Task.

Most work in relevance theory so far has focused on the interpretation rather than the production of utterances. However, the theory also has testable implications for the production process. Speakers often fail to be relevant to their audience, and sometimes do not even make the effort to be relevant. Still, utterances could not effectively convey the presumption of their own relevance unless speakers were aiming at optimal relevance most of the time, and achieving it often enough. In section 13.5, we describe a series of experiments designed to test how far speakers were actually aiming at optimal relevance.

13.3 Testing the cognitive principle of relevance with relational reasoning tasks

In most studies on reasoning, psychologists analyse the successful or unsuccessful performance of participants in reasoning tasks. They look at the percentages of correct conclusions or the time taken to draw such a conclusion. They investigate factors that impede or enhance correct performance, such as the content or complexity of the premises, the task instructions, or IQ. They use this evidence to test various theories of the inferential machinery that underlies our reasoning ability. Some argue that people reason by constructing mental models of the premises (Johnson-Laird and Byrne 1991). Others support the idea that people reason by applying general inference rules (Rips 1994; Braine and O'Brien 1998). Still others have proposed that reasoning relies on domain-specific procedures (Cheng and Holyoak 1985; Cosmides 1989).

Relevance theory claims that comprehension is based on a domain-specific inferential procedure, but it is not, in and of itself, a theory of human reasoning.

It is, in fact, compatible with the view that an important role is played in reasoning by mental models, by inference rules, or by both, or by still other kinds of procedures in a domain-general or domain-specific way.[3] Nevertheless, relevance theory may make a direct contribution to the study of reasoning by suggesting testable claims, not about the procedures used in reasoning processes (except in the case of comprehension) but about their goals.

Standard approaches to the study of reasoning have had little to say about what causes people to engage in reasoning (that is, when they are not asked to do so by an experimenter), what expectations they have in doing so, and what kinds of conclusions satisfy these expectations, bringing the process to a close.[4] What guides reasoners to infer a specific conclusion? At first sight, one might argue that people aim to infer a conclusion that *follows logically* from the premises. However, from any given set of premises, there is an infinity of such conclusions, most of which are of no interest at all. For instance, nobody would bother to infer, from the single premise *P*, the logical conclusion *Not (not (not (not P)))*. Harman has formulated this idea as a *principle of clutter avoidance*: 'It is not reasonable or rational to fill your mind with trivial consequences of your beliefs, when you have better things to do with your time, as you often do' (Harman 1995: 186).

For a conclusion to be worth inferring, logical validity is not enough. Some valid conclusions are too trivial ever to be derived, and others may be derived in some circumstances and not in others. From the same set of premises, we might derive a particular conclusion in one situation, another conclusion in a second situation, or no conclusions at all in a third. In a recent study, we proposed that the conclusions people are inclined to draw are those, if any, that seem relevant enough in the context (Van der Henst, Sperber and Politzer 2002). This, of course, is a direct consequence of the cognitive principle of relevance.

In this study, we compared so-called 'determinate' and 'indeterminate' relational problems such as the following:

Determinate problem	Indeterminate problem
A is taller than B	A is taller than B
B is taller than C	A is taller than C

Such relational problems have been empirically investigated in many studies (see Evans, Newstead and Byrne 1993 for a review). Determinate problems are so-called because the one relation between the three terms A, B, and C which is not explicitly described in the premises – that between A and C – is nevertheless inferable from them: in our example, A is taller than C. Indeterminate problems are so-called because the one relation which is not described in the premises is not inferable from them: in our example, B might be taller than C or C might be taller than B. Hence, nothing follows from the premises about the relation between B and C. The goal of most studies on relational problems has been to describe how the premises are mentally represented and processed by reasoners. Typically, participants have had to answer a specific question like 'What is the relation between A (or B) and C?' and the evidence comes from the rate of correct answers. The correct answer for the determinate problem above would be: *A is taller than C*. The correct answer for the indeterminate problem would be: *It is impossible to tell*. Indeterminate problems tend to yield a lower rate of correct answers than determinate ones.[5]

In our study, the aim was not to assess and explain the relative difficulty posed by determinate and indeterminate problems. Instead of asking a question about a specific relation between the two terms mentioned in the premises, we just asked *What, if anything, follows from the premises?* We were interested in what causes some participants, particularly with indeterminate problems, to answer, *Nothing follows*.

As noted above, it is always possible to infer conclusions from a given set of premises. Moreover, some of these conclusions are quite obvious: for instance, from two premises *P* and *Q*, their conjunction *P-and-Q* trivially follows. So when people say that nothing follows from a given set of premises, either they are just failing to see the obvious, or, we suggest, they mean that nothing *relevant* follows. If so, *Nothing follows* answers are evidence about people's intuitions of relevance. In particular, if a problem creates the expectation that the most relevant conclusion to be derived should be of a certain type, but it fails to warrant any conclusion of this type, people may be tempted to answer that nothing follows. We tried to show that this is what happens with indeterminate relational problems.

What conclusion could participants expect to infer from two relational premises in the context of a reasoning task? In determinate and indeterminate relational problems such as those above, there are three terms, A, B, and C, one type of asymmetric and transitive relation, e.g. *taller than*, and thus three possible relations of this type, between A and B, B and C, and A and C. Two of these relations are described in the premises. Given the communicative principle of relevance, these relations are presumed to be relevant in the context of the task, and, more specifically, the two relations given in the premises are expected to be relevant by allowing the third relation to be inferred. Of course, it could be correctly pointed out that in these experimental situations, the premises on which participants are asked to reason are arbitrary and bear no relation to their real-life concerns, so that neither the premises nor the conclusions that can be derived from them have any genuine relevance. Still, we would argue, just as participants reason under the pretence that the premises are true (that, say, the premise 'Jim is taller than Paul' is about two actual people), they reason under the pretence that the premises, and the conclusions they are expected to derive from them, might be relevant in some ordinary context of knowledge about the individuals or the entities described in the premises. It is not hard, for instance, to pretend that it might be relevant to know that Jim is taller than Paul and that Paul is taller than Dick, and to assume then that it would be relevant to draw the conclusion that Jim is taller than Dick.

Participants' expectations of relevance are easily satisfied in the case of determinate problems, but not in the case of indeterminate ones, where the relation that is not specified in the premises cannot be inferred from them. Hence, with indeterminate problems, participants may be tempted to answer that nothing follows. This is indeed what we observed. In our studies, 43 per cent of the participants gave a *nothing follows* response to indeterminate problems, while only 8 per cent did so with determinate problems. This difference in the rate of *nothing follows* answers between determinate and indeterminate problems is not, of course, surprising. However, it had never been demonstrated before, and, more importantly, only relevance theory provides a simple and direct explanation of this difference. When participants say that nothing follows, what they mean, we suggest, is not that it is impossible to infer anything at all from the two premises, but that it is impossible to derive a conclusion relevant enough to be worth deriving, i.e. a conclusion about the third undescribed relation among the three items mentioned in the premises.

Nevertheless, faced with a situation where what would be the most relevant conclusion cannot be inferred, about half of the participants do offer some positive conclusion. Are they giving up on relevance and just looking for any logically valid conclusion, or are they still guided by considerations of relevance? As we will show, the answer can be found by examining the specific conclusions they actually derive.

Consider the determinate conclusion *A is taller than B and C*, or equivalently, *A is the tallest*, derived from our Indeterminate Problem. This conclusion simply involves merging the two premises into a single sentence. It may seem trivial, especially in the context of a reasoning experiment where participants are generally eager to demonstrate their reasoning skills to the experimenter. However, a conclusion such as *A is the tallest* may have some relevance of its own. There are ordinary situations where it would be relevant to know which item in a set ranks higher than the others with respect to some given property (e.g. *who is the tallest*). In fact, in many situations, knowing which item in a set ranks higher than all the others with respect to some comparative property is more relevant than knowing the relative positions of two other items in the set which are lower on the comparison scale. For instance, suppose you have a choice among three different cars, all of which would satisfy your needs, and you just want to buy the cheapest. You will probably be more interested in knowing which of the three is the cheapest than in knowing which of the other two is the cheaper. Hence, inferring *A is more ... than B and C* has some relevance since, assuming a quite ordinary context, it may be a step on the way to deriving further contextual implications (e.g. about which car to buy).

Here, someone might raise the following objection: How can deductively deriving a conclusion and adding it to (or substituting it for) an initial set of premises yield a more relevant point of departure for further reasoning, given that nothing can be derived from this conclusion that wasn't already derivable from the initial premises? In other words, how can such a conclusion be relevant at all, in a context where the premises on which it is based are already given? The fact that relevance is defined not just in terms of effect but also in terms of processing effort provides a simple answer. A set of premises supplemented with some deductively derived conclusion could not carry more cognitive effects than the initial set, and could not therefore be more relevant on *the effect side*; however, it can be more relevant on *the effort side* by yielding the same effects for less effort. The deduction of some specific conclusion from a set of premises may be a preliminary and effort-costly necessary step towards deriving cognitive effects from this set of premises. In that case, the conclusion is just as relevant as the premises on the effect side, and more relevant on the effort side.

We frequently encounter information which we think is likely to prove useful in the future. We then retain this information, and often process it in such a way as to optimise its potential usefulness. Suppose, for instance, that you arrive in a holiday resort where you plan to spend a month with your family. You learn that there are three doctors in the resort, Smith, Jones and Williams. You also learn the following two pieces of information: {*Smith is a better doctor than Jones, Jones is a better doctor than Williams*}. At the time, you don't need a doctor, but you might need one in the future, and would then want to visit the best doctor in town. So the information is potentially relevant to you. You might simply store the two pieces of information above, but from a cognitive point of view it would be more efficient to draw the conclusion *Smith is the best doctor* straight away. By drawing this conclusion now, you prepare for future circumstances in which you might need a doctor. By adding this conclusion to the two initial premises, you are left with a set of premises for future inference which has a greater expected relevance, since its exploitation will require fewer inferential steps. Moreover, if you expect not to need information about the other two doctors, it may be enough to remember just the conclusion *Smith is the best doctor*, replacing the initial two-premise set with the single derived conclusion, thus reducing memory load.

If what makes a conclusion seem relevant is that it saves effort for the possible derivation of cognitive effects, then it follows that the more effort it saves for such possible derivations, the greater its perceived relevance will be. In our initial study (Van der Henst, Sperber and Politzer 2002), we manipulated the relevance of a relational conclusion of the form *A is more ... than B and C* by formulating the premises so as to make the derivation of such a conclusion more or less effortful. In one type of problem, the derivation of this conclusion was very easy, and thus the effort saved for the possible derivation of cognitive effects was quite low, whereas with another type of problem, the conclusion was harder to derive, and thus the effort saved was greater. The problems we used were the following:[6]

Problem 1:
A is taller than B
A is taller than C

Problem 2:
B is taller than A
C is taller than A

In both cases, the relation between B and C is indeterminate. However, in each case it is possible to derive a variety of conclusions. For instance, from Problem 1, conclusions (9a) and (9b) can be inferred, and from Problem 2, conclusions (10a) and (10b) can be inferred:

(9)   a. A is taller than B and C
        b. B and C are shorter than A

(10)   a. A is shorter than B and C
        b. B and C are taller than A

With the usual element of pretence involved in the experimental study of reasoning, such conclusions can be seen as having some relevance in that they may facilitate the derivation of further cognitive effects, given some plausible context.

Deriving the single-subject conclusion (9a) from the premises of Problem 1 involves hardly any inferential effort. Since the grammatical subject (A) and the comparative term (*taller than*) are the same in both the conclusion and the premises, all that is required is to merge the two premises into a single sentence. Deriving the single-subject conclusion (10a) from the premises of Problem 2, by contrast, involves some genuine inferential effort: the grammatical object in the premises (A) has to be put in subject position, and the comparative term (*taller than*) has to be converted into its opposite (*shorter than*). In this case, it is the double-subject conclusion (10b) that simply involves merging the two premises. If participants simply went for the less effort-demanding conclusion, they should choose (9a) and (10b). By contrast, if they are guided by consid-erations of relevance, they should choose (9a) and (10a).

Conclusions (9a) and (9b) are logically equivalent, and would therefore yield the same effects in any context; the same applies to conclusions (10a) and (10b). However, in most contexts, it would cost less effort to derive these effects using the single-subject conclusions (9a) and (10a) as premises than using the double-subject conclusions (9b) or (10b) as premises. Why? Because most pieces of knowledge transmitted, constructed and stored in human cognition have a single entity or a single category, rather than a pair of entities or categories, as their topic (for fairly obvious reasons having to do with cognitive efficiency). We are more likely, for instance, to encounter a contextual conditional premise of the form (11a) than one of the form (11b):

(11)   a. If A is taller than B and C, then . . .
        b. *If B and C are shorter than A, then . . .*

By using either (9a) or (9b) together with either (11a) or (11b) as premises, the same conclusions can be derived; however, the derivation will be more direct if the minor premise of this conditional syllogism, i.e. (9a) or (9b), matches the antecedent of the major premise, i.e. (11a) or (11b). In other words, in most realistic contexts, single-subject conclusions such as (9a) and (10a) are likely to prove more relevant than double-subject conclusions such as (9b) and (10b). We therefore predicted that, in both Problem 1 and Problem 2, participants, guided by considerations of relevance, would derive more single-subject than double-subject conclusions.

There is a further reason, specific to the premises of Problem 2, why (10a) should be perceived as more potentially relevant than (10b). The extra effort involved in deriving (10a) as compared to (10b) is effort spent in the right direction, since it can be seen as preparatory to the derivation of a cognitive effect. The same point does not apply to (9a) and (9b) in Problem 1. As noted above, the derivation of (9a), unlike that of (9b), involves virtually no effort. In other terms, the derivations of both (9a) and (10a) are steps in the right direction, but the derivation of (10a) is a much bigger step, and therefore a more useful one. This suggests that Problem 2 should be perceived as yielding a relevant enough conclusion more frequently than Problem 1.

For the reasons just described, we expected that participants who produced a conclusion with Problems 1 and 2 would predominantly produce a single-subject conclusion, and that there would be more such conclusions, and fewer *nothing follows* answers, with Problem 2 than with Problem 1. Note that there is nothing intuitively obvious about these predictions, which follow quite directly from the cognitive principle of relevance as applied to this particular reasoning problem, and from no other approach we are aware of. Our findings, presented in Table 13.1, confirmed these predictions.

Another way to increase the relevance of a conclusion *A is more . . . than B and C* derived from indeterminate relational premises is to act on the effect side. As noted above, a conclusion cannot yield a greater cognitive effect than the premises from which it is deductively derived. However, the information contained in the premises of a problem can yield greater or smaller cognitive effects depending on the wider context. The greater these effects are, the more useful it will be to derive a conclusion which is a step on the way to achieving these effects,

Table 13.1. *Percentage of conclusion types for Problems 1 and 2*

	Problem 1	Problem 2	Total
	A is taller than B *A is taller than C*	*B is taller than A* *C is taller than A*	
Single-subject conclusions	26%	45%	35%
Double-subject conclusions	14%	15%	14%
Nothing follows	54%	31%	43%
Other	6%	9%	8%

and hence the more relevant this conclusion will be. Here, acting on the effect side means providing or suggesting a context in which a conclusion derived from the premises of a problem might yield greater or smaller cognitive effects.

In Problem 2, the conclusion *A is taller than B and C* has a modicum of potential relevance. However, the cognitive effects that such a conclusion might yield remain rather vague as long as no context is provided. The relevance of this conclusion can be increased by manipulating the effect factor in the way suggested above: in particular, by providing a context in which this conclusion will have clear contextual implications. Imagine, for instance, that the premises of Problem 2 are processed with the knowledge that whoever is the tallest out of A, B and C is the tallest person in the world. In this context, deducing that *A is taller than B and C* is a necessary step towards inferring that *A is the tallest person in the world.*

We predict that people should be more inclined to produce the conclusion *A is more . . . than B and C* when an appropriate context is provided than when no context, or a less appropriate or inappropriate context is given. We tested this prediction in three experiments carried out in an unpublished study with Guy Politzer.

In the first experiment, participants were given either a problem with no explicit context provided (Problem 3) or a problem with an explicit context provided (Problem 4), and were asked to produce a conclusion:

Problem 3:
Premises: A is ahead of B
            A is ahead of C

Problem 4:
Context: *A, B and C were the top three finishers in the race last Sunday.*
Premises: A is ahead of B
            A is ahead of C

In both cases, it follows from the premises that *A is ahead of B and C*. However, in the race context, deriving the logical conclusion *A is ahead of B and C* is a step towards deriving the contextual implication *A won the race*. The possibility of deriving this contextual implication makes the logical conclusion *A is ahead of B and C* more relevant than it would be in the absence of any explicit context. Since the conclusion that A is ahead of B and C has greater relevance in the race context, it should be more frequently derived, and participants should produce more determinate conclusions and fewer *nothing follows* answers. Our results do indeed show that Problem 4 resulted in a higher rate of determinate conclusions than Problem 3 (54% vs. 70%, $\chi^2(1) = 5.59$, p < 0.02). Moreover, in the race context, there were three times as many determinate conclusions referring to the race context, such as *A is the first* or *A is the winner*, than conclusions simply integrating the two premises, such as *A is ahead of B and C* or *B and C are behind A*.

In a second experiment, we manipulated the effect factor by using two different explicit contexts, both of which increased the relevance of the conclusion *A is more ... than B and C*. However, the context provided in Problem 5 (which was almost identical to that in Problem 4) produced a greater increase in relevance than the context provided in Problem 6:

Problem 5:
Context: *A, B and C were the first three finishers in the race last Sunday.*
Premises: A arrived before B
              A arrived before C

Problem 6:
Context: *A, B and C were the last three finishers in the race last Sunday.*
Premises: A arrived before B
              A arrived before C

In Problem 5, the context explicitly focuses on people who were the first three in a race; if this is relevant at all, knowing who was *the* first should be even more relevant. The premises of the problem can thus achieve relevance by making it possible to infer exactly who arrived first and who did not. Deriving the conclusion that A arrived before B and C allows one to infer three contextual implications: *A won the race*, *B did not win the race*, and *C did not win the race*. In Problem 6, the context focuses on people who arrived last in a race. In contrast with Problem 5, deriving the conclusion that A arrived before B and C makes it possible to infer only one contextual implication: *A did not arrive last*. Because the relation between B and C is indeterminate, it is impossible to infer who arrived last. The conclusion that A arrived before B and C has some relevance in Problem 6, but less than in Problem 5, and it should therefore be

Table 13.2. *Percentage of conclusion types for Problems 5 and 6*

	Problem 5	Problem 6
	N = 90	N = 91
Determinate conclusions	94.4	74.7
Nothing follows	3.3	18.7
Errors and weird answers	2.2	6.6

produced less often. Our results (see Table 13.2) indeed show that people derived more determinate conclusions in Problem 5 than in Problem 6 (94.4% vs. 74.7%, χ^2 (1) = 13.45, p < 0.001).

Any explicit context evokes a wider *implicit* context of general knowledge. For instance, the explicit context in problem 5, *A, B and C were the first three finishers in the race last Sunday*, evokes background knowledge about racing, about the value attributed to winning, about prizes or medals given to winners, and so on. So, inferring from the explicit context the conclusion that A has won the race makes it possible to derive from the implicit context the further conclusions that A is likely to be pleased, that he may be given a medal or a prize, and so on.

In a third experiment, we manipulated relevance by evoking different implicit contexts. In general, when a context is explicitly provided, participants may expect the premises of a problem to be relevant in this explicit context, or at least in the wider context implicitly evoked by this explicit context. If the explicit and implicit contexts are related in content to the premises, this should strengthen the expectation of relevance and encourage participants to derive positive conclusions from the premises rather than answering that nothing follows. Inversely, if the explicit and implicit contexts are unrelated in content to the premises, this should reduce participants' expectations of relevance and encourage them to say that nothing follows. Here is how we tested this prediction.

Consider Problems 7 and 8:

Problem 7:

Context: *A, B and C, who were measured during a medical examination, are not of the same height*

Premises: A is taller than B
        A is taller than C

Table 13.3. *Percentage of conclusion types for Problems 7 and 8*

	Problem 7	Problem 8
	N = 162	N = 168
Determinate conclusions	76.5	42.9
Nothing follows	19.8	50.6
Errors and weird answers	3.7	6.5

Problem 8:

Context: *A, B and C did not win the same amount of money in the last lottery*
Premises: A is taller than B
                A is taller than C

The explicit context in Problem 7, by mentioning height measurements as part of a medical examination, evokes an implicit context of common knowledge about the implications of height differences for health, performance, access to certain jobs, and so on. This should encourage participants to see the conclusion *A is taller than B and C* as potentially relevant in this implicit context. The explicit context in Problem 8, by mentioning the winning of money in a lottery, evokes an implicit context of common knowledge in which individual height plays no role at all. We should therefore observe a much lower rate of determinate conclusions for Problem 8 than for Problem 7. Our results (see Table 13.3) confirmed that there were many more determinate conclusions for Problem 7 (76.5%) than for Problem 8 (42.9%, χ^2 (1) = 38.8, p < 0.0001).

The experiments presented in this section give support to the cognitive principle of relevance, i.e. the claim that human cognition tends to be geared to the maximisation of relevance, by corroborating some of its consequences in the area of psychology of reasoning. More specifically, the choice of whether or not to draw conclusions from a given set of premises, and the choice of which particular conclusion (if any) to draw, are guided by considerations of relevance. People are inclined to draw a specific conclusion from a set of premises to the extent that this conclusion seems potentially relevant. This is a non-trivial consequence of the cognitive principle of relevance. It has, in turn, non-trivial consequences for the study of reasoning in general. In particular, the failure of participants to derive some specific conclusion in a reasoning task may be due not to poor logical capacities or to pragmatic problems with comprehension of the task, but to their failure to see the relevance of the conclusion they were intended to draw, or, more subtly, their failure to see the relevance of some intermediate inferential step necessary for deriving the intended conclusion. In spontaneous inference, being guided by considerations of relevance should contribute to the overall efficiency of inferential processes, but it may also, on occasion, prevent one from reaching some highly relevant conclusion because some crucial intermediate steps did not seem relevant at all.

13.4   Testing the communicative principle of relevance with the Wason Selection Task

Wason's Selection Task (Wason 1966) has been the most commonly used tool in the psychology of reasoning (see Manktelow 1999). Genuine versions of Wason's Selection Task share the same basic four-component structure:

(i) An introduction (sometimes in narrative form);

(ii) A conditional statement known as the 'rule', with the linguistic form 'If P, then Q', and either a descriptive content stating how things are, or a deontic content stating how they should be;

(iii) Four cards: one representing a case where P is satisfied, one where P is not satisfied, one where Q is satisfied, and one where Q is not satisfied (known respectively as the P, the not-P, the Q, and the not-Q cards). When the card displays information about P, information about Q is hidden, and conversely.

(iv) The instruction to select all and only those cards where the hidden information must be made visible in order to judge whether the rule is true (in descriptive versions) or is being obeyed (in deontic versions).

For example, the text of an 'abstract' descriptive selection task might be: 'Here are four cards. Each has a number on one side and a letter on the other side. Two of these cards here have the letter side up, and two have the number side up. Indicate which of these cards you need to turn over in order to judge whether or not the following rule is true: "If there is a 6 on one side, there is an E on the other side".' The cards are as shown in Figure 13.1.

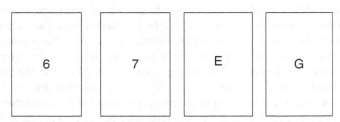

Figure 13.1 A typical four-card task

With such an abstract version of the task, typically only about 10 per cent of participants make the correct selection of the 6 and G cards, that is, the cards that represent the P case and the not-Q case.

In a typical example of a deontic version of the task (Griggs and Cox 1982), participants are presented with a rule such as 'If a person is drinking beer, then that person must be over 18 years of age', and cards representing four individuals in a bar, with what they are drinking indicated on one side of the cards, and their age on the other side. The four cards represent, respectively, a person drinking beer, a person drinking soda (with the age of these first two persons hidden), a person aged 29, and a person aged 16 (with the drink hidden for these other two). Participants are instructed to select the cards that must be turned over to see whether any of these four people is breaking the rule. Typically, the correct card combination (i.e. the P-card 'This person is drinking beer' and the not-Q card 'This person is 16 years old') is selected by well over 50 per cent of the participants.

Work on the selection task has been used as the basis for a variety of claims about human reasoning and rationality. In particular, it has been taken to show that most individuals do not in general reason in accordance with the rules of logic, not even the elementary rules of propositional calculus, as evidenced by their failure to select the P and the not-Q cards in descriptive versions of the task (e.g. Cheng and Holyoak 1985; Griggs and Cox 1982). Does the selection task really provide a tool for testing general claims about human reasoning? Evans (1989) maintained that participants understand the task as one of identifying the *relevant* cards, and that for this, they use heuristic cues of relevance rather than deductive reasoning. Extending this insight, Sperber, Cara and Girotto (1995) put forward a general explanation of the selection task based on relevance theory. They argued that participants' performance on the selection task is best explained on the assumption that (1) the linguistic comprehension process itself provides participants with intuitions of relevance, (2) these intuitions, just like comprehension generally, are highly content- and context-dependent, and (3) participants trust their intuitions of relevance and select cards accordingly. In standard versions of the task, these intuitions are misleading. In other versions, in particular many deontic versions, people's intuitions of relevance point towards the correct selection of cards. If pragmatic comprehension mechanisms determine participants' responses in the selection task, and thus pre-empt the use of whatever domain-general or domain-specific reasoning mechanisms people are endowed with, the task cannot be a good tool for the study of these reasoning mechanisms. On the other hand, it may be of some use in studying people's intuitions of relevance.

Participants presented with a Wason Selection Task approach the text of the problem, and in particular the conditional rule, in the same way that they approach all utterances in conversation or reading. They make use of their standard comprehension abilities. The very fact that a text is presented to them raises expectations of relevance, and they search for an interpretation that satisfies these expectations (which, given the artificiality of the task, may be quite modest). In doing so, they follow the relevance-guided comprehension procedure explained above in (8): that is, they follow a path of least effort in constructing interpretive hypotheses and stop when their expectations of relevance are satisfied. More specifically, this is what participants do with the conditional rule in the selection task: guided by expectations of relevance, they derive from it consequences that might justify these expectations.

The rule itself, being a conditional statement, is not directly testable. Merely by looking at the two sides of a card, you can check the truth or falsity of a straightforward atomic statement or a conjunction of atomic statements such as 'There is a 6 on one side of this card and an E on the other side'. It is true if it matches your observations, and false otherwise. However, you cannot confirm a conditional statement such as 'If there is a 6 on one side, then there is an E on the other side' by matching it to your observations. The truth of a conditional statement is tested indirectly, by deriving from it consequences that are directly testable, and testing these. Participants therefore have two reasons for deriving consequences from the rule. The first is in order to interpret it in a way that satisfies their expectation of relevance. The second is to find directly testable consequences of the rule in order to give a sensible response to the experimenter. What they do in practice is give a response based on the consequences they spontaneously derived in interpreting the rule, without looking for other consequences that might provide a better test of the rule. What they *should* do, in principle, is make sure not only that the consequences they derive are entailed by the rule, but also that, conversely, the rule is entailed by these consequences. Otherwise, the consequences might be true and the rule false. However, this would involve more than simply reasoning in accordance with the rules of propositional calculus. It would also require higher-order reasoning about the structure of the problem. People's failure to engage in such reasoning shows not that they are illogical when presented with such a problem, but that they are unreflective, or at least insufficiently reflective, and overconfident in their intuitions of relevance. In the case of the abstract task described above, from the rule 'If there is a 6 on one side, there is an E on the other side', participants may infer that the card with a 6 must have an E on the other side. They may also infer from the rule that there are cards with a 6 and an E (otherwise the rule would be irrelevant). Including either or both of these consequences as part of one's interpretation of the rule contributes to its relevance by indicating what one might expect to see on turning over the cards. If participants use the first of these two consequences in deciding which cards must be turned over to see whether the rule is true or false, they will select just the card with a 6 (the P card). If they use only the second consequence, or if they use both, they will turn over the card with a 6 and the one with an E (the P card and the Q card). These are indeed the most frequent selections with standard versions of the selection task. In a deontic case such as the drinking-age problem ('If a person is drinking beer, then that person must be over 18 years of age'), in order to satisfy their expectations of relevance, participants might derive from the rule the consequence that there should be no beer drinker under 18. They would then select the card representing a beer drinker (the P card) and the one representing a person under 18 (the not-Q card), which is, as it happens, the correct selection.

Why should the consequences derived in the two cases be different? Because they are derived in order of accessibility until expectations of relevance are satisfied, and both order of accessibility and expected level of relevance are context-dependent. In both problems – and in general with conditional statements – the most accessible consequence is the *modus ponens* one: in the abstract problem, it is that the card with a 6 should have an E on the other side, and in the drinking-age problem, it is that the beer drinker should be 18 or over. In both cases, this implication determines the selection of the P card, which is indeed selected by most participants in both experiments. Why, then, do many participants also select the Q card in the abstract version, and the majority of participants select the not-Q card in the drinking-age problem (as in most deontic versions of the task)? In the abstract problem above, the implication 'There are cards with a vowel and an even number' is much more easily accessed than the implication 'There are no cards with a vowel and without an even number', and satisfies the low expectations of relevance raised by this artificial problem. In the drinking-age problem, on the other hand, the implication that there should not be underage beer drinkers is the most accessible one, and the only one that satisfies expectations of relevance: common-sensically, the point of a normative rule such as 'If a person is drinking beer, then that person must be over 18' is not to make adult beer drinkers more common, but to make underage beer drinkers less common.

By pairing rules and contexts more appropriately, the order of accessibility of consequences and expectations of relevance can be manipulated, and it should be possible to elicit different patterns of selection, including logically correct selections. Sperber and colleagues (1995) produced several *descriptive* versions of the task which elicited a higher percentage of correct responses than had ever been found before with such versions. They showed that – contrary to what was generally believed at the time – good performance is not restricted to deontic versions.[7] Girotto, Kemmelmeir, Sperber and Van der Henst (2001) provided further evidence for the relevance approach by demonstrating how it can be used to manipulate *deontic* versions of the task and obtain at will either the common correct P and not-Q selections or incorrect P and Q selections (more commonly found in descriptive versions). Further experiments and comparisons with the approach of Leda Cosmides and her collaborators (Cosmides

1989; Fiddick, Cosmides and Tooby 2000) can be found in Sperber and Girotto (2002, 2003). Here, by way of illustration, we give just two examples of these experiments, one succinctly, and the other in greater detail.

Girotto, Kemmelmeir, Sperber and Van der Henst (2001) used the following problem (adapted from Cheng and Holyoak 1985): 'Imagine that you work in a travel agency and that the boss asks you to check that the clients of the agency have obeyed the rule "If a person travels to any East African country, then that person must be immunised against cholera", by examining cards representing these clients, their destinations and their immunisations.' The four cards showed 'Mr Neri. Destination: Ethiopia', 'Mr Verdi. Destination: Canada', 'Immunisations done: Cholera' and 'Immunisations done: None', respectively, and as usual, participants were asked which cards had to be examined in order to find out whether the clients of the agency had obeyed the rule. In this context, the relevance of the rule is to prevent people without cholera immunisation from travelling to East African countries. We predicted, therefore, that participants would choose the P card (a traveller to an East African country) and the not-Q card (a person without cholera immunisation). This prediction is not specific to relevance theory: it would be shared by all researchers in the area, whatever their theoretical viewpoint. After all, it reiterates common findings, which have been explained, for instance, by proposing that people have pragmatic schemas for reasoning about obligations and permission (Cheng and Holyoak 1985), or that they have an evolved 'Darwinian algorithm' for reasoning about social contracts (Cosmides 1989).

According to the relevance-theoretic approach, what causes the selection of the P and not-Q cards in this deontic scenario is that the presence of individuals violating the cholera rule among the people represented by the cards would be more relevant than the presence of individuals obeying the rule. Could this relative relevance of cases of violation as opposed to cases of conformity be reversed by altering the context – which, if the relevance approach is correct, should cause participants to choose the P and the Q cards? To achieve this, we used the same scenario, with a twist. The narrative stated that, contrary to what the boss of the agency had thought, cholera immunisation is no longer required when travelling to East Africa. The boss is now worried that she may have misinformed clients and caused them to follow a rule that is no longer in force. She therefore asks the employee to see whether or not clients have obeyed the rule 'If a person travels to any East African country, then that person must be immunised against cholera', by looking at cards similar to those used in the previous condition. In this context, what is relevant is that some clients may have followed the false rule and been immunised unnecessarily (and might then sue the agency, for instance). On the other hand, the case of clients who have ignored the rule is no longer relevant. We predicted, therefore, that participants would select the P card (a traveller to an East African country) and the Q card

Table 13.4. *Percentage of the main selection patterns in the true and false cholera-rule selection task*

Pattern	True rule	False rule
P and not-Q	62	15
P and Q	26	71
Other	12	14

(a person with cholera immunisation). Note that this prediction is non-standard, but follows from the relevance-based explanation of the selection task. This prediction was confirmed. Table 13.4 shows the results we obtained in a within-participants design. (We also obtained practically the same results with a between-subjects design.)

This cholera-rule experiment gives what we hope is an intuitively clear illustration of the role of relevance in participants' responses to selection task problems. However, it remains too intuitive to provide a genuinely specific confirmation of the communicative principle of relevance. In particular, it throws no light on the respective roles of effect and effort in guiding participants' intuitions of relevance and selection of cards.

In their Experiment 4, Sperber and colleagues (1995) aimed to take apart the two factors affecting relevance, effect and effort, in order to test their respective roles and ascertain whether relevance, which combines the effort and the effect factors in a principled manner, is more explanatory than either effort or effect taken alone. To achieve this, they created four scenarios, varying the effect and effort factors separately in four conditions, which they called **effect−/effort+**, **effect−/effort−**, **effect+/effort+**, and **effect+/effort−** (see Figure 13.2).

All four scenarios involved a machine that manufactures cards with a number on one side and a letter on the other. A character, Mr Bianchi, asserts: 'If a card has a 6 on the front, it has an E on the back.' In all conditions, the four cards had respectively a 6, a 4, an E and an A on the visible side, and participants were asked which card or cards had to be turned over to check whether what Mr Bianchi says is true.

From the conditional 'If a card has a 6 on the front, it has an E on the back' participants are sure to derive consequence (12). They may also derive either or both of (13) and (14):

(12)   The card with a 6 has an E on the other side

(13)   There are cards with a 6 and an E

Effect–/Effort +	*Effect–/Effort–*	*Effect+/Effort+*	*Effect+/Effort–*
	A machine manufactures cards. It is programmed to print at random, on the front of each card,		
a number	a 4 or a 6	a number	a 4 or a 6
On the back of each card, it prints a letter at random.	On the back of each card, it prints either an E or an A at random.	On the back of each card, it prints a letter: – When there is a 6, it prints an E. – When there is not a 6, it prints a letter at random.	On the back of each card, it prints a letter: – When there is a 6, it prints an E. – When there is a 4, it prints an E or an A at random.
		One day, Mr Bianchi, the person in charge, realises that the machine has produced some cards it should not have printed. On the back of the cards with a 6, the machine has not always printed an E:	
		sometimes it has printed any letter at random.	sometimes it has printed an A instead of an E.
The person in charge, Mr Bianchi, examines the cards and has the strong impression that the machine does not really print letters and numbers at random. I think, he says, that		Mr Bianchi fixes the machine, examines the newly printed cards and says: don't worry, the machine works fine,	
	if a card has a 6 on the front, it has an E on the back		

Figure 13.2 The four possible conditions of the machine experiment (Sperber, Cara and Girotto 1995)

(14)   There are no cards with a 6 and without an E

In the two **effort+** conditions, (13) is easier to derive than (14), which involves two negations. Moreover, (14) does not carry any obvious effect that is worth the extra effort. So we should expect participants to base their selections either on (12), thus selecting just the E, or on (12) and (13), thus selecting both the E and the 6.

To increase the probability that participants would derive consequence (14) before (13), we could act on either the effort side or the effect side. To act on the effort side, we had the machine, in the two **effort–** conditions, print only 6s and 4s on one side and Es and As on the other. Thus, instead of an indefinite number of possible number–letter combinations (e.g. $9 \times 26 = 234$ if only numbers from 1 to 9 are used), we now have four possible combinations: 6 and E, 6 and A, 4 and E, and 4 and A, which are all equally easy to represent. This makes it possible to simplify (14) and replace it with (14′)

(14′)   There are no cards with a 6 and an A

We predicted that, since (14′) is easier to represent than (14), more participants would derive it in the **effort–** conditions than in the **effort+** conditions, and would, accordingly, select the card with an A rather than the card with an E.

To increase the probability that participants' expectations of effect would be satisfied by an interpretation of the rule as implying (14) rather than (13), in the two **effect+** conditions we extended the scenario as follows. The machine was supposed to print an E on the back of cards with a 6; however, it malfunctioned and began printing cards with a 6 and a letter other than an E. After having it repaired, Mr Bianchi asserted: 'If a card has a 6 on the front, it has an E on the back.' In this context, the relevance of Mr Bianchi's assertion went via the implication that there were no cards with a 6 and a letter other than an E (in other terms, consequence (14)). By contrast, in this context, consequence (13) does not contribute to the relevance of the conditional. We therefore predicted that in the two **effect+** conditions, participants would infer (14) and select the 6 and the A card more often than in the **effect–** conditions.

The two **effect+** conditions on the one hand, and the two **effect–** conditions on the other hand, differ from one another only on the effort side, while the two **effort+** and the two **effort–** conditions differ from one another only on the effect side. Given this, the predictions that follow from the relevance-theoretic account of the task are self-evident: the best performance should be with the **effect+/effort–** condition, and the worst should be with the **effect–/effort+** condition. The performance on the **effect+/effort+** and the **effect–/effort–** conditions should be at an intermediate level between the other two conditions. Moreover, the effect and effort factors should each make a separate contribution to good performance. The results are summarised in Figure 13.3.

These results confirm our prediction. Both factors affecting relevance – effect and effort – were shown to play a role in performance. These results show how effort and effect factors can be manipulated independently or jointly so as to favour one interpretation of a conditional statement over another. The advantage of the selection task paradigm in this context is that participants' interpretations of the rule are revealed by their selection of cards.

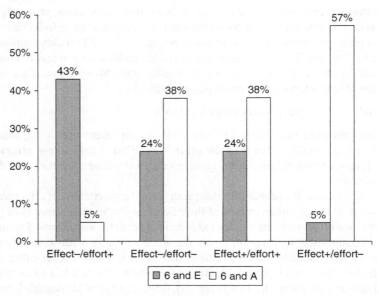

Figure 13.3 Percentage of 6 and E (incorrect) and 6 and A (correct) responses in the four conditions of the machine problem

13.5   Testing the communicative principle of relevance with a speech production task

According to the communicative principle of relevance, utterances convey a presumption of their own optimal relevance, and they do so whether or not they actually are optimally relevant. Speakers may fail to achieve relevance, or they may not even try, and in such cases, the presumption of optimal relevance is unjustified. But whether or not it is justified, this presumption is automatically conveyed by every utterance used in communication, and it guides the comprehension process. Accordingly, most research designed to explore the consequences of the communicative principle of relevance has focused on the comprehension process itself. Still, the communicative principle could not be correct – and relevance could not guide the comprehension process – if speakers were not, often enough, trying to be optimally relevant, and generally succeeding. In the study reported in this section, we investigate the degree to which speakers actually aim at being relevant, even when talking to perfect strangers from whom they have little to expect in return.

Imagine the following exchange between two strangers in the street:

(15)   MR X: Hello, do you have the time, please?
         MRS Y: Oh yes, it's 4.30.

In fact, Mrs Y's watch shows not 4.30 but 4.28. She has chosen to round her answer even though she could have been more accurate. Rounding numbers is quite common. People round when talking about money, distance, time, weight, and so on. What explains this behaviour? We recently argued that rounding is in part explained by considerations of relevance (Van der Henst, Carles and Sperber 2002). A rounded answer is generally more relevant than an accurate one, and speakers round in order to be relevant to their hearer.

In a few situations, for instance when taking a train, someone who asks for the time is better off with an answer that is accurate to the minute. If your train leaves at 4.29, and you are told that it is 4.30 when in fact it is 4.28, you may think you have missed the train when you could actually still catch it. On the other hand, if you were told that it is 4.25, you might end up missing your train, thinking that you still had four minutes left to board it. In most situations, however, the conclusions you would draw from a time rounded to the nearest multiple of five minutes are the same as those you would draw from a time that is accurate to the minute. So, in general, rounding does no harm. Does it do any good? A rounded number requires less *processing effort*: 4.30 is easier to manipulate than 4.28. Producing rounded numbers may thus be a way of providing addressees with an optimally relevant answer by reducing their processing effort without compromising any cognitive effect likely to be derived.

In most situations then, a speaker who is asked what time it is and wishes to be as relevant as possible would round her answer. However, she might be rounding for other reasons. In particular, if she is wearing an analogue watch that shows only numbers that are multiples of five, it may be easier for her to round than not to round. She might then round in order to minimise not her audience's effort, but her own. In fact, a sceptic might argue, the goal of minimising the audience's effort might make no contribution at all to people's tendency to give a rounded answer when asked for the time.

In order to find out whether a tendency to optimise relevance was a factor in rounding the time, we went up to people on the campus of the University of Paris VII and simply asked them: 'Hello, do you have the time please?' (Van der Henst, Carles and Sperber 2002). We noted their response, and also the type of watch they were wearing (analogue or digital), and divided them into two groups, the 'analogue' and the 'digital' group. For people with a digital watch, it requires less effort simply to read aloud the exact time shown on the watch than to round it to the closest multiple of five. If people were just trying to minimise their own effort when asked for the time, then they should always round if their watch is analogue, and never round if it is digital. On the other hand, if people are also motivated by the goal of reducing their audience's effort, then not only those with analogue watches, but also a significant percentage of those with digital watches should round.

What we found is that people rounded in both conditions. The percentage of rounders is calculated on the basis of the percentages of responses which give the time in a multiple of five minutes. If people never rounded, there should be 20 per cent of such responses (this is the theoretical distribution of numbers which are multiples of 5). However, the percentages we observed in the two conditions were much higher: 98 per cent of answers were multiples of 5 in the analogue group, and 65.8 per cent in the digital group. This means that 97 per cent of people rounded in the analogue condition and 57 per cent in the digital one[8] (see Figure 13.4). Hence, even though participants in the digital group rounded less than those in the analogue group, remarkably, a majority of them did make an extra effort in order to reduce their audience's effort.

Some people with analogue watches may round just to save their own effort, but the case of people with digital watches shows that a majority of people are disposed to round, even when this means making an extra effort. We saw this disposition as part of a more general disposition to try to produce optimally relevant utterances. However, an alternative explanation might be that people round in order to minimise their commitment: they may not be sure that their watch is accurate to the minute, although they are more confident that it is accurate within a five-minute interval. Indeed, this desire to minimise commitment may account for some of the rounding we observed; but could it be enough to make the relevance-based explanation superfluous? To investigate this possibility, we created a situation where accuracy manifestly contributed to relevance.

Although rounded answers are easier to process than non-rounded ones, there are some situations, for instance when someone wants to catch a train as described above, where optimal relevance depends on cognitive effects that are carried only by a more accurate answer. Speakers guided by the goal of producing an optimally relevant answer should, in this condition, provide a more precise answer if they can, than in the ordinary kind of situation in which our first experiment took place.

We tested this prediction in Experiment 2 with two groups of people. In the control group, participants were approached in the same way as in the previous experiment and simply asked for the time. In the experimental group, the request was framed in a context where an accurate answer was obviously more relevant. The experimenter went up to the participant with a watch in his hand and said: 'Hello! My watch isn't working properly. Do you have the time please?' In this context, it was clear that the experimenter was asking for the time in order to set his own watch, and that for this purpose an answer that was accurate to the minute would be more relevant. Only answers from participants with an analogue watch were recorded. Participants had therefore to make an extra effort in order to provide an accurate answer. We found that participants were much more accurate in the experimental than in the control

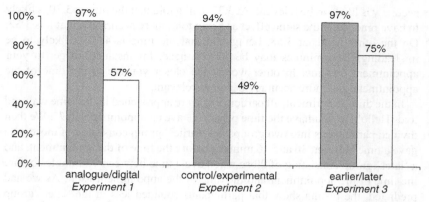

Figure 13.4 Percentage of rounders in the three rounding experiments (Van der Henst, Carles and Sperber 2002). In Experiment 1, participants in the 'analogue' group wore analogue watches, and those in the 'digital' group wore digital watches; in Experiment 2, participants in the 'control' group were simply asked for the time, while those in the 'experimental' group were asked for the time by an experimenter setting his watch; in Experiment 3, participants in the 'earlier' group were asked for the time more than 15 minutes before the time of the appointment mentioned by the experimenter, while those in the 'later' group were asked for the time less than 15 minutes before the stated time of the appointment.

condition: there were 94 per cent of rounders in the control condition and only 49 per cent in the experimental one (see Figure 13.4, Experiment 2). This means that 51 per cent of participants in the experimental group gave the requester a time that was accurate to the minute. Note that rounded answers may still have satisfied the presumption of optimal relevance: even an approximate answer would be relevant enough to be worth the hearer's attention, as required by the first clause of the presumption, and moreover, as required by the second clause, they may have been the most relevant ones compatible with the speakers' abilities (if they had doubts about the accuracy of their watch), or preferences (if they were reluctant to work out a more precise answer). Our results show in any case that a majority of participants not only understood that accuracy was more relevant in this condition, but were also willing and able to make the extra effort to give an accurate answer.

It is easy enough to see that accuracy to the minute is relevant to someone setting a watch: it need not involve the kind of refined concern for relevance presupposed by relevance theory. In a third experiment, we manipulated the relationship between relevance and accuracy in a much subtler way.

Suppose you want to know how much time you have left before an appointment at 4.00 p.m. The closer you get to the time of the appointment, the more accuracy is likely to be relevant. At 3.32, being told that the time is 3.30 is likely to have practically the same effect as being told, more accurately, that it is 3.32. On the other hand, at 3.58, being told that the time is 4.00 is likely to be misleading. Two minutes may be all you need, for instance, to get to your appointment on time. In other words, the closer you are to the time of the appointment, the more accuracy becomes relevant.

In the third experiment, all participants were approached in the same way and told 'Hello! Do you have the time please? I have an appointment at T'. We then divided participants into two groups: an 'earlier' group consisting of those who gave a time between 30 and 16 minutes before the time of the appointment, and a 'later' group consisting of those who gave a time between 14 minutes before the time of the appointment and the time of the appointment itself. As we had predicted, the results show that participants rounded less in the 'later' group (75% of participants) than in the 'earlier' group (97%). A 22 per cent difference may not seem so impressive until you realise that those people in the later group who did give an accurate answer were not only willing to make the effort to read their analogue watch more carefully, and confident enough of its accuracy, but also made the extra effort to take the perspective of the stranger who was addressing them and infer that accuracy, at this point in time, would contribute to the relevance of their utterance.

The experiments described in this section show how subtle aspects of people's spontaneous speech behaviour can be predicted on the basis of the communicative principle of relevance: speakers tend to produce utterances that justify the presumption of optimal relevance these utterances automatically convey.

13.6   Conclusion

The studies reported in this chapter tested and confirmed predictions directly inspired by central tenets of relevance theory and, in particular, by the cognitive and communicative principles of relevance. Of course, it would take many more successful experiments involving a variety of aspects of cognition and communication to come anywhere near a compelling experimental corroboration of relevance theory itself. Still, from a pragmatic point of view, we hope that the few experiments we have presented here, together with others we have mentioned, show how imagining, designing and carrying out experiments helps expand and sharpen pragmatic theory. From an experimental psychology point of view, these experiments illustrate how a pragmatic theory that is precise enough to have testable consequences can put previous experimental research in a novel perspective and suggest new experimental paradigms.

14   The why and how of experimental pragmatics: the case of 'scalar inferences'

Ira Noveck and Dan Sperber

Although a few pioneers in psycholinguistics had taken an experimental approach to various pragmatic issues for more than twenty years, it is only in the past few years that investigators have begun using experimental methods to test pragmatic hypotheses (see Noveck and Sperber 2004). We see this emergence of a proper experimental pragmatics as an important advance, with great potential for further development. In this chapter we want to illustrate what can be done with experimental approaches to pragmatic issues by considering one example, the case of so-called 'scalar inferences', where the experimental method has helped sharpen a theoretical debate and provided uniquely relevant evidence. We will focus on work done by the first author and his collaborators, or work closely related to theirs, but other authors have also made important contributions to the topic (e.g. Papafragou and Musolino 2003; Guasti, Chiercha, Crain, Foppolo, Gualmini and Meroni 2005; De Neys and Schaeken 2007).

14.1   Methodological background: the limits of pragmatic intuitions as evidence

Theoretical work in pragmatics relies heavily – often exclusively – on pragmatic intuitions. These are rarely complemented with observational data of a kind more common in sociologically oriented pragmatics. Use of statistical data from corpuses or experiments is even less common. This is partly a result of the fact that most theoretical pragmaticists are trained in departments of linguistics, where linguistic intuitions are quite often the only kind of data considered. Optimally, of course, one would want pragmaticists to use whatever kind of data might significantly confirm or disconfirm hypotheses. Moreover, a sensible desire for methodological pluralism is not the only reason to diversify the types of evidence used in pragmatics. There are also principled limits to the use of pragmatic intuitions.

It makes sense (although it is not entirely uncontroversial) to judge a semantic description by its ability to account for semantic intuitions. Of course the use of semantic intuitions, and of linguistic intuitions generally, raises methodological problems, and calls for methodological caution. For instance, a linguist's intuitions may be biased by prior theoretical commitments. One can also mistake what are in fact pragmatic intuitions for semantic ones (as ordinary language philosophers systematically did, according to Grice). Still, there are good reasons why semantic intuitions are so central to semantics. Semantic intuitions are not just *about* semantic facts; they are themselves semantic facts. For instance, the intuition that sentence (1) entails (2) is not *about* some semantic property that this sentence would have anyhow, whether or not it was accessible to speakers' intuitions.

(1)   John knows that it is raining.

(2)   It is raining.

Rather, for (1) to have the meaning it has *is* (among other things) for it to be intuitively understood as entailing (2). A semantic analysis of linguistic expressions that accounts for all the speaker–hearer's semantic intuitions about these expressions may not be the best possible one, but it is descriptively adequate (in Chomsky's sense). By contrast, an explanatorily adequate description of the semantics of a given language involves hypotheses about the capacities involved in the acquisition of this semantics, and here observational and experimental evidence should be of relevance.

The use of pragmatic intuitions raises the same methodological problems as the use of semantic intuitions, and more besides. It is a mistake to believe that the type of pragmatic intuitions generally used in pragmatics are data of the same kind as the semantic intuitions used in semantics. Genuine pragmatic intuitions are the intuitions hearers have about the intended meaning of utterances addressed to them. However, the pragmatic intuitions appealed to in theoretical pragmatics are not normally about actual utterances addressed to readers of a pragmatics article, but about hypothetical cases involving imaginary or generic interlocutors. Pragmatic intuitions about hypothetical utterances have proved useful in a variety of ways, but it is important to keep in mind that they are not intuitions about how an utterance is interpreted, but about how an utterance *would be* interpreted if it were produced in a specific situation by a speaker addressing an actual hearer, with referring expressions being assigned actual referents, and so on. These intuitions are educated guesses – and no doubt generally good ones – about hypothetical pragmatic facts, but they are not themselves pragmatic facts, and they may well be in error. That is, we may be wrong about how we would in fact interpret a given utterance in a given context.

Apart from helping to compensate for the inherent limitations of pragmatic intuitions, an experimental approach can provide crucial evidence that helps to choose between alternative theories which may assign the same interpretive content to utterances, but have different implications for the cognitive mechanisms used in arriving at these interpretations. To make a worthwhile contribution, of course, experimentalists must conform to fairly strict methodological criteria and measure exactly what they are aiming to measure – typically the effect of one 'independent' variable on another 'dependent' variable without other uncontrolled variables affecting the results. We will show how this plays out in the study of 'scalar inferences'.

14.2   Theoretical background: scalar implicatures as Generalised Conversational Implicatures (GCIs)

The experiments we will present are relevant to the study of so-called 'scalar implicatures'. Here we briefly remind readers of the main features of the Gricean and neo-Gricean accounts of these, and focus on the claim that scalar implicatures are Generalised Conversational Implicatures, or GCIs. Scalar implicatures are illustrated by examples such as (3a), which is said to implicate (3c), or (4a), said to implicate (4c):

(3)   a. It is possible that Hillary will win.
          b. It is certain that Hillary will win.
          c. It is not certain that Hillary will win.

(4)   a. Some of the guests have arrived.
          b. All of the guests have arrived.
          c. Not all of the guests have arrived.

Proposition (3b) is more informative than (3a), which it entails. If the more informative proposition would make a greater contribution to the common purpose of the conversation, then a speaker obeying Grice's first Maxim of Quantity ('Make your contribution as informative as is required') would be expected to express it unless she were unable to do so without violating the Supermaxim of Quality ('Try to make your contribution one that is true'). Thus, on a Gricean account, a speaker uttering (3a) typically implicates (3c) (i.e. the negation of (3b)). For the same reasons, a speaker uttering (4a) typically implicates (4c) (i.e. the negation of (4b)).

These implicatures are described as 'scalar' because, according to an account developed by neo-Griceans, and in particular by Laurence Horn (1972), their derivation draws on pre-existing linguistic scales consisting of a set of alternate terms or expressions ranked by order of informativeness: <*possible, certain*> and <*some, all*> are examples of such scales. When a less informative term on a scale is used in a way that appears not to satisfy the first Maxim of Quantity, the speaker can be taken to implicate that the proposition that would have been expressed by use of a stronger term is false. This account of the type of implicatures carried by (3a) or (4a) extends to a wide variety of cases, and has some intuitive appeal. However, it should not be seen as obviously correct or as having no alternative. In particular, its implications for processing are less attractive. According to this account, the inference from the utterance to its scalar implicature goes through a consideration not only of what the speaker said and the context, but also of what the speaker might have said but did not. It is this type of effort-demanding inference that makes the Gricean account of implicature derivation seem implausible from a cognitive and developmental point of view.

Levinson draws on another idea of Grice's, that of Generalised Conversational Implicatures, to propose an account that might offer a solution to the problem posed by the derivational complexity of scalar implicatures. Grice noted that some implicatures are generally valid (from a pragmatic rather than a logical point of view, of course) and could therefore be inferred without taking the context into account, except in the small number of cases where the context happens to make them invalid. Grice contrasted these Generalised Conversational Implicatures with Particularised Conversational Implicatures, which are valid only in certain contexts. In his book *Presumptive Meanings: The Theory of Generalized Conversational Implicature* (Levinson 2000), Levinson elaborates Grice's original and somewhat vague notion. For Levinson, GCIs are *default inferences*, that is, inferences which are automatically generated but can be cancelled in certain contexts. Levinson treats scalar implicatures as paradigm cases of GCIs (whereas Grice's own examples of GCIs do not include scalar implicatures). This proposal has the advantage of making the derivation of these implicatures a relatively simple one-step process, which needs no access either to contextual premises or to the full Gricean rationale for their derivation.

Levinson's own rationale for GCIs so conceived has to do with the optimisation of processing. The existence of GCIs speeds up the communication process, which Levinson argues is slowed down by the need for phonetic articulation: some unencoded aspects of the speaker's meaning can be inferred from metalinguistic properties of the utterance such as the choice of a given word from a set of closely related alternatives. For instance, the speaker's choice of 'some' rather than the stronger 'all' in (4a) ('Some of the guests have arrived') justifies the inference that (4c) is part of her meaning. These are non-demonstrative inferences, of course. There are cases where they would be invalid. For instance, if it is clear in the context that the speaker of (4a) has only partial information about the arrival of the guests, then (4c) would not be part of her meaning. Still, given that GCIs are valid in most contexts (or so it is assumed), the overall increase in the speed of communication brought about by their automaticity is not compromised by the rare cases where they have to be cancelled for contextual reasons.

The theory of scalar implicatures as default GCIs makes four claims:

(a) These inferences are made by default, irrespective of the context, and cancelled when required by the context.

(b) The fact that these inferences are made by default adds to the speed and efficiency of communication.

(c) These inferences contribute to utterance interpretation at the level of implicatures, rather than as enrichments of its explicit content (in Grice's terms, *what is said*, or in relevance theory's terms, its *explicatures*).

(d) These inferences are scalar: they exploit pre-existing scales such as <*some, all*>, <*or, and*>, <*possible, necessary*>.

We doubt all four claims. The bulk of this chapter will be devoted to explaining how experimental evidence has cast strong doubts on claim (a). First, however, we briefly present an argument which also casts doubt on (b), and outline the relevance-theoretic approach, which is in contradiction with all four claims.

This idea that default implicatures or GCIs would increase the speed and efficiency of communication may seem sensible and capable of lending support to the whole theory. However, it raises the following empirical issue. If GCIs had to be cancelled too often, their cost would offset the benefit of deriving them by default. Suppose, for instance, that a certain type of GCI had to be cancelled a third of the time. The total cost of using such a GCI would be the cost of deriving it by default in all cases, plus the cost of cancelling it in a third of cases. This would have to be compared with the cost of deriving the implicature as a 'particularised conversational implicature' – that is, in a context-sensitive and therefore costlier way – in two-thirds of the cases, but without the cost of default derivation followed by cancellation in the other third of cases. It is not clear that, given such frequencies, the proposed rationale for GCIs in terms of economy would make much sense.

To show that this kind of calculus is not unrealistic, consider the example of 'P or Q' and its alleged GCI *not (P and Q)*. We are not aware of any statistical data on the frequency of exclusive uses of 'or', and we share the common intuition that often, when people utter a sentence of the form 'P or Q' they can be taken to exclude the possibility that both *P* and *Q* are true. However, it does not follow that this is part of their meaning. In most cases, the fact that *P and Q* is excluded follows from real world knowledge and not from the interpretation of 'or', as illustrated in (5)–(7):

(5)   He is a bachelor or he is divorced.

(6)   Jane is in Paris or in Madrid.

(7)   Bill will arrive Monday or Tuesday.

If 'P or Q' implicates by default that *not (P and Q)*, then in cases such as (5)–(7) where the two disjuncts cannot both be true for common-sense reasons, people will compute a GCI that makes them understand the speaker as redundantly implicating what is already part of the common ground, and this is surely a cost without an associated benefit. Moreover, if we are careful to exclude cases where the mutual exclusivity of the disjuncts is self-evident and need not be communicated, and look only at cases such as (8)–(10), where neither the inclusive nor the exclusive interpretation is ruled out a priori, it is not at all obvious that the exclusive interpretation of 'or' is dominant:

(8)   She wears sunglasses or a cap.

(9)   Our employees speak French or Spanish.

(10)   Bill will sing or play the piano.

We have no hard statistical data to present, but it seems less than obvious that a disposition to understand utterances of the form 'P or Q' by default as implicating *not (P and Q)* would increase the speed or efficiency of communication. More generally, the effect that GCIs would have on the efficiency of communication should be investigated rather than assumed.   '

14.3   Relevance theory's approach

We will assume that the basic tenets of relevance theory are familiar (Sperber and Wilson 1995; see also Wilson and Sperber 2004 for a recent restatement), and focus on how it applies to what neo-Griceans call 'scalar implicatures'. Two basic ideas play a crucial role here:

(a) Linguistic expressions serve not to *encode* the speaker's meaning but to *indicate* it. The speaker's meaning is inferred from the linguistic meaning of the words and expressions used, together with the context.

(b) The speaker's explicit and implicit meaning (her explicatures and implicatures) are inferred not sequentially but in parallel. The final overall interpretation of an utterance results from mutual adjustment of implicatures and explicatures guided by expectations of relevance

Here is a simple illustration of these two points:

(11)   HENRY: Do you want to go on working, or shall we go to the cinema?
         JANE: I'm tired. Let's go to the cinema.

Jane's description of herself as 'tired' achieves relevance by explaining why she is accepting Henry's suggestion. It must therefore be understood as conveying not simply that she is tired, but that she is too tired to go on working, while at the same time not too tired to go to the cinema. The word 'tired' is used to indicate an *ad hoc* concept TIRED*, with an extension narrower than that of the linguistically encoded concept TIRED. Whereas TIRED extends from a minimal level of tiredness to complete exhaustion, TIRED* extends only over those levels of tiredness that explain why Jane would rather go to the cinema than work. Henry correctly understands Jane's explicature to be (12) and her implicature to be (13), the result being an optimally relevant interpretation:

(12)   I am TIRED*

(13)   The reason why I would rather go to the cinema than work is that I am TIRED*

Note that the explicature in (12), and in particular the interpretation of 'tired' as indicating TIRED*, is calibrated so as to justify the implicature in (13). The explicature could therefore only be inferred once the implicature had been tentatively assumed to be part of Jane's meaning. The overall interpretation results from a process of mutual adjustment between explicature and implicature.

Consider now an expression such as 'some of the Xs', which is generally seen as giving rise to 'scalar implicatures'. From a semantic point of view, 'some of the Xs' denotes the set of subsets of n Xs where n is at least two and at most the total number of Xs. From a relevance-theoretic point of view, an expression of the form 'some of the Xs' – like any linguistic expression – is used not to encode the speaker's meaning, but to indicate it. In particular, the concept indicated by a given use of 'some of the Xs' may be an *ad hoc* concept SOME OF THE Xs* whose denotation differs from that of the literal SOME OF THE Xs. Rather than ranging over all subsets of Xs between two and the total number of Xs, the extension of SOME OF THE Xs* may be narrowed at either end, or it may be broadened to include subsets of one.

Imagine (14) uttered in a discussion of the spread of scientific knowledge in America:

(14)   Most Americans are creationists and some even believe that the Earth is flat.

Clearly, the speaker is understood as meaning that a number of Americans much greater than two believe that the earth is flat. Two Americans with this belief – say two inmates in a psychiatric hospital – would be enough to make her utterance literally true, but not (and by a wide margin) to make it relevant. Since we can assume that the speaker regards it as common knowledge that not all Americans believe the earth is flat, there is no reason to think that this is part of her meaning (inferring it would involve a processing cost without increasing cognitive effects, so it would detract from relevance). On the other hand, the speaker's contrastive use of 'most' and 'some' and her use of 'even' do make it part of her meaning that fewer Americans believe the earth is flat than believe in creationism (this, of course, entails that not all Americans believe that the earth is flat, but not every entailment of a speaker's meaning is part of that meaning). So the denotation indicated by the use of 'some' in (14) is narrower at both ends than the literal denotation: it includes those subsets of Americans which are large enough to be relevant (and hence much larger than sets of two Americans), but smaller than the set of American creationists.

Let us now go back to a version of example (4). Jane and Henry have invited a few friends to a dinner party. Suppose, first, that they have agreed that Henry will go and pick up the dessert from the *patisserie* as soon as the guests begin to arrive. Henry is in the garage; he hears the bell ring, and then Jane shouts (15):

(15)   JANE [*to Henry*]: Some of the guests have arrived

Henry does not know how many of the guests have arrived, or indeed whether Jane has opened the door and seen how many there are, and the question need not even occur to him. What makes Jane's utterance relevant is that it implies that he should go and buy the dessert now, and this does not depend on the number of guests at the door. Henry's construal of 'some' is compatible with any number of guests having arrived, even a single one, and it therefore involves a broadening of the literal meaning.

Consider now a different scenario. Henry is alone in the kitchen cooking. Jane comes in and tells him (15). The implications that Henry derives are that he should come and greet the guests and bring the finger food he has made as an appetizer. The value of 'some' is taken to be one for which these are the main consequences. If all the guests had arrived, the implications would be not just that he should greet the guests and bring the finger food, but also, and more importantly, that he should put the fish in the oven and make the final preparations for the meal itself. The fact that Jane's utterance achieves relevance without bringing to mind consequences more typical of the arrival of all the guests causes Henry to construe 'some' with some vague cardinality above one and below all. He need not actively exclude *all*; he may simply not even consider it. On the other hand, if he had been wondering whether all the guests have arrived, then he will take Jane's utterance to license the inference that not all of them have. Moreover, if he had asked Jane whether all the guests had arrived, or if he knew she was aware that it was particularly relevant to him at this point in time, he would take that to be an intended inference. The same would happen if she had put a contrastive stress on 'some', causing him extra effort and suggesting an extra effect. In other words, if there is some mutually manifest, actively represented reason to wonder whether all the guests have arrived, then (15) can be taken to implicate that not all of them have.

From a relevance theory point of view, (11), (14) and (15) are just ordinary illustrations of the fact that linguistic expressions serve to indicate rather than encode the speaker's meaning, and that the speaker's meaning is quite often a narrowing or broadening of the linguistic meaning. Taking 'some' to indicate not *at least two and possibly all* but *at least two and fewer than all* is a common narrowing of the literal meaning of 'some' at the level of the explicature of the utterance. It is not automatic, but takes place when the implications that make the utterance relevant as expected are characteristically carried by this narrowed meaning.

We are not denying that a statement of the form '. . . some . . .' may in some cases carry an implicature of the form . . . *not all* . . . (or, in other cases we will not discuss here, an implicature of the form . . . *some* . . . *not* . . .). This happens when the utterance containing 'some' achieves relevance by answering a tacit or explicit question about whether *all* items satisfy the predicate. The fact that it does not give a positive answer *implicates* a negative answer, and therefore a narrowed construal of 'some' as excluding all. Standard accounts of 'scalar implicatures' fail to distinguish between cases where the explicature merely entails . . . *not all* . . . and the much less frequent cases where the utterance also implicates . . . *not all* . . . .

In all cases where the meaning of 'some' in an utterance is narrowed to exclude *all*, this is the result of an inferential process which looks at consequences that might make the utterance relevant as expected, and which adjusts the meaning indicated by 'some' so as to yield these consequences. In particular, if what would make the utterance relevant is an implication that is true of some but not all Xs, then the meaning of 'some' is adjusted to exclude *all*. These inferential processes result from the hearer's automatic search for an interpretation that meets his expectation of relevance, and they all follow the same heuristics. There is nothing distinctive about the way 'scalar' inferences are drawn. Moreover, the class of cases described in the literature as scalar inferences is characterised by an enrichment at the level of the explicature (where, for instance, 'some' is reinterpreted in a way that excludes *all*), and only in a small sub-class of these is the exclusion of the more informative concept not just entailed but also implicated.

According to relevance theory, then, so-called 'scalar implicatures' are neither scalar nor necessarily implicatures. Of course, it would be possible to redefine the notion of 'scalar implicature' to cover just those cases where there is an explicit or implicit question about whether the use of a more informative expression by the speaker (e.g. 'all' instead of 'some') would have been warranted; here, a denial of the more informative claim can indeed be implicated by use of the less informative expression. However, 'scalar implicatures' in this restricted sense depend on contextual premises (linked to the fact that the stronger claim was being entertained as a relevant possibility) rather than a context-independent scale, and are therefore not candidates for the status of GCI.

From the point of view of relevance theory, then, the classical neo-Gricean theory of scalar implicatures can be seen as a mistaken generalisation of the relatively rare case where a weaker claim genuinely *implicates* the denial of a stronger claim which is under consideration in the context, to the much more common case where the denotation of an expression is narrowed to exclude marginal or limiting instances with untypical implications. For instance, 'possible' as in (3a) ('It is possible that Hillary will win') is often construed as excluding, on the one side, mere metaphysical possibility with a very low empirical probability, and, on the other, certainty and quasi-certainty. The trimming of 'possible' at both ends results in an enriched and generally more relevant meaning. Since the trimming at the very high probability end is no different from the trimming that takes place at the very low probability end, both should be explained in the same way. This rules out the scalar aspect of the 'scalar implicature' account, which works (if at all) only at the upper end. By contrast, if (3a) were uttered in reply to the question: 'Is it certain that Hillary will win?', then it would indeed implicate (3c) ('It is not certain that Hillary will win'), because it would achieve relevance by implicitly answering in the negative a question that had been asked. From a relevance theory point of view, the two cases should be distinguished.

This is not the place to compare in detail the GCI and relevance-theoretic approaches. Instead, we focus on a testable difference in their predictions. According to Levinson, 'GCI theory clearly ought to make predictions about process. But here the predictions have not yet been worked out in any detail' (Levinson 2000: 370). However, there is one prediction about process that follows quite directly from GCI theory, since it amounts to little more than a restatement of some of the tenets of the theory. According to the theory, GCIs are computed by default, and are contextually cancelled when necessary. Both the computation and the cancellation of GCIs are processes, and each should therefore take some time and effort (even if the default nature of GCIs should make their computation quite easy and rapid). Everything else being equal, less effort should be required, and less time taken, in the normal case where a GCI is computed and not cancelled, than in the exceptional case where a GCI is first computed and then cancelled. Relevance theory predicts just the opposite pattern.

From a relevance-theoretic perspective, the speaker's meaning is always inferred, even when it involves a literal interpretation of the linguistic expressions used. However, the inferences may differ in the time and effort they require. Both sentence meaning and context contribute to making some interpretations easier to derive than others. If sentence meaning were the only factor to be taken into account, one could predict that the smaller the distance between it and the speaker's meaning it is used to indicate, the less time and effort would be required to bridge the gap between sentence meaning and speaker's meaning. However, contextual factors must also be taken into account. For instance, an enriched interpretation may be primed by the context, and may therefore be easier to infer than a literal interpretation. Consider a variant of example (11):

(16)   HENRY: You look tired. Let's go to the cinema.
          JANE: I am tired, but not too tired to go on working.

A natural interpretation of Henry's utterance involves the *ad hoc* concept TIRED*, where being TIRED* is a sufficient reason to stop working but not a sufficient reason to stay at home. Jane could have replied, 'No, I am not tired: I'll go on working', meaning that she was not TIRED* (as discussed above).

Table 14.1. *Contrasting predictions of GCI Theory and relevance theory about the speed of interpretation of scalar terms (when an enriched construal is not contextually primed)*

Interpretation of the scalar term	GCI theory	relevance theory
literal	default enrichment + context-sensitive cancellation, *hence slower*	no enrichment, *hence faster*
enriched	default enrichment, *hence faster*	context-sensitive enrichment, *hence slower*

When Jane asserts instead that she *is* tired, Henry is primed to interpret 'tired' as TIRED*. However, a relevant interpretation of Jane's utterance as a whole imposes a broader, more literal and, in this situation, more effortful construal of the term.

Even when an enriched interpretation of an utterance is not primed by the context, it may require less processing effort than the literal interpretation, because the contextual implications that make the enriched interpretation relevant are easier to derive than those that would make the literal interpretation relevant. This typically occurs with metaphorical utterances, where a relevant literal interpretation is often hard, or even impossible, to construct.

In the absence of contextual factors that would make an enriched interpretation of an utterance easier to arrive at, relevance theory predicts that a literal interpretation, which merely involves the attribution to the speaker of a meaning already provided by linguistic decoding, should require shallower processing and take less time than an enriched one, which involves a process of meaning construction. This is the case in particular in the experiments we describe below.

The difference in predictions between GCI theory and relevance theory can be presented in table form (see Table 14.1). This difference is of a type that lends itself to experimental investigation.

14.4 Methodological considerations in experimental approaches to 'scalar inferences'

In the experimental study of scalar inferences,[1] there are four methodological considerations to bear in mind. First, one wants to be sure that a given result (e.g. the rate of responses indicating a pragmatic enrichment, or the mean reaction time associated with such an enrichment) is a consequence of the intended target of the experiment and not of other contextual variables. For example, one wants to be sure that the understanding of a disjunctive statement of the form *P or Q* as excluding *P and Q* is due to pragmatic enrichment of the term 'or' (from an inclusive to an exclusive interpretation) rather than to some other feature. It is therefore best to avoid investigating utterances which invite an exclusive understanding of the situation described, as opposed to an exclusive understanding of the description itself. In example (6) above ('Jane is in Paris or in Madrid'), the exclusive understanding is based on our knowledge that a person cannot be in two places at once, and need not involve any pragmatic enrichment of the meaning of the word 'some'. In devising experimental material, it is thus important to invent examples where an enriched interpretation is not imposed by extra-pragmatic considerations. This can be done by using examples where the participants' knowledge is equally compatible with a literal or an enriched interpretation of a scalar term, or where knowledge considerations might bias participants in favour of a literal interpretation. In either case, if the results provide evidence of enrichment, one can be confident that it comes from a pragmatic inference about what the utterance meant, rather than a mere understanding of how the world is.

Second, it is best to use a paradigm that allows for two identifiable outcomes, so that the presence of an enrichment can be indicated by a unique sort of response, while a non-enrichment is indicated by a different response. This is why most of the experiments on scalars described here involve a scenario that could be described by use of a more informative utterance than the test utterance (produced by a puppet or some other interlocutor). Imagine, for example, being shown five boxes, each containing a token, and being told, 'Some boxes contain a token'. If you interpret 'some' literally (i.e. as compatible with *all*), you would agree with the statement; if you enrich 'some' so as to be incompatible with *all*, you would have to disagree. In these conditions, a participant's response (agrees or disagrees) is revealing of a particular interpretation.

Third, one wants every assurance that an effect is robust. That is, one wants to see the same result over and over again, across a variety of comparable tasks. When two similar studies (for instance, two studies investigating different scalar terms, but in equivalent ways) produce comparable outcomes, each strengthens the findings of the other. By contrast, if two very similar experiments fail to produce the same general effects, something is wrong. This does not mean that negative results are necessarily fatal for an experimental paradigm. A carefully modified experiment which prompts a different sort of outcome than previous ones (and in a predictable way) can help determine the factors underlying a certain effect. This happens with the developmental findings to be described below, which have generally shown that children are more likely than adults to *agree* with a weak statement (e.g. 'Some horses jumped over a fence') when a stronger one would be pragmatically justified (because in fact all the horses jumped over a fence). All sorts of follow-up studies have been designed to put this effect to the test. In general, the effect has been resilient, but there are a few studies showing that one can get children to appear more adult-like by using specific sorts of modifications. For example, experimenters have tried to confirm the effect in conditions where participants are given some prior training, or using scenarios designed to highlight the contrast between the weak utterance and the possibility of making a stronger claim. The net result is that the outcomes of these tests do indeed help identify the factors that can encourage scalar inference-making.

Fourth, it is important for any experiment to include as many reasonable controls as possible. These are test questions which are similar to the main items of interest, but are used basically to confirm that there is nothing bizarre in the task. For example, if participants' responses indicate that they enrich 'some', but it is also found that the same participants endorse the use of the word 'some' to describe a scene where 'none' would be appropriate, then there is something questionable about the experiment. This rarely happens (the above example is presented for illustrative purposes only), but it is important to provide assurances for oneself and for readers that such bizarreness can be ruled out. Any decent task will include several controls which lead to uncontroversial responses and are designed, in effect, to contextualise the critical findings. The studies we will discuss exemplify the four methodological considerations we have just discussed.

14.5   Developmental studies

The experimental study of scalar inferences began in the framework of developmental studies on reasoning. Noveck (2001) investigated the responses children gave (by agreeing or disagreeing) to a puppet who produced several statements, including one that could ultimately lead to a pragmatic enrichment. All the statements, even those used as controls to confirm that the participants understood the task, concerned the contents of a covered box, and were presented by a puppet (handled by the experimenter). Participants were told that the contents of the covered box resembled those of one or other of two further boxes, both of which were open and had their contents in full view. One open box contained a parrot, and the other contained a parrot and a bear. The participants then heard the puppet say:[2]

(17)   A friend of mine gave me this (covered) box and said, 'All I know is that whatever is inside this box (the covered one) looks like what is inside this box (the one with a parrot and bear) or what is inside this box (the one with just a parrot)'.

The participant's task was to say whether or not he agreed with further statements produced by the puppet. The key item was ultimately the puppet's 'under-informative' statement:

(18)   There might be a parrot in the box.

Given that the covered box *necessarily* contained a parrot, the statement in (18) can be answered in one of two ways. The participant can 'agree' if she interprets 'might' literally (so that ... *might* ... is compatible with ... *must* ...) or she can 'disagree' if she interprets *might* in an enriched way (where ... *might* ... is incompatible with ... *must* ...). Adults tended to be equivocal with respect to these two interpretations (35% agreed with the statement), while children (five-, seven- and nine-year-olds) tended to interpret this statement in a minimal way, i.e. literally. Collectively, 74 per cent of the children responded by agreeing with the statement in (18). However, not all children were alike.

The five-year-olds agreed with (18) at a rate of 72 per cent (a percentage unlikely to occur by chance – which would yield a rate of 50 per cent in such agree/disagree contexts). Nevertheless, they failed to answer many control questions at such convincing rates. For example, when asked to agree or disagree with statements about the bear ('There has to be a bear', 'There might be a bear', 'There does not have to be a bear', 'There cannot be a bear') they answered at levels comparable to those predicted by chance (55% correct across the four questions). Seven-year-olds, on the other hand, did manage to answer practically all seven control questions at rates indicating that they understood the task overall (77%). This is why Noveck (2001) reported that seven-year-olds were the youngest to demonstrate competence with this task while at the same time revealing that they preferred the literal interpretation of 'might' (at a rate of 80%, which is statistically distinguishable from expectations based on chance). The seven-year-olds thus provided the strongest evidence that those linguistically competent children who performed well on the task overall still interpreted 'might' in an unenriched way. As might be expected, the nine-year-olds also answered control problems satisfactorily. Response rates indicating unenriched interpretations of 'might' were high (69%), and much higher than the adults', but were nevertheless statistically indistinguishable from predictions based on chance, which suggests that these children were *beginning* to appear adult-like with respect to (18). Overall, these results were rather surprising for a reasoning study, because they indicated that children were more likely than adults to produce a logically correct evaluation of the under-informative modal statement. This sort of response is surprising and rare, but thanks to a pragmatic analysis – where pragmatically enriched interpretations are seen as likely to result from a richer inferential process than minimal interpretations that add nothing to semantic decoding – these results had a ready interpretation.

Despite taking every precaution (using numerous control items and sampling many children), one can never exclude the possibility that these effects might be a result of some subtle factor beyond the experimenter's intention or control.

That is why – especially when faced with counterintuitive results like these – it pays to do follow-ups. These have essentially been of two sorts.

The first sort of follow-up is designed to confirm that the effect exists. In one experiment (Noveck 2001: Experiment 2), five-year-olds, seven-year-olds and adults were given the same task as the one above, but all participants received more thorough training to ensure that they understood the parameters of the task. The training involved an identical scenario (one box containing a horse and a fish and another just a horse), but participants were asked pointed questions about the covered box (e.g. *Could there be a fish by itself in the box?*). Overall, such training increased rates of minimal interpretations of 'might' across all three ages when participants were given the task in Experiment 1. Agreement with a statement such as (18) was now 81 per cent for five-year-olds, 94 per cent for seven-year-olds, and 75 per cent for adults. Although rates of such minimal interpretations were statistically comparable across ages, the same trends are found as in the first experiment reported above. Seven-year-olds again demonstrated (through their performance with the control problems) that they were the youngest to show overall competence with the task while *tending* to be more likely than adults to choose a literal interpretation of the weak scalar term. The data also revealed that the extra training encourages adults to behave more 'logically' (to stick to the literal meaning of 'might'), like the children.

In an attempt to establish the reliability and robustness of the developmental effect, Noveck (2001: Experiment 3) took advantage of an older study which unintentionally investigated weak scalar expressions in four- to seven-year-old children and which also failed to show evidence of pragmatic enrichment. Smith (1980) presented children with statements such as 'Some giraffes have long necks' and reported that it was surprising to find the children accepting them as true. In a third experiment, therefore, Noveck (2001) essentially continued from where Smith left off. The experiment adopted the same technique as Smith (which included pragmatically felicitous statements such as 'Some birds live in cages' as well as statements with 'all') in order to confirm that the developmental findings of the first two experiments were not flukes. The only differences in this third experiment were that the children were slightly older than in the first two studies (eight and ten years old), and that the experimenter was as 'blind' to the purpose of the study as the participants (the student who acted as experimenter thought that unusual control items such as 'Some crows have radios' or 'All birds have telephones' were the items of interest). The results showed that roughly 87 per cent of children accepted statements like 'Some giraffes have long necks', whereas only 41 per cent of adults did. Again, adults were more likely than children to enrich the interpretation of the under-informative statements (understanding … *some* … to exclude … *all* …) and thus tended to reject them (since all giraffes have long necks). All participants answered the five sorts of control items (25 items altogether) as one would expect.

These data prompted Noveck (2001) to revisit other classic studies that serendipitously contained similar scenarios (where a stronger statement would be appropriate but a weaker one is made) to determine whether they tell the same story as 'might' and 'some'. In fact, three studies with 'or' (Paris 1973; Sternberg 1979; Braine and Rumain 1981), where a conjunctive situation is described with a weaker disjunction, provide further confirming evidence. The authors of these studies also reported counter-intuitive findings which show younger children being, in effect, more logical than adults (children tend to treat 'or' inclusively more often than adults). None of these authors, lacking a proper pragmatic perspective, were able to make sense of these data at the time. All told, this effect appeared robust.

Other follow-up studies have actually taken issue with Noveck's *interpretation* of the findings. In fact, Noveck (2001: 184) emphasised that his data show that children are ultimately less likely than adults to pragmatically enrich under-informative items across tasks; this did not amount to a claim that children lacked pragmatic competence. Still, there has been a lot of work designed to show that young children are more competent than it might appear. These studies usually take issue with Noveck's Experiment 3 (the one borrowed from Smith 1980), because it involves the quantifier 'some' (which is of more general interest than 'might'), and because the items used in that task are admittedly unusual (see Papafragou and Musolino 2003; Chierchia, Guasti, Gualmini, Meroni, Crain and Foppolo 2004; Feeney, Scrafton, Duckworth and Handley 2004; Guasti, Chierchia, Crain, Foppolo, Gualmini and Meroni 2005).

We highlight here the main advances made in these studies. In two sets of studies, Papafragou and colleagues (Papafragou and Musolino 2003; Papafragou and Tantalou 2004) attempted to show that children as young as five are generally able to produce implicatures if the circumstances are right. In fact, Papafragou and Musolino (2003: Experiment 1) first confirmed the developmental effect summarised above by showing that five-year-olds are less likely than adults to produce enrichments with 'some', 'start' and 'three' in cases where a stronger term (namely, 'all', 'finished' and a 'larger number', respectively) was called for. They then modified the experimental setup in two ways in preparing their second experiment. First, before they were tested, participants received training designed to enhance their awareness of pragmatic anomalies. Specifically, children were told that the puppet would say 'silly things' and that the point of the game was to help the puppet say it better (e.g. they would be asked whether a puppet described a dog appropriately by saying 'This is a little animal with four legs'). In the event that the child did not correct the puppet, the experimenter did. Second, the paradigm put the focal point on a protagonist's performance. Unlike in their Experiment 1, where participants were asked to evaluate a quantified statement like 'Some horses jumped over the fence' (when in fact all the horses did), the paradigm in Experiment 2 creates the expectation that the stronger statement (with 'all') might be true. Participants would hear a test statement like, 'Mickey put some of the hoops around the pole' (when he had been shown to succeed with all of the hoops), and they were also told that Mickey claims to be especially good at this game and that this is why another character challenges him to get all three hoops around the pole. With these changes, five-year-olds were more likely to produce enrichments than they were in the first experiment. Nevertheless, the five-year-olds, even in the second experiment, still produced enrichments less often than adults did. This indicates that – even with training and with a focus on a stronger contrast – pragmatic enrichments require effortful processing in children.[3]

Guasti, Chierchia, Crain, Foppolo, Gualmini and Meroni (2005) argue that pragmatic enrichments should be as common among five-year-olds as among adults, and further investigated the findings of Noveck (2001) and Papafragou and Musolino (2003). In their first experiment, they replicated the finding of Noveck (2001: Experiment 3) on 'some' in seven-year-olds, and used this as a baseline for studying independently the role of the two factors manipulated by Papafragou and Musolino (2003). One factor was the role of training and its effect on children's proficiency at computing implicatures (Experiments 2 and 3), and the other was the role of increasing emphasis on the outcome of a scalar implicature (Experiment 4). Their Experiments 1 through 3 showed that training young participants to produce the most specific description of a given situation can indeed have a major effect on performance. While their initial experiment showed that seven-year-olds accept statements such as 'Some giraffes have long necks' 88 per cent of the time (as opposed to 50% for adults), when trained in this way their acceptance rate becomes adult-like and drops to 52 per cent. Nonetheless, this effect is short-lived, i.e. it does not persist when the same participants are tested a week later (Experiment 3). In the last experiment, the authors made the *all* alternative more salient in context. They did this, for instance, by presenting participants with a story in which several characters have to decide whether the best way to go and collect a treasure is to drive a motorbike or ride a horse. After some discussion, all of them choose to ride a horse. In this way, it is made clearer that the statement participants have to evaluate ('Some of the characters chose to ride horse') is under-informative. The results indicated that children are more likely to produce an enriched interpretation in an adult-like manner when the context makes this enrichment highly relevant.

This last finding shows that one can create situations that encourage children to pragmatically enrich weak-sounding statements, and to do so in an adult-like way. It does not alter the fact that in less elaborate scenarios, where cues to enrichment are less abundant, seven-year-olds do not behave in this way, and it does not tell us what younger children do. Overall, the developmental effect shows that pragmatic enrichments require some effort. In experimental settings, the effort required can be somewhat reduced, or the motivation to perform it increased, but in the absence of such contextual encouragements, younger children faced with a weak scalar term are more likely to stick with its linguistically encoded meaning.

If children had been found to perform scalar inferences by default, this would have been strong evidence in favour of the GCI theory approach. However, taken together, the developmental data suggest that for children, enriched interpretations of scalar terms are not default interpretations. This sort of data is not knock-down evidence against GCI theory, since it is compatible with two hypotheses: (1) scalar inferences are not default interpretations for adults either (even if adults are more likely to derive them because they take relatively less effort, and because adults are more inclined to invest effort in the interpretation of an utterance given their greater ability to derive cognitive effects from it). Or, (2) in the course of development, children become not only capable of performing scalar inferences by default, but also disposed to perform such inferences. The first hypothesis is consistent with the relevance theory approach, while the second is consistent with the GCI approach. To find out which approach has more support, further work had to be done with adults.

14.6   Time course of comprehension among adults

As mentioned above, GCI theory implies that a literal interpretation of a scalar term, produced by cancelling a default enrichment, should take longer than an enriched interpretation; by contrast, relevance theory, which denies that enrichment takes place by default, implies that an enriched interpretation, inferred when required to meet contextual expectations of relevance, should take longer than a literal one. What is needed to test these contrasting predictions are experiments manipulating and measuring the time course of the interpretation of statements with weak scalar terms.

The same methodological considerations apply here as in the developmental tasks: it is important to make sure that enriched interpretations are clearly identifiable through specific responses, that the tasks used include a variety of controls, and that the effect is reliable and robust. One way of identifying enriched vs. literal interpretations is provided by earlier studies where participants were asked to make true/false judgements about statements (e.g. 'Some elephants are mammals') which could be construed as literally true but underinformative, or enriched (to imply ... *not all* ...) and judged as false. Hence the participants' truth-value judgements reflect their literal or enriched interpretation.

As indicated above, prior work is often critical to developing the appropriate measures. In fact, Rips (1975) unintentionally included the right sort of cases when looking at other issues of categorisation using materials such as 'Some congressmen are politicians'. He examined the effect of the interpretation of the quantifier by running two studies, one where participants were asked to treat 'some' as meaning *some and possibly all*, and another where they were asked to treat 'some' as meaning *some but not all*. The results showed that participants given the *some but not all* instruction in one experiment responded more slowly than those given the *some and possibly all* instruction in another. Despite these indications, Rips modestly hedged in concluding that 'of the two meanings of *Some*, the informal meaning *may* be the more difficult to compute' (italics added). To make sure that Rips's data were indeed indicative of a slowdown related to *some but not all* readings, Bott and Noveck (2004) ran a series of four experiments that followed up on Rips (1975) and essentially confirmed that enriched interpretations take longer than literal ones.

Bott and Noveck's categorisation task involved the use of under-informative items (e.g. 'Some cows are mammals') and five controls that varied the quantifier (*some* and *all*) and the category–subcategory order, as well as proper membership. The six types of statements are illustrated below with the six possible ways of using the subcategory *elephants*, but it is worth pointing out that the paradigm was set up so that the computer randomly paired a given subcategory with a given category while verifying that, at the end of each experimental session, there were nine instances of each type:

(19)   a. Some elephants are mammals (Under-informative).
       b. Some mammals are elephants.
       c. Some elephants are insects.
       d. All elephants are mammals.
       e. All mammals are elephants.
       f. All elephants are insects.

In the first experiment, a sample of twenty-two participants was given the same task twice, once with the instruction to treat 'some' as meaning *some and possibly all*, and once with the instruction to treat 'some' as meaning *some but not all* (and of course the order of presentation was varied). When participants were under instruction, in effect, to engage the scalar inference, they were shown to be less accurate and take significantly longer to respond to the Under-informative items (like those in (19a)). Specifically, when the instructions called for a *some but not all* interpretation, rates of correct responses to the Under-informative item (i.e. judging the statement 'false') were roughly 60 per cent; when the instructions called for a *some and possibly all* interpretation, rates of correct responses to the Under-informative item (i.e. judging the statement 'true') were roughly 90 per cent. For the control items, rates of correct responses were always above 80 per cent and sometimes above 90 per cent. It is clear that the Under-informative case in the *some but not all* condition provides exceptional data.

The reaction time data showed that the correct responses to the Under-informative item in the *some but not all* condition were exceptionally slow. It took roughly 1.4 seconds to correctly evaluate the Under-informative statements in the *some but not all* condition and around 0.8 seconds in the *some and possibly all* conditions. Responses to the control items – across both sorts of instructions – took at most 1.1 seconds, but more often around 0.8 to 0.9 seconds. Thus, the Under-informative statement in the *some but not all* condition is the one most affected by the instructions. All this confirms Rips's initial findings. More importantly, there is not a single indication that interpreting 'some' to mean *some but not all* is an effortless or quasi-effortless step. Again, a default view of scalar inference would predict that under the *some but not all* instruction, responses to Under-informative statements should take less time than responses under the *some and possibly all* instruction. According to an account based on relevance theory, the opposite should be found. The data more readily support the relevance-theoretic account.

A potential criticism of this experiment might go as follows. Given that the correct response to the Under-informative statement with the *some and possibly all* instruction is to say 'True', while the correct response to the Under-informative statement with the *some but not all* instruction is to say 'False', the reduced accuracy and slowdown in reaction times in the second type of case might be due to a response bias favouring positive rather than negative responses. To alleviate concerns about such a potential response bias, Bott and Noveck demonstrated experimentally that the effects linked to pragmatic effort are not simply due to hitting the 'False' key.

In a second experiment, the paradigm was modified so that the same overt response could be compared across both sorts of instructions; that way, the participants' response choice (True vs. False) could not explain the observed effects. To make these comparisons possible, participants were not asked to agree or disagree with first-order statements such as those in (19), but with second-order statements about these first-order statements. For example, participants were presented with the two statements: 'Mary says the following sentence is false' / 'Some elephants are mammals.' They were then asked to agree or disagree with Mary's second-order statement. In this case, participants instructed to treat 'some' as meaning *some but not all* should agree, whereas participants instructed to treat 'some' as meaning *some and possibly all* should disagree, reversing the pattern of positive and negative responses in the previous experiment.

The results of this second experiment were nevertheless remarkably similar to those of the first one. Here, when participants were, in effect, under instruction to draw the scalar inference, they were less accurate and took significantly longer to respond correctly to the Under-informative item. When 'agree' was linked with the instruction to use a *some but not all* interpretation, rates of correct responses were roughly 70 per cent; when 'agree' was linked with the instruction to use a *some and possibly all* interpretation, rates of correct responses were roughly 90 per cent. For all control items, rates of correct responses were always above 85 per cent, and often above 90 per cent. It is clear that, once again, the Under-informative case in the *some but not all* condition provides exceptional data. The reaction-time data also showed that the correct 'agree' responses to the Under-informative item in the *some but not all* condition were exceptionally slow. It took nearly 6 seconds to evaluate the Under-informative statements correctly when 'agree' was linked with the instruction to use a *some but not all* interpretation, and around 4 seconds when 'agree' was linked with the instruction to use a *some and possibly all* interpretation (all reaction times were longer than in the previous experiment due to the *Mary says* statement). The control items across both sorts of instructions took on average around 4.5 seconds, and never more than 5 seconds. Again, the experiment demonstrated that any response that requires a pragmatic enrichment implies extra effort.

Both these experiments, though inspired by previous work, are arguably unnatural. It is unusual to instruct participants in a conversation about how they should interpret the word 'some', as was done in Experiment 1; the second experiment doubles the complexity by requiring participants to make meta-linguistic judgements based on statements like *Mary says the following is false.* Bott and Noveck's third experiment simplified matters by asking participants to make true/false judgements about the categorical statements (e.g. those in (19)) themselves, and with no prior instruction. When the issue is presented in this way, there is no useful sense in which a response is 'correct' or not. Rather, the responses reveal the participant's literal or enriched interpretation, and can be compared in terms of reaction times.

Roughly 40 per cent of participants responded 'true' to Under-informative items and 60 per cent responded 'false'. This corresponds to the rates found among adults in Noveck's developmental studies (see also Noveck and Posada 2003; Guasti, Chierchia, Crain, Foppolo, Gualmini and Meroni 2005). The main finding was that mean reaction times were longer when participants responded 'false' to the Under-informative statements than when they responded 'true' (3.3 seconds versus 2.7 seconds, respectively). Furthermore, 'false' responses to the Under-informative statements appear to be slower than responses to all the control statements (including three, (19c), (19e) and (19f), that require a 'false' response). The 'true' response was made at a comparable speed to all of the control items.

In their last experiment, Bott and Noveck varied the time available to participants for responding to the statements. The rationale for this design was as follows: if, as implied by GCI theory, literal interpretations of weak scalar terms take longer than the default enriched interpretations, then limiting the time available should decrease the rate of literal interpretations and increase the rate of enriched ones. By contrast, if, as implied by relevance theory, enriched interpretations take longer, then limiting the time should have the opposite effect (i.e. shorter lags should be associated with higher rates of literal interpretations). Using the same general procedure as in the previous experiments (asking participants to make true/false judgements about categorical statements), the paradigm manipulated the time available for the response. In one condition, participants had a relatively short time (0.9 seconds) to respond, while in the other they had a relatively longer time (3 seconds). Only the time to *respond* was manipulated. To control for uptake, participants were presented with the text one word at a time, and at the same rate in both conditions; there is thus no possibility that participants in the 'Short-lag' condition spent less time reading the statements than those in the 'Long-lag' condition.

Bott and Noveck reported that when participants had a shorter period of time available to respond, they were more likely to respond 'True' to Underinformative statements (indicating a literal interpretation): 72 per cent of participants responded 'True' in the Short-lag condition, and 56 per cent did so in the Long-lag condition. This strongly implies that they were less likely to derive the scalar inference when they were under time pressure than when they were relatively pressure-free. As in all the prior experiments, control statements provide a context in which to appreciate the differences found among Underinformative statements. The results showed that performance on control statements in the Short-lag condition was quite good overall (rates of correct responses ranged from 75% to 88%) and that, as one would expect, rates of correct performance on the control items *increased* when more time was available (by 5% on average). The contrast between a percentage that drops with extra time (as is the case for the Under-informative statements) and percentages that increase over time provides a unique sort of interaction, confirming that time is needed to provoke scalar inferences.

The experiments we have described so far take into account the four methodological considerations discussed above, with well-controlled dependent variables: the rate of literal vs. enriched interpretations of weak scalar terms, and the speed with which they are derived. Together, they provide strong evidence that an enriched interpretation of a weak scalar term requires more processing time than an unenriched, literal interpretation, as predicted by relevance theory and contrary to the prediction implied by GCI theory.

Still, it might be argued that the categorisation tasks used in these experiments, even if they are methodologically sound from an experimental psychology point of view, are too artificial to be used in testing pragmatic hypotheses. If the claim were that laboratory tasks are somehow irrelevant to pragmatics, we would argue that the onus of the proof is on the critics: after all, participants bring their ordinary pragmatic abilities to bear on experimental verbal tasks, just as they do in any unusual form of verbal exchange. In particular, if it is part of adult pragmatic competence to make scalar inferences by default, it would take some argument to make it plausible that an experimental setting somehow inhibits this basic disposition. On the other hand, if the claim is that fairly artificial laboratory experiments are not enough, and that they should be complemented with more ecologically valid designs, we agree. Happily, Breheny, Katsos and Williams (2006) have provided just this kind of welcome complement.

Following up on a procedure from Bezuidenhout and Cutting (2002), Breheny *et al.* presented disjunctive phrases (e.g. 'the class notes or the summary') in two kinds of contexts: Lower-bound contexts (where the literal reading of a scalar term is more appropriate, as in (20) below), and Upper-bound contexts (where the enriched reading of the scalar is more appropriate, as in (21) below). These were presented as part of short vignettes (along with many 'filler' items to conceal the purpose of the study) and participants' reading times were measured. More specifically, participants were asked to read short texts presented on a computer screen one fragment at a time, and to read the next fragment by hitting the space bar (the slashes in (20) and (21) delimit fragments).

(20)   *Lower-bound context*
        John heard that / the textbook for Geophysics / was very advanced. / Nobody understood it properly. / He heard that / if he wanted to pass the course / he should read / *the class notes or the summary.*

(21)   *Upper-bound context*
        John was taking a university course / and working at the same time. / For the exams / he had to study / from short and comprehensive sources. / Depending on the course, / he decided to read / *the class notes or the summary.*

In such a task, if shorter reading times were found in the Upper-bound contexts, which call for scalar inferences, than in the Lower-bound contexts, where the literal interpretation is more appropriate, this would support the GCI claim that scalar inferences are made by default. Findings in the opposite direction would support the relevance theory account. What Breheny *et al.* found is that phrases like *the class notes or the summary* took significantly longer to process in Upper-bound contexts than in Lower-bound contexts, a result consistent with findings reported above.

14.7   Conclusion

The experimental work we have summarised here confirms predictions derived from relevance theory, and falsifies predictions derived from GCI theory. Does this mean that relevance theory is true and GCI theory is false? Of course not.

Nevertheless, these results should present a serious problem for GCI theorists. It is quite possible that they will find a creative solution to this problem. For instance, they might be able to show that, despite the methodological precautions described above, the reported studies failed to eliminate some uncontrolled factor, and that better studies provide evidence that points in the opposite direction. More plausibly, they might revise their theory in order to accommodate these results. One line of revision would be to reconsider the idea that GCIs are default inferences (or to water down the notion of default to the point where it no longer has implications for processing time). After all, not all neo-Griceans agree with Levinson's account of GCIs (see in particular Horn 2004, 2006). Still, it is worth noting that, if scalar inferences are not truly default inferences and invariably involve consideration of what the speaker chose not to say, then we are back to the worry that such inferences are excessively effort-demanding. Generally speaking, experimental findings such as those we have summarised here should encourage neo-Griceans to work out precise and plausible implications of their approach at the level of cognitive processing.

Relevance theorists are not challenged in the same way by the work we have described – after all, their prediction is confirmed – but they should bear in mind that the same prediction could be made from quite different theoretical points of view: it follows from relevance theory, but relevance theory does not follow from it. They might then try to develop aspects of these experiments that could give positive support to more specific aspects of the theory. For instance, according to the theory, hearers look for an interpretation that satisfies their expectations of relevance, and the relevance of an interpretation varies inversely with the effort needed to derive it. It should then be possible to make participants choose a more or a less parsimonious interpretation by increasing or decreasing the cognitive resources available to participants for the interpretation process. Bott and Noveck's fourth experiment can be seen as a first suggestive step in this direction.[4]

As we have just explained, we do not expect readers to form a final judgement on the respective merits of GCI theory and relevance theory on the basis of the experimental evidence presented. What we do hope to have done is to convince you that, alongside other kinds of data, properly devised experimental evidence can be highly pertinent to the discussion of pragmatic issues, and that pragmaticists – and in particular students of pragmatics – might benefit greatly from becoming familiar with relevant experimental work, and contributing to it (perhaps in interdisciplinary ventures).

15 A pragmatic perspective on the evolution of language

Dan Sperber and Gloria Origgi

15.1 Introduction

Suppose you overhear someone of whom you know nothing say, 'It was too slow'. You have no problem understanding the sentence, but how much does that help you understand what the speaker means in uttering it? Very little. You don't know what the pronoun 'it' refers to, what time span is indicated by this use of past tense 'was', and from what point of view 'it' was 'too slow'. The speaker might have uttered this sentence in order to convey an indefinite variety of meanings: for example, that the chemical reaction in the lab that afternoon had been too slow compared to what she had expected, that the decrease in unemployment had been too slow in France when Jospin was Prime Minister to help him win the presidential election, or that Jack's car was too slow (so that, last weekend, they had borrowed Peter's).

'It was too slow' is an ordinary sentence. Most – arguably all – sentences in any human language likewise underdetermine their interpretation. The grammar of a language, even if it is taken to include not only syntax but also phonology and semantics, does not on its own provide a sufficient basis for understanding utterances. In understanding an utterance, humans do not just associate a linguistic meaning to the sound of a sentence: they also use information about the speech situation, the interlocutors, their past interactions, the background knowledge they share, and so on. Without this contextualisation, an utterance provides only fragments of meaning without a definite import.

A new branch of linguistics, pragmatics, has developed over the past forty years, which studies the interpretation of utterances in context.[1] Work in pragmatics has at least established that contextual factors play a major role in the interpretation of every utterance, at both the explicit and implicit levels. Recognition of the highly context-dependent nature of interpretation leads to a rethinking of the role of language in linguistic communication. This rethinking has a variety of implications for related fields, and for semantics in particular. Here we discuss the implications of a pragmatic perspective for the evolution of language.

15.2   Two models of communication

Two models of linguistic communication stand in sharp contrast: the classical, or 'code', model, and the much more recent 'inferential' model. According to the code model, the sentences of a language are sound–meaning pairs. In order to convey her meaning, all the speaker has to do is encode it into a sound structure which is paired to it in the language, and all the hearer has to do is decode the sound back into the meaning. According to the inferential model, based on the work of the philosopher Paul Grice (1957, 1989) and developed in particular in relevance theory (Sperber and Wilson 1995; Carston 2002a), the linguistic decoding of an utterance provides no more than a semantic structure that falls considerably short of determining the speaker's intended meaning, and instead provides a piece of evidence from which this meaning can be inferred.

Both the code and the inferential models agree that human languages are codes which pair phonetic structures with semantic structures by means of a recursive grammar. It is often pointed out that, thanks to their grammar and their huge lexicons, human languages are incomparably richer codes than the small repertoires of signals used in animal communication. Another striking difference – but one that is hardly ever mentioned – is that human languages are quite defective when regarded simply as codes. In an optimal code, every signal must be paired with a unique message, so that the receiver of the signal can unambiguously recover the initial message. Typically, animal codes (and also artificial codes) contain no ambiguity. Linguistic sentences, on the other hand, are full of semantic ambiguities and referential indeterminacies, and do not encode at all many other aspects of the meaning they are used to convey. This does not mean that human languages are inadequate for their function. Instead, what it strongly suggests is that the function of language is not to encode the speaker's meaning, or, in other terms, that the code model of linguistic communication is wrong.

According to the inferential model, understanding the speaker's meaning is an inferential process for which the premises are, on the one hand, the fact that the speaker has uttered a certain sentence with semantic properties assigned to it by the grammar of the language, and, on the other, contextual information. Grice (1957) first suggested this perspective by reanalysing the notion of speaker's meaning. A speaker's meaning, in Grice's analysis, is a complex communicative intention which must be recognised by the hearer in order to be fulfilled. It is an intention to achieve a certain effect on the mind of the hearer by means of the hearer's recognition of the very intention to achieve this effect.

Seen this way, communication depends on the ability of humans to attribute mental states to others: that is, it depends on their 'naive psychology', or 'theory of mind'. This ability has been the subject of considerable work in developmental psychology and the study of the evolution of social behaviour.[2] Humans spontaneously interpret one another's behaviour not as simple bodily movements, but as the belief-guided fulfilment of intentions. Living in a world inhabited not only by physical objects and living bodies but also by mental states, humans may want to act upon these mental states. They may seek to change the desires and beliefs of others. This can happen unbeknownst to the person one seeks to influence. It can also be carried out overtly – by making it manifest that one is trying to cause the hearer to believe or desire something – and this is communication proper. Overt communication is achieved by giving the hearer evidence of the meaning one intends to communicate. This evidence can be of any sort – gestures, mimicry, demonstrations – and it may or may not be coded. What matters is that the evidence provided, together with the context, allows the addressee to infer the communicator's meaning.

In inferential communication, the communicator seeks to fulfil her intention by making it manifest to the hearer. This procedure carries a clear risk: the addressee, recognising that the communicator intends to act on his mental states, can easily foil this intention. On the other hand, precisely because it is overt, inferential communication has two advantages which make it much more powerful in general than all the other ways of acting on people's mental states. While a mistrustful hearer may refuse to be influenced, a hearer who trusts the communicator's competence and honesty will make an effort to understand a message which he assumes is relevant and is also disposed to accept. More importantly still, whereas the manipulation of the mental states of others by non-communicative means is relatively costly and always imprecise, overt communication, where both the communicator and the addressee are intent on achieving comprehension, makes it possible to transmit, at very little cost, contents as rich and precise as one wants.

The role of language in inferential communication is to provide the communicator with evidence, as precise and complex as she wishes, of the content she wants the hearer to accept. It is not necessary for the utterance to encode this content *in extenso* and unambiguously. Quite commonly, a fragmentary, ambiguous and loose coding is enough, in the context, to indicate a complete and unequivocal meaning. In this respect, inferential comprehension is no different from any other cognitive non-demonstrative inference process which draws relatively reliable conclusions from fragmentary evidence open to multiple interpretations by relying on both empirical regularities and the context. The main task of pragmatics is to explain how such inferences are carried out in the particular case of linguistic communication. What empirical regularities guide the process? How are the linguistic properties of the utterance, on the one hand, and contextual information on the other, put to use? Although different pragmatic theories give different answers to these questions (see Horn and Ward 2004), they share two basic assumptions: that comprehension is inferential, and that its goal is, by drawing on both the sentence meaning and the context, to discover the speaker's intended meaning.

15.3   The evolution of language and the two models of linguistic communication

Clearly, the classical code model and the inferential model being developed in pragmatics assign different functions to language in linguistic communication. To different functions there should correspond, in the history of the species, different selective pressures and hence different hypotheses about the biological evolution of language. However, scholars working on the evolution of language have generally paid little or no attention to pragmatics (Dessalles 2000 is an exception). A few who are aware of pragmatic aspects of language use (e.g. Pinker 1994: chapter 7; Jackendoff 2002) treat them as marginal, and in practice accept the code model as a very good approximation. Indeed, many scholars consider the evolution of language without worrying much about its specific properties, whether grammatical or pragmatic. In some cases, this is because their contribution consists in explaining the emergence of language on the basis of some biological function that could be fulfilled by any language-like system, whatever its precise properties (e.g. Dunbar 1996). In others (see Kirby 2002 for a review), it is because their work on modelling the possible evolutionary emergence of codes in a population of artificial agents is progressing so satisfactorily at the formal level that they tend to take its empirical relevance for granted.

Coded communication works best when emitter and receiver share exactly the same code. Any difference between the emitter's and receiver's codes is a possible source of error in the communication process. In animal communication, where in most cases the code is genetically specified, a mutation affecting an individual's code is likely to produce a mismatch between its signals and those of its conspecifics. Such a mismatch compromises the individual's ability to act as either an emitter or a receiver of information, and is therefore counter-adaptive.

More generally, since a code must be shared by a population in order to be advantageous, evolution cannot easily 'experiment' with modifications which not only (as with the effect of any random mutation) have a very low chance of being advantageous, but which, moreover, only start to be advantageous when the modification is sufficiently widespread in the population to be of use: that is, one or several generations after the initial mutant. The most plausible modifications to a genetically transmitted code involve the addition of new signals (for example, an alarm signal for a new species of predators in the environment), which do not modify the structure of the pre-existing code. The small size of codes in animal communication suggests that such additions are themselves quite rare. Indeed, animal communication codes, which (unlike human languages) really do work according to the code model, are typically tiny, lacking in syntax, and highly stable within a given species. The great majority involve no learning (and when learning is involved, as in the case of songbirds, it usually involves only a single signal which serves to distinguish local populations of the same species and which therefore cannot be fully genetically specified).

In the case of inferential communication, the situation is quite different. The success of inferential communication does not require the communicator and audience to have the same semantic representation of the utterance (or other type of communicative behaviour). All that is necessary is for the utterance, however they may represent it, to be seen as evidence for the same conclusion. Take the following trivial dialogue, for example:

(1)   JOHN: I'm beat!
        LISA: OK, let's go home.

It is of little importance whether the meaning that John and Lisa associate with the word 'beat' is the same. It may be that 'beat', for John, means extreme fatigue, while for Lisa, it is simply a synonym of 'tired'. In any event, John says, 'I'm beat' not in order to indicate a degree of fatigue that this term might encode, but in order to indicate contextually both his wish to return home and the reason for it, namely his fatigue. The level of fatigue that may justify one's desire to return home depends on the situation: it is not the same at a party among friends, while taking a stroll, or at work. In John's utterance, then, 'beat' indicates not a level of fatigue encoded by the word, but the level of fatigue which, in the situation of the utterance, is relevant in that it justifies John's wish. This *ad hoc* meaning is contextually constructed. If, in John's lexicon, 'beat' encodes extreme fatigue, then he is using the term hyperbolically. If, in Lisa's lexicon, 'beat' is simply a synonym of 'tired', she understands John's use of it literally. All the same, John and Lisa communicate successfully. Classifying usages as literal, loose, or figurative plays no part in the real-time comprehension process.

As we have just illustrated, it is not necessary for the interlocutors to have identical codes. It is not sufficient, either. Consider the following dialogue:

(2)   JOHN: Can you fix my watch?
        WATCHMAKER: That will take some time.

The semantics of 'will take some time' is trivial (or at least let us suppose that it is for John and the watchmaker, and trivial in the same way): everything that has non-zero duration takes time. Yet in uttering this truism, the watchmaker sets John on the way to a non-truistic and relevant interpretation. Repairing the watch will take not just any amount of time, but an amount of time that it is relevant to draw to John's attention. If John is expecting the repair to take at least a week, he will understand the utterance to mean that the repair will take several weeks. On the other hand, if the watchmaker thinks John is expecting the repair to be done that very day, she will choose that same form of utterance to convey that the repair will be a matter of days rather than hours. The fact that the words 'take', 'some' and 'time' have the same meaning in their lexicons does not protect John and the watchmaker from the possibility of misunderstanding.

According to the inferential model, it is neither necessary nor sufficient for the interlocutors' codes to be near-identical if they are to communicate effectively. In these conditions, a mutation that affects the language faculty and causes the mutant's grammar to diverge from that of her interlocutors will not necessarily be detrimental to her ability to communicate. As we will now show, such a mutation may even be advantageous.

Suppose that a change in the language faculty leads to the internalisation of a grammar which attributes more structure to utterances than they superficially realise – say, by projecting unexpressed constituents onto them. This might facilitate inferential comprehension.

Consider a protolanguage with only word-size sound–meaning pairs, with no syntactic structure. The word 'drink' in this protolanguage designates the action of drinking and nothing else (it is not a two-place predicate, unlike the word 'drink' in English); the word 'water' designates the substance water and nothing else, and so on. With such a limited code, the fact that the hearer can decode the meaning associated with the word the speaker has used would not ensure successful communication between them. A hearer who associates the utterance 'Water' with the concept of water is not thereby informed of anything at all. Even a concatenation of expressions such as 'drink water' in such a language would not be decoded in the way we spontaneously tend to decode it on the basis of our understanding of English. In this protolanguage, 'drink water' does not denote the action of drinking water. It simply activates two concepts, the concept of drinking and the concept of water, without linking them syntactically or semantically. The mental activation of a single concept, or a few concepts with no linguistically determined semantic linkage between them, does not denote a state of affairs or an action described by associating these two concepts; and it falls even farther short of expressing an attitude such as belief or desire.

In these conditions, such a protolanguage could be of use only to beings capable of inferential communication. For these individuals, the activation of even a single concept via decoding could easily provide enough evidence for the reconstruction of a full-fledged meaning, the speaker's meaning. Imagine two speakers of this protolanguage, let us call them John and Lisa, walking in the desert. John points to the horizon and utters, 'Water'. Lisa correctly infers from this that he means something like, *There is water over there*. Just when they reach the water hole, John collapses, exhausted, and mutters, 'Water'. Lisa correctly infers that he means something like, *Give me some water*. In the case of animal communication – which is entirely coded – such a range of interpretive constructions would not be possible for a single signal.

Suppose now that Lisa is in fact a mutant whose language faculty is more complex than those of her fellow creatures, and had enabled her as a child to analyse the words of the protolanguage she was acquiring as either arguments or one- or two-place predicates. She had therefore categorised 'drink' as a two-place predicate, 'water' as an argument, and so on. When Lisa the mutant sees John collapse and mutter, 'Water', what is activated in her mind is not only the concept of water, but a syntactic structure with an unexpressed predicate that is capable of taking 'water' as an argument. She thus decodes more than John had in fact encoded. John is not a mutant, and therefore expresses himself in the rudimentary language of their community, without mentally imposing an under-lying syntactic structure on it. However, this mismatch between John's and Lisa's representations of the utterance is not detrimental to communication. Even if she were not a mutant, in order to understand what John meant, Lisa would have had to mentally (though not linguistically) represent not only water but also an action that had water as its object. Lisa the mutant is immediately set on the right path thanks to the syntactic structure she falsely (though usefully) attributes to John's utterance.

When she speaks, Lisa the mutant, using signals which are homonymous to those of her community, encodes not only atomic concepts but also predicate–argument structures. When she says, 'Water', her utterance also encodes the unexpressed placeholder for a predicate which would take 'water' as an argu-ment. When she says 'Drink', her utterance encodes the unexpressed place-holder for the two arguments of 'drink'. When she says 'Drink water', her utterance encodes not only the two concepts DRINK and WATER, but also the complex concept DRINK SOME WATER (plus the unexpressed placeholder for the argument-subject of 'drink'). Lisa's interlocutors do not recognise these under-lying structures in her utterances, but they arrive at the intended interpretations all the same, by an inferential path that is linguistically less specified.

Now if Lisa is a second-generation mutant, and her interlocutors include some of her brothers and sisters who are also mutants, and who therefore speak and comprehend as she does, then she and her co-mutants will communicate more effectively than the other members of their community. They communi-cate, in fact, using a language whose utterances, although phonologically identical to those of the non-mutants, are syntactically and semantically more complex, and therefore easier to deal with pragmatically. In the language of these mutants, new linguistic signs may emerge and stabilise by a process of grammaticalisation which is unavailable to non-mutants. For example, pro-nouns could come to take the place of unspecified arguments.

This imaginary example illustrates how a more advanced language faculty, which leads those who possess it to internalise a richer code than the one present in their community, may emerge and evolve. This can only happen in a system based on inferential communication. In a code-based system, every departure from the common grammar will be disadvantageous, or at best neutral: it will never be advantageous.

These considerations apply not only to the initial emergence of the language faculty, but to all possible stages in its evolution. A disposition to treat uncoded communicative behaviour as a coded signal may facilitate inferential comprehension of the communicator's intentions and lead to the stabilisation of this kind of behaviour as a signal.

15.4   Conclusion

The human mind is characterised by two cognitive abilities with no real equivalent in other species on Earth: language and naive psychology (that is, the ability to represent the mental states of others). We have suggested here that it is because of the interaction between these two abilities that human communication was able to develop and acquire its incomparable power (cf. Origgi and Sperber 2000; Sperber 2000a; Origgi 2001; Sperber and Wilson 2002). From a pragmatic perspective, it is quite clear that the language faculty and human languages, with their richness and flaws, are only adaptive in a species that is already capable of naive psychology and inferential communication. The relatively rapid evolution of languages themselves, and their relative heterogeneity within one and the same linguistic community – we see these two features as linked – can only be adequately explained if the function of language in communication is to provide evidence of the speaker's meaning, and not to encode it.

In these conditions, research on the evolution of the language faculty must be closely linked to research on the evolution of naive psychology. Similarly, research on the evolution of languages must take their pragmatic dimension systematically into account.

Notes

1 INTRODUCTION: PRAGMATICS

1. In Grice's original formulation, '"[Speaker] meant something by x" is (roughly) equivalent to "[Speaker] intended the utterance of x to produce some effect in an audience by means of the recognition of this intention"' (Grice 1957/1989: 220). For discussion and reformulation, see Strawson (1964); Searle (1969, 1983); Schiffer (1972); Recanati (1986, 1987); Grice (1982); Bach (1987); Neale (1992); Sperber and Wilson (1995: chapter 1).
2. For nuanced discussion of different varieties of contextualism, see Carston (2009, 2010).
3. The wording of this maxim (and perhaps of the supermaxim of Manner) is a nice illustration of Grice's playfulness.
4. In this chapter, we will focus on the recovery of explicit truth-conditional content and implicatures; for brief comments on the treatment of presupposition and illocutionary force, see section 1.5 and note 16.
5. On generalised implicatures and the neo-Gricean approach, see Horn (1984, 1992, 2004, 2005); Levinson (1983, 1987, 2000); Hirschberg (1991); Carston (1995, 1998a); Green (1995); Matsumoto (1995); Sperber and Wilson (1995: 276–78).
6. Grice himself does not seem to have seen the distinction between generalised and particularised implicatures as theoretically significant. For discussion, see Carston (1995, 1998a, 2002a); Sperber and Wilson (1995); for experimental evidence on default inference, see Noveck (2001); Chierchia, Crain, Guasti, Gualmini and Meroni (2001); Bezuidenhout and Morris (2004); Papafragou and Musolino (2003); Noveck and Sperber (2004, 2007); Breheny, Katsos and Williams (2006).
7. On the saying–implicating distinction, see Carston (2002a: section 2.2, 2004); Wilson and Sperber (2002: section 7); Recanati (2004a: chapter 1). For representative collections on the semantics–pragmatics distinction, see Turner (1999); Szabó (2005).
8. Karttunen and Peters (1979) extend Grice's notion to other non-truth-conditional items such as 'even'. Blakemore (1987, 2002) and Bach (1999) criticise the notion of conventional implicature and offer alternative accounts; on non-truth-conditional meaning, see section 1.5.
9. Hedges are necessary because Grice does occasionally suggest that what is said may go beyond the literal meaning. See his comments on 'dictiveness without formality' in Grice (1989: 361).

10. Decoding and inferential elaboration actually overlap in time as online comprehension proceeds, with linguistic constituents providing input to elaboration as soon as they are decoded. Moreover, disambiguation, i.e. the selection of one of several decoding hypotheses, is typically affected by pragmatic enrichment or elaboration.

11. For accounts along these lines, see Carston (1988, 2002a); Recanati (1989, 2004a); Sperber and Wilson (1995, 1998a, 2008); Wilson and Sperber (2002); Neale (2004, in press). Alternative, more literalist accounts have been defended in Stanley (2000, 2002); Stanley and Szabó (2000).

12. We are considering here only what we call basic or first-level explicatures. We also claim that there are higher-level explicatures incorporating speech-act or propositional-attitude information; for discussion, see section 1.5.

13. For discussion of the relevance-theoretic account of explicatures and alternative views on the explicit–implicit distinction, see Bach (1994a, 2004); Levinson (2000: 186–98); Horn (2004, 2005); Stanley (2000, 2002); see also Carston (2002a: section 2.5); Recanati (2004a). Bach introduces a notion of 'impliciture', distinct from implicature, to cover those aspects of what is said that are not linguistically encoded. He rejects the notion of explicature on the ground that pragmatic inferences are cancellable and that nothing cancellable can be explicit. By this criterion (on which the explicit–implicit distinction essentially reduces to the coding–inference or semantics–pragmatics distinction), not even disambiguation and reference assignment can contribute to explicit content, and the resulting notion falls well short of Grice's notion of what is said.

14. On the explicit–implicit distinction in relevance theory, see Sperber and Wilson (1995: chapter 4, sections 2 and 4); Carston (2002a: section 2.3); Wilson and Sperber (2004). For a more detailed analysis of the mutual adjustment process for (6b), see Wilson and Sperber (2002: Table 1).

15. Definite descriptions such as 'the rent' in (9b) have been treated in the pragmatic literature as cases of 'bridging implicature' (Clark 1977) and analysed using relevance theory by Matsui (2000), Wilson and Matsui (2000); Noveck and Sperber (2004).

16. To the extent that pragmatic 'presuppositions' can be analysed as implicated (or accommodated) premises (cf. Grice 1981; Atlas 2004), the mutual adjustment process also sheds light on their derivation. On other types of 'presuppositional' effect, see Sperber and Wilson (1995: chapter 4, section 5) and section 1.5 below.

17. Here we will consider metaphor and related phenomena. For analyses of irony and understatement, see Sperber and Wilson (1981, 1990a, 1995: chapter 4, sections 7 and 9, 1998b); Wilson and Sperber (1992); Wilson (2006).

18. See for instance Strawson (1964); Searle (1969, 1975a); Katz (1977); Recanati (1987); Tsohatzidis (1994); Sadock (2004).

19. See for example Stalnaker (1974); Wilson (1975); Gazdar (1979); Karttunen and Peters (1979); Grice (1981); Anscombre and Ducrot (1983); Blakemore (1987, 2002); Wilson and Sperber (1993); Bruxelles, Ducrot and Raccah (1995); Sperber and Wilson (1995: section 4.5); Horn (1996); Kadmon (2001); Atlas (2004); Hall (2004, 2007); Iten (2005).

20. For an account of interjections within this framework, see Wharton (2003a, 2009).

3 TRUTHFULNESS AND RELEVANCE

1. In this chapter we will focus on metaphor, hyperbole and a range of related phenomena. For analyses of irony and understatement, see Sperber and Wilson (1981, 1990a, 1995: chapter 4, sections 7, 9, 1998b); Wilson and Sperber (1992).
2. For discussion, see Gross (1998).
3. Since what we are calling 'loose uses' shade off into figurative uses such as hyperbole and metaphor, it might be argued that Lewis's analysis of vagueness could be saved by treating 'run' and certain other cases which present problems for his analysis as falling on the figurative side (cf. Gross 1998). But this would merely transfer them from one problematic category to another since, as we have argued, neither Lewis nor Grice has proposed a satisfactory analysis of tropes. Moreover, the move would be *ad hoc* since, as we have also shown, these uses have little in common with standard examples of metaphor and hyperbole recognised in the literature on rhetoric.
4. A positive cognitive effect is a genuine improvement in knowledge. When false information is mistakenly accepted as true, this is a cognitive effect, but not a positive one: it does not contribute to relevance (though it may seem to the individual to do so). For discussion, see the Postface to the second edition of *Relevance* (Sperber and Wilson 1995), section 3.2.1.
5. A hearer's expectations of relevance may be more or less sophisticated. In an unsophisticated version, presumably the one always used by young children, what is expected is actual optimal relevance. In a more sophisticated version, used by competent adult communicators who are aware that the speaker may be mistaken about what is relevant to the hearer, or in bad faith and merely intending to appear relevant, what is expected is a speaker's meaning that it may have seemed to the speaker would seem optimally relevant to the hearer. Adult communicators may nevertheless expect actual optimal relevance by default. Here we will ignore these complications, but see Sperber (1994a); Wilson (2000).
6. In the case of deliberate equivocation, where an utterance is intentionally constructed so that two apparently satisfactory competing interpretations occur to the hearer and he is unable to choose between them, neither interpretation is directly accepted. Rather, it is the fact that the speaker has produced such an utterance that is seen as a communicative act. It receives a higher-order interpretation, which may involve endorsing both lower-order interpretations (if they are compatible), or rejecting both (if they are not). For examples and discussion, see Sperber and Wilson (1987b: 751).
7. For instance, Jorgensen, Miller and Sperber (1984); Happé (1993); Sperber, Cara and Girotto (1995); Politzer (1996); Gibbs and Moise (1997); Hardman (1998); Matsui (1998, 2000); Nicolle and Clark (1999); van der Henst (1999); Noveck, Bianco and Castry (2001); Girotto, Kemmelmeir, Sperber and van der Henst (2001); van der Henst, Carles and Sperber (2002); van der Henst, Sperber and Politzer (2002). As noted above, van der Henst, Carles and Sperber (2002) provides a direct experimental test of the claim that considerations of relevance outweigh considerations of truthfulness in verbal communication.
8. This is a variant of an example introduced in the first edition of *Relevance* (cf. Sperber and Wilson 1986a: 189–90) – there it was 'I have had breakfast' – which has been much discussed (e.g. Recanati 1989; Bach 1994a; Carston 1998b, 2002a; Taylor 2001).

9. We are using 'concept' in the psychological sense, to mean (roughly) the mental representation of a property.

10. There is now a considerable literature on hidden constituents (and more generally, on possible pragmatic contributions to explicit content). See, for example, Bach (1994a, 1997; 2000); Groefsema (1995b); Bezuidenhout (1997); Stainton (1997, 1998); Carston (1998b, 2002a); Neale (2000); Stanley (2000); Stanley and Szabo (2000); Taylor (2001); Recanati (2002a).

11. This will obviously involve some rethinking of the notion of explicitness itself; we do this in section 3.7 below.

12. In fact, for a large country, being FLAT* is incompatible with being flat: if Holland were flat, travelling from the centre to the borders would involve going upwards, that is, further away from the centre of the Earth.

13. See Grice (1989: 359–68) on the centrality of the intuitive notion of *saying*, which he characterised in what he acknowledged was 'a certain favored, and maybe in some degree artificial, sense' (Grice 1967/1989: 118).

14. We are considering here only what we call basic or first-level explicatures. We also claim that there are higher-level explicatures which do not normally contribute to the truth conditions of the utterance (Wilson and Sperber 1993; Sperber and Wilson 1995; Ifantidou 2001; Carston 2004).

15. Whatever the proposition expressed by a literal utterance of (38), it entails the existentially quantified proposition *There is a relationship between the referent of 'his' and a unique car, and there is a criterion of size, such that this car is too big by this criterion*. However, this proposition is never the utterance meaning of (38), and it would be highly counterintuitive to treat it as its literal meaning.

16. See, for example, Travis (1985); Carston (1988, 1998b, 2002a, 2004); Recanati (1989, 2004a); Bach (1994a, 1997, 2000).

17. Note that, in order to ground a clear notion of literalness, the notion of enrichment itself must be properly defined. It cannot be defined in terms of entailment since, presumably, literalness of use is maintained under negation or embedding (e.g. in the antecedent of a conditional), whereas entailment relations are not: *I have eaten* is entailed by *I have eaten supper tonight*, but *I have not eaten* is not entailed by *I have not eaten supper tonight*; similarly with *If I have/haven't eaten (supper tonight), then P*).

18. Although her notion of a convention, and of the role of intention in communication, differs from those of Lewis or Grice, Ruth Millikan (1984) also bases her philosophy of language on a version of the norm of truthfulness (see Origgi and Sperber 2000 for discussion).

19. For further discussion of the relation between truth and relevance, see the Postface to the second edition of *Relevance* (Sperber and Wilson 1995), section 3.2.1.

4 RHETORIC AND RELEVANCE

1. For elaboration of this point, see Sperber (1985: chapter 1).

2. See Sperber and Wilson (1986a). For a more detailed account of looseness and metaphor, see Sperber and Wilson (1986b). For a more detailed account of irony, see Sperber and Wilson (1981).

3. For further discussion, see Wilson and Sperber (1988a).

5 A DEFLATIONARY ACCOUNT OF METAPHORS

1. See for instance Lakoff and Johnson (1980); Sperber and Wilson (1986b, 1990a, 1995); Lakoff (1987, 1994); Lakoff and Turner (1989); Carston (1997, 2002a); Fauconnier (1997); Glucksberg, Manfredi and McGlone (1997); Kintsch (2000); Talmy (2000); Glucksberg (2001); Fauconnier and Turner (2002); Wilson and Sperber (2002).

2. See Gibbs (1994a, 1994b, 1998) and also his debate with Gregory Murphy (Murphy 1996, 1997; Gibbs 1996).

3. Some authors (e.g. David Lewis 1975) treat figurative meanings as linguistically encoded rather than pragmatically inferred; however, this vastly increases both the ambiguity of language and its gross defectiveness as a code.

4. For many (perhaps most) speakers of English today, 'temperature' may be ambiguous between a general sense and a narrower one equivalent to *fever*. For these speakers, 'temperature' in (8) would have to be disambiguated rather than narrowed. Historically, however, this narrower linguistic meaning will have been lexicalised as a result of repeated pragmatic narrowings of a single general meaning. In this case, and in others where a narrowed and/or broadened meaning of a term may have undergone lexicalisation, we are discussing how it would be interpreted in dialects where it has not yet become lexicalised. In fact, far from being an objection to a pragmatic account, the frequent occurrence of lexicalised narrowings and broadenings of lexical meanings calls for a pragmatic account as a crucial component of historical lexicology.

5. Strictly speaking, only propositions have implications. When we talk (as we will) of a concept's having implications, we have in mind the implications that propositions carry in virtue of having this concept as a constituent.

6. On the notion of a literal interpretation, see Sperber and Wilson (1995: chapter 4, sections 6–7). On this account, when a metaphorical use becomes lexicalised, an interpretation that requires the presence of exactly this concept in the explicit content will be strictly literal.

7. It might be argued that a stretch of land is flat in a second, lexicalised sense if every point on its surface is at the same distance from the centre of the earth (as opposed to being on a plane), so that someone can travel across it without climbing up or down. A problem for this view is that the statement 'If all the land on earth were at sea level, the earth would be flat' should then be true on one reading, whereas in fact it seems simply false.

8. This intuition underlies many classical rhetorical treatments, and also appears to motivate Grice's analysis of hyperbole (Grice 1967/1989: 34).

9. The distinction between literal and non-literal utterances may be relevant to normative concerns, as in law, for instance (see Wilson and Sperber 2002: section 7).

10. See, for instance, Martinich (1984), Tourangeau and Rips (1991), Becker (1997), Gineste, Indurkhya and Scart (2000), Carston (2002a), Vega Moreno (2004, 2007), Wilson and Carston (2006).

11. For an interesting proposal to handle emergent properties by augmenting the relevance-theoretic account with the machinery of domain mappings, see Gibbs and Tendahl (2006). The relations between 'domain mapping' accounts of metaphor and fully inferential accounts deserve fuller exploration than we can give them here. For now, we simply note that if emergent properties are derivable using only the

independently motivated inferential mechanisms outlined above, then domain mappings may be best seen as a result of, rather than a prerequisite to, the interpretation of linguistic metaphors, and as contributing to the interpretation process on the effort side, by altering the accessibility of contextual assumptions and implications, rather than playing the central role assigned to them in most cognitive linguistic accounts (see Wilson and Carston 2006).

12. In fact, most contextual implications are typically probabilified rather than made certain by a premise that contextually implies them, since the implication depends on the truth of other contextual premises which are generally less than certain. Implying some conclusion with certainty may be seen as a limiting case of strongest possible contextual implication (see Sperber and Wilson 1995: chapter 2).

13. Actually, even in this case, you would have to make some estimate of how precise your answer would have to be to achieve optimal relevance: could you save your hearer some processing effort without any loss on the effect side by rounding the time to the nearest multiple of five minutes, or would it be better to give an answer that is accurate to the minute? And from the hearer's perspective, would it be better to take an answer such as 'It's ten past five' as an approximation or to treat it as accurate to the minute? In most ordinary situations, mutual adjustment of the explicit content and the implicit presumption of relevance will yield an interpretation in which the response is understood as rounded (see Van der Henst, Carles and Sperber 2002).

14. Incidentally, we believe that pragmatic approaches which idealise away differences in the strength of implicatures (as most do), are ignoring a central aspect of language use.

6 EXPLAINING IRONY

1. Falsity is not the only kind of inadequacy that may be indicated by irony: ironical questions are neither true nor false and ironical understatements are typically true, but both are inadequate because of their blatant irrelevance when taken at face value.

2. See e.g. Winner (1988); Capelli, Nakagawa and Madden (1990); Happé (1993); Sullivan, Winner and Hopfield (1995); Creusere (1999, 2000); Keenan and Quigley (1999); Dennis, Purvis, Barnes, Wilkinson and Winner (2001); Nakassis and Snedeker (2002); Pexman and Glenwright (2007).

3. See e.g. Smith and Tsimpli (1995); Winner, Brownell, Happé, Blum and Pincus (1998); McDonald (1999, 2000); Dennis, Purvis, Barnes, Wilkinson and Winner (2001); Giora, Zaidel, Soroker, Batori and Kasher (2000); Langdon, Davies and Coltheart (2002); Adachi et al. (2004); MacKay and Shaw (2004); Brüne (2005); Shamay-Tsoory, Tomer and Aharon-Peretz (2005); Wang, Lee, Sigman and Dapretto (2006); Chevallier (2009), Chevallier, Noveck, Happé and Wilson (2011).

4. See e.g. Gibbs (1986, 1994a); Dews and Winner (1999); Schwoebel, Dews, Winner and Srinivas (2000); Giora (2003); Glucksberg (2001).

5. A terminological point: in those early days of relevance theory, we used 'mention' (in an extended sense of the term) to describe what we would later call 'interpretive use' (of which attributive uses are a subtype – see section 6.3). In the first edition of *Relevance* (1986a), we gave up this use of 'mention' and have talked since then of the 'echoic' theory of irony.

6. That is, any act of communication in which the linguistically encoded meaning makes an essential contribution to the content of what is communicated.

7. Attributive use is one of several sub-varieties of a more general category of *interpretive* use; see Sperber and Wilson (1995); Sperber (1997, 2000a); Wilson (2000, 2006).

8. The tacit reports in (12) and (13) display some features typical of free indirect discourse (e.g. lack of subordination, shifted tense and reference, use of 'now' with past tense verbs, etc.); see e.g. McHale (1978); Banfield (1982); Sternberg (1982a); Fludernik (1993); Mey (1999); Blakemore (2009).

9. Moreover, in echoing Jack's utterance, Sue is obviously not trying to *remind* Jack of what he has just said. This is why we do not agree with Kreuz and Glucksberg's (1989) view that an ironical echo always has the function of a reminder.

10. For further exposition of the echoic account, see Sperber and Wilson (1990a, 1995); Wilson and Sperber (1992); Sperber and Wilson (1998b); Wilson (2006).

11. See e.g. Onishi and Baillargeon (2005); Surian, Caldi and Sperber (2007); Southgate, Chevallier and Csibra (2010).

12. The correlation Happé found between irony comprehension and success in second-order false-belief tests has proved fairly robust, and has been confirmed in a variety of conditions (see note 2). By contrast, later studies suggest that, if anything, the orders of ability required for metaphor comprehension should be revised downwards: while some metaphors may presuppose the ability to pass standard first-order false-belief tests, others are understood by people who do not pass standard false-belief tests at all (Giora, Zaidel, Soroker, Batori and Kasher 2000; Langdon, Davies and Coltheart 2002; Martin and McDonald 2004; Norbury 2005; Mo, Su, Chan and Liu 2008).

13. Clark and Gerrig, drawing on the etymology of the Greek word *eironeia*, do, however, suggest that the idea of pretence is present in classical theories. Still, the fact is that in both classical rhetoric and Grice's account, irony serves to convey the opposite of the literal meaning of the utterance, and evocations of pretence are mere marginal subtleties.

14. For critical discussion of the echoic account and responses to some objections, see Clark and Gerrig (1984); Sperber (1984); Giora (1995); Hamamoto (1998); Yamanashi (1998); Seto (1998); Sperber and Wilson (1998b); Curcó (2000); Currie (2006, 2008); Wilson (2006); Colston and Gibbs (2007).

15. As shown in section 6.3, according to the echoic account, as long as the 'allusion' is based on resemblance in content, this would be enough to make the utterance echoic.

16. Even on the narrow interpretation used by Kumon-Nakamura *et al.*, the utterances (21)–(23) could also be seen as echoic. We have argued (Sperber and Wilson 1981: 311–12), that over-polite requests such as (23) can be ironical echoes of the sort of deferential utterance that (it is implied) the hearer sees as his due. Sarcastic offers such as (22) can be seen as ironically echoing the sort of utterance a good host is expected to produce, or that a guest who thinks his greed has not been noticed might be expecting to hear; and so on.

17. That is, not by directly quoting the speaker.

18. In later work, Currie (2008) suggests that the 'restrictive or defective view of the world' which is the target of the irony need not actually be attributed to anyone. For reasons of space, we will leave discussion of Currie's reservations about the echoic account to another time.

7 LINGUISTIC FORM AND RELEVANCE

1. For further discussion and a range of additional examples, see Carston (1988).
2. It might be argued that Grice's maxim of brevity could account for these examples, *ka* being longer than *a*. Such an analysis would be empirically distinguishable from ours. We claim that the pragmatic differences between (6a) and (6b) result not from the fact that *ka* is longer than *a* but from the fact that (6b) contains extra, phonetically unrealised syntactic material. Even if *ka* and *a* were identical in length, (6b) would be costlier to process and thus, on our account but not on Grice's, should still have the implications described.
3. For discussion of Carston's proposals, see Recanati (1989).
4. Within a relevance-theoretic framework, Ruth Kempson has been developing a procedural approach to anaphora (see Kempson 1988b; see also Ariel 1990; Kleiber 1990; Reboul 1990). The analysis of pronouns thus looks like providing an important source of evidence about the nature of procedural constraints on interpretation.
5. In a suitably attenuated sense on which to *say that P*, for example, is to make no commitment to the truth of *P*. See Sperber and Wilson (1986a: chapter 4, section 10).

8 PRAGMATICS AND TIME

1. See, for example, Dowty (1986); Lascarides (1992); Lascarides, Asher and Oberlander (1992); and Lascarides and Oberlander (1993).
2. For Gricean solutions to the sequencing problem, see Harnish (1976); Gazdar (1979); Posner (1980); Levinson (1983); Comrie (1985); Green (1989); and Horn (1989); for critical discussion see Carston (1988, 1993a, 1993b, 1998b); and Recanati (1989, 1993, 1994).
3. Some experimental confirmation of the claims of this section is provided by Gibbs and Moise (1996). While the contribution of pragmatics to truth-conditional content is now increasingly acknowledged, there is still some debate about how the results are to be described. Sperber and Wilson (1986a) introduce a notion of *explicature*, which is broader than Grice's notion of *what is said* and covers the types of case discussed above. Levinson (1987) retains the term 'implicature' but distinguishes two subtypes: those that contribute to truth-conditional content and those that do not. Bach (1994a, 1994b) distinguishes *implicitures*, which contribute to truth-conditional content, from *implicatures*, which do not. For discussion, see Carston (1998b).
4. For further discussion of these issues, see Sperber (1994a); Wilson (1998b).
5. For some discussion, see Sperber, Premack and Premack (1995).
6. For general discussion of the notions of exemplification and restatement within relevance-based and coherence-based frameworks, see Blakemore (1997).

9 RECENT APPROACHES TO BRIDGING: TRUTH, COHERENCE, RELEVANCE

1. For further discussion, see Reboul (1994); Reboul *et al.* (1997).
2. For further discussion of topic-based approaches to coherence, see Wilson (1998b).

3. For further discussion of coherence-based approaches, see Moeschler and Reboul (1994); Moeschler (1998).
4. In fact, coherence theory imposes a second arbitrary cut-off point between repetitions of full sentences which are adjacent in discourse and those separated by other utterances. Generally, coherence relations are only seen as holding between adjacent units of discourse. Coherence-based approaches must thus provide separate accounts not only of intra-sentence repetitions, but also of intra-discourse repetitions that are not adjacent.
5. For further discussion of the relations between truth and relevance, see Wilson and Sperber (1998b, 2002). For more detailed exposition of the arguments of this chapter, see Matsui (1995, 1998, 2000, 2001).

10 MOOD AND THE ANALYSIS OF NON-DECLARATIVE SENTENCES

1. On the semantic notion of mood, see Lyons (1977: sections 16.2 and 16.3); Palmer (1986).
2. For discussion of some non-literal, non-serious cases, see below; for arguments that force-based analyses of mood are inadequate to deal with embedded cases, see Pendlebury (1986).
3. McGinn also argues convincingly against the claim that truth-conditional semantics can deal directly with non-declaratives. Although we will not consider this claim explicitly here, the notion of interpretive use developed in sections 10.3 and 10.4 lies well beyond the scope of truth-conditional semantics.
4. Karttunen and Peters (1976) propose to account for these differences by appeal to the notion of conventional implicature.
5. For the moment, we will ignore echoic questions, and make the simplifying assumption that interrogatives always reflect the speaker's estimations of desirability. In section 10.5, this simplifying assumption will be dropped.
6. This is not the only way to deal with exam questions and guess questions within our framework, but it is the simplest. When the full range of data is taken into account, a more complex treatment, involving triply interpretive use, may be needed.

11 METAREPRESENTATION IN LINGUISTIC COMMUNICATION

1. Arguably, the child with Asperger's syndrome quoted in section 11.2, who failed to understand the word 'mat' as intended to pick out a rug, was unable to go beyond a strategy of Naive Optimism to one of Cautious Optimism.
2. Or at least deducible from assumptions explicitly represented. Since the full set of metarepresentations in a Gricean speaker's meaning are not deducible from any finite subset, I will ignore this complication here (see Sperber and Wilson 1990b for discussion.)
3. These are perhaps the clearest cases in which the mindreading ability contributes directly to the communicated content, by providing access to information about the speaker's mental states, which may then be picked out by the relevance-theoretic comprehension procedure and attributed as part of the speaker's meaning.
4. See Martin (1992) and Sperber and Wilson (1998b) for discussion of such cases, which (like many of my previous examples) present problems for traditional (non-attributive) analyses of irony.

5. Even overtly metarepresentational devices may leave a lot to be inferred, as illustrated by the example with 'disappointed' in section 11.2.

13 TESTING THE COGNITIVE AND COMMUNICATIVE PRINCIPLES OF RELEVANCE

1. See for instance Sperber, Cara and Girotto (1995); Politzer (1996); Gibbs and Moise (1997); Hardman (1998); Nicolle and Clark (1999); Matsui (2000, 2001); Girotto, Kemmelmeir, Sperber and Van der Henst (2001); Noveck (2001); Noveck, Bianco and Castry (2001); Van der Henst, Sperber and Politzer (2002); Van der Henst, Carles and Sperber (2002); Noveck and Posada (2003); Ryder and Leinonen (2003).
2. 'Effort' as used here refers to any expenditure of energy in the pursuit of a goal. It is not restricted to conscious effort.
3. Sperber, however, has been defending the view that the human mind is 'massively modular' (Sperber 1994b), and Sperber and Wilson (2002) have argued that linguistic comprehension is modular.
4. See Johnson-Laird and Byrne (1991: 20–22) for a notable exception.
5. Supporters of mental model theory explain this by pointing out that the mental representation of indeterminate problems calls for two mental models (to represent the two possible relations between B and C) as opposed to one model for the determinate problems (Byrne and Johnson-Laird 1989).
6. All the experiments reported in this section were carried out in French.
7. Other studies have confirmed this: e.g. Green and Larking (1995); Johnson-Laird and Byrne (1995); Love and Kessler (1995); Liberman and Klar (1996); Hardman (1998).
8. To calculate the percentage of rounders we used the following formula: *Percentage of rounders* $= (M - 20)/80$, where M is equal to the percentage of answers given as a multiple of five. When M is equal to 20, the percentage of rounders is equal to 0, and when it is equal to 100, so is the percentage of rounders.

14 THE WHY AND HOW OF EXPERIMENTAL PRAGMATICS: THE CASE OF 'SCALAR INFERENCES'

1. From now on, for ease of exposition, we will use the term 'scalar' without quotes to refer to the phenomena so described in the neo-Gricean approach. This of course implies no theoretical commitment on our part.
2. The contents of parentheses were not uttered, but indicated.
3. Papafragou and Tantalou (2004) aim to show that five-year-olds can be encouraged to produce scalar inferences, and at adult levels. We do not discuss their results here because their data are based on a non-standard paradigm in which participants are given no justifiable reason to accept the 'minimal' interpretation of a term such as 'some'. In other words, the paradigm does not provide participants with two clear options. Moreover, many of the claims in the study are based on children's self-reports, and even these lead to the conclusion that at most 56% of Papafragou and Tantalou's participants derived scalar inferences.
4. For other experimental explorations based on relevance theory, see Van der Henst and Sperber (2004).

15 A PRAGMATIC PERSPECTIVE ON THE EVOLUTION OF LANGUAGE

1. See for instance Ducrot (1972); Levinson (1983, 2000); Horn (1989); Grice (1989); Sperber and Wilson (1995); Stalnaker (1999); Carston (2002a); Recanati (2004a); Atlas (2005); Szabó (2005).
2. See for instance Byrne and Whiten (1988); Carruthers and Smith (1996); Whiten and Byrne (1997); Baron-Cohen, Tager-Flusberg and Cohen (1993/2000); Leslie, Friedman and German (2004).

References

Ackerman, B. 1983. Form and function in children's understanding of ironic utterances. *Journal of Experimental Child Psychology* **35**: 487–508.

Adachi, T., Koeda, T., Hirabayashi, S., Maeoka, Y., Shiota, M., Wright, E. and Wada, A. 2004. The metaphor and sarcasm scenario test: A new instrument to help differentiate high functioning pervasive developmental disorder from attention deficit/hyperactivity disorder. *Brain and Development* **26**: 301–6.

Anscombre, J. and Ducrot, O. 1983. *L'argumentation dans la langue*. Brussels: Mardaga.

Ariel, M. 1990. *Accessing Noun Phrase Antecedents*. London: Routledge.

Asher, N. and Lascarides, A. 1995. Lexical disambiguation in a discourse context. *Journal of Semantics* **12**: 69–108.

1998. The semantics and pragmatics of presupposition. *Journal of Semantics* **15**: 239–99.

2003. *Logics of Conversation*. Cambridge University Press.

Asher, N. and Wada, H. 1988. A computational account of syntactic, semantic and pragmatic principles for anaphora resolution. *Journal of Semantics* **6**: 309–44.

Astington, J., Harris, P. and Olson, D. (eds.) 1988. *Developing Theories of Mind*. Cambridge University Press.

Atlas, J. 2004. Presupposition. In Horn and Ward (eds.), pp. 29–52.

2005. *Logic, Meaning, and Conversation: Semantical Underdeterminacy, Implicature, and their Interface*. Oxford University Press.

Austen, J. [1990]. *Persuasion*. World's Classics. Oxford University Press. (First published 1818.)

Bach, K. 1987. On communicative intentions: A reply to Recanati. *Mind & Language* **2**: 141–54.

1994a. Conversational impliciture. *Mind & Language* **9**: 124–62.

1994b. Semantic slack: What is said and more. In Tsohatzidis (ed.), pp. 267–91.

1997. The semantics–pragmatics distinction: What it is and why it matters. *Linguistische Berichte* **8**: 33–50.

1999. The myth of conventional implicature. *Linguistics and Philosophy* **22**: 327–66.

2000. Quantification, qualification and context: A reply to Stanley and Szabó. *Mind & Language* **15**: 262–83.

2001. You don't say? *Synthese* **127**: 11–31.

2004. Pragmatics and the philosophy of language. In Horn and Ward (eds.), pp. 461–87.

Bach, K. and Harnish, R. M. 1979. *Linguistic Communication and Speech Acts.* Cambridge, MA: MIT Press.

Banfield, A. 1982. *Unspeakable Sentences: Narration and Representation in the Language of Fiction.* London: Routledge.

Barkow, J., Cosmides, L. and Tooby, J. 1995. *The Adapted Mind: Evolutionary Psychology and the Generation of Culture.* Oxford University Press.

Bar-Lev, S. and Palacas, A. 1980. Semantic command over pragmatic priority. *Lingua* **51**: 137–46.

Baron-Cohen, S. 1995. *Mindblindness: An Essay on Autism and Theory of Mind.* Cambridge, MA: MIT Press.

Baron-Cohen, S., Leslie, A. and Frith, U. 1985. Does the autistic child have a 'theory of mind'? *Cognition* **21**: 37–46.

Baron-Cohen, S., Tager-Flusberg, H. and Cohen, D. (eds.) 1993. *Understanding Other Minds: Perspectives from Autism.* Oxford University Press (2nd edition 2000).

Barsalou, L. 1987. The instability of graded structure: Implications for the nature of concepts. In U. Neisser (ed.) *Concepts and Conceptual Development: Ecological and Intellectual Factors in Categorization*, pp. 101–140. Cambridge University Press.

Bartsch, K. and Wellman, H. 1995. *Children Talk about the Mind.* Oxford University Press.

Becker, A. 1997. Emergent and common features influence metaphor interpretation. *Metaphor and Symbol* **12**: 243–59.

Bell, M. 1975. Questioning. *Philosophical Quarterly* **25**: 193–212.

Bender, J. and Wellbery, D. (eds.) 1990. *The Ends of Rhetoric: History, Theory, Practice.* Stanford University Press.

Benveniste, E. 1966. *Problèmes de linguistique générale.* Paris: Gallimard.

Bezuidenhout, A. 1997. Pragmatics, semantic underdetermination and the referential–attributive distinction. *Mind* **106**: 375–409.

Bezuidenhout, A. and Cutting, J. 2002. Literal meaning, minimal propositions, and pragmatic processing. *Journal of Pragmatics* **34**: 433–56.

Bezuidenhout, A. and Morris, R. 2004. Implicature, relevance and default inferences. In Noveck and Sperber (eds.), pp. 257–82.

Bezuidenhout, A. and Sroda, M.-S. 1996. Disambiguation of reference by young children: An application of relevance theory. Paper presented at Relevance Theory Workshop, Tokyo, March 1996.

  1998. Children's use of contextual cues to resolve referential ambiguity: An application of relevance theory. *Pragmatics and Cognition* **6**: 265–99.

Blakemore, D. 1987. *Semantic Constraints on Relevance.* Oxford: Blackwell.

  1988. *So* as a constraint on relevance. In Kempson (ed.), pp. 183–95.

  1991. Performatives and parentheticals. *Proceedings of the Aristotelian Society* **91**: 197–213.

  1992. *Understanding Utterances.* Oxford: Blackwell.

  1994. Echo questions: A pragmatic account. *Lingua* **4**: 197–211.

  1997. Restatement and exemplification: A relevance-theoretic reassessment of elaboration. *Pragmatics and Cognition* **5**: 1–19.

  2002. *Relevance and Linguistic Meaning: The Semantics and Pragmatics of Discourse Markers.* Cambridge University Press.

2009. Parentheticals and point of view in free indirect style. *Language and Literature* **18**: 129–53.

Blass, R. 1989a. Pragmatic effects of co-ordination: the case of 'and' in Sissala. *UCL Working Papers in Linguistics* **1**: 32–51.

1989b. Grammaticalisation of interpretive use: The case of *rε* in Sissala. *Lingua* **79**: 299–326.

1990. *Relevance Relations in Discourse: A Study with Special Reference to Sissala.* Cambridge University Press.

Bloom, L. 1991. *Language Development from Two to Three.* Cambridge University Press.

Bloom, P. 1997. Intentionality and word learning. *Trends in Cognitive Sciences* **1**: 9–12.

2000. *How Children Learn the Meanings of Words.* Cambridge, MA: MIT Press.

2002. Mindreading, communication, and the learning of names for things. *Mind & Language* **17**: 37–54.

Blutner, R. and Zeevat, H. (eds.) 2003. *Optimality Theory and Pragmatics.* Basingstoke: Palgrave.

Bolinger, D. 1978. *Yes–no* questions are not alternative questions. In Hiz (ed.), pp. 87–105.

Booth, W. 1961. *The Rhetoric of Fiction.* Chicago University Press.

1974. *A Rhetoric of Irony.* University of Chicago Press.

Bott, L. and Noveck, I. 2004. Some utterances are under-informative: The onset and time course of scalar inferences. *Journal of Memory and Language* **51**: 437–57.

Braine, M. and O'Brien, D. 1998. *Mental Logic.* Mahwah, NJ: Lawrence Erlbaum.

Braine, M. and Rumain, B. 1981. Children's comprehension of 'or': Evidence for a sequence of competencies. *Journal of Experimental Child Psychology* **31**: 46–70.

Breheny, R. 2002. The current state of (radical) pragmatics in the cognitive sciences. *Mind & Language* **17**: 169–87.

Breheny, R., Katsos, N. and Williams, J. 2006. Are generalized scalar implicatures generated by default? An on-line investigation into the role of context in generating pragmatic inferences. *Cognition* **100**: 434–63.

Bretherton, I. 1991. Intentional communication and the development of an understanding of mind. In Frye and Moore (eds.), pp. 49–75.

Bretherton, I. and Beeghly, M. 1982. Talking about internal states: The acquisition of an explicit theory of mind. *Developmental Psychology* **18**: 906–21.

Brockway, D. 1981. Semantic constraints on relevance. In H. Parret, M. Sbisa and J. Verschueren (eds.) *Possibilities and Limitations of Pragmatics*, pp. 57–78. Amsterdam: John Benjamins.

Brüne, M. 2005. 'Theory of mind' in schizophrenia: A review of the literature. *Schizophrenia Bulletin* **31**: 21–42.

Bruxelles, S., Ducrot, O. and Raccah, P.-Y. 1995. Argumentation and the lexical topical fields. *Journal of Pragmatics* **24**: 99–114.

Bryant, G. and Fox Tree, J. 2005. Is there an ironic tone of voice? *Language and Speech* **48**: 257–77.

Burton-Roberts, N. 1989. *The Limits to Debate: A Revised Theory of Semantic Presupposition.* Cambridge University Press.

(ed.) 2007. *Pragmatics.* Basingstoke: Palgrave.

Butler, K. 1995. Content, context and compositionality. *Mind & Language* **10**: 3–24.

Byrne, R. and Johnson-Laird, P. 1989. Spatial reasoning. *Journal of Memory and Language* **28**: 564–75.

Byrne, R. and Whiten, A. (eds.) 1988. *Machiavellian Intelligence: Social Expertise and Evolution of Intellect in Monkeys, Apes and Humans.* Oxford University Press.

Capelli, C., Nakagawa, N. and Madden, C. 1990. How children understand sarcasm: The role of context and intonation. *Child Development* **61**: 1824–41.

Cappelen, H. and Lepore, E. 1997a. Varieties of quotation. *Mind* **106**: 429–50.

1997b. On an alleged connection between indirect speech and theory of meaning. *Mind & Language* **12**: 278–96.

Caramazza, A. and Grober, E. 1976. Polysemy and the structure of the subjective lexicon. In C. Rameh (ed.) *Semantics: Theory and Application.* Georgetown University Round Table on Language and Linguistics, pp. 181–206. Washington, DC: Georgetown University Press.

Carruthers, P. and Boucher, J. (eds.) 1998. *Language and Thought: Interdisciplinary Themes.* Cambridge University Press.

Carruthers, P. and Chamberlain, A. (eds.) 2000. *Evolution and the Human Mind: Language, Modularity and Social Cognition.* Cambridge University Press.

Carruthers, P. and Smith, P. (eds.) 1996. *Theories of Theories of Mind.* Cambridge University Press.

Carston, R. 1988. Implicature, explicature and truth-theoretic semantics. In Kempson (ed.), pp. 155–81. (Reprinted in Davis (ed.) 1991, pp. 33–51; Kasher (ed.) 1998, vol. IV, pp. 464–79.)

1993a. Conjunction, explanation and relevance. *Lingua* **90**: 27–48.

1993b. Conjunction and pragmatic effects. In R. Asher (ed.) *The Encyclopaedia of Language and Linguistics*, pp. 692–8. Oxford: Pergamon Press.

1995. Quantity maxims and generalised implicature. *Lingua* **96**: 213–44.

1996. Metalinguistic negation and echoic use. *Journal of Pragmatics* **25**: 309–30.

1997. Enrichment and loosening: Complementary processes in deriving the proposition expressed? *Linguistische Berichte* **8**: 103–27.

1998a. Informativeness, relevance and scalar implicature. In Carston and Uchida (eds.), pp. 179–236.

1998b. Pragmatics and the Explicit–Implicit Distinction. PhD thesis, University of London. (Revised version published as Carston 2002a.)

2002a. *Thoughts and Utterances: The Pragmatics of Explicit Communication.* Oxford: Blackwell.

2002b. Linguistic meaning, communicated meaning and cognitive pragmatics. *Mind & Language* **17**: 127–48.

2004. Explicature and semantics. In S. Davis and B. Gillon (eds.) *Semantics: A Reader*, pp. 817–45. Oxford University Press.

2009. The explicit/implicit distinction in pragmatics and the limits of explicit communication. *International Review of Pragmatics* **1**: 35–62.

2010. Explicit communication and 'free' pragmatic enrichment. In B. Soria and E. Romero (eds.) *Explicit Communication: Robyn Carston's Pragmatics*, pp. 217–85. Basingstoke: Palgrave.

Carston, R. and Uchida, S. (eds.) 1998. *Relevance Theory: Applications and Implications.* Amsterdam: John Benjamins.

Chafe, W. and Nichols, J. (eds.) 1986. *Evidentiality: The Linguistic Coding of Epistemology.* Norwood, NJ: Ablex.

Cheng, P. and Holyoak, K. 1985. Pragmatic reasoning schemas. *Cognitive Psychology* **17**: 391–416.

Chevallier, C. 2009. Communication in Asperger's Syndrome. PhD thesis, University of Lyon 2.

Chevallier, C., Noveck, I., Happé, F. and Wilson, D. 2011. What's in a voice? Prosody as a test case for the Theory of Mind account of autism. *Neuropsychologia* **49**: 507–17.

Chierchia, G., Crain, S., Guasti, M., Gualmini, A. and Meroni, L. 2001. The acquisition of disjunction: Evidence for a grammatical view of scalar implicatures. *BUCLD 25 Proceedings*, pp. 157–68. Somerville, MA: Cascadilla Press.

Chierchia, G., Guasti, T., Gualmini, A., Meroni, L., Crain, S. and Foppolo, F. 2004. Adults' and children's semantic and pragmatic competence in interaction. In Noveck and Sperber (eds.), pp. 283–300.

Clark, B. 1991. Relevance Theory and the Semantics of Non-declaratives. PhD thesis, University of London.

　1993. A relevance-theoretic analysis of pseudo-imperatives. *Linguistics and Philosophy* **16**: 79–121.

Clark, H. 1977. Bridging. In P. Johnson-Laird and P. Wason (eds.) *Thinking: Readings in Cognitive Science*, pp. 411–20. Cambridge University Press.

　1993. *Arenas of Language Use*. Stanford, CA: CSLI.

　1996. *Using Language*. Cambridge University Press.

Clark, H. and Carlson, T. 1981. Context for comprehension. In J. Lang and A. Baddeley (eds.) *Attention and performance* vol. IX, pp. 313–30 Hillsdale, NJ: Lawrence Erlbaum.

Clark, H. and Gerrig, R. 1984. On the pretense theory of irony. *Journal of Experimental Psychology: General* **113**: 121–6.

　1990. Quotations as demonstrations. *Language* **66**: 764–805.

Clark, H. and Haviland, S. 1977. Comprehension and the Given–New Contract. In R. Freedle (ed.) *Discourse Production and Comprehension*, pp. 1–40. Norwood, NJ: Ablex.

Clark, H. and Marshall, C. 1981. Definite reference and mutual knowledge. In A. Joshi, B. Webber and I. Sag (eds.) *Elements of Discourse Understanding*, pp. 10–63. Cambridge University Press.

Cohen, L. J. 1971. Some remarks on Grice's views about the logical particles of natural language. In Y. Bar-Hillel (ed.) *Pragmatics of Natural Languages*, pp. 50–68. Dordrecht: Reidel.

Cohn, D. 1978. *Transparent Minds: Narrative Modes for Presenting Consciousness in Fiction*. Princeton University Press.

Cole, P. (ed.) 1981. *Radical Pragmatics*. New York: Academic Press.

Cole, P. and Morgan, J. (eds.) 1975. *Syntax and Semantics 3: Speech Acts*. New York: Academic Press.

Coleridge, S. T. 1907. *Biographia Literaria*, edited by J. Shawcross. London: Oxford University Press.

　1987. *The Collected Works, vol. V: Lectures 1808–1819, On Literature*. Princeton University Press.

Colston, H. and Gibbs, R. 2007. A brief history of irony. In Gibbs and Colston (eds.), pp. 3–21.

Comrie, B. 1985. *Tense*. Cambridge University Press.

Cosmides, L. 1989. The logic of social exchange: Has natural selection shaped how humans reason? Studies with the Wason Selection Task. *Cognition* **31**: 187–276.

Coulmas, F. (ed.) 1986. *Direct and Indirect Speech*. Berlin: Mouton de Gruyter.

Creusere, M. 1999. Theories of adults' understanding and use of irony and sarcasm: Applications to and evidence from research with children. *Developmental Review* **19**: 213–62.

2000. A developmental test of theoretical perspectives on the understanding of verbal irony: Children's recognition of allusion and pragmatic insincerity. *Metaphor and Symbol* **15**: 29–45.

Culler, J. 1981. *The Pursuit of Signs: Semiotics, Literature, Deconstruction*. Ithaca, NY: Cornell University Press.

Curcó, C. 1998. Indirect echoes and verbal humour. In Rouchota and Jucker (eds.), pp. 305–25.

2000. Irony: Negation, echo and metarepresentation. *Lingua* **110**: 257–80. (Reprinted in Gibbs and Colston (eds.) 2007, pp. 269–93.)

Currie, G. 2002. *Recreative Minds: Imagination in Philosophy and Psychology*. Oxford University Press.

2006. Why irony is pretence. In S. Nichols (ed.) *The Architecture of the Imagination*, pp. 111–33. Oxford University Press.

2008. Echo et feintise: quelle est la différence et qui a raison? *Philosophiques* **35**: 13–23.

Dancy, J., Moravcsik, J. and Taylor, C. C. W. (eds.) 1988. *Human Agency: Language, Duty and Value*. Stanford University Press.

Dascal, M. 1981. Contextualism. In H. Parret, M. Sbisà and J. Verschueren (eds.) *Possibilities and Limitations of Pragmatics*, pp. 153–77. Amsterdam: John Benjamins.

Davidson, D. 1968. On saying that. *Synthese* **19**: 130–46. (Reprinted in Davidson 1984, pp. 93–108.)

1979a. Quotation. *Theory and Decision* **11**: 27–40. (Reprinted in Davidson 1984, pp. 79–92.)

1979b. Moods and performances. In A. Margalit (ed.) *Meaning and Use*, pp. 9–20. Dordrecht: Reidel. (Reprinted in Davidson 1984, pp. 109–21.)

1984. *Inquiries into Truth and Interpretation*. Oxford University Press.

Davies, M. and Stone, T. (eds.) 1995a. *Mental Simulation: Philosophical and Psychological Essays*. Oxford: Blackwell.

(eds.) 1995b. *Folk Psychology*. Oxford: Blackwell.

Davis, S. (ed.). 1991. *Pragmatics: A Reader*. Oxford University Press.

Deane, P. 1988. Polysemy and cognition. *Lingua* **75**: 325–61.

de Neys, W. and Schaeken, W. 2007. When people are more logical under cognitive load: Dual task impact on scalar implicature. *Experimental Psychology* **54**: 128–33.

Dennis, M., Purvis, K., Barnes, M., Wilkinson, M. and Winner, E. 2001. Understanding of literal truth, ironic criticism, and deceptive praise following childhood head injury. *Brain and Language* **78**: 1–16.

Dessalles, J.-L. 2000. *Aux origines du langage. Une histoire naturelle de la parole*. Paris: Hermès.

Dews, S. and Winner, E. 1999. Obligatory processing of literal and non-literal meanings in verbal irony. *Journal of Pragmatics* **31**: 1579–99.

Dickens, C. [1996] *Bleak House*. Penguin Classics. Harmondsworth: Penguin. (First published 1852–3.)

Dowty, D. 1986. The effects of aspectual class on the temporal structure of discourse: Semantics or pragmatics? *Linguistics and Philosophy* 9: 37–61.

Ducrot, O. 1972. *Dire et ne pas dire*. Paris: Hermann.

1973. *Le preuve et le dire*. Paris: Mame.

1980. Analyses pragmatiques. *Communications* 32: 11–60.

1983. *Puisque*: Essai de description polyphonique. In M. Herslund, O. Mordrup and F. Sorensen (eds.) *Analyse grammaticale du français*. Special issue of *Revue romane* 24: 166–85.

1984. *Le dire et le dit*. Paris: Minuit.

Dunbar, R. 1996. *Grooming, Gossip and the Evolution of Language*. London: Faber and Faber.

Erku, F. and Gundel, J. 1987. The pragmatics of indirect anaphors. In Verschueren and Bertuccelli-Papi (eds.), pp. 533–45.

Escandell-Vidal, V. 1998. Metapropositions as metarepresentations. Paper delivered to the Relevance Theory Workshop, Luton, September 1998. (Revised version published as Escandell-Vidal 2002.)

2002. Echo-syntax and metarepresentations. *Lingua* 112: 871–900.

Evans, J. St. B. T. 1989. *Bias in Human Reasoning: Causes and Consequences*. Hove: Lawrence Erlbaum.

Evans, J. St. B. T., Newstead, S. and Byrne, R. 1993. *Human Reasoning. The Psychology of Deduction*. Hove: Lawrence Erlbaum.

Fauconnier, G. 1975. Pragmatic scales and logical structure. *Linguistic Inquiry* 6: 353–75.

1985. *Mental Spaces: Aspects of Meaning Construction in Natural Language*. Cambridge, MA: MIT Press/Bradford Books.

1997. *Mappings in Thought and Language*. Cambridge University Press.

Fauconnier, G. and Turner, M. 2002. *The Way we Think: Conceptual Blending and the Mind's Hidden Complexities*. New York: Basic Books.

Feeney, A., Scrafton, S., Duckworth, A. and Handley, S. 2004. The story of *some*: Everyday pragmatic inference by children and adults. *Canadian Journal of Experimental Psychology* 58: 121–32.

Fiddick, L., Cosmides, L. and Tooby, J. 2000. No interpretation without representation: The role of domain-specific representations in the Wason Selection Task. *Cognition* 77: 1–79.

Fillmore, C. 1990. Epistemic stance and grammatical form in English conditional sentences. *Chicago Linguistic Society* 26: 137–62.

Fludernik, M. 1993. *The Fictions of Language and the Languages of Fiction*. London: Routledge.

Fodor, J. 1975. *The Language of Thought*. New York: Crowell.

1983. *The Modularity of Mind*. Cambridge, MA: MIT Press.

1992. A theory of the child's theory of mind. *Cognition* 44: 283–96.

Fodor, J. and Lepore, E. 1998. The emptiness of the lexicon: Critical reflections on J. Pustejovsky's *The Generative Lexicon*. *Linguistic Inquiry* 29: 269–88.

Franks, B. 1995. Sense generation: A 'quasi-classical' approach to concepts and concept combination. *Cognitive Science* 19: 441–505.

Franks, B. and Braisby, N. 1990. Sense generation or how to make a mental lexicon flexible. *Proceedings of the 12th Annual Conference of the Cognitive Science Society*. Cambridge, MA: MIT Press.

Fridlund, A. 1994. *Human Facial Expression: An Evolutionary View*. New York: Academic Press.

Frith, U. and Happé, F. 1999. Theory of mind and self-consciousness: What is it like to be autistic? *Mind & Language* 14: 1–22.

Frye, D. and Moore, C. (eds.) 1991. *Children's Theories of Mind: Mental States and Social Understanding*. Hillsdale, NJ: Lawrence Erlbaum.

Garnham, A. and Perner, J. 1990. Does manifestness solve problems of mutuality? *Behavioral and Brain Sciences* 13: 178–9.

Garver, N. 1965. Varieties of use and mention. *Philosophy and Phenomenological Research* 26: 230–8.

Gazdar, G. 1979. *Pragmatics: Implicature, Presupposition and Logical Form*. London: Academic Press.

Gelman, S. and Markman, E. 1986. Categories and induction in young children. *Cognition* 23: 183–209.

Gernsbacher, M. (ed.) 1994. *Handbook of Psycholinguistics*. New York: Academic Press.

Gibbs, R. 1986. On the psycholinguistics of sarcasm. *Journal of Experimental Psychology: General* 115: 3–15. (Reprinted in Gibbs and Colston (eds.) 2007, 173–200.)

　　1987. Mutual knowledge and the psychology of conversational inference. *Journal of Pragmatics* 11: 561–88.

　　1994a. *The Poetics of Mind: Figurative Thought, Language and Understanding*. Cambridge University Press.

　　1994b. Figurative thought and figurative language. In Gernsbacher (ed.), pp. 411–46.

　　1996. Why many concepts are metaphorical. *Cognition* 61: 309–19.

　　1998. The fight over metaphor in thought and language. In N. Katz, C. Cacciari, R. Gibbs and M. Turner (eds.) *Figurative Language and Thought*, pp. 88–118. New York: Oxford University Press.

Gibbs, R. and Colston, H. (eds.) 2007. *Irony in Language and Thought: A Cognitive Science Reader*. Hillsdale, NJ: Lawrence Erlbaum.

Gibbs, R. and Moise, J. 1997. Pragmatics in understanding what is said. *Cognition* 62: 51–74.

Gibbs, R. and Tendahl, M. 2006. Cognitive effort and effects in metaphor comprehension: Relevance theory and psycholinguistics. *Mind & Language* 21: 379–403.

Gigerenzer, G., Todd, P. M. and the ABC Research Group. 1999. *Simple Heuristics that Make us Smart*. Oxford University Press.

Gineste, M.-D., Indurkhya, B. and Scart, V. 2000. Emergence of features in metaphor comprehension. *Metaphor and Symbol* 15: 117–35.

Giora, R. 1995. On irony and negation. *Discourse Processes* 19: 239–64.

　　1997. Discourse coherence and theory of relevance: Stumbling blocks in search of a unified theory. *Journal of Pragmatics* 27: 17–34.

　　2003. *On our Mind: Salience, Context and Figurative Language*. New York: Oxford University Press.

Giora, R., Zaidel, E., Soroker, N., Batori, G. and Kasher, A. 2000. Differential effects of right- and left-hemisphere damage on understanding sarcasm and metaphor. *Metaphor and Symbol* 15: 63–83.

Girotto, V., Kemmelmeir, M., Sperber, D. and Van der Henst, J.-B. 2001. Inept reasoners or pragmatic virtuosos? Relevance and the deontic selection task. *Cognition* 81: 69–76.

Glucksberg, S. 2001. *Understanding Figurative Language*. Oxford University Press.

Glucksberg, S., Manfredi, D. and McGlone, M. 1997. Metaphor comprehension: How metaphors create new categories. In T. Ward, S. Smith, and J. Vaid (eds.) *Creative Thought: An Investigation of Conceptual Structures and Processes*, pp. 327–50. Washington, DC: American Psychological Association.

Gombert, J. 1990. *Metalinguistic Development*. Sussex: Harvester Press.

Gopnik, A. and Wellman, H. 1992. Why the child's theory of mind really is a theory. *Mind & Language* **7**: 145–71.

Goschke, T. and Koppelberg, D. 1991. The concept of representation and the representation of concepts in connectionist models. In W. Ramsey, S. Stich and D. Rumelhart (eds.) *Philosophy and Connectionist Theory*, pp. 129–61. Hillsdale, NJ: Erlbaum.

Green, D. and Larking, R. 1995. The locus of facilitation in the abstract selection task. *Thinking and Reasoning* **1**: 183–99.

Green, G. 1989. *Pragmatics and Natural Language Understanding*. Hillsdale, NJ: Lawrence Erlbaum.

Green, M. 1995. Quantity, volubility, and some varieties of discourse. *Linguistics and Philosophy* **19**: 83–112.

Grice, H. P. 1957. Meaning. *Philosophical Review* **66**: 377–88. (Reprinted in Grice 1989, pp. 213–23.)

   1967. *Logic and Conversation*. William James Lectures, Harvard University. In Grice 1989, pp. 3–143.

   1969. Utterer's meaning and intentions. *Philosophical Review* **78**: 147–77. (Reprinted in Grice 1989, pp. 86–116.)

   1981. Presupposition and conversational implicature. In Cole (ed.), pp. 183–98. (Reprinted in Grice 1989, pp. 269–82.)

   1982. Meaning revisited. In N. Smith (ed.) *Mutual Knowledge*, pp. 223–43. London: Academic Press. (Reprinted in Grice 1989, pp. 283–303.)

   1989. *Studies in the Way of Words*. Cambridge, MA: Harvard University Press.

Griggs, R. and Cox, J. 1982. The elusive thematic-materials effect in Wason's Selection Task. *British Journal of Psychology* **73**: 407–20.

Groefsema, M. 1995a. 'Can', 'may', 'must' and 'should': A relevance-theoretic approach. *Journal of Linguistics* **31**: 53–79.

   1995b. Understood arguments: A semantic/pragmatic approach. *Lingua* **96**: 139–61.

Gross, S. 1998. Essays on Linguistic Context-Sensitivity and its Philosophical Significance. PhD dissertation, Harvard University.

   2001. *Essays on Linguistic Context-Sensitivity and its Philosophical Significance*. London: Routledge.

Grosz, B. 1981. Focusing and description in natural language dialogues. In A. Joshi, B. Webber and I. Sag (eds.) *Elements of Discourse Understanding*, pp. 85–105. Cambridge University Press.

Grosz, B. and Sidner, C. 1986. Attention, intentions and the structure of discourse. *Computational Linguistics* **12**: 175–204.

Guasti, M. T., Chierchia, G., Crain, S., Foppolo, F., Gualmini, A. and Meroni, L. 2005. Why children and adults sometimes (but not always) compute implicatures. *Language and Cognitive Processes* **20**: 667–96.

Gunderson, K. (ed.) 1975. *Language, Mind and Knowledge*. Minnesota Studies in the Philosophy of Science, vol. VII. Minneapolis: University of Minnesota Press.

Gutt, E.-A. 1991. *Translation and Relevance*. Oxford: Blackwell.

Hall, A. 2004. The meaning of 'but': A procedural reanalysis. *UCL Working Papers in Linguistics* **16**: 199–236.

2007. Do discourse connectives encode concepts or procedures? *Lingua* **117**: 149–74.

Hamamoto, H. 1998. Irony from a cognitive perspective. In Carston and Uchida (eds.), pp. 257–70.

Hamblin, C. 1973. Questions in Montague English. *Foundations of Language* **10**: 41–53.

Happé, F. 1993. Communicative competence and theory of mind in autism: A test of relevance theory. *Cognition* **48**: 101–19.

1994. *Autism: An Introduction to Psychological Theory*. Cambridge, MA: Harvard University Press.

Happé, F. and Loth, E. 2002. 'Theory of mind' and tracking speakers' intentions. *Mind & Language* **17**: 24–36.

Hardin, C. 1988. *Color for Philosophers*. New York: Hackett.

Hardman, D. 1998. Does reasoning occur in the selection task? A comparison of relevance-based theories. *Thinking and Reasoning* **4**: 353–76.

Hare, R. M. 1970. Meaning and speech acts. *Philosophical Review* **79**: 3–24. (Reprinted in Hare 1971, pp. 74–93.)

1971. *Practical Inferences*. London: Macmillan.

Harman, G. 1995. Rationality. In E. Smith and D. Osherson (eds.) *Thinking: An Invitation to Cognitive Science*, vol. III, pp. 175–211. (2nd edition) Cambridge, MA: MIT Press.

Harnish, R. M. 1976. Logical form and implicature. In T. Bever, J. Katz, and D. T. Langendoen (eds.) *An Integrated Theory of Linguistic Ability*, pp. 313–91. New York: Crowell. (Reprinted in Davis (ed.) 1991, pp. 316–64.)

1994. Mood, meaning and speech acts. In Tsohatzidis (ed.), pp. 407–59.

Hauser, M. 1996. *The Evolution of Communication*. Cambridge, MA: MIT Press.

Hawkins, J. 1978. *Definiteness and Indefiniteness: A Study in Reference and Grammaticality Prediction*. London: Croom Helm.

Hirschberg, J. 1991. *A Theory of Scalar Implicature*. New York: Garland.

Hirschfeld, L. and Gelman, S. 1994. *Mapping the Mind: Domain Specificity in Cognition and Culture*. Cambridge University Press.

Hiz, H. (ed.) 1978. *Questions*. Dordrecht: Reidel.

Hobbs, J. 1979. Coherence and coreference. *Cognitive Science* **3**: 67–90.

1985. On the coherence and structure of discourse. Report CSLI85–37. Menlo Park, CA: CSLI.

2004. Abduction in natural language understanding. In Horn and Ward (eds.), pp. 724–41.

Hobbs, J., Stickel, M., Appelt, D. and Martin, P. 1993. Interpretation as abduction. *Artificial Intelligence* **63**: 69–142.

Horn, L. 1972. On the Semantic Properties of Logical Operators in English. PhD Dissertation, UCLA.

1984. Towards a new taxonomy for pragmatic inference: Q- and R-based implicature. In D. Schiffrin (ed.) *Meaning, Form, and Use in Context*, pp. 11–42. Washington, DC: Georgetown University Press.

1985. Metalinguistic negation and pragmatic ambiguity. *Language* **61**: 121–74.

1989. *A Natural History of Negation*. University of Chicago Press.

1992. The said and the unsaid. *SALT II: Proceedings of the Second Conference on Semantics and Linguistic Theory*, pp. 163–202. Ohio State University Linguistics Department.

360　　　References

1996. Presupposition and implicature. In S. Lappin (ed.) *The Handbook of Contemporary Semantic Theory*, pp. 299–320. Oxford: Blackwell.

2000. From IF to IFF: Conditional perfection as pragmatic strengthening. *Journal of Pragmatics* **32**: 289–326.

2004. Implicature. In Horn and Ward (eds.), pp. 3–28.

2006. The Border wars: A neo-Gricean perspective. In K. Turner and K. von Heusinger (eds.) *Where Semantics Meets Pragmatics*, pp. 21–48. Amsterdam: Elsevier.

Horn, L. and Ward, G. (eds.) 2004. *The Handbook of Pragmatics*. Oxford: Blackwell.

Hornsby, J. 1988. Things done with words. In Dancy, Moravcsik and Taylor (eds.), pp. 27–46.

Hovy, E. 1990. Parsimonious and profligate approaches to the question of discourse structure relations. In K. McKeown, J. Moore and S. Nirenburg (eds.) *Proceedings of the 5th International Workshop on Natural Language Generation, Pittsburgh 1990*: 128–36.

Hugo, V. [1985] *Oeuvres complètes: Poésie II*. Paris: Robert Laffont. (First published 1880–92.)

Huntley, M. 1984. The semantics of English imperatives. *Linguistics and Philosophy* **7**: 103–33.

Ifantidou, E. 1993. Parentheticals and relevance. *UCL Working Papers in Linguistics* **5**: 193–210.

1994. Evidentials and Relevance. PhD thesis, University of London. (Revised version published as Ifantidou 2001.)

2001. *Evidentials and Relevance*. Amsterdam: John Benjamins.

Ifantidou-Trouki, E. 1993. Sentence adverbials and relevance. *Lingua* **90**: 69–90.

Itani, R. 1990. Explicature and explicit attitude. *UCL Working Papers in Linguistics* **2**: 52–64.

1996. *Semantics and Pragmatics of Hedges in English and Japanese*. Tokyo: Hituzi Syobo.

Iten, C. 2005. *Linguistic Meaning, Truth Conditions and Relevance: The Case of Concessives*. Basingstoke: Palgrave.

Iwata, S. 1998. Some extensions of the echoic analysis of metalinguistic negation. *Lingua* **105**: 49–65.

Jackendoff, R. 2002. *Foundations of Language: Brain, Meaning, Grammar, Evolution*. Oxford University Press.

Jackson, F. (ed.) 1991. *Conditionals*. Oxford University Press.

Johnson-Laird, P. and Byrne, R. 1991. *Deduction*. Hove: Lawrence Erlbaum.

1995. A model point of view. *Thinking and Reasoning* **1**: 339–50.

Jorgensen, J., Miller, G. and Sperber, D. 1984. Test of the mention theory of irony. *Journal of Experimental Psychology: General* **113**: 112–20.

Joyce, J. [1960] *Ulysses*. London: The Bodley Head. (First published 1922.)

Kadmon, N. 2001. *Formal Pragmatics: Semantics, Pragmatics, Presupposition and Focus*. Oxford: Blackwell.

Kaplan, D. 1989. Demonstratives. In J. Almog, J. Perry and H. Wettstein (eds.) *Themes from Kaplan*, pp. 481–563. Oxford University Press.

Karttunen, L. 1977. The syntax and semantics of questions. *Linguistics and Philosophy* **1**: 3–44. (Reprinted in Hiz 1978: 165–210.)

Karttunen, L. and Peters, S. 1976. What indirect questions conventionally implicate. In S. Mufwene, C. Walker and S. Steever (eds.) *Chicago Linguistic Society: Papers from the Twelfth Regional Meeting*, pp. 351–68. Chicago Linguistic Society.

1979. Conventional implicature. In C.-Y. Oh, and D. Dineen (eds.) *Syntax and Semantics 11: Presupposition*, pp. 1–56. New York: Academic Press.

Kasher, A. 1976. Conversational maxims and rationality. In A. Kasher (ed.) *Language in Focus: Foundations, Methods and Systems*, pp. 197–211. Dordrecht: Reidel. (Reprinted in Kasher (ed.) 1998, vol. IV, pp. 181–214.)

1982. Gricean inference revisited. *Philosophica* **29**: 25–44.

1984. Pragmatics and the modularity of mind. *Journal of Pragmatics* **8**: 539–57. (Revised version published in Davis (ed.) 1991, pp. 567–82.)

(ed.) 1998. *Pragmatics: Critical Concepts*, vols. I–VI. London: Routledge.

Katz, J. 1977. *Propositional Structure and Illocutionary Force*. New York: Crowell.

1990. *The Metaphysics of Meaning*. Cambridge, MA: MIT Press.

Keefe, R. and Smith, P. (eds.) 1997. *Vagueness: A Reader*. Cambridge, MA: MIT Press.

Keenan, T. and Quigley, K. 1999. Do young children use echoic information in their comprehension of sarcastic speech? A test of echoic mention theory. *British Journal of Developmental Psychology* **17**: 83–96.

Kempson, R. (ed.) 1988a. *Mental Representation: The Interface between Language and Reality*. Cambridge University Press.

1988b. On the grammar–cognition interface: The principle of full interpretation. In Kempson (ed.), pp. 199–224.

Khalfa, Jean. (ed.) 1994. *What is Intelligence?* Cambridge University Press.

Kintsch, W. 2000. Metaphor comprehension: A computational theory. *Psychonomic Bulletin and Review* **7**: 257–66.

Kiparsky, C. and Kiparsky, P. 1971. Fact. In D. Steinberg and L. Jakobovits (eds.) *Semantics: An Interdisciplinary Reader*, pp. 345–69. Cambridge University Press.

Kirby, S. 2002. Natural language from artificial life. *Artificial Life* **8**: 185–215.

Kleiber, G. 1990. Marqueurs référentiels et processus interprétatifs: pour une approche 'plus sémantique'. *Cahiers de linguistique française* **11**: 241–58.

Kreuz, R. and Glucksberg, S. 1989. How to be sarcastic: The echoic reminder theory of verbal irony. *Journal of Experimental Psychology: General* **118**: 374–86.

Kumon-Nakamura, S., Glucksberg, S. and Brown, M. 1995. How about another piece of pie: The allusional pretense theory of discourse irony. *Journal of Experimental Psychology: General* **124**: 3–21. (Reprinted in Gibbs and Colston (eds.) 2007, pp. 57–95.)

Lakoff, G. 1987. *Women, Fire, and Dangerous Things: What Categories Reveal about the Mind*. University of Chicago Press.

1994. Conceptual metaphor home page. Available at: http://cogsci.berkeley.edu/lakoff/MetaphorHome.html.

Lakoff, G. and Johnson, M. 1980. *Metaphors we live by*. Chicago University Press. (New edition with Afterword, 2003.)

Lakoff, G. and Turner, M. 1989. *More than Cool Reason: A Field Guide to Poetic Metaphors*. University of Chicago Press.

Langdon, R., Davies, M. and Coltheart, M. 2002. Understanding minds and understanding communicated meanings in schizophrenia. *Mind & Language* **17**: 68–104.

Lascarides, A. 1992. Knowledge, causality and temporal representation. *Linguistics* **30**: 941–73.

Lascarides, A. and Asher, N. 1993. Temporal interpretation, discourse relations and common-sense entailment. *Linguistics and Philosophy* **16**: 437–93.

Lascarides, A., Asher, N. and Oberlander, J. 1992. Inferring discourse relations in context. In *Proceedings of the 30th Annual Meeting of the Association for Computational Linguistics, Delaware, June 1992*, pp. 1–8. Stroudsburg, PA: Association for Computational Linguistics.

Lascarides, A. and Oberlander, J. 1993. Temporal coherence and defeasible knowledge. *Theoretical Linguistics* **19**: 1–37.

Lascelles, M. 1939. *Jane Austen and her Art*. Oxford University Press. (2nd edition 1965.)

Lasersohn, P. 1999. Pragmatic halos. *Language* **75**: 522–51.

Leech, G. and Short, M. 1981. *Style in Fiction: An Introduction to English Fictional Prose*. London: Longman.

Lehrer, A. 1990. Polysemy, conventionality and the structure of the lexicon. *Cognitive Linguistics* **1–2**: 207–46.

Leslie, A. 1987. Pretense and representation: The origins of 'theory of mind'. *Psychological Review* **94**: 412–26.

   1991. The theory of mind impairment in autism: Evidence for a modular mechanism of development? In Whiten (ed.), pp. 63–78.

Leslie, A., Friedman, O. and German, T. 2004. Core mechanisms in 'theory of mind'. *Trends in Cognitive Sciences* **8**: 528–33.

Leslie, A. and Happé, F. 1989. Autism and ostensive communication: The relevance of metarepresentation. *Development and Psychopathology* **1**: 205–12.

Levelt, W. 1989. *Speaking: From Intention to Articulation*. Cambridge, MA: MIT Press.

Levinson, S. 1983. *Pragmatics*. Cambridge University Press.

   1987. Minimization and conversational inference. In Verschueren and Bertuccelli-Papi (eds.), pp. 61–129.

   2000. *Presumptive Meanings: The Theory of Generalized Conversational Implicature*. Cambridge, MA: MIT Press.

Lewis, C. and Mitchell, P. (eds.) 1994. *Children's Early Understanding of Mind: Origins and Development*. Hillsdale, NJ: Lawrence Erlbaum.

Lewis, D. 1970. General semantics. *Synthese* **22**: 18–67. (Reprinted in Lewis 1983, pp. 189–232.)

   1975. Languages and language. In Gunderson (ed.), pp. 3–35. (Reprinted in Lewis 1983, pp. 163–88.)

   1979. Scorekeeping in a language game. *Journal of Philosophical Logic* **8**: 339–59. (Reprinted in Lewis 1983, pp. 233–49.)

   1983. *Philosophical Papers*, vol. I. Oxford University Press.

Liberman, N. and Klar, Y. 1996. Hypothesis testing in Wason's Selection Task: Social exchange, cheating detection or task understanding. *Cognition* **58**: 127–56.

Lock, A. 1980. *The Guided Reinvention of Language*. New York: Academic Press.

Love, R. and Kessler, C. 1995. Focussing in Wason's Selection Task: Content and instruction effects. *Thinking and Reasoning* **1**: 153–82.

Luscher, J.-M. 1989. Connecteurs et marques de pertinence: l'exemple de *d'ailleurs*. *Cahiers de linguistique française* **10**: 101–45.

1994 Les marques de connexion: Des guides pour l'interprétation. In Moeschler et al. (eds.), pp. 17–227.

Lyons, J. 1977. *Semantics*, vol. 2. Cambridge University Press.

MacKay, G. and Shaw, A. 2004. A comparative study of figurative language in children with autistic spectrum disorders. *Child Language, Teaching and Therapy* **20**: 13–32.

Manktelow, K. 1999. *Reasoning and Thinking*. Hove: Psychology Press.

Mann, W. and Thompson, S. 1988. Rhetorical structure theory. Toward a functional theory of text organisation. *Text* **8**: 243–48.

Martin, I. and McDonald, S. 2004. An exploration of causes of non-literal language problems in individuals with Asperger syndrome. *Journal of Autism and Developmental Disorders* **34**: 311–28.

Martin, R. 1992. Irony and universe of belief. *Lingua* **87**: 77–90.

Martinich, A. P. 1984. A theory for metaphor. *Journal of Literary Semantics* **13**: 35–56. (Reprinted in Davis (ed.) 1991, pp. 507–18.)

Matsui, T. 1995. Bridging and Relevance. PhD thesis, University of London. (Revised version published as Matsui 2000.)

  1998. Pragmatic criteria for reference assignment: A relevance-theoretic account of the acceptability of bridging. *Pragmatics and Cognition* **6**: 47–97.

  2000. *Bridging and Relevance*. Amsterdam: John Benjamins.

  2001. Experimental pragmatics: Towards testing relevance-based predictions about anaphoric bridging inferences. In V. Akman, P. Bouquet, R. Thomason and R. Young (eds.) *Modeling and Using Context, Lecture Notes in Artificial Intelligence*, pp. 248–60. Berlin: Springer-Verlag.

Matsumoto, Y. 1995. The conversational condition on Horn scales. *Linguistics and Philosophy* **18**: 21–60.

McCawley, J. 1991. Contrastive negation and metalinguistic negation. In L. Dobrin, L. Nichols and R. Rodriguez (eds.) *Chicago Linguistic Society 27, Parasession on Negation*, pp. 189–206. Chicago Linguistic Society.

McDonald, S. 1999. Exploring the process of inference generation in sarcasm: A review of normal and clinical studies. *Brain and Language* **69**: 486–506.

  2000. Neuropsychological studies of sarcasm. *Metaphor and Symbol* **15**: 85–98. (Reprinted in Gibbs and Colston (eds.) 2007, pp. 217–30.)

McGinn, Colin. 1977. Semantics for non-indicative sentences. *Philosophical Studies* **32**: 301–11.

McHale, B. 1978. Free indirect discourse: A survey of recent accounts. *PTL: A Journal for Descriptive Poetics and Theory of Literature* **3**: 249–87. (Reprinted in M. Bal (ed.) 2004 *Narrative Theory: Critical Concepts and Cultural Studies*, vol. I, pp. 187–222. London: Routledge.)

Medin, D., Coley, J., Storms, G. and Hayes, B. 2003. A relevance theory of induction. *Psychonomic Bulletin and Review* **10**: 517–32.

Mey, J. 1999. *When Voices Clash: A Study in Literary Pragmatics*. Berlin: Mouton de Gruyter.

Millikan, R. 1984. *Language, Thought and Other Biological Categories*. Cambridge, MA: MIT Press.

  1998. Language conventions made simple. *Journal of Philosophy* **95**: 161–80.

Mitchell, P., Robinson, E. and Thompson, D. 1999. Children's understanding that utterances emanate from minds: Using speaker belief to aid interpretation. *Cognition* **72**: 45–66.

Mo, S., Su, Y., Chan, R. and Liu, J. 2008. Comprehension of metaphor and irony in schizophrenia during remission: The role of theory of mind and IQ. *Psychiatry Research* **157**: 21–9.

Moeschler, J. 1989a. *Modélisation du dialogue: Représentation de l'inférence argumentative*. Paris: Hermès.

1989b. Pragmatic connectives, argumentative coherence and relevance. *Argumentation* **3**: 321–39.

1998. Les relations entre événements et l'interprétation des énoncés. In J. Moeschler, J. Jayez, M. Kozlowska, J.-M Luscher, L. de Saussure and B. Sthioul (eds.) *Le Temps des événements: Pragmatique de la référence temporelle*, pp. 293–321. Paris: Kimé.

Moeschler, J. and Reboul, A. 1994. *Dictionnaire encyclopédique de pragmatique*. Paris: Seuil.

Moeschler, J., Reboul, A., Luscher, J. and Jayez, J. (eds.) 1994. *Langage et pertinence: Référence temporelle, anaphore, connecteurs et métaphore*. Presses Universitaires de Nancy.

Morris, A. and Sloutsky, V. 1998. Understanding of logical necessity: Developmental antecedents and cognitive consequences. *Child Development* **69**: 721–41.

Morris, C. 1938. *Foundations of the Theory of Signs*. University of Chicago Press.

Muecke, D. 1970. *Irony*. London: Methuen.

Murphy, G. 1996. On metaphoric representation. *Cognition* **60**: 173–204.

1997. Reasons to doubt the present evidence for metaphoric representation. *Cognition* **62**: 99–108.

Nakassis, C. and Snedeker, J. 2002. Beyond sarcasm: Intonation and context as relational cues in children's recognition of irony. In A. Greenhill, M. Hughs, H. Littlefield and H. Walsh (eds.) *Proceedings of the Twenty-Sixth Boston University Conference on Language Development*, pp. 429–40. Somerville, MA: Cascadilla Press.

Neale, S. 1990. *Descriptions*. Cambridge, MA: MIT Press.

1992. Paul Grice and the philosophy of language. *Linguistics and Philosophy* **15**: 509–59.

2000. On being explicit: Comments on Stanley and Szabó, and on Bach. *Mind & Language* **15**: 284–94.

2004. This, that and the other. In A. Bezuidenhout and M. Reimer (eds.) *Descriptions and Beyond*, pp. 68–182. Oxford University Press.

in press. *Linguistic Pragmatism*. Oxford University Press.

Nicolle, S. and Clark, B. 1999. Experimental pragmatics and what is said: A response to Gibbs and Moise. *Cognition* **66**: 337–54.

Noh, E.-J. 1998a. Echo questions: Metarepresentation and pragmatic enrichment. *Linguistics and Philosophy* **21**: 603–28.

1998b. The Semantics and Pragmatics of Metarepresentations in English: A Relevance-theoretic Approach. PhD thesis, University of London. (Revised version published as Noh 2000.)

1998c. A relevance-theoretic account of metarepresentative uses in conditionals. In Rouchota and Jucker (eds.), pp. 271–304.

2000. *Metarepresentation: A Relevance-Theoretic Approach*. Amsterdam: John Benjamins.

Nølke, H. 1990. Pertinence et modalisateurs d'énonciation. *Cahiers de linguistique française* **11**: 105–26.

Norbury, C. 2005. The relationship between Theory of Mind and metaphor: Evidence from children with language impairment and autistic spectrum disorder. *British Journal of Developmental Psychology* **23**: 383–99.

Noveck, I. 2001. When children are more logical than adults: Experimental investigations of scalar implicature. *Cognition* **78**: 165–88.

Noveck, I., Bianco, M. and Castry, A. 2001. The costs and benefits of metaphor. *Metaphor and Symbol* **16**: 109–21.

Noveck, I., Ho, S. and Sera, M. 1996. Children's understanding of epistemic modals. *Journal of Child Language* **23**: 621–43.

Noveck, I. and Posada, A. 2003. Characterizing the time course of an implicature: An evoked potentials study. *Brain and Language* **85**: 203–10.

Noveck, I. and Sperber, D. (eds.) 2004. *Experimental Pragmatics*. Basingstoke: Palgrave.

2007. The why and how of experimental pragmatics. In Burton-Roberts (ed.), pp. 184–212. (Chapter 14, this volume.)

Nunberg, G. 1996. Transfers of meaning. In Pustejovsky and Boguraev (eds.), pp. 109–32.

Nuti, M. 2003. Ethnoscience: Examining Common Sense. PhD thesis, University of London.

Onishi, K. and Baillargeon, R. 2005. Do 15-month-old infants understand false beliefs? *Science* **308**: 255–8.

Origgi, G. 2001. Interpretare il linguaggio e interpretare gli altri: una o due teorie? *Sistemi Intelligenti* **8**: 171–88.

Origgi G. and Sperber, D. 2000. Evolution, communication and the proper function of language. In Carruthers and Chamberlain (eds.), pp. 140–69.

Overton, W. (ed.) 1990. *Reasoning, Necessity and Logic: Developmental Perspectives*. Hillsdale, NJ: Lawrence Erlbaum.

Palmer, F. 1986. *Mood and Modality*. Cambridge University Press.

Papafragou, A. 1998a. Modality and the Semantics–Pragmatics Interface. PhD thesis, University of London. (Revised version published as Papafragou 2000.)

1998b. Inference and word meaning: The case of modal auxiliaries. *Lingua* **105**: 1–47.

1998c. The acquisition of modality: Implications for theories of semantic representation. *Mind & Language* **13**: 370–99.

2000. *Modality: Issues in the Semantics–Pragmatics Interface*. Amsterdam: Elsevier Science.

2002. Mindreading and verbal communication. *Mind & Language* **17**: 55–67.

Papafragou, A. and Musolino, J. 2003. Scalar implicatures: Experiments at the semantics–pragmatics interface. *Cognition* **86**: 253–82.

Papafragou, A. and Tantalou, N. 2004. Children's computation of implicatures. *Language Acquisition* **12**: 71–82.

Paris, S. 1973. Comprehension of language connectives and propositional logical relationships. *Journal of Experimental Child Psychology* **16**: 278–91.

Partee, B. 1973. The syntax and semantics of quotations. In S. Anderson and P. Kiparsky (eds.) *A Festschrift for Morris Halle*, pp. 410–18. New York: Holt, Rinehart and Winston.

Pendlebury, M. 1986. Against the power of force: Reflections on the meaning of mood. *Mind* **95**: 361–72.

Perner, J., Frith, U., Leslie, A. and Leekam, S. 1989. Explorations of the autistic child's theory of mind: Knowledge, belief, and communication. *Child Development* **60**: 689–700.

Pexman, P. and Glenwright, M. 2007. How do typically developing children grasp the meaning of verbal irony? *Journal of Neurolinguistics* **20**: 178–96.

Pilkington, A. 2000. *Poetic Effects: A Relevance Theory Perspective*. Amsterdam: John Benjamins.

Pinkal, M. 1995. *Logic and Lexicon*. Dordrecht: Kluwer.

Pinker, S. 1994. *The Language Instinct*. New York: Penguin.

Politzer, G. 1996. A pragmatic account of a presuppositional effect. *Journal of Psycholinguistic Research* **25**: 543–51.

Posner, R. 1980. Semantics and pragmatics of sentence connectives in natural language. In J. Searle, F. Kiefer and M. Bierwisch (eds.) *Speech Act Theory and Pragmatics*, pp. 168–203. Dordrecht: Reidel.

Predelli, S. 1998. Utterance, interpretation and the logic of indexicals. *Mind & Language* **13**: 400–14.

Pustejovsky, J. 1995. *The Generative Lexicon*. Cambridge, MA: MIT Press.

Pustejovsky, J. and Boguraev, B. (eds.) 1996. *Lexical Semantics: The Problem of Polysemy*. Oxford: Clarendon Press.

Reboul, A. 1990. Rhétorique de l'anaphore. In G. Kleiber and J. Tyvaert (eds.) *L'anaphore et ses domaines*, pp. 279–300. Paris: Klincksieck.

  1994. L'anaphore pronominale: le problème de l'attribution des référents. In Moeschler, Reboul, Luscher and Jayez (eds.), pp. 105–73.

Reboul, A. and the CERVICAL group. 1997. Le projet CERVICAL: Représentations mentales, référence aux objets et aux événements. Ms., CRIN-CNRS and INRIA-Lorraine.

Recanati, F. 1986. On defining communicative intentions. *Mind & Language* **1**: 213–42.

  1987. *Meaning and Force*. Cambridge University Press.

  1989. The pragmatics of what is said. *Mind & Language* **4**: 295–329. (Reprinted in Davis (ed.) 1991, pp. 97–120.)

  1993. *Direct Reference: From Language to Thought*. Oxford: Blackwell.

  1994. Contextualism and anti-contextualism in the study of language. In Tsohatzidis (ed.), pp. 156–65.

  1995. The alleged priority of literal interpretation. *Cognitive Science* **19**: 207–32.

  1998. Pragmatics. In E. Craig (ed.) *Routledge Encyclopaedia of Philosophy* **7**, pp. 620–33. London: Routledge.

  2000. *Oratio Obliqua, Oratio Recta: The Semantics of Metarepresentations*. Cambridge, MA: MIT Press.

  2002a. Unarticulated constituents. *Linguistics and Philosophy* **25**: 299–345.

  2002b. Does linguistic communication rest on inference? *Mind & Language* **17**: 105–26.

  2004a. *Literal Meaning*. Cambridge University Press.

2004b. Semantics and pragmatics. In Horn and Ward (eds.), pp. 442–62.

2007. Indexicality, context and pretence. In Burton-Roberts (ed.), pp. 213–29.

Reinhart, T. 1981. Pragmatics and linguistics: An analysis of sentence topics. *Philosophica* **27**: 53–94.

Richards, I. A. 1936. *The Philosophy of Rhetoric*. London: Oxford University Press.

Rips, L. 1975. Quantification and semantic memory. *Cognitive Psychology* **7**: 307–40.

1994. *The Psychology of Proof*. London: MIT Press.

Rockwell, P. 2000. Lower, slower, louder: Vocal cues of sarcasm. *Journal of Psycholinguistics Research* **29**: 483–95.

Rouchota, V. and Jucker, A. (eds.) 1998. *Current Issues in Relevance Theory*. Amsterdam: John Benjamins.

Ryder, N and Leinonen, E. 2003. Use of context in question answering by 3-, 4- and 5-year-old children. *Journal of Psycholinguistic Research* **32**: 397–415.

Sadock, J. 2004. Speech acts. In Horn and Ward (eds.), pp. 53–73.

Saka, P. 1998. Quotation and the use–mention distinction. *Mind* **107**: 113–35.

Salmon, N. 1986. *Frege's Puzzle*. Cambridge, MA: MIT Press.

Samet, J. and Schank, R. 1984. Coherence and connectivity. *Linguistics and Philosophy* **7**: 57–82.

Sanders, T., Spooren, W. and Noordman, L. 1992. Toward a taxonomy of coherence relations. *Discourse Processes* **15**: 1–35.

1993. Coherence relations in a cognitive theory of discourse representation. *Cognitive Linguistics* **4**: 93–133.

Sanford, A. 2002. Context, attention, and depth of processing during interpretation. *Mind & Language* **17**: 186–206.

Sanford, A. and Garrod, S. 1981. *Understanding Written Language*. Chichester: John Wiley.

Sanford, A., Moar, K. and Garrod, S. 1988. Proper names as controllers of discourse focus. *Language and Speech* **31**: 43–56.

Schiffer, S. 1972. *Meaning*. Oxford: Clarendon Press.

Schmerling, S. 1975. Some remarks on symmetric and asymmetric conjunctions. In Cole and Morgan (eds.), pp. 211–32.

1982. How imperatives are special, and how they aren't. In R. Schneider, K. Tuite and R. Chameltzy (eds.) *Chicago Linguistic Society: Parasession on Nondeclaratives*, pp. 202–218. Chicago Linguistic Society.

Scholl, B. and Leslie, A. 1999. Modularity, development and 'theory of mind'. *Mind & Language* **14**: 131–53.

Schwoebel, J., Dews, S., Winner, E. and Srinivas, K. 2000. Obligatory processing of the literal meaning of ironic utterances: Further evidence. *Metaphor and Symbol* **15**: 47–61. (Reprinted in Gibbs and Colston (eds.) 2007, pp. 253–67.)

Searle, J. 1969. *Speech Acts*. Cambridge University Press.

(ed.) 1971. *The Philosophy of Language*. Oxford University Press.

1975a. A taxonomy of illocutionary acts. In Gunderson (ed.), pp. 334–69. (Reprinted in Searle 1979, pp. 1–29.)

1975b. Indirect speech acts. In Cole and Morgan (eds.), pp. 59–82.

1979. *Expression and Meaning*. Cambridge University Press.

1980. The background of meaning. In J. Searle, and F. Kiefer (eds.) *Speech-Act Theory and Pragmatics*, pp. 221–32. Dordrecht: Reidel.

1983. *Intentionality*. Cambridge University Press.

Seto, K. 1998. On non-echoic irony. In Carston and Uchida (eds.), pp. 239–55.

Shamay-Tsoory, S., Tomer, R. and Aharon-Peretz, J. 2005. The neuroanatomical basis of understanding sarcasm and its relation to social cognition. *Neuropsychology* **19**: 288–300.

Sidner, C. 1983. Focusing in the comprehension of definite anaphora. In M. Brady and R. Berwick (eds.) *Computational Models of Discourse*, pp. 267–330. Cambridge, MA: MIT Press.

Sigman, M. and Kasari, C. 1995. Joint attention across contexts in normal and autistic children. In C. Moore, and P. Dunham (eds.) *Joint Attention: Its Origins and Role in Development*, pp. 189–203. Hillsdale, NJ: Lawrence Erlbaum.

Smith, C. L. 1980. Quantifiers and question answering in young children. *Journal of Experimental Child Psychology* **30**: 191–205.

Smith, N. V. (ed.) 1982. *Mutual Knowledge*. London: Academic Press.

Smith, N. V. and Tsimpli, I.-M. 1995. *The Mind of a Savant: Language Learning and Modularity*. Oxford: Blackwell.

Southgate, V., Chevallier, C. and Csibra, G. 2010. Seventeen-month-olds appeal to false beliefs to interpret others' referential communication. *Developmental Science* **16**: 907–12.

Sperber, D. 1984. Verbal irony: Pretense or echoic mention? *Journal of Experimental Psychology: General* **113**: 130–6.

  1985. *On Anthropological Knowledge*. Cambridge University Press.

  1994a. Understanding verbal understanding. In J. Khalfa (ed.) *What is Intelligence?*, pp. 179–98. Cambridge University Press.

  1994b. The modularity of thought and the epidemiology of representations. In Hirschfeld and Gelman (eds.), pp. 39–67.

  1996. *Explaining Culture: A Naturalistic Approach*. Oxford: Blackwell.

  1997. Intuitive and reflective beliefs. *Mind & Language* **12**: 67–83.

  2000a. Metarepresentations in an evolutionary perspective. In Sperber (ed.), pp. 117–37.

  (ed.) 2000b. *Metarepresentations: A Multidisciplinary Perspective*. Oxford University Press.

  2001. In defense of massive modularity. In E. Dupoux (ed.) *Language, Brain and Cognitive Development: Essays in Honor of Jacques Mehler*, pp. 45–57. Cambridge, MA: MIT Press.

Sperber, D., Cara, F. and Girotto, V. 1995. Relevance theory explains the selection task. *Cognition* **57**: 31–95.

Sperber, D. and Girotto, V. 2002. Use or misuse of the selection task? Rejoinder to Fiddick, Cosmides, and Tooby. *Cognition* **85**: 277–90.

  2003. Does the selection task detect cheater-detection? In K. Sterelny and J. Fitness (eds.) *From Mate to Mentality. Evaluating Evolutionary Psychology*, pp. 197–225. New York: Psychology Press.

Sperber, D., Premack, D. and Premack, A. (eds.) 1995. *Causal Cognition: A Multidisciplinary Debate*. Oxford: Clarendon Press.

Sperber, D. and Wilson, D. 1978. Les ironies comme mentions. *Poétique: Revue de Théorie et d'Analyse Littéraire* **36**: 395–412.

  1981. Irony and the use–mention distinction. In Cole (ed.), pp. 295–318. (Reprinted in Davis (ed.) 1991, pp. 550–63.)

1982. Mutual knowledge and relevance in theories of comprehension. In Smith (ed.), pp. 61–87. (Reprinted in Kasher (ed.) 1998, vol. IV, pp. 369–82.)

1986a. *Relevance: Communication and Cognition.* Oxford: Blackwell and Cambridge MA: Harvard University Press. (1st edition; 2nd edition published as Sperber and Wilson 1995.)

1986b Loose talk. *Proceedings of the Aristotelian Society* **86**: 153–71. (Reprinted in Davis (ed.) 1991, pp. 540–9.)

1987a. Précis of *Relevance: Communication and Cognition. Behavioral and Brain Sciences* **10**: 697–710. (Reprinted in Kasher (ed.) 1998, vol. V, pp. 82–115.)

1987b. Presumptions of relevance. *Behavioral and Brain Sciences* **10**: 736–53.

1990a. Rhetoric and relevance. In Bender and Wellbery (eds.), pp. 140–56. (Chapter 4, this volume.)

1990b. Spontaneous deduction and mutual knowledge. *Behavioral and Brain Sciences* **13**: 179–84.

1995. *Relevance: Communication and Cognition.* (2nd edition, with a new Postface) Oxford: Blackwell.

1998a. The mapping between the mental and the public lexicon. In Carruthers and Boucher (eds.), pp. 184–200. (Chapter 2, this volume.)

1998b. Irony and relevance: A reply to Drs Seto, Hamamoto and Yamanashi. In Carston and Uchida (eds.), pp. 283–93.

2002. Pragmatics, modularity and mindreading. *Mind & Language* **17**: 3–23. (Chapter 12, this volume.)

2005. Pragmatics. In F. Jackson and M. Smith (eds.) *Oxford Handbook of Contemporary Analytic Philosophy,* pp. 468–501. Oxford University Press. (Chapter 1, this volume.)

2008. A deflationary account of metaphors. In R. Gibbs (ed.) *The Cambridge Handbook of Metaphor and Thought,* pp. 84–105. Cambridge University Press. (Chapter 5, this volume.)

Stainton, R. 1997. Utterance meaning and syntactic ellipsis. *Pragmatics and Cognition* **5**: 51–78.

1998. Quantifier phrases, 'Meaningfulness in Isolation', and ellipsis. *Linguistics and Philosophy* **21**: 311–40.

Stalnaker, R. 1974. Pragmatic presuppositions. In M. Munitz and P. Unger (eds.) *Semantics and Philosophy.* New York University Press. (Reprinted in Stalnaker 1999, pp. 47–62.)

1999. *Context and Content: Essays on Intentionality in Speech and Thought.* Oxford University Press.

Stanley, J. 2000. Context and logical form. *Linguistics and Philosophy* **23**: 391–434.

2002. Making it articulated. *Mind & Language* **17**: 49–68.

Stanley, J. and Szabó, Z. 2000. On quantifier domain restriction. *Mind & Language* **15**: 219–61.

Sternberg, M. 1982a. Proteus in quotation-land: Mimesis and the forms of reported discourse. *Poetics Today* **3**: 107–56.

1982b. Point of view and the indirections of direct speech. *Language and Style* **15**: 67–117.

Sternberg, R. 1979. Developmental patterns in the encoding and combination of logical connectives. *Journal of Experimental Child Psychology* **28**: 469–98.

Stich, S. 1990. *The Fragmentation of Reason: Preface to a Pragmatic Theory of Cognitive Evaluation*. Cambridge, MA: MIT Press.

Strawson, P. 1952. *Introduction to Logical Theory*. London: Methuen.

1964. Intention and convention in speech acts. *Philosophical Review* **73**: 439–60. (Reprinted in Searle (ed.) 1971, pp. 170–89.)

Sullivan, K., Winner, E. and Hopfield, N. 1995. How children tell a lie from a joke: The role of second-order mental state attributions. *British Journal of Developmental Psychology* **13**: 191–204.

Surian, L., Caldi, S. and Sperber, D. 2007. Attribution of beliefs by 13-month-old infants. *Psychological Science* **18**: 580–6.

Sweetser, E. 1990. *From Etymology to Pragmatics: Metaphorical and Cultural Aspects of Semantic Structure*. Cambridge University Press.

Szabó, Z. (ed.) 2005. *Semantics versus Pragmatics*. Oxford University Press.

Talmy, L. 2000. *Toward a Cognitive Semantics* (2 vols.). Cambridge, MA: MIT Press.

Taylor, K. 2001. Sex, breakfast and *descriptus interruptus*. *Synthese* **128**: 45–61.

Tomasello, M. and Kruger, A. 1992. Joint attention in action: Acquiring verbs in ostensive and non-ostensive contexts. *Journal of Child Language* **19**: 311–33.

Tourangeau, R. and Rips, L. 1991. Interpreting and evaluating metaphors. *Journal of Memory and Language* **30**: 452–72.

Travis, C. 1975. *Saying and Understanding*. Oxford: Blackwell.

1985. On what is strictly speaking true. *Canadian Journal of Philosophy* **15**: 187–229.

2001. *Unshadowed Thought: Representation in Thought and Language*. Cambridge, MA: Harvard University Press.

Tsohatzidis, S. (ed.) 1994. *Foundations of Speech Act Theory: Philosophical and Linguistic Perspectives*. London: Routledge.

Turner, K. (ed). 1999. *The Semantics–Pragmatics Interface from Different Points of View*. Oxford: Elsevier Science.

Unger, P. 1975. *Ignorance: A Case for Scepticism*. Oxford: Clarendon Press.

Urmson, J. 1963. Parenthetical verbs. In C. Caton (ed.) *Philosophy and Ordinary Language*, pp. 220–40. Urbana, IL: University of Illinois Press.

van der Auwera, J. 1981. *What do we Talk about When we Talk? Speculative Grammar and the Semantics and Pragmatics of Focus*. Amsterdam: John Benjamins.

1985. *Language and Logic. A Speculative and Condition-Theoretic Study*. Amsterdam: John Benjamins.

1986. Conditionals and speech acts. In E. Traugott, A. ter Meulen, J. Reilly and C. Ferguson (eds.) *On Conditionals*, pp. 197–214. Cambridge University Press.

1997. Conditional perfection. In A. Athanasiadou, and R. Dirven (eds.) *On Conditionals Again*, pp. 169–90. Amsterdam: John Benjamins.

Van der Henst, J.-B. 1999. The mental model theory and spatial reasoning re-examined: The role of relevance in premise order. *British Journal of Psychology* **90**: 73–84.

Van der Henst, J.-B., Carles, L. and Sperber, D. 2002. Truthfulness and relevance in telling the time. *Mind & Language* **17**: 457–66.

Van der Henst, J.-B. and Sperber, D. 2004. Testing the cognitive and communicative principles of relevance. In Noveck and Sperber (eds.), pp. 141–71. (Chapter 13, this volume.)

Van der Henst, J.-B., Sperber, D. and Politzer, G. 2002. When is a conclusion worth deriving? A relevance-based analysis of indeterminate relational problems. *Thinking and Reasoning* **8**: 1–20.

van der Sandt, R. 1991. Denial. In L. Dobrin, L. Nichols and R. Rodriguez (eds.) *Chicago Linguistic Society 27, Parasession on Negation*, pp. 331–44. Chicago Linguistic Society.

Vanderveken, D. 1990–91. *Meaning and Speech Acts* (2 vols.). Cambridge University Press.

van Rooy, R. 2003. Questioning to resolve decision problems. *Linguistics and Philosophy* **26**: 727–63.

Vega Moreno, R. 2004. Metaphor interpretation and emergence. *UCL Working Papers in Linguistics* **16**: 197–222.

2007. *Creativity and Convention: The Pragmatics of Everyday Figurative Speech*. Amsterdam: John Benjamins.

Verschueren, J. and Bertuccelli-Papi, M. (eds.) 1987. *The Pragmatic Perspective*. Amsterdam: John Benjamins.

von Frisch, K. 1967. *The Dance Language and Orientation of Bees*. Cambridge, MA: Belknap Press of Harvard University Press.

Wade, E. and Clark, H. 1993. Reproduction and demonstration in quotations. *Journal of Memory and Language* **32**: 805–19.

Walton, K. 1976. Points of view in narrative and depictive representation. *Nous* **10**: 49–61.

1990 *Mimesis as Make-believe: On the Foundations of the Representational Arts*. Cambridge, MA: Harvard University Press.

Wang, A., Lee, S., Sigman, M. and Dapretto, M. 2006. Neural basis of irony comprehension in children with autism: The role of prosody and context. *Brain* **129**: 932–43.

Wason, P. 1966. Reasoning. In B. Foss (ed.) *New Horizons in Psychology*, pp. 135–51. Harmondsworth: Penguin.

Wellman, H. 1990. *The Child's Theory of Mind*. Cambridge, MA: MIT Press.

Werth, P. (ed.) 1981. *Conversation and Discourse*. London: Croom Helm.

Wharton, T. 2003a. Interjections, language and the 'showing/saying' continuum. *Pragmatics and Cognition* **11**: 39–91.

2003b. Natural pragmatics and natural codes. *Mind & Language* **18**: 447–77.

2009. *Pragmatics and Non-Verbal Communication*. Cambridge University Press.

Whiten, A. (ed.) 1991. *Natural Theories of Mind: Evolution, Development and Simulation of Everyday Mindreading*. Oxford: Blackwell.

Whiten, A. and Byrne, R. (eds.) 1997. *Machiavellian Intelligence II: Evaluations and Extensions*. Cambridge University Press.

Willey, L. H. 1999. *Pretending to be Normal: Living with Asperger's Syndrome*. London: Jessica Kingsley.

Williams, D. 1992. *Nobody Nowhere*. New York: Avon Books.

Williamson, T. 1994. *Vagueness*. London: Routledge.

Wilson, D. 1975. *Presuppositions and Non-Truth-Conditional Semantics*. London: Academic Press. (Reprinted by Gregg Revivals, Aldershot, 1991.)

1998a. Linguistic structure and inferential communication. In B. Caron (ed.) *Proceedings of the 16th International Congress of Linguists*, Paris, 20–25 July 1997. Oxford: Elsevier Sciences.

1998b. Discourse, coherence and relevance: A reply to Rachel Giora. *Journal of Pragmatics* **29**: 57–74.

2000. Metarepresentation in linguistic communication. In Sperber (ed.), pp. 411–48. (Chapter 11, this volume.)

2003. Relevance and lexical pragmatics. *Italian Journal of Linguistics/Rivista di Linguistica* **15**: 273–91.

2006. The pragmatics of verbal irony: Echo or pretence? *Lingua* **116**: 1722–43.

Wilson, D. and Carston, R. 2006. Metaphor, relevance and the 'emergent property' issue. *Mind & Language* **21**: 404–33.

2007. A unitary approach to lexical pragmatics: Relevance, inference and ad hoc concepts. In Burton-Roberts (ed.), pp. 230–59.

Wilson, D. and Matsui, T. 2000. Recent approaches to bridging: Truth, coherence, relevance. In J. de Bustos Tovar, P. Charaudeau, J. Alconchel, S. Iglesias Recuero and C. Lopez Alonso (eds.) *Lengua, Discurso, Texto*, vol. 1, pp. 103–132. Madrid: Visor Libros. (Chapter 9, this volume.)

Wilson, D. and Sperber, D. 1981. On Grice's theory of conversation. In Werth (ed.), pp. 155–78. London: Croom Helm. (Reprinted in Kasher (ed.) 1998, vol. IV, pp. 347–68.)

1986. Pragmatics and modularity. In A. Farley, P. Farley and K.-E. McCullough (eds.) *Chicago Linguistic Society 22, Parasession on Pragmatics and Grammatical Theory*, pp. 67–84. Chicago Linguistic Society. (Reprinted in Davis (ed.) 1991, pp. 583–95.)

1988a. Mood and the analysis of non-declarative sentences. In Dancy, Moravcsik and Taylor (eds.), pp. 77–101. (Reprinted in Kasher (ed.) 1998, vol. II, pp. 262–89.) (Chapter 10, this volume.)

1988b. Representation and relevance. In Kempson (ed.), pp. 133–53.

1992. On verbal irony. *Lingua* **87**: 53–76. (Reprinted in Gibbs and Colston (eds.) 2007, pp. 35–55.)

1993. Linguistic form and relevance. *Lingua* **90**: 1–25. (Chapter 7, this volume.)

1998a. Pragmatics and time. In Carston and Uchida (eds.), pp. 1–22. (Chapter 8, this volume.)

1998b. Truthfulness and relevance. Paper delivered to the San Marino conference on Grice's Heritage, May 1998. (Revised version published as Wilson and Sperber 2002.)

2002. Truthfulness and relevance. *Mind* **111**: 583–632. (Chapter 3, this volume.)

2004. Relevance theory. In Horn and Ward (eds.), pp. 607–32.

Winner, E. 1988. *The Point of Words: Children's Understanding of Metaphor and Irony.* Cambridge, MA: Harvard University Press.

Winner, E., Brownell, H., Happé, F., Blum, A. and Pincus, D. 1998. Distinguishing lies from jokes: Theory of Mind deficits and discourse interpretation in right-hemisphere brain-damaged patients. *Brain and Language* **62**: 89–106.

Yamanashi, M. 1998. Some issues in the treatment of irony and related tropes. In Carston and Uchida (eds.), pp. 271–82.

Index

acceptability, 56–8, 178, 188, 197, 209
  and manipulation of effects, 203–5
  and relevance-based approach, 199–200
accessibility, 188
  and ambiguity, 195
  of bridging assumptions, 191–2
  and coherence, 197–9
  of consequences, 297–8
  factors affecting, 189
  of linguistic antecedents, 189–91
  and use of *prefer*, 193, 194–5
  See also processing effort
accidental information transmission, 151
accidental relevance, 239–40
accommodation for comparative salience rule, 193
accommodation of assumptions, 15
achievability in imperatives and infinitival clauses, 216–18
ad hoc concepts, 20–2, 41, 42, 45–6, 73–4, 107, 110, 115, 120–2, 312–13, 316, 335
adverbials, illocutionary, 162–4
allusional pretence account of irony, 137
ambiguity
  and code model of communication, 98–9, 332
  and coherence-based approach, 206–8
  in illocutionary adverbials, 163–4
  and reference assignment, 195
analytic and contextual implications, 218–19
and
  and reverse-causal interpretation, 184–6

temporal and causal connotations, 154, 156, 170–2, 185
antecedents, linguistic
  accessibility, 189–91
approximations, 19–20, 54–6, 106
  acceptability, 56–7
  expectations of truthfulness, 60–1
  false, 59–60
  interpretation of meaning, 70, 71–5
  vagueness, 20, 57–9
  and violation of maxims, 56
Asher, N. and A. Lascarides, 206–8
assumptions, accommodation of, 15
attention
  and cognitive efficiency, 271–2
  and manipulation of mental states, 273–5
  and mindreading ability, 272–3
attitude in irony, 126–7, 141–2
attribution and autism, 254
attributive uses of language, 128–9, 345
  in echoic utterances, 130–1
attributive–pretence account of irony
  and normative bias, 142
  and tone of voice, 144
  See also irony
Austin, J. L., 20
autism
  and attribution, 254
  and mindreading ability, 235–6
  and Naive Optimism, 240–1

Bach, K., 7, 163, 221, 231, 255, 264, 339, 340, 341, 342, 346
Banfield, A., 252
Bar-Lev, S. and A. Palacas, 184, 185